1990

Who's Who in British Radio

Edited by Dawn C. Rusling

Associate Editor   Paul A. Rusling

First edition

Published by
Eurobroadcast Publications
P O Box 12, Willerby, HULL. UK HU10 7YT

Published and Copyright owned by
Eurobroadcast Publications, 1995
ISBN 1 900401 00 2

Typeset in Times Roman by
Business Data Limited, P O Box 12 Hull, HU10 7YT

Printed and bound by
J Bootyman Limited, 242 Hessle Road, Hull HU3 3DB

First Published 1995
First edition, December 1995

©Eurobroadcast Publications

Eurobroadcast Publications, P O Box 12, Willerby, Hull. HU10 7YT

FOREWORD

As the daughter of someone whose entire life revolves around radio broadcasting, ever since I could talk I've had to answer our telephone to, and had the pleasure to meet, a bewildering variety of people from the world of radio. Disc-jockeys, station managers and engineers, not to mention receptionists, jingle singers and many others. They've all been so polite and friendly I've often been embarrassed to admit that I'd forgotten who they are, or what they do.

I've built a database of the people who work not only on the radio, but those who support them behind the scenes. That forms the basis of this book, which attempts to not only record the existence of those in the industry, but to give an insight into their personalities.

To make the book as comprehensive as possible we invited every radio station in the UK and hundreds of individuals to supply information for the book. Some didn't bother to respond and their entries reflect this, but most of the true 'radio' people were very helpful. I must thank those who supplied information on others, the station managers and secretaries, especially those at smaller and understaffed stations who took the time to help me assemble the information.

One of the most interesting parts of the information provided was in answer to my question "how did you get into radio?" Hopefully this will not only amuse readers but help anyone trying to get that important first break into the business.

There is so much movement and change and the response has been so encouraging, that we have decided to publish the book annually. As the radio business grows, each edition will become bigger, more detailed and even more comprehensive.

I hope you send me have your ideas and comments - please enjoy reading !

Dawn Rusling

P.S. Please send all 'updates' to us as early as possible as an electronic version is to be made available regularly. Full details of this and other products and information of interest to radio enthusiasts, can be found in the section at the back of the book.

Who's Who in British Radio

Chris A'COURT

Chris was a news producer at *BBC Radio Devon* and *Dorset FM,* from where he moved to BBC Radio Oxford - now *BBC Radio Thames Valley.*

John ABBOTT

Audio Unit Manager for *BBC Midlands.*

Mike ABBOTT

Sports Producer at *BBC Scotland.*

Nick ABBOT

Nick's first job was on the Virgin in-house station, after which *Radio Luxembourg* asked him to do a late-night phone-in. He later returned to Virgin - currently at *Virgin 1215.*

Ray ABBOTT

Producer of programmes at *BBC Radio Three.*

Mr ABIE

Presenter at *Radio Clyde 2.*

Gloria ABRAMOFF

Gloria is an editor at *BBC Radio GLR.*

Jenny ABRAMSKI

Controller of News and Sport at the BBC and largely responsible for the establishment of *Radio Five Live.*

Fran ACHESON

Educational Producer at the BBC.

Nigel ACHESON

BBC Arts & Science Features producer.

Katriona ACHOSTA

Producer for the BBC Educational Directorate.

Christa ACKROYD

Born in Halifax towards the end of the fifties, Christa went to school in her home town and in nearby Bradford. Her career began in local newspapers in West Yorkshire following which she joined *Pennine Radio* in Bradford as the station's Morning Editor.

She became nationally known for her thorough network coverage of the Yorkshire Ripper case, and then joined *BBC Radio Four* where she was the Northern presenter of 'Women's Hour' in the 1970s.

In 1981 Christa joined the new Leeds station, *Radio Aire,* as News Editor and after three years became Programme Director.

Under Christa's control, Aire became an industry leader in speech and news programming and Christa's work won her four Sony awards.

After seven years at Radio Aire, Christa resigned and she joined Yorkshire Television as a news reporter. She's since become one of the region's best known women, as co-anchor of the news magazine programme 'Calendar' and presenter of many other programmes on the channel.

Christa's role in radio has been recognised in her being invited to judge the Sony Awards and she recently worked on two major applications for new services in Yorkshire.

Harry ADAIR

Editor at the BBC Northern Ireland regional broadcasting centre.

Caroline ADAM

Assistant Head of Religious Programmes at BBC *Radio Scotland.*

Darren ADAM

Educated in Nairn, Darren got into radio by making a nuisance of himself at *Moray Firth Radio* in Inverness. There he worked on various on-air shifts as well as production tasks at *Moray Firth Radio,* and stood in for most of the station's regular jocks.

Darren recently went into broadcasting full time at *Forth FM* in Edinburgh and is also a prolific commercial voice-over artist.

Bernard ADAMS

Educational Directorate Producer for the BBC.

Colin ADAMS

Head of Regional Broadcasting (BBC Radio) based in Manchester.

Colin ADAMS

Head of News at *Radio Clyde.*

Dave ADAMS

Presenter of Club Music programmes at *Heartland FM.*

Jeremy ADAMS

Presenter of the 'Spotlight' programme for the BBC in *Northern Ireland.*

Kaye ADAMS

Weekday presenter at *Scot FM.*

4

Larry ADAMS
Country music producer at *BBC Radio Kent*.

Martin ADAMS
Born in Birkenhead, Martin worked as a car sales rep' until he got into radio "after meeting a guy in a pub!" Martin's first broadcast was on *Sud Radio* in Andorra back in 1969, and he's since worked in hospital radio (Clutterbridge) and on a string of pirates in the early 1980's.

He was fundamental in setting up *Radio Maldwyn* where he is now Sales Manager and still finds time to host a 'Family Favourites' programme for three hours each Sunday lunchtime where he's known as the dirty old man in a raincoat!. Likes lots of scotch but not the hangover afterwards.

Michael ADAMS
Educated at Sheffield University, Michael joined *Radio Hallam* in Sheffield in 1974 as the first engineering graduate trainee in the independent radio network. At Radio Hallam, he became proficient in presentation, scripting, newsreading, commercial presentation, studio technical operations and outside broadcasts.

With the development of Radio Hallam's systems division, later to become Audionics Limited, he has been involved in the design construction and commissioning of some twenty independent radio services as well as broadcast studios for the BBC.

He is also the designer of the SMS control centre routing system, which provides a large proportion of the U.K's independent radio network with news and advertising.

At Canford Audio, Michael is now responsible for the selection of new products for inclusion in the company's 600 page catalogue of some 9,000 audio and broadcast-related products.

Rick ADAMS
Rick is a popular daytime presenter on 2CR's *Classic Gold 828* station, in Bournemouth.

Robin ADAMS
Robin is the Director of Development at the *World Radio Network*, an international programme consolidation station based in London and heard all around the world.

Stacey ADAMS
Executive Producer at the BBC Educational Directorate.

Tony ADAMS
Presenter for *Island FM* in the Channel Islands.

John ADAMSON
Senior Engineer with the BBC, based in Nottingham, and he is also responsible for *BBC Radio Norfolk*.

Peter ADAMSON
A Geordie who also worked as a teacher in Liverpool, he became a cult figure at BBC *Radio Humberside* in the eighties and nineties. He presents the weekly jazz programme for all the BBC North local stations, and a weekday lunchtime phone-in programme on *Radio Humberside* for which he received a Sony Gold Award for 'Local Radio Personality of the Year'.

Tony ADAMSON
Golf correspondent for BBC Radio sports.

John ADDERLEY
John is now a news and programme producer at *BBC Radio Devon* and *Dorset FM*.

Kate ADIE
Began her broadcasting career at *BBC Radio Bristol* and is now chief overseas reporter with BBC News. She has been awarded an OBE for service to news reporting.

Roger AGARD
Head of Sales at *WNK Radio* in North London.

Richard AGGUS
Senior Executive at the London HQ of Starbird Satellite Services.

Iain AGNEW
Iain is a Producer, specialising in travel programmes at *BBC Radio Scotland*.

John AGNEW
John is a sports correspondent (mainly cricket commentaries) for BBC Radio Sport.

UPDATES Please fax to 01 482 658227

Mike AHERN

Mike Ahern was born in Waterloo, Liverpool and was educated with Kenny Everett. His first job was in a menswear shop, but due to a serious mishap involving a suit worth 30 guineas, he moved to another job after just three months. A variety of jobs followed, including him being a barman, a clerk and a factory hand. When a colleague of his opened a pub, Mike acted as a compere and a part-owner. He also worked at the Cavern Club, Liverpool with DJ Bob Wooler.

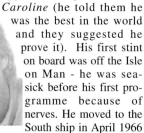

In 1964 Mike applied for a job on *Radio Caroline* (he told them he was the best in the world and they suggested he prove it). His first stint on board was off the Isle on Man - he was seasick before his first programme because of nerves. He moved to the South ship in April 1966 where he was the regular mid-morning jock for 15 months, during which time he had a successful fan club through which he received many proposals of marriage! He made his television debut in June 1966 as a presenter of 'New Faces'

Mike was one of the original team of DJs on *BBC Radio 1* when it first opened in September 1967 and achieved a record for being the shortest - surviving jock on the station, leaving shortly afterwards for Australia. There he worked at *4BC* in Brisbane , *6PM* at Perth, *3UZ* in Melbourne, *2KO* in Newcastle and *7HT* in Hobart. In the late eighties Mike returned to the UK and *Capital Gold* until September, 1995.

JOE AHEARNE

Joe is the Company Secretary of *Atlantic 252*.

Patrick AHERNE

Presenter of Sunday g programmes on Signal.

Therese AHERNE

Publisher of magazines at BBC Enterprises.

Rahil AHMAD

Received a law degree as a photographer and got into radio by sending in a 4 line letter and photo to *Spectrum Radio* - he says it was the luck of timing ! Currently works at *Spectrum Radio* as a news presenter and journalist and also at *BBC Radio WM* as a news reviewer.

Karen AINLEY

News Producer at *BBC Radio Essex*.

Adrian AIR

Presenter at *RAM FM* in Derby.

Donald AIRD

Senior Engineer at *Moray Firth Radio* in Inverness.

Sally AITCHISON

Sales Director at *TFM Radio*, part of the Metro Group, in Stockton.

William AITKEN MBE DL

Company Secretary for *South West Sound FM*.

Miriam AKHTAR

Producer, based at Southampton for BBC radio.

Tom ALBAN

Tom is a senior news reporter for *BBC Radio Hereford and Worcester*.

Robert ALBURY

Producer at BBC Educational Directorate.

Chris ALDRED

Born 16th April 1942 in Chislehurst, Kent. Began radio career with *BFBS* Malta in 1975 as an alternative to getting bored lying in the sun all day. When her husband was posted back to UK two years later, Chris joined *BBC Radio 2* as newsreader and continuity and she became regular host of 'You, the Night & The Music'.

Ian ALDRED

Born in Manchester in 1949 and first radio programme was in 1978. Has worked at BBC *Radio Scotland*, and on the Corporation's first four national networks. His most embarrassing moment was playing a record at the wrong speed on *Radio 3* - he now lives in Edinburgh.

David E ALEXANDER

David is a Director of the *Downtown Radio / Cool FM* stations in Belfast.

Diane ALEXANDER
Service manager at Country 1035 in London.

Jackie ALEXANDER
Director of resources at BBC Enterprises.

Kay ALEXANDER
Presenter with BBC in the Midlands.

Mike ALEXANDER
Mike was a news reporter at *BBC Radio Humberside* in the 1980s.

Paul ALEXANDER
Paul worked as a club DJ and resident comic until joining Radio Caroline International, where he hosted the breakfast-time

 "Multicolourbound Showgramme", the "Sleep-walkers Spectacular" and various other extravagantly-titled programmes on *Radio Caroline International* in the early 70s.

He also broadcast on the BBC and various stations overseas, such as *Swiss Radio International* -his full name is Paul Alexander Rusling (qv).

Sue ALEXANDER
News Producer for *Wiltshire Sound* until 1994 when she became the station's Assistant Editor.

Ali AL-HADAITHI
Chief Executive of Middle East Broadcasting.

Ansar ALI
News producer at *BBC Radio Peterborough* and host of 'Asian Voice' each Friday, 7pm.

Erkan ALI
Chairman of Turkish Radio (Cable station).

Andy ALIFFE
Andy is a Senior Producer of Light Entertainment programmes for the BBC.

David ALLAN
Born 7th August, 1944 in Bury, Lancashire, David began his broadcasting career on *Radio 390* where he hosted country-music flavoured programmes.

David moved to the ship based *Radio 355* very briefly when Ted Allbeury took over the station and in 1968 he joined *BBC Radio Two*.

He stayed at the station hosting country music programmes and a Sunday Morning Breakfast Show until 1992 when he moved across to BBC Television as a continuity announcer.

As well as BBC domestic radio and television channels David's voice is also heard hosting similar music programmes on five airlines, including British Airways, and the BBC World Service. In 1990 David received the award for 'Most Popular European Country Music DJ' in a poll organised by a leading country Music Newspaper, an award he still proudly holds.

Grae ALLAN
Managing Director *Radio Clyde* 1 and 2 .

Richard ALLAN
Operations coordinator Executive at *Radio Tay.*

Steve ALLAN
Sales Manager at *Moray Firth Radio.*

Stu ALLAN
Presenter at *Key 103.*

John ALLARD
Sports Editor at *BBC Radio Cleveland.*

Ted ALLBEURY
Ted had a long and distinguished career in the SOE (Special Operations Executive) which gave him much material for his later exploits as a novelist. He's written a dozen or more best sellers and the spy-thrillers can be seen on every newsstand in the English-speaking world.

His contribution to radio was immense; he was Managing Director of *Estuary Radio Limited*, the company which operated *Radio 390* from a fort off Whitstable for several years. Ted broadcst on the station himself and was the regular host of 'Red Sands Rendevous'.

When Radio 390 was prosecuted for broadcasting within UK waters, even though 8 miles off the coast, Ted moved further out to sea. The new location was 4 miles off the coast (who said the law is an ass?) and the ship-borne station called *Radio 355*, another 'easy listening' operation.

In the early 1970s he was involved in licence applications, such as that for Newcastle, along with Bill MacDonald(qv).

Ted is now retired and enjoying life at his home in Kent, but still follows the radio business with great interest.

Adrian ALLEN
Presenter and Head of Music for *Red Rose Gold*.

Brian ALLEN
Began his career as a club DJ in Denmark and joined *Radio Caroline* in 1983. Brian now runs a very successful restaurant in Denmark.

Donald ALLEN
Born in 1930 and educated at Southall, he was in the Forces and then the Diplomatic Service in Holland in the1950s and later in Panama and France, before joining the Broadcast Complaints Commission in 1990.

Janet ALLEN
Producer at *BBC Radio Scotland.*

Joe ALLEN
Country Producer with a Sunday evening show on *BBC Radio Northampton*

John ALLEN
An editor for BBC News & Current Affairs.

Liz ALLEN
A Halifax-born girl who got into radio by becoming secretary to a drama producer at BBC Radio Leeds. She's also worked as a hostess on the QE2, as a TV extra and a freelance journalist as well as a prolific novelist. Liz moved into radio proper with Bradford ILR *Pennine Radio* in 1975 where she hosted arts and music programmes before moving back to the BBC and *Radio Leeds* "for a rest" before taking her talents to national *Radio 2*.

Louise ALLEN
Programme Producer at *BBC Radio Cleveland.*

Mike ALLEN (1)
Began his radio career at *Capital Radio* in London in the 1970's and then moved across town to be present of night-time shows at *LBC / Newstalk Radio* until it closed in late 1994.

Mike ALLEN (2)
A Producer/ presenter at *BBC Radio Devon* and Dorset until he joined *Gemini Radio* In Exeter where he is now the programme manager of the station's AM service.

Paul ALLEN (1)
Presenter of an arts programme on *Radio Four.*

Paul ALLEN (2)
Programme controller and host of some programmes on *2CR in* Bournemouth.

Pete ALLEN
Presents a jazz music programme on *BBC Wiltshire Sound.*

Richard ALLEN
Presenter of programmes about arts and video on *Radio Tay* in Dundee where he is also the station's Operation s Coordinator.

Scott ALLEN
Presenter at *Radio Borders.*

Steve ALLEN
Mike's parents were both in the Forces and had another son; Mike was schooled mainly in Newbury and left prep' school aged 15. His first job was selling soft furnishings and carpets in Newbury where he also helped out in the funeral department!

Steve was running his own mobile disco for several years and in 1970 went off to Denmark to work in clubs there, but didn't fit in with either clubs or the continentals, so he returned home.

Dale Winton (qv), who he worked with in a London club, suggested he join the *United Biscuit Network* (in-factory cable radio station, based in Uxbridge) and four years later sent an audition tape to LBC. Alan King (qv) hired him after an interview in a pub off Fleet Street during which radio was never discussed, and stayed with the station for the next sixteen years - in fact until it closed hosting the afternoon programme.

After LBC Steve did some work for the *UK Living* TV channel and then joined *VIVA 963* in February 1995. At first he was the only man in the line-up and scheduled to do a four hour programme. While he was voicing Viva's test transmissions, *London News Radio*, who'd taken over the LBC frequencies, offered him some work.

Viva 963 decided they couldn't envisage any of their presenters appearing on a rival station so dispensed with his services!

After a period doing holiday relief for Robbie Vincent on LNR he was given a daily lunchtime slot and hopes he'll be there for sixteen years!

Stu ALLEN
DJ at *Piccadilly Gold* In Manchester

Tim ALLEN
Tim is one of the regular presenters at *Northants Radio* in Northampton.

Vince ALLEN

Born in 1937, six feet tall Vince became a paratrooper during National Service and on leaving the army became the manager of an RnB group. He was hired by Roy Bates (qv) to manage a new venture in 1965 - *Radio Essex*.

Vince broadcast on the station himself and, after Radio Essex was closed down in early 1967, he moved to Yorkshire and took over programming at *Radio 270* where he rapidly became one of the station's most popular broadcasters.

He used a curious recording of galloping horses and cowboy calls as a theme and was far better known as 'Rusty' Allen, thanks to his flaming hair, usually worn in a Teddy Boy quiff.

Rusty's was the last voice heard on *Radio 270* when the station closed and, after a period working in clubs, he took a job with in local government administration in his native Essex.

Richard ALLINSON
A 1958 baby, he was given his first record "Love Me Do" for his third birthday and ten years later was running a mobile disco business. He spent most of his time at Lancaster University in the campus radio station, which obviously gave him a good grounding as he graduated straight into *Capital Radio* in August 1980 - the only jock to ever join Capital with no experience! A long stint on

the station's early shift and as a swing jock followed; he has also accurately predicted the last three Christmas number one chart hits.

In 1983 Richard won his first Sony Gold Award. He likes tennis, Japanese food and real ale, and hates Ford Capris! Married with a son and lives in Camden.

David ALLISON
Journalist at *BBC Radio Berkshire*.

John ALLISON CBE
John is a director of *Swansea Sound*.

Rupert ALLISON
On - air presenter on Orchard FM

Julian ALLITT
Managing Director of *BAY 96 FM* in Lancaster and Morecambe.

Nick ALLRIGHT
Presented a series of overnight shows on *Essex FM* in 1994 and currently presents an early breakfast show on sister station *Breeze AM*. His most humourous event was playing the part of Humphrey Bogart in front of an all American audience which he now thinks is "not advisable!"

Paul ALLWRIGHT
His first broadcast was in May '93 where he presented weekend overnight shows on *Essex FM*. Since January '94 Paul has presented weekday early breakfast shows on *Breeze*, a subsidiary of Essex Radio plc.

Nick ALLMARK
Head of Production, Business and Finance for the BBC, based in Southampton.

Marcus ALTON
News producer at *BBC Radio Derby*.

Monique AMAUDRY
Director of Corporate Communications at MTV.

Liz AMBLER
Joined the BBC as a secretary after leaving Bradford Girls Grammar School, Liz was one of the first local radio broadcasters in Britain, at the then VHF only *BBC Radio Leeds* in June 1968. Presented the mid morning show as well as a Sunday phone-in programme on *Radio*

Leeds until recently.

Barry AMIS

Religious Producer and programme presenter (weekends) at *BBC Three Counties Radio.*

John AMIS

Presenter of 'My Music' on *Radio Four.*

Geoff AMOS

Hosts a Saturday lunchtime gardening programme on *BBC Radio Leicester.*

Jon AMOS

Presenter at *BBC Radio Cambridgeshire.*

Alison ANDERSON

Planning organiser at *BBC Radio Four.*

Arthur ANDERSON

Head of Production at *BBC Radio Scotland.*

Bill ANDERSON

Sports reporter at *Moray Firth Radio* in Inverness.

Billy ANDERSON

Head of Sales for Glasgow area at *Scot FM.*

Brian ANDERSON

Brian's radio career began as a panel operator at *Radio Caroline* in 1973, followed by *Radio Mi Amigo* and *Radio North Sea International.*

In 1975 Brian came ashiore to work in ILR and joined *Radio Tees* in Stockton, where he remained until moving north of the border to *Moray Firth Radio.*

He stayed at MFR eventually being placed in charge of programmes, until the early 1990s, when he moved to Shanghai in China and, sadly, has not been heard of since.

Ian ANDERSON

Head of Engineering at *Premier Radio*, London.

Jerry ANDERSON

Presenter on BBC Northern Ireland.

Iain ANDERSON

Producer at *BBC Radio Scotland* and presents 'Sport on Scotland' each Saturday.

Ian ANDERSON

Engineer in charge at *BBC Radio Bristol.*

Ian J. D. ANDERSON

Born in Lerwick, Shetland and educated on the Island and in Edinburgh. His career from 1969 includes *Radio 428* (from Andorra) and *Radio Geronimo, Radio Nordsee International* and other offshore stations. After coming ashore he joined *Radio Forth,* Edinburgh.

Ian freelanced for BBC and ILR for a time and from 1976 until 1985 was also a freelance author and writer. he then established the *Shetland Islands Broadcasting Company* which has been broadcasting since 1987. The station is jointly owned by Ian and his wife Inga Walterson (see separate entry).

He is company secretary of SIBC, where his responsibilities also include news, finance and engineering.

Ian ANDERSON

Engineer-in-charge at *BBC Radio Bristol.*

John ANDERSON

Presents a programme at BBC Northern Ireland.

Leslie ANDERSON

Home affairs correspondent at *BBC Radio Scotland.*

Ray ANDERSON (1)

A long time radio enthusiast, Ray started 'East Anglian Productions' in 1968 whilst still at school. It is now one of the longest established production companies in the UK.

His first broadcasts were on ship-borne *Radio Atlantis* in 1974 as Ray Warner, pre-recording his programme from one turntable at his home in Frinton!

In the same year he started 'Jumbo Records' which releases radio documentaries. In the seventies and eighties he was a leading supplier of radio memorabilia.

In 1986 he bought the ship 'Communicator after its arrest for non-payment of staff, and relaunched it as *Laser Hot Hits.* Technical difficulties ensued, as did other problems - including a boarding by would be operators!

Ray now presents an excellent juke-box programme on *Mellow 1557,* an ILR srtation which was, until 1995, based at Ray's well known 'Radio House' building in Frinton Essex. He is currently working on a film about radio ships called 'Rock The Boat'.

Ray ANDERSON (2)
Presenter on *Great North Radio* (Newcastle).

Tom ANDERSON
Tom's radio career began in the 1970s on *Radio Caroline*. he was the first voice on air on the new 1980s *Caroline 319* which launched on 20th August 1983, and responsible for the station's 'Overdrive' service, which majored on new music, especially reggae. In 1993 he moved to *Riviera Radio* in Monte Carlo, where he was later appointed Programme Director.

Val ANDERSON
Editor of English output at *BBC World Service*.

Paul ANDREW
Presenter on GWR FM East.

David ANDREWS
Got into radio by way of hospital radio in Chelmsford and in June 1985 joined *Radio Caroline* for a year before a similar length gig at *Energy 103* in Dublin.

In July 1987 he set off to *Riviera Radio* in Monaco for a six month stay, returning to the UK to join *Chiltern Radio* in early 1988. David stayed there until joining *Capital Gold* in September 1994 - the highlight of his career.

Ian ANDREWS
Non executive director of *Classic Gold 828* in Bournemouth.

James ANDREWS
Presenter at *The Pulse* in West Yorkshire.

Leighton ANDREWS
Head of Public Affairs at the BBC's Corporate Affairs section, based at Broadcasting House.

Sue ANDREWS
Finance Manager at *Melody Radio* in London.

Phil ANGELL
Presenter of the Breakfast show at *Fox FM* in Oxford where, in 1995 he became the station's programme controller.

Natalie ANGLESY
Host of an afternoon programme from 1.00 until, 4pm at weekends on *London Newstalk 1152*.

Paul ANGUS
Chief Executive at *Devonair Radio*.

Steve ANSELL
Head of Personnel at BBC Scotland.

Elizabeth ANSTEE
Senior Producer of Light Entertainment (radio) based at Broadcasting House.

Paul ANTHONY
Presenter of the Saturday lunchtime and Sunday breakfast shows on *Signal One,* in Stoke.

Peter ANTONY
As a sixties child, Peter Antony grew up with a great love of pop music and only one ambition - to become a disc jockey. Some twenty years on, he was signed by Europe's largest commercial radio station - *Radio Luxembourg*.

In 1978, Peter moved to London and was taken on by a DJ agency. Soon after being the resident DJ in several night clubs in the South East, Peter landed one of the top DJ jobs in London - resident DJ at Stringfellows, probably the most famous discotheque in the world.

In 1985 Peter's appointment to the Luxembourg team followed freelance work with the company over the previous months.

Michael APICHELLA
After several years as a newspaper journalist and columnist, Michael spent ten years at BBC Radio Oxford as a religious producer. His radio documentary 'The Old Rugged Cross' won a Christian Broadcasters Council award in 1994.

In 1995 he joined *Premier Radio*, London's new Christian station as their senior producer. Michael has also written three books and over a hundred articles about religion and travel.

Abigail APPLETON
Producer of Science and Features, BBC Radio.

John APPLEYARD
Presenter at *BBC Radio York* in mid eighties.

Mike APPLEYARD
Chief Engineer at *Radio City*, ILR station in Liverpool, in the nineties.

Dickie ARBITER
Born in 1940 in London, Dickie went into acting in South Africa and in 1959 moved across to radio. He then had a stint doing radio and TV news reporting in Rhodesia and moved to London as LBC became the capital's first commercial radio station 1973.

He became a well known voice on LBC in its glory years and known to millions around the UK as one of the most distinctive newsreaders on IRN. - including anchor coverage of the Royal Wedding in 1981.

Alicia ARCE
Producer at *BBC Radio Cambridgeshire*.

Andy ARCHER

 Andy was born at Terrington St Clements in Norfolk on 22nd January, 1946, and was educated at the West Norfolk College of Art and Technology. He was bitten by the radio bug on hearing Tom Lodge (qv) on Radio Caroline and visited the *Radio City* offices in London, before making a short trip out to the fort. He then joined the RAF and became an air traffic controller, but decided to buy himself out and get into radio.

He joined *Radio Caroline* just after the Marine Offences Act and was on board the ship when it was towed away by the tender company in lieu of unpaid bills. Two years later was one of the team who launched *Radio North Sea* .

In the early seventies he was involved in the return of *Radio Caroline* off the Dutch coast and was Programme Director of the station's Dutch service as well as one of the most popular DJs on its International service. He became the first British DJ to be prosecuted under the Marine Offences Act in 1975.

He also broadcast on associate station *Radio Atlantis* before returning to the UK where he worked at Radio Orwell in Ipswich and as a continuity announcer at *Tyne Tees TV* using his real name Andrew Dawson.

Andy then moved south to Devonair and on to Ireland in the 1980s where he worked at Sunshine Radio and at ERI in Cork, before returning to the UK and a job at Centre Radio in Leicester. In the early 80s was lured back to Radio Caroline but after being apprehended on an illegal tender trip into the UK he decided to come ashore permanently and joined County Sound in Guildford.

He then moved back to *Radio Orwell* and then, in 1990, to *Invicta Supergold* in Kent as Programme Controller. Andy then moved to *CN103* in Cambridge when the station launched and, more recently, he has been heard recently on BBC local stations in East Anglia.

John ARCHER
Head of Music and Arts at *BBC Radio Scotland*.

Jonathan ARENDT
Commercial Director of *London Newstalk FM*.

Rob ARENSTEIN
Head of Commercial Production at *TFM Radio* .

Stewart ARGO
Director at *Heartland FM*.

ARIF
Drive time presenter on new station *Radio XL*-AM in the Midlands.

Usha ARMAR
Programme Controller and Chief Executive at *Sunrise Radio* in London, Bradford and Leicester.

Lucy ARMITAGE
Producer of lunchtime programmes during 1995 at *BBC Radio One*.

Janice ARMSTRONG
A radio journalist at the former BBC *Radio Berkshire*, now merged with Radio Oxford to form *Radio Thames Valley*.

Mike ARMSTRONG
Senior engineer at *BBC Wiltshire Sound*.

Susan ARMSTRONG
Environment specialist at *Heartland FM*.

Who's Who in British Radio

Tim ARNOLD
Producer / presenter at *BBC Radio Devon.*

Sue ARON
Producer at the BBC Educational Directorate.

Belinda ARTINGSTALL
Presenter and producer at *BBC Radio Cumbria.*

David ARSCOTT
Applied to BBC after University and presented the afternoon programme on BBC *Radio Brighton* in the early 1980s.

Chris ARUNDELL
Born in York, Chris trained to be a biologist, but by 1981 the radio bug had bitten and he set sail on the *Voice of Peace* "somewhere in the Mediterranean".

In the 1980's he worked at no less than 18 radio stations, travelling around the UK, and in 1989 he settled at BBC *Radio Humberside*, becoming district reporter for the northern part of the station's editorial area, based in Bridlington. Chris is regularly heard on the station on a variety of programmes..

As well as broadcasting he also writes about travelling and gardening, and thinks the highlight of his radio career has yet to come. He likes all kinds of good music, botany, drinking good beer and running, but hasn't much time for designer spectacles and people who don't think for themselves.

Frank ASH
Producer at the BBC Educational Directorate.

Janie ASH
Sales Manager at *The Bay,* in Lancaster.

Andy ASHBY
Hosts a Sunday early morning (midnight to 6am) programme at *Fox FM* in Oxford.

Denise ASHBY
Promotions Manager at *Southern FM.*

Clare ASHFORD
Care is now the host of weekend/overnight shows on *Capital FM.*

Chris ASHLEY
Phone-in host and programme producer on *BBC Radio Cambridgeshire* in 1995.

Hugh ASHLEY
Presenter at *BBC Radio Solent.*

Stephen ASHLEY-KING
Administrator of the BBC Singers at *Radio Three.*

David ASHTON
News producer at *BBC Radio Cumbria.*

Lindsey ASHWOOD
In 1995, newsroom manager at *Orchard FM .*

Phil ASHWORTH
Assistant Editor at *BBC Radio Cumbria.*

Michael ASPEL
Born 12th January 1933 in London and held down a variety of posts before some amateur dramatics involvement led to his appearing on Children's Hour on the *Home Service* now *Radio Four)* in 1954. He began his career as an actor with BBC Radio in Cardiff.

Michael then moved to the BBC's West region to embark on a career in continuity announcing, and later television newscasting. That led to his hosting *Crackerjack* on BBC TV, his own series *Ask Aspel* as well as being the resident host of *Miss World.*

In 1974 he joined *Capital Radio* for a (then) huge sum and presented a daily show for almost two decades.

David ASPER
Director of *Talk Radio UK.*

Gordon ASTLEY
Born in Lancashire, Gordon was one of the presenters on cult children's TV programme 'Tiswas' in the early 80's, before joining *Beacon Radio.*

While there he developed a taste for magic and music halls, and hosted a weekday breakfast programme.

He moved to BBC *Radio WM* with his morning programme and in 1995 was presenting a morning programme (9am to 1 pm) at *Southern Counties Radio,* serving the area south of London.

Nick ASTLEY-COOPER
Nick is the Assistant Director of Engineering at the Radio Authority.

13

John ASTON

After a two hour audition with Mike Raven, John was hired for *King Radio* as a disc-jockey using the name John Stewart. When King closed down and became *Radio 390* he changed his name to Chris Stewart, as Equity already had a John Stewart on their books.

Later in 1965 he moved to nearby *Radio Essex*, but joined *Radio Caroline North* the following year as a newsreader. Caroline already had Bob Stewart, so yet another name change was in order - and he became John Aston.

Then followed a spell selling airtime for *Radio England*, another brief spell for Radio *Caroline* on their south ship, and then a move to Yorkshire and *Radio 270* at Easter, 1967. It was on 270 he became known as 'Action' John Aston, but didn't settle there either, moving back south to *Radio 355*. While there his cabin was used for a live broadcast from the ship by the then unknown singer Jose Feliciano.

John then went into the voice over business doing documentaries and training films and eventually joined a film company as production manager. In 1975 he returned to radio providing facilities for Swansea Sound OB programmes and then set up a sound effects studio, providing audio for the series 'Space 1999'. He also worked on 'Revenge of the Pink Panther', 'Return of the Jedi' and several other films and appeared on sc reen himself for 35 seconds as a five star General!

A good example of his work can be heard on the film 'Jewel of the Nile' and recently he was working on a new version of 'Frankenstein'. He now lives in Berkshire with his wife Christine and two children.

Trevor ASTON

Senior producer of daily programmes at BBC South - Network radio, based Southampton.

David ASTOR

Joint chief executive of *Golden Rose*, which launched and operated *Jazz FM*. Then applied for and won North West regional licence in summer 1993, due on air in late 1994 with Jazz music format.

Pete ATKIN

Head of BBC Network Radio (South), based in Bristol.

Neal ATKINSON

In 1993 he was a presenter at *Radio City FM* in Liverpool.

Roy ATKINSON

Head of Music (PM) on *Moray Forth Radio* in Inverness, Scotland.

Syd ATKINSON

Producer of dance band music at *Moray Firth Radio*.

Lord ATTENBOROUGH, CBE

President of *Capital Radio Group Plc.*

Lambros ATTESHLIS

Producer at BBC Educational Directorate.

Tony ATTWATER

Head of News and Sport at *Beacon Radio* in Wolverhampton.

Henry AUBREY-FLETCHER

Director of *Fox FM*, Oxford.

George AUCKLAND

Producer at BBC Educational Directorate.

John AUMONIER

John became Managing Director of *Radio Mercury* and the Allied Radio Group, as well as overseeing operation of the ill-fated *Airport Information Radio*. He was involved in the launch of *Virgin 1215* and *TalkRadio UK*, leaving the INR 3 station in July 1995 "to pursue other broadcasting interests". He is a director of Phoenix Radio, which bid for the Reigate ILR licence in Autumn 1995.

Dave AUSTIN

Presents a weekly programme on BBC Radio Kent.

Mark AUSTIN

A director of *1170 - AM* in High Wycombe.

Philip AUSTIN

Company Secretary of *Spectrum International*.

Richard AUSTIN

Born on 22nd May in 1948 and educated at Winchester Choir School, Richard became a teacher before joining the BBC as an education producer. He then worked as a trainer at the BBC's famed Local Radio Unit and was also among the first local radio voices with *Radio Durham* (now a part of *Radio Cleveland*).

Who's Who in British Radio

By the early 1980s Richard was producing the breakfast programme on BBC *Radio Cumbria* and is now a senior producer at BBC *Somerset Sound*.

Wendy AUSTIN
Presenter at *BBC Radio Ulster*.

Justin AVIS
Promotion manager at *Southern Sound* in Brighton.

Ian AXTON
Sports Producer at *Spire FM* in Wiltshire.

Margaret AYERS
A director of *Red Rose Radio* in Preston.

Mike AYLING
Chief Engineer at *2 CR* and sister station *Classic Gold 828*, both in Bournemouth.

Richard AYRE
Controller of Editorial Policy at the BBC Policy Department, Broadcasting House.

John AYRES
News editor at *Devonair Radio*.

Margaret AYRES
Director of *Red Rose Radio* in Preston.

Henry AYRTON
Presents a folk music programme each Monday evening on *BBC Radio Leeds*.

Nick BABB

Nick was working as a mobile DJ by the time he was 14 and also worked in the record department at Woolworths for a while.

He became a 'paid' helper on a late night show at *Radio Aire* after being a guest on a programme in 1989 and his first broadcast came one snowy night in 1991 - a case of being in the right place at the right time. Since then he's presented a variety of programmes on Aire and sister station, *Magic 828*.

As well as radio work, 22 year old Nick runs his own PA and light equipment business and also coordinates promotions at *Radio Aire*. The highlight of his career was appearing on stage in front of 45,000 people in Leeds and, like most presenters, lists his likes as food, drink and women.

Tim BACKSHALL
News producer at *BBC Radio Cumbria*.

John BACON
Group Insurance Officer at *Capital Radio*.

Louise BADGER
Manager of the BBC Symphony Orchestra for BBC *Radio Three*.

Simon BAGGE
Assistant New Editor at BBC Midlands.

David L BAGLEY
Managing Director of *BRMB* Group and Head of Sales and Marketing at *Xtra AM*.

Alan BAGULEY
Operations Manager for *BBC Radio Wales*.

Gwyn BAILEY
Choral Presenter on *Swansea Sound*.

Nick BAILEY
Began his radio career with *Radio Caroline* and in 1993 joined *Classic FM* where he has presented the station's breakfast sequence since the station's launch.

Richard BAILEY
Sports reporter and commentator at *BBC Radio Sheffield* in the eighties and nineties.

Robin BAILEY
Attended Thorpe St Andrew Grammar school in Norwich after which he became a newspaper journalist for six years. In 1987 he joined *Radio Broadland* as a sports and news reporter, making his first broadcast in October.

Three years later he joined BBC Radio sport and then moved to *Radio Two* as a rugby producer for three years. In Summer 1995 came the highlight so far of his radio career, when he moved to *Radio Five* to become a regular 'Sport on Five' presenter.

Tim BAILEY
Newsroom Editor at BBC's News and Current Affairs (Radio) department.

Who's Who in British Radio

Trevor BAILEY
Director of *Essex Radio Group*.

Eileen BAINES
Promotion manager at *Jazz FM*, Manchester.

Paul BAJORIA
News Producer at *BBC Radio Newcastle* and producer of programmes for disabled people.

Anthony BAKER
Director of *Yorkshire Broadcasting Co Ltd*, applicant for ILR licences in 1995.

Cheryl BAKER
Member of Eurovision winning group 'Buck's Fizz' before becoming a TV presenter. She has appeared on many radio stations and is now a regular weekend show presenter for *BBC Radio 5*.

Colin BAKER
News Editor at *Leicester Sound FM*.

Danny BAKER
Originally a presenter with Michael Aspel on a weekly Thames TV programme, also Danny was a presenter on GLR in the early 1990s where he did the weekend breakfast programmes.

He moved to *Radio One* in 1994 for a Sunday morning programme and caused controversy when he objected to a trailer on Remembrance Sunday, and hosted a series of DAZ TV commercials.

Danny's favourite group is Earth,Wind and Fire and he supports Millwall F.C. He currently hosts a Saturday morning programme on BBC R*adio One*.

David BAKER

After leaving school, David managed a record shop in Dublin and, when he was just 13, David made his first broadcast on radio reading sports results on Saturday afternoons. He then worked for *Radio City* and things took off from there.

He also worked for several other stations in Dublin, including *Kiss FM* and *Radio Leinster*.

He now works at Breeze AM, where he hosts a weekday evening programme and has been there since its launch in July 1989. He also works for Sky Sports at the weekend.

The highlight of his career was when he won an award "For service to the Irish Radio industry." His other work is reporting from football matches from various venues around the country and does commentary and video work for football clubs such as Q.P.R. FC.

Elaine BAKER
Music Organiser at TFM Radio in Stockton.

Jack BAKER
An Oldham, Lancashire, boy, Jack was born on 16th June in 1947 and educated at Stockport Grammar School, the Pembroke College in Cambridge and Manchester Polytech'. A disco promoter, encyclopedia salesman and lecturer in English, he got into radio by way of working the club scene and getting a slot on BBC *Radio Manchester* in their 'New Voices' programme which showcased nightclub jocks.

The BBC didn't hire anyone connected with clubs in those days if they could help it, so Jack applied to the last of the first wave of ILR stations - *Pennine Radio*, who wouldn't hire anyone as a DJ either, but took him on as a 'presenter'.

A more Yorkshire sounding name of JULIUS K. SCRAGG was adopted and he became a star of the 70s, with one of his programmes being nominated Best Light Entertainment Show in Local Radio' in 1981. He then moved fifty miles down the M1 to BBC *Radio Sheffield* to become a producer as well as DJ and was responsible for some of its best output in the eighties, including an excellent Pop Quiz series.

Jack's biggest claim to fame is his notorious 'striptease on radio' at *Pennine Radio* where listeners pledged cash for charity) for him to peel off his shoes, socks and other apparel. It took just 20 minutes before he was stark naked, and a photo by the station's MD found its way to the national *Daily Star*. His first love is his family, radio, computers and music.

He then moved to *BBC Radio Sheffield* where he presents a weekday afternoon programme.

John BAKER

After a period working in sales at *Fox FM* in Oxford, John moved to *Wessex FM* in Dorchester in October 1995 to be the station's Sales and Marketing Manager.

Keith BAKER

Head of News and Current Affairs at *BBC Radio Ulster*.

Mike BAKER

A former *Radio Caroline* DJ, Mike was the first voice on the air at *Beacon Radio* when the station launched in 1976, he stayed there throughout the eighties, hosting programmes such as 'Love in the Afternoon'.

He joined joined the new regional station *Heart FM* when it launched in Birmingham in 1994. He currently hosts the station's afternoon programme from 1pm until 4pm.

Pete BAKER

A Londoner who pursued his love of radio and electronics while at Bath University, Pete also worked at the *BBC World Service* and used the Corporation's facilities to assemble an audition tape which impressed *Piccadilly Radio* so much they hired him as an all-round swing jock.

He hosted children's programmes, late night programmes and regular day-time strips and also became head of music in the early 1980s.

Peter BAKER

In the 1990s Peter was a Senior Producer at *BBC Radio Oxford*, which has now merged with Radio Berkshire to become *Radio Thames Valley*.

Richard BAKER

Born June 1925 in North London, he worked as a school teacher and actor, before finding himself out of work in 1950. He joined the BBC ("I thought it would be fun for a few months, and stayed ever since") as a continuity announcer and has hosted many programmes over his forty four years or so there.

Currently presenting a weekly programme each Saturday evening called 'Comparing Notes' on *Radio Four* and programmes such as 'Baker's Dozen' on airline in-flight headset channels.

Richard Anthony BAKER

First job was a reporter on the London 'Evening Standard' , but he also found time to play in several jazz bands. He then joined the *World Service* as a journalist and his first programme was on *BBC Radio London.*

He has also written for and produced programmes for Radio 2, 3 and 4 and in the 1980s moved to the live side of the microphone to host programmes, having to add his middle name to avoid confusion with the well known *Radio Four* presenter with a similar name!

Rodney BAKER-BATES

Director of Finance at BBC, based at Broadcasting House.

Neil BALDOCK

Senior Programme Producer at *BBC Essex*.

Graham BALDWIN

Graham is one of the Directors of cable station *Community Radio Milton Keynes*.

Peter BALDWIN CBE

Born on 19th February, 1927, Peter was educated at in Chelmsford and enlisted in the regular Army and Royal Signals,. He saw service in World War II, The Korean War and (including Berlin airlift) Joined IBA as Deputy Director of Radio and Chief Executive of Radio Authority from February 1990 until summer 1995.

Adrian BALL

Adrian is the Programme Organiser at Severn Sound in Gloucestershire.

David BALL

Company secretary for Mid Anglia Radio Plc and Chairman of CN103 in Cambridge.

G BALL

Company Secretary at *Leicester Sound FM*.

Martin BALL

Martin is now a London sales executive for *London News Radio*.

John-Paul BALLANTINE

Head of Music and Station promotion activities at *Downtown Radio* and *Cool FM* in Belfast.

17

Martin BALLARD

Producer at *BBC Radio Leicester* and host of daily mid-morning programme.

Penny BALLARD

Promotions Manager at *Trent FM* and *GEM-AM*.

Ally BALLINGALL

Programme Controller at *Radio Tay* and also presents folk music programmes as 'Ally Bally'.

Judith BANBURY

Senior officer at the BBC Educational Directorate.

Greg BANCE

One of the most distinctive voices in the business, Greg's career began as a disc-jockey on offshore radio stations around the UK coast under the name 'Roger Scott', beginning with *Radio Essex* in 1966.

Then came a spell at *Radio 270* before moving on to *Radio Caroline North*. He was also a continuity announcer and occasional local feature presenter at several regional ITV companies; HTV, Anglia, Tyne Tees, Granada, Southern, ATV and LWT.

Greg has always been an active freelance and he's been heard on hundreds of commercials and AV productions. In the early 1970's he joined *Radio North Sea International* where he was known as 'Arnold Layne' (who said the Pink Floyd weren't ahead of their time!) and after finally coming ashore he joined *LBC* and began using his 'real' name - leaving the path clear for another talented broadcaster to take up the 'Roger Scot' moniker.

Greg moved to Ipswich ILR *Radio Orwell* where he became a full time senior presenter and producer, hosting a variety of slots, from breakfast to intimate late night sequences. In the 1980's he was regularly heard on BBC Radio London, and also returned to regional TV, becoming known as "The Voice of Anglia".

He spent periods at *Beacon Radio, Two Counties Radio*, and then back to LBC. In addition he's run the newsroom at BFBS single handed and more recently has been heard as a regular presenter at Essex Radio's *Breeze-AM*, where he currently hosts weekday evenings and Sunday afternoon strips.

David BANKS

Host of a programme each Sunday morning from 10 to Non on *London Newsradio FM*.

Margaret BANKS

Margaret was the Station Secretary and administrator at *Wear FM* until June, 1995.

Robin BANKS (1)

After a career which included being a leading light in the Free Radio Association, which campaigned for commercial radio to be introduced to the UK, and wielding a screwdriver for several radio station, Robin Adcroft was persuaded to host programmes on *Radio Caroline's* International service in 1973.

A larger pay packet lured Robin across to the nearby 'Mebo II' where he broadcast on *Radio Noordzee*, as Robin Banks to millions all over Europe. Robin stayed with the station when it changed its name to *Radio Nova* and sailed to the Mediterranean, but moved back into engineering wielding that trusty screwdriver once again for many stations all over the continent and even further afield.

Now a highly regarded station engineer he is currently setting up a network of FM stations in Africa, leaving his 'Robin Banks' name available for anyone who wants to pick up his tax bills! And some one did -

Robin BANKS (2)

The second Robin Banks got his first job in radio when he visited a pirate station while only 14 years old - the regular DJ had' turned up (he was later found locked in the toilet). After leaving school Robin went to the *Voice of Peace*.

The advent of the Gulf War and the prospects of a scud missile attack provoked a sense of nostalgia for dear old Blighty, so Robin returned for a gig at *Radio Nova*, then the first UK satellite station broadcasting from

Camberley. The station soon closed due to lack of advertising so, after turning down a gig with a South African station, Robin headed off to Ireland and *Atlantic 252*.

While there he came to the attention of *Virgin, 1215*, where he now presents weekday overnights.

Boni BANNARD

Educated at Leicester Polytechnic, Boni started her radio career as a reporter/ producer at BBC Radio Cambridgeshire.Also has been a local education correspondent and has worked at 6 other radio stations.Her highlight of her career was having the first interview with John Major when he became Prime Minister.

Roderic BANNATYNE

A Director of *Country 1035* in London.

Graham BANNERMAN

Presenter of Multitrack music programmes on the *BBC World Service*.

Richard BANNERMAN

Editor and Producer with B*BC Radio Three*.

Matthew BANNISTER

Born on the 16th March, 1957, Matthew was educated in Sheffield and at the University of Nottingham. In 1978 he joined *BBC Radio Nottingham*, 1978 and three years later moved to *Capital Radio* as a news reporter. In 1983 he moved to the *Radio One* 'Newsbeat' programme but returned to Capital Radio two years later as Head of News and Talks. In 1988 he was appointed Managing Editor of *BBC Radio London* and oversaw its change into *GLR*.

He coordinated the BBC's Charter Renewal project and the Corporation's Programme Strategy Review for which he was rewarded with the 'Network Controller - Radio One' role in July 1993. A first actions were most Radio One personalities with former GLR colleagues (e.g. Chris Evans, Trevor Dann, ...) and moving the music and presentation policies towards a younger style. His recreations include opera, the theatre and collecting books.

Sharon BANNOFF

Editor of topical features at the BBC Arts and Science section.

Rahila BANO

Producer of Asian programmes at *BBC GMR*.

Jim BANVILLE

Director of *Essex Radio* Group Plc.

Steve BANYARD

Sports Editor at *Hallam FM*

Roger BARA

Sports editor of *BBC Radio Jersey*.

Des BARBER

Des was a presenter at *KCBC* in Kettering, Northamptonshire until 1995.

Martin BARBER

Presents a Sunday morning show on *BBC Radio Northampton*.

Ronnie BARBOUR

Born in Scotland, Ronnie hosts weekend programmes on *BBC Radio Cambridgeshire* and in 1995 he joined *TalkRadio UK*.

Bill BARCLAY

Although Bill's first broadcast was on a 'Folk on Friday' programme for the BBC back in 1968, it wasn't until 1974 that he got into radio professionally. At that time he was on tour with Rod Stewart and *Radio Clyde* asked him to present a Sunday Night programme.

He spent the last twenty years with the group and can now be heard on the *Max AM* station. He's also appeared in many radio and TV plays and sit-coms and has toured most parts of the world including the USA, Canada, Middle East and the Falklands, but among his highlights are 'Snowline' broadcasts.

Likes life, but not getting up in the morning and is currently writing a screen play for TV.

Barclay BARCLAY-WHITE

A Weybridge dentist, who was on holiday on the Essex coast and listened to *Radio North Sea* with his children. Their reaction to the all music station encouraged Barclay to set up a company called *Capital Radio* to bid for licences when they became available. They won the second ILR licence to be offered, London's 'general entertainment' station, *Capital Radio* and Barclay has remained a board member ever since.

Ron BARDEN

A director of *Northants Radio*.

Brian BARFIELD
The Head of Planning at *BBC Radio Three*.

Geoff BARKER
Presenter at *2CR / Classic Gold*.

Mrs J BARKER OBE
Mrs Barker is a director of Mid Anglia Radio.

Kate BARKER
Parliamentary Correspondent for BBC News and Current Affairs.

Kent BARKER
An old Felstead boy, Kent also schooled in Connecticut USA, he got into radio in college radio in Los Angeles. Eventually borrowed a tape recorder and gate-crashed a reception for 'That's Entertainment' and got an interview with Gene Kelly and Liza Minelli, which he sold to Capital Radio. He tried almost every local radio station in England before Dave Cousins, then PD at *Radio Tees* took him on.

Peter BARKER
A Trained chorister (at Southwell cathedral School) he became a BBC announcer in 1962 when such a role meant shifts across all three national networks.

When network dedicated announcers came into vogue he chose *Radio 3* and was one of the station's best known voices for many years. Lives with his wife Eileen in London.

Dilly BARLOW
Programme Producer at *BBC Radio 4*.

Boni BARNARD
Became a print journalist after attending Leicester Polytechnic and then joined *BBC Radio Cambridgeshire* where she became a news producer. An education specialist she also reports on that subject for BBC TV news and on other local stations in the BBC East group.

She was the first person to interview John Major after he became Prime Minister and has written a book on the media. Boni doesn't like local radio speech "twangs" but loves enthusiasm on the air.

John BARNES
In 1994 John was the news editor at Red Rose Radio in Preston. He is now the Station Manager at *Radio Maldwyn* in Powys, Wales and presenter of a lunchtime weekday programme.

Nick BARNES
Sports producer at *BBC Radio Cumbria*

Paul BARNES
Well known BBC TV East presenter and also late night presenter on BBC Local Radio in East Anglia until early 1995. He returned to the station in Autumn 1995 to host one late night programme each week.

Richard BARNES
Engineer in charge at *BBC Radio Leeds*.

Sam BARNES
Promotion executive at *Chiltern* in Bedford.

Steve BARNES
Born in the late 1940's, Steve was born in Burnley and, after a career with the Electricity Board, Philips Group and the IBA, became one of the first employees of *Piccadilly Radio*, being hired as an engineer in early 1974 to help build the studios in Manchetser.

In 1979 he became the station's Chief Engineer and in 1987 took on the role of General Manager. He's recently undertaken a complete refurbishment of the station's equipment and is now working on its move to new premises.

Susie BARNES
A Lincolnshire girl she was educated at Kesteven High School and London College, before becoming a BBC Secretary. After a spell in admin she moved into production in talks and Current Affairs, before moving to the 'Popular Music' department.

Her first broadcast was reading listeners' letters on 'Woman's Hour', but she has also worked on programmes at *BBC Radio One* and presented own programmes on *Radio 2* and BBC GLR. She became well known as 'The Action Girl' on Tony Blackburn's programme.

John BARNETT
Managing Director of *The Wave* in Blackpool.

Peter BARNETT
Peter is the Chief Engineer at *Q102.9 FM* in Northern Ireland.

Simon BARNETT
Simon hosts a music programme each Sunday night from 7pm on *GLR* in London.

Elaine BARONE
Assistant Editor for *BBC Radio Bedfordshire.*

Andrew BARR
Head of Religious Programme at *BBC Radio Scotland.*

Felicity BARR
Journalist and newsreader at Network News,

Shelley BARR
Assistant Administration. Personnel and Finance Officer at *BBC Essex.*

Nick BARRACLOUGH
Presenter of weekday early morning programmes on *BBC Radio Cambridgeshire* and recently hosting a Saturday afternoon programme on *BBC Radio Two.*

Richard BARRANCE
Marketing Controller at *Heartland FM* in Pitlochry, Scotland.

Dave BARRETT
Presenter on *GWR (East)*FM.

Simon BARRETT
Born in Bromley in June 1954, Simon was educated at Dulwich Prep School and the City of London Public School. He joined Record Mirror as a trainee journalist in 1971 and after about eight months became a club DJ in Spain.

In 1973 he joined the BBC as Assistant Publicity Officer at *Radio One*, and the twoards the end of 1974 joined *Radio Caroline*. Over the next year he had an eventful life, even being arrested when the Caroline ship drifted into British waters but continued broadcasting.

Simon later wrote about his experiences on the ship called 'SOS - 10 days in the Life of a Lady". He then returned to the UK to continue his broadcasting career.

Dick BARRIE
Born in Glasgow and educated at Allan Glen's School, he has extensive experience of cargo management at Glasgow Airport. In 1977 he was recruited to present the 'Flightwatch' broadcasts on *Radio Clyde, Radio Forth* and

BBC Radio Scotland and the following year graduated to hosting his own programme on *Radio Forth.*

Since then he's hosted regular country-flavoured programmes on Radio Forth and also programme inserts on motorsports and speedway on Radio Clyde.

As well as radio, Dick has presented pieces for ITV's World of Sport and the highlight of his career was interviewing his boyhood here, Phil Everly. Likes good music, hot weather and laughing, but not cold weather and dishonesty in business.

'Always available' - call his agent, 0141 638 1670.

Mike BARRY
Director at *CRMK* in Milton Keynes.

Quintin BARRY
Managing Director of *Invicta Radio* in Kent.

Sheila BARTER
Sheila began her career in newspaper journalism, and spent several years freelancing before joining BBC Radio news department.

She worked extensively at *Radio Two* as producer on the Jimmy Young Programme and for *Radio Four* and 'Woman's Hour', before joining *Premier Radio,* as a producer in early 1995.

Christopher BARTLETT
Producer / presenter at *BBC Radio Devon*

Patrick BARTLETT
Parliamentary correspondent for local stations, based at BBC Politics Unit, Westminster.

Louise BASCH-GREENBERG
Chief Producer for BBC Radio's Arts, Science and Features Department, based in London.

Sameena BASHEY
Cultural affairs producer at *Radio Newcastle.*

Kerry BASSETT
Daytime presenter at *Touch AM* in Wales.

Louise BATCHELOR
Bi-media environment correspondent at BBC Radio Scotland, based in Glasgow.

Terry BATE
Terry gained substantial marketing experience in canada and came to the UK in the mid six-

ties where he was hired by Ronan O'Rahilly to head up the *Radio Caroline* sales operation. After Caroline closed down he joined Jocelyn Stevens (qv) on the United Newspapers campaign to have commercial radio legalised in the UK and later lobbying the Government after the White Paper was published.

As he was still technically under contract to Radio Caroline, terry returned briefly to the Caroline fold in early 193 to help relaunch the International service, but was also very busy assisting and consulting with applications for the new ILR franchises in the UK. Among those he helped bid for were the LBC station in London.

Terry was one of the founders of Broadcast Marketing Services, which became leading rep' house BMS, selling airtime on Radio City (Liverpool) and Radio Clyde. As well as being a shareholder in several stations (such as Pennine Radio and Radio City) Terry was instrumental in launching seminars and training on sales and it was his dynamism, creativity and vision which many of today's senior sales executives and station manager acknowledge persuaded them to make a car4eer in the UK radio industry.

Terry then went back to Canada for several years, he has interests in several stations there, especially in British Columbia.

Terry He was brought back in when BMS began to founder in the 1980s but is now happier spending his time skiing and sailing, in the Caribbean and in Canada.

Terry opened his own radio station on Gozo, Malta on Yorkshire Day, 1993 (1st August) called *Radio Calypso*.

Derek BATEMAN (1)
Producer of 'People and Power' on *BBC Radio Scotland*

Derek BATEMAN (2)
Head of Sales at *Wessex FM* in Dorchester.

Susannah BATEMAN
Susannah is a Newsreader on *BBC GLR*

Dick BATES
Financial Controller of Regional Broadcasting, BBC, based at Broadcasting House.

Mick BATES
Presenter of a farming programme on *Radio Maldwyn* in Wales.

Roy BATES
Former Desert Rat and Southend fisherman who commandeered a former radar outpost in the Thames Estuary and began operations as Radio Essex in 1965. He was responsible for launching the careers of many well known broadcasters including Mark Wesley and Dick Palmer.

When the fort was judged to be in UK waters he closed the station and took over a similar structure off Harwich, over which he's claimed sovereignty for almost thirty years. In the mid-eighties he announced plans for a TV channel and three radio stations from the fort on the Terry Wogan TV show, but his backers have since been proved to be professional con-men.

His family still occupy the structure, which they call Sealand, and issue stamps and passports.

Simon BATES
Simon moved to New Zealand in 1965 after struggling with university and spent four years working on radio and television in the capital, Wellington. In 1969, Simon left Wellington and went to Australia.

In Sydney he joined a television station and spent the next two years travelling round the Pacific making programmes. In 1971 he returned to Europe and joined the BBC, presenting the early morning show on *Radio One* and *Radio Two* sporadically for two years.

He took over his first daily show in November 1977 and hosted *Radio One*'s mid morning strip for thirteen years, some programme elements becoming almost a national institution.

A victim of the purge on older jocks in 1993/1994, he was reputed to be joining *Atlantic 252* but surfaced on some ILR stations with a syndicated programme. In September 1995 Simon joined *Talkradio UK* where he now hosts the station's weekday breakfasts, with a six-figure sponsorship deal on his 'Our Tune' feature and his face on the boxes of Kleenex tissues.

Michael BATH
Presenter of BBC Radio Kent's teatime "Scene & Heard" show.

Bruce BATTEN
Producer of programmes at *BBC Radio Ulster*.

Graham BATTYE
Producer of the 'Late Night' programmes on *BBC Radio WM*.

Howard BAUGH
Chairman of *Choice FM* in South London.

Gillian BAXTER
News producer at *BBC Radio Leeds*.

Jenny BAXTER
Senior Producer of 'PM' on BBC *Radio Four*.

Travis BAXTER
Born on 26th September, 1957 in Lincolnshire, Travis got into radio via the hospital route and made his first full broadcast on *Plymouth Sound*. He then switched his presentation duties to S*wansea Sound* and in 1979 became a producer at *Capital 602*, a leading station on South Africa's 'Wild Coast'.

On returning to the UK, Travis joined *Devonair* and later moved to the BBC's *Radio Devon*.

It wasn't long before the mandarins at Broadcasting House snapped him up to produce programmes on their national station, *Radio Two*, and in the late eighties he joined a new project at Radio Luxembourg, then called Radio Tara and, for a brief period, Radio Five. The BBC already had plans for a new station called Radio Five, so Travis had Luxembourg come up with a new name for their project - it became *Atlantic 252* and launched in September 1989 - and Travis has been the station's Managing Director ever since, steering it to become the UK's most listened to independent station.

As well as his Atlantic 252 duties, Travis is also MD of Luxembourg's other radio interests in the UK as well as a new network of stations in Sweden. In November, 1995, he took over as Managing Director of *Talkradio UK*. Travis is a total radio person, has no dislikes and thinks the funniest radio event he's ever heard is him broadcasting.

Jeremy BEADLE
Born on the 12th April, 1948, in Hackney, this well known TV prankster has appeared on eight major TV series and published three books. In 1995 he moved into radio and was one of the original presenters on *Talkradio UK* with a regular Sunday night programme.

Rosemary BEALE
Sales and Marketing Director at *The Bay*, in Lancaster and Morecambe.

Simon BEALE
Presenter at *Invicta FM* in Kent.

Adrian BEAN
Drama Producer at *BBC Radio Four*.

Tony BEARD
Tony hosts a weekly request show each Dunsay Lunchtime (12 until 2) on *BBC Radio Dorset and Devon*.

Paul BEASLEY
Presenter and Traffic Manager at *Mix 96* in Aylesbury, Buckinghamshire.

Phillippa BEAUMONT
News Reporter at *BBC Radio Essex*.

Maureen BEBB
Chief Assistant and senior administrator at Bush House for BBC World Service.

Craig BECK
Presenter at *Mercia FM* in Coventry.

Douglas BECK
Director of *South West Sound*, ILR station in Dumfries and Galloway.

Jason BECK
Journalist Jason worked at *Wessex FM* and also at *2CR* in Bournemouth, before joining the Fareham newsroom of *Ocean FM* in 1995.

Suzi BECKER
Presenter at *BRMB FM* in Birmingham.

Viv BEEBY
Producer at BBC Radio production centre in Southampton.

Keith BEECH
keith was a Senior Producer at *BBC Radio Gloucester* and in 1994 was promoted to be assistant editor at the station.

Sandy BEECH
Sandy had his name chosen for him by *Atlantic*

252, from where he moved to *Virgin 1215* when it launched, and now is Programme Director at the Invicta network in Kent.

Graham BEECROFT

The head boy at Bowlington School, Graham began work in the tactical planning unit with Lever Brothers at Port Sunlight before becoming a quantity surveyor. His first broadcast was a football commentary and in 1982 he joined the staff of *BBC Radio Merseyside* where he later became Sports Editor.

In 1989 he moved across town to join Liverpool's ILR station, *Radio City* in a similar role.

Graham is a regular contributor to the Sky Sports TV channel and also is the commentator on Everton's annual video. he likes good food, wine and theatre as well as playing sport, but hates bigots, rude people and anyone who hogs the centre lane on motorways.

Johnny BEERLING

Born 12th April, 1937, Johnny attended Sir Roger Manwod's GS School at Sandwich in kent and joined the RAF as a wireless fitter in 1955. he started in radio in 1955 running a station in Aden for the RAF where he doubled as station manager, studio engineer and early morning disc-jockey.

In 1957 he joined the BBC as Terrchnical Operator , then Studio Manager, before becoming a producer for the *Light Programme.* When *Radio One* was set up he was heavily involved in the process, devising jingles, recruiting most of the DJ talent and he produced the first ever show with Tony Blackburn.

In 1971 he set the tone for the Network's rock documentaries with a 14 hour documentary - 'The History of the Beatles'. This established a style of programming which has continued for 26 years with an average of 50 new musical documentaries being produced each year.

Two years later he conceived and launched the famous Radio One Roadshow, which grew from a small caravan operation to an 80 foot mobile stage iin a series of articulated trucks. Each season more than a million people took part in the OBs from resorts around the UK.

In the mid seventies he co-authored (which involved writing most of the manuscript and turning Rosko's notes into English!) 'Emperor Rosko's DJ Handbook', a book which, for many years, has been regarded as the essential instruction manual for budding (and practicing!) disc-jockeys.

In 1983 Johnny became the Head of Programmes on the network. Two years later he was appointed Controller of Radio One and oversaw its move to the FM band in the late 1980s and adoption of a new name - *One FM*.

Johnny retired from the BBC in 1993 to spend more time on his many pastimes (which include photography, skiing and angling). Johnny is an active member of the Radio Academy, which in March 1992 awarded him the Ferguson Award for 'Outstanding contribution to Music Radio' - the first non-broadcaster to receive it.

In 1993 he completed a year as President of the TV and Radio Industry Club of Great Britain and in May 1994 was appointed a Governor of the Brits School for pPerforming Arts and Technology. The same month he received a Sony Award for 'Outstanding Services to the Radio Industry'.

As a former studio engineer, Johnny has always had a keen interest in audio developments and was a leading member of a committee to consider the future of stereo and quadrophonic sound in broadcasting. He was a staunch supporter of getting a permanent FM outlet for Radio One so the station could broadcast in stereo. Since 1995 he has been responsible for the BBC's involvement in developing RDS (Radio Data System). He chaired the EBI Programme experts group all the time he was with the BBC and is still co-chairman of the RDS Forum, an international meeting ground for broadfcasters and manufacturers.

In 1995 he took on a new position as Chairman of Uniques 'Special Projects' division where he is also responsible for developing new presenter talent.

Who's Who in British Radio

Howard BEESTON
Managing Director of 'Travel News', the new ITN traffic service for local radio stations.

Mike BEESTON
Presenter at *Southern FM*, Brighton.

Alex BELL
Alex is a long-serving Presenter of the breakfast programme on *BBC Radio Scotland*.

Alison BELL
Regional producer for *BBC World Service*, based in Glasgow.

Chris BELL

Born in Kingston-upon-Hull, in the days when radio was wireless and DAB was something to do with sherbert, Chris first began broadcasting with *BBC Radio Humberside* at the end of the 'Seventies where he started his career as a Technical Operator.

After 8 years, he moved across to ILR, joining Yorkshire Radio Network's *Viking Radio* in the mid-eighties, as well as working on sister stations *Pennine Radio* and *Radio Hallam*.

Chris then moved sideways (he has other strange habits!) into the organisation's new invenstion - *Viking Gold*, later to become *Classic Gold*, where he became Presentation Controller until the take-over of YRN by the Metro Group, after which Chris returned to BBC local radio for a short period.

Chris is the proud holder of the prestigious SONY/ TRIC 'Local Radio Personality of the Year' award , which he gained whilst working at *Viking FM*. In the 1990's he took part in several RSL's in the Hull area and is still looking for a permanent radio role in his beloved East Yorkshire. Until then he delights in driving buses and currently works as a controller with the Humberside Police.

Clinton BELL
Clinton is the Station Controller of the Virgin Megastores in house station.

Colin BELL
Presenter of own programme each weekday evening on *BBC Radio Scotland*.

Graham BELL
News reporter and presenter on *Manx Radio*, Isle of Man.

Ian BELL
Producer of history and travel programmes for BBC Network Radio, based in Southampton.

John BELL
Director of *Marcher Gold* in Wrexham.

Lyn BELL
Sales Promotion Manager at *TFM* in Stockton.

Marianne BELL
Marianne is now a radio production assistant working on several programmes at *BBC Radio Thames Valley*, formerly *Radio Berkshire*.

Neil BELL
Co-presents mid-afternoon Sunday Sports show on BBC *Radio Kent*.

Phil BELL
Head of News at *Southern FM* in Brighton.

Tom BELL
Educated at Falkirk and Denny Hugh School, he's had a variety of jobs, including a musician, singer, grocer and a technical progress officer. He got into radio by sending a demo tape to the Programme Controller after hosting a launch party for *Radio Forth* in 1975 and made his first broadcast around Valentine's day that year- one very memorable Saturday morning. Since 1990 Tom has been a mainstay of the station's *MAX-AM* outlet and for several years was their Head of Music.

As well as radio presentation he also hosts cabaret and roadshows and is a presenter and roadshow coordinator for *Central FM*. The highlights of his career were broadcasting from the Ark Royal and other Royal Navy ships. He once spent some time on a swap feature trying to talk a listener into taking up ice skating before discovering that he only had one leg! Likes genuine people and hates back-stabbing.

David BELLAN

Began his radio career in the Middle East where he ran an english language station based in Jeddah, Saudi Arabia for several years. came to the UK in the 1970s and joined the *BBC World Service*, where he's remained ever since. Currently produces much acclaimed 'Science in Action' series.

Jules BELLERBY

Presenter at *BBC Radio Humberside* and *BBC Radio Essex* in the mid-eighties, he is believed to have left radio.

Liz BELLINGALL

Dorset producer at *BBC Radio Devon & Dorset.*

David BELLINGER

Producer of specialist music programmes for BBC Radio, based in the East Midlands.

Kate BELLINGHAM

After getting a BA Hons in Physics at Queens, Oxford, Kate worked for three years as a computer programmer and then three years as an electronics engineer.

In 1989 she joined BBC Television to present the 'Techno' series and the following year became a presenter on 'Tomorrow's World' - she was there from 1990 to 1994.

In September 1994 she joined *Radio Five Live* to host 'The Acid Test', a popular weekly science and technology magazine show and she also produces and presents 'Chain reaction'.

The highlight of Kate's career was going to CERNB, the particle physics centre in Switzerland, for 'The Acid Test' and the funniest event of her radio career was "introducing a guest, then discovering she hadn't yet arrived and so having to fill in until she did. No one realised!"

Kate likes fascinating facts but abhorrs unfunny jokes and patronising programmes.

David BENEDICTUS

David is a Drama Producer for *Radio Four*, based in London.

Barbara BENJAMIN

Assistant in the BBC Press and Information Unit, based at Broadcasting House.

Alan BENNETT

Alan is a news and sports producer and reporter at Mix 96 in Aylesbury.

Carole BENNETT

Sales promotion manager at *TFM* in Stockton.

Chris BENNETT

News Journalist and programme producer with *BBC Radio Berkshire.*

Clive BENNETT

Senior Producer with special responsibilities for opera at *BBC Radio Three.*

David BENNETT

Senior Producer at BBC *Dorset FM.*

Jill BENNETT

Assistant editor at *BBC Radio Norfolk.*

John BENNETT

Producer and Presenter at *BBC Radio Ulster.*

Neil BENNETT

Journalist at *BBC Radio Gloucester.*

Nick BENNETT

Station Engineer at Gemini Radio in Exeter.

Roger BENNETT

Presenter of BBC radio's 'Morning West' programme for over two decades, he was voted local radio broadcaster of the Year in 1983 and is also a keen jazz afficionado, playing in a band called the Blue Notes. Currently at *BBC Radio Solent* and hosting the morning show at *Radio Bristol.*

Owen BENNETT-JONES

Owen is a Presenter of news programmes on BBC World Service.

Grant BENSON

Worked on the *Voice of Peace* where he was programme director, and on *Radio Caroline* in 1983.

Mark BENSON

Began his radio career at *Radio Top Shop* in 1990 and did some freelance work at *SGR* in Suffolk. Then moved to *Power FM* in

Hampshire and finally, the highlight of his career so far, a move to *Capital FM* where he remains to day.

He once got lost his security pass and had to break down the door at a radio station! Likes eating out and hates trains.

Neil BENTLEY

Attended school in his home town of Portsmouth and got into radio by complete accident - making bacon sandwiches overnight! His first broadcast was overnight on *Power FM*. He then moved to drive time with *Horizon Radio* where he says the highlight of his career was developing the station's mid morning show.

His most humourous moment came when he was doing a gig at a bowling centre and got caught up in the machine. From Horizon Neil moved to nearby *Northants FM* where he now does the station's breakfast programme.

Owen BENTLEY

Head of Radio, BBC Midlands.

Jon BENYON

Swansea born, he was schooled in Corby and Kettering and first broadcast with BFDBS in Germany,where he presented 'Family Favourites'. When he returned to the UK he joined *BBC Radio Wales* and then moved to *BBC Radio Nottingham.*

Paul BERESFORD

Once had ambitions to become a farmer but after an unfortunate incident when he set a tractor alight he moved to London and enrolled on an acting course. He also became a stunt man for a while and worked in a milk bar and as a watch salesman.

In 1965 he joined *Radio 390* for the station's launch and stayed there until after the station closed. he didn't get off the fort quickly enough and was struck by lighting one day, which may have prompted him to emigrate to South Africa where he worked in the music business for several years.

Michael BERNARD

Michael began his career in media, marketing and advertising at the Sunday Express. He became Sales Group Head for AIR Services before moving to Independent Radio Sales where he became Regional Sales Manager.

In 1985 he was recruited by the MSB group as General Manager initially working on existing local newspaper businesses but with the brief to develop a new radio sales company. In 1992 he joined *Virgin Radio* as Marketing Controller.

Ralph BERNARD

After a long career in local radio, Ralph is now Group Chief Executive of *GWR Group, the* Group Financial Controller of the Association of independent radio Companies and sits on the board of many GWR stations.

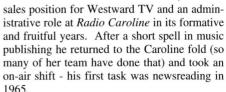

Claudia BERRY

Producer / reporter at *BBC Radio Worcester.*

Colin BERRY

Born 29th January 1946 at Welwyn Garden City, Colin attended Wembley Grammar School and began his career as an administrator with Granada TV, before a sales position for Westward TV and an administrative role at *Radio Caroline* in its formative and fruitful years. After a short spell in music publishing he returned to the Caroline fold (so many of her team have done that) and took an on-air shift - his first task was newsreading in 1965.

By 1971 Colin had moved back to TV, this time newsreading at Harlech Television and he then moved to the BBC and began making trailers for *Radio 1* and *Radio 2*, when there was little difference. He joined *BBC Radio 2* in 1973 as continuity announcer and presented almost every programme on the station, including all the main line shows. He has deputised for all the station's household names - Jimmy Young, Terry Wogan and David Hamilton included.

On the TV front, Colin has co-hosted 'Top of

the Pops', been a mystery guest on the 'Generation Game' and is known all over Europe for his excellent chairing of 'European Pop Jury', an EBU networked programme.

In 1987 he appeared on the Wogan TV programme and has also been seen on 'Blankety Blank', 'Going Live' and hosted programmes on *BBC Radio Bedfordshire*.

Colin wrote and produced several music series for *BFBS* and recently for In-flight airline programmes. He likes the Isle of Wight, Victoria Wood, oysters and real ale, hates most folk music and cricket. Married to Sandra and has two children, Marina and Jonathan.

Patrick BERRY
Managing Director of *Choice FM* in South London and the Chairman of the station's sister station in Birmingham.

Bert BERTONLINI
Director of *Oasis Radio* in St Albans, Herts.

Mark BERTRAND
Music Producer at *BBC Radio Guernsey*.

Chris BEST
After a period at *Great Northern Radio*, Chris now presents the breakfast show on *Essex FM*.

Allan BESWICK
Presents mid morning shows weekdays (from 9 to 12) on *BBC Radio GMR* (Manchester).

Barry BETHELL
DJ on *Invicta Supergold* in Kent.

Mike BETTISON
Assistant editor at *BBC Radio Derby*.

Michael BETTON
The Managing Director at *Ocean Sound* from its launch until he moved to Lincolnshire, where he wrote the successful application for *Lincs FM* and has been Managing Director since the station's launch.

He is also the chairman of the technical committee of the Association of Independent Radio Companies.

Teleri BEVAN
Head of Programmes at *Radio Ceredigion*.

Trevor BEVINS
Producer at *BBC Radio Dorset and Devon*.

Fred BEWICK
Secretary at *Wear FM*.

Julia BICKNELL
Julia has a journalism background second to none, having worked with the BBC at regional, national and international levels, most recently with the BBC's current affairs department, serving the *World Service* and *Radio 4*. In early 1995 she joined London's new Christian radio station, *Premier* where she is editor and presenter of breakfast programmes.

Jenny BILD
Executive Producer for the BBC World Service.

Mark BILSBY
Radio career began with hospital radio and then ILR where he pioneered an interactive morning show. He loves OB work and phone-ins, but doesn't like missing shows and the prima-donnas in the industry. Mark also works as a stage hypnotist, sings, acts (Equity member) and currently hosts a Saturday morning show at *Wey Valley Radio* in Hampshire.

Norman BILTON
Managing Director at *Radio Wyvern*.

Richard BILTON
Initially a new reporter at *BBC Essex,* he is now a News Producer.

Miranda BIRCH
Senior producer in charge of all weekend output at *BBC Radio Solent*.

Philip BIRCH.
Born in 1927, Philip was reputedly the youngest commissioned officer in the War - her served with the Royal West kent regiment while only 18 years old. After being demob bed he went to the USA and worked in new York and Detroit with the advertising giant J. Walter Thompson. In 1964 he was headhunted by a consortium of Texans who had seen the impact of Radio Caroline and decided to operate an even more commercial station.

Philip wanted to call the new station *Radio*

Galaxy and the Americans wanted to call *KLIF-London* and operated as a branch of a leading station in Dallas.

Philip Birch anglified the operation and managed it from plush offices in Mayfair. Within months, Radio London became the highest earning offshore station ever and spawned most of the best radio jocks the UK has ever heard, including Dave Cash, Duncan Johnson and Kenny Everett.

After Radio London was forced off the air, Philip launched Piccadilly Radio in Manchester, which he ran until the 1980s. he is now retired and lives in California.

Therese BIRCH

Born 15th April 1954 in Surrey, attended the St Mauer's Convent in Weybridge from where she joined the 'Surrey Herald'. Her first broadcast was on *LBC* in June 1974 (reading a children's story) where she became a late night favourite for many years before progressing into television for Granada TV and Channel 4.

When LBC lost its licence in 1994 she was quickly snapped up by its successor, *London News Radio* for weekend programmes. As well as radio, Therese also hosts a childrens Saturday morning show for ITV and two series on *Channel Four*. She is also in demand for syndicated radio tapes and audio-visuals.

Jonathan BIRCHALL

Singapore Foreign Correspondent for The BBC World Service News.

John BIRT

Born on 10th December, 1944, and educated at St Mary's College in Liverpool and at St Catherine's College in Oxford. In 1968 he was the producer of Kenny Everett's first ever TV series on Thames TV, "Nice Time'.

He then moved to 'World in Action' and finally became Director of programmes at LWT for five years, until 1987 when he moved to the BBC. After five years as deputy Director-General, he became the Corporation's Director General in 1992 and has been responsible for shedding civil service attitudes and reshaping the BBC.

John is a member of the Media Law Group and has sat on many committees on the future of broadcast legislation. He is married to Jane, an American, and has a son and a daughter.

Louise BIRT

Producer/Reporter for *BBC Radio Worcester*.

Mark BISHOP

News journalist and editor at *Orchard FM*.

Stephen BISHOP see Johnny Lewis.

Alan BLACK

Born on 15th January, 1943 in Rosyth, Fife, he joined a band of itinerant gypsies on leaving school before joining an illustration studio and later a well known comic publisher in Dundee.

After a trip to London he decided to join the then newly launched station, *Radio Scotland* and later moved south to the American-owned *Swinging Radio England*. Alan then transferred to SRE's sister station *Britain Radio* and was Programme Controller by the time the station closed in August 1967.

Alan then joined *Radio One* and was a regular DJ on 'Midday SPin' but decided that the life of an artist was less demanding. He's had cartoons published in many publications, including the 'Radio Times' and was one of the team who worked on the Beatles' film 'Yellow Submarine'.

Bill BLACK

Presents a music show for *BBC Clyde 2*.

David BLACK

Sales Director at *Touch AM* in South Wales.

Johnny BLACK

Host of late night weekend programmes on *BBC Southern Counties Radio*.

Rev Len BLACK

A director at *Moray Firth Radio*.

Liz BLACK

Host of a religious show on *Brunel Classic Gold*.

Peter BLACK

Head of Presentation at *Melody Radio*.

John BLACKBURN

Company Secretary at *Wear FM* until 1995.

Tony BLACKBURN

Born 29th January 1943 in Guildford, he was schooled at Millfield and began his showbiz

career singing with a band in Bournemouth (called Tony Blackburn and the Rovers - his first corny joke?) which included Al Stewart, later to achieve fame with his 'Year of the Cat' album.

In Summer 1964 he read about *Radio Caroline* in the NME and successfully auditioned for a job, remaining on the south ship where he presented the 'Big Line Up' for over a year before joining rival pirate ship *Radio London*. He continued to pursue a singing career and had several singles released in the sixties, but none achieved great sales levels despite being very competently performed - probably because other DJS jealously ignored them and gave no air play?

Tony achieved notoriety on Caroline and Big L for making up own sung ID jingles and cracking the most awful corny jokes, a trade mark he took with him to the BBC when he abandoned offshore radio in 1967 for the *Light Programme*. His real reason for joining the BBC was to present the prime-time breakfast show on the BBC's new network, *Radio One*.

A move to *BBC Radio London* gave him more creative freedom, (and a lie-in), as well as a chance to use all his old Big L jingles, but still keeping a weekly programme on Radio One.

He quickly became a cult figure, appearing at nightclubs in London, often garbed in a leopard skin leotard, and becoming very suggestive on his programme talking to housewives, his own audience who'd grown up with his breakfast programme. When this went he moved to Capital Radio for their new AM service, *Capital Gold*.

In the USA he would have been a perfect pitchman, but in the UK his talent has been stifled and often wasted, as his television appearances have occasionally shown. An undoubted master of the craft, he is often ridiculed, something he actively encourages by acting the clown, but in reality Tony knows the radio business better and is far more competent than most others.

Tim BLACKMORE
Tim was a producer at *BBC Radio One* and then at *Capital Radio* for many years, before joining *Unique Broadcasting* in the 1990s.

Eddie BLACKWELL
Eddie qualified as a Member of the Advertising Association in 1955 and joined Fleetway Publications and later 'Woman's Mirror' where he was senior Executive.

He then moved to the National Magazine Company where he was responsible for 'Good Housekeeping' and, in September 1964, eddie joined a company called Radlon Sales at its new offices in Mayfair.

The company was about to revolutionise radio in the UK - it opened as *Radio London* three months later and Eddie was the station's Senior Sales Executive.

In the 1970's Eddie became Sales Manager and then Station Manager at Southend-based *Essex Radio*. He is now the Group Operations Manager for *Brunel Classic Gold* and as keen a jazz fan as ever.

Julian BLACKWELL
Chairman of *Fox FM*.

Mark BLADES
With an early career as a hairdresser, Mark is one of the few people who onto the air by dropping an 'h' (from 'hair to air) ! He worked initially on the satellite station *UCB* before joining London's AM Christian radio station *Premier* in early 1995 to host their overnight shifts.

David BLAKE
Chairman of *Red Dragon FM/Touch AM*

Edward BLAKEWELL
Co-Presents a regular programme called Musical Encounters on *BBC Radio 3*.

Ian BLAKEY
A former director of the *Yorkshire Radio Network*, Ian is now the Chairman of the

Minster group of stations, and also of the *Voice of Yorkshire*.

Zelda BLAKEY
News Producer for *BBC Wiltshire Sound*.

Mary BLANCE
Senior Producer/Presenter in Shetland for *BBC Scotland*.

Colin BLANE
BBC Foreign Correspondent in Nairobi,and a regional correspondent in Scotland for the BBC News and current affairs.

Ric BLAXILL
Producer of 'Top of The Pops and also of programmes at *BBC Radio One*.

Steve BLEARS
News Coordinator at *TFM*.

Alan BLEASDALE
As a 24 years old teacher in Liverpool, Alan's break into writing came at BBC Radio Merseyside, where he turned up with eight short stories in a brown paper bag. The station manager liked them and they were broadcast, leading to his later success with series such as 'The boys from the black stuff.'

Helen BLENKINSOP
Senior Producer for BBC News/Current affairs.

James BLESSING
Born on the 1st October, 1971 in Barrow in Furness, James attended Alma Park School, and Aquinas Sixth Form College in Stockport before the University of Kent at Canterbury where he achieved a B Sc in Physics with astro-physics.

He got into radio partly by accident, partly through his perseverance having done three years at the campus station UKC, becoming embroiled in all forms of station operation, programming engineering and sales, as well as managing the station for a while.

In 1994 he got a place at the Radio Training Unit and produced a drive time programme with presenter Ray Teret (qv) on RSL station *Oldham FM* and also presented programmes on another RSL *Reach FM*.

He then joined *Kiss 102* as a station assistant, producing weekend programmes and the highlight of his career was hearing his first programme on the air at Kiss. James' first programme had to be done from a rickety disco deck after the main studio went off line. He likes music, people, Manchester, sleeping and computers, but hates raw tomato and style gurus.

Tony BLEWITT
As the presenter of Luxembourg's top rated show on weekday evenings Tony has built up enormous listener loyalty during his time with the radio station .In the early days he performed a complete comedy cabaret act with a friend when they were booked as DJs. They released a record called *"Chip Shop Rapping"* and also a comedy reggae version of the Crossroads theme. They are still together writing comedy songs and are planning a record release soon.

Sarah BLIZZARD
Presenter at the *New Leicester Sound FM*.

Antony BLOND
Company Secretary for Manchester stations *Piccadilly Gold/Key 103*.

Jonty BLOOM
Business Journalist for the BBC News and Current Affairs.

Michael BLOOD
Producer of religious programmes for *BBC Radio WM/WCR*.

Lawrie BLOOMFIELD
Managing Editor and Station Manager at *BBC Radio Shropshire*.

Sir Kenneth BLOOMFIELD
National Governor for Northern Ireland for the British Broadcasting Corporation.

Alvin BLOSSOM
Educated at Bradford Technical College, he had a variety of roles before his break into radio, which came on the hospital radio service at Leeds General Infirmary. He eventually got four shows on *Radio Hallam*, who rejected him due to 'lack of experience', so he took the hard route helping out at *BBC Radio Leeds*.

Well remembered for his zany off the wall humour, he became very popular there until the BBC bureaucracy squeezed him out. A sad loss to radio.

Hester BLOTT
Hester is the Publicity Manager at *BBC Radio 2*.

Chris BLOUNT
First radio job was as a technical operator at the BBC World Service; he then became a cameraman in White City and then out to Plymouth (he's a Cornishman, this was akin to going home for him) as a floor manager at TV Centre. there. He then became a producer and presenter at BBC *Radio Oxford*, before moving back to Plymouth again.

His dream came true on 17th January 1983, when he launched *BBC Radio Cornwall* by arriving at the station's Truro Wharfside HQ by boat. This is home to Chris and he's been there now for the last dozen or so years, currently hosting the station's mid morning weekday show. His main love (after wife Kay and the children) is model railways and the one thing Chris hates is over-zealous news reporting.

Steve BLOWER
News Producer at *BBC Radio Newcastle*.

Joanna BLYTHEMAN
Host of a food programme about food and nutrition every sunday on *BBC Radio Scotland*.

Helen BOADEN
Editor of a programme for BBC News and Current Affairs and also editor of a show called 'File on Four' for BBC Radio 4.

Christine BOAR
Produces regular midweek evening shows on *BBC Radio 1*.

Martin BOASE
Martin is the chairman of *Kiss FM*.

Susanna BOCCACCIO
Presenter for *Radio Wave* which transmits from the top of Blackpool Tower.

Andy BOCKING
Area Engineer at *BBC Radio Solent*.

Kevin BOCQUET
Regional Correspondent in the Manchester area for BBC News and Current Affairs.

Wayne BODKIN
Born in Stourbridge in the Midlands, Wayne's radio career began in hospital radio. He hosted a phone-in programme on *Beacon Radio* in the 1980s.

Chris BODLE
Chief Engineer at *BBC Radio Devon and Dorset*.

Gail BOLAM
Reporter for *BBC Radio Devon* and *Dorset FM*.

Jane BOLGER
News Producer for *BBC Radio Merseyside*.

Sean BOLGER
Breakfast host at *Talkradio UK* in early 1995 and then moved to the afternoon women's magazine programme on the station.

Tristran BOLITHO
Station and programme organiser at the regional dance station based in Bristol, *Galaxy FM*.

Kate BOLTON
Kate produces a Saturday lunchtime show on *BBC Radio 3*.

Peter BOLTON
Executive Chairman of *Wessex FM*.

Angela BOND
Hull-born Angela was the daughter of a Sea Captain, born and raised in Hong Kong. and the UK. She passed extra mural exams in music singing and the spoken word and at 15 was a church soloist and a member of the group The Carol Levis Discoveries.

She began her broadcasting career in Kenya as a copywriter and artist and then moved to the Seychelles, producing a major documentary there.

In Nigeria, Angela edited the Government's daily press releases and was a media studies tutor at the University. In 1959, she joined Rediffusion in Hong Kong as a duty announcer and interviewer, as well as acting as a programme and commercial producer. Her first programme as a DJ on *Radio Hong Kong* was

Gramophone Department, assembling music programmes for all three national networks and the World Service. Among her output was 'Housewives Choice', 'What's New' and 'Family Favourites' and a series with David Frost.

In 1967 she was one of the small team who wrote the manifesto for the forthcoming national pop channel - *Radio One*, for which Angela devised and scripted the first Radio One jingles and devised the 'nursery' lunchtime programmes from which new Radio One DJs were selected.

For four years Angela produced the Kenny Everett programmes, spending a lot of time apologising to the BBC hierarchy for his misdemeanours. She also produced Pete Murray's Open House (trebling its audience to 7.5 million in just three months!) and 'Pick of The Pops' with Alan Freeman.

In 1973 when Radios One and Two separated she moved to *Radio Two* to introduce more adult contemporary music to its output and was the first to propose computer assistance for music programming. In 1980 the BBC rewarded her for increasing audiences with a three months paid tour of the USA, where she became an honorary citizen of Nashville.

The following year Angela proposed that the Corporation adopt computer-assisted music scheduling and in 1982 she was selected by Aubrey Singer (qv) Managing Director of BBC Radio to be the first Music Programming Adviser to the BBC's network of 33 stations.

In 1987 she was head-hunted by Radio Computing Services of New York (world leaders in radio software) to introduce their system to UK and Irish markets - the result is that their scheduler 'Selector' is now in use at most ILR stations and in Radio One and Radio Two, plus MTV and VH1.

Angela continues to be involved in programme making and directs live music and dance spectaculars. She also lectures on music programming for the EBU, Dutch and some Scandinavian radio authorities.

James BOND
Sports producer at *BBC Radio Shropshire*.

Marc BOND
Sales manager at *Spire FM* and station manager of *Gold Radio*, a satellite station of Spire.

Philip BOND
Chief Engineer at *Melody Radio* in London.

Caroline BOON
Caroline is the General Administrator responsible for the smooth running of *Minster FM* and subsidiary stations, since 1992.

Sue BONNER
Senior Producer of 'The World This Weekend' at BBC Radio Four.

Jeff BONSER
General Secretary of the Churches Advisory Council for Local Broadcasting and a member of the Board of Directors at London station *Premier Radio*.

Susan BOOKBINDER
Journalist with *Independent Radio News*.

Anthony BOORE
Director of *Piccadilly Radio* when owned by Transworld Radio

Kelvin BOOT
Presenter of natural history programmes on *BBC Radio Four*.

Julia BOOTH
Presented the afternoon drive-time show on *BBC Radio Essex* when it launched in the mid-eighties and later moved to *Radio York*, where she now hosts several programmes.

Mel BOOTH
Head of sales at *Red Rose Radio* in Preston.

Robert BOOTH
Presenter of Sunday programme on *Classic FM*.

Phil BOREHAM
Manager of Resources Department at the BBC, based in Bristol.

Angela BORGNANA
Angela began her radio career at the end of 1983 by answering the phones and making tea at *BBC Radio Bristol*, her first programme was there presenting a showbiz programme called "As Time Goes By' with Gerry Parker. She was a co-founder of *Spectrum radio* in London in 1990 and presenter of the station's Italian Programme, for which her BA in Italian Studies has proved most useful.

The highlight of her career was promotion to Programme Controller at Spectrum and she is very proud of her achievements at the station, especially in increasing figures and the Asian programmes. her most humourous moment came after a stunt interviewing a fake Italian Minister - hordes of listeners besieged the station afterwards wanting a word with him!

Angela likes food, Carey Grant and R'n'B music, but hates limp handshakes and pretentiousness. Currently working with a dozen different personalities at Spectrum International.

Martin BORLEY
News producer at *BBC Radio Northampton*.

Yolanda BORNEO
Admn' manager at the Radio Academy.

Radek BOSHETY.
Presenter of classical music programmes on *BBC World Service*.

Louise BOTTING
Journalist and presenter with BBC, working on *Radio Four* and *Radio Five*. In 1995 she chaired *New 102 FM*, an applicant for the Stratford on Avon ILR licence.

Rt Hon.Virginia BOTTOMLEY
Mrs Bottomley was elected as MP for Surrey South East in a by-election in 1984, and became a Parliamentary Private Secretary to Chris Patten when he was Minister of Overseas Development. She then became a PPS to Sir Geoffrey Howe while he was Foreign Secretary and became a Minister herself in 1988.

While at the Health Ministry she became a nationally known figure and in July 1995 was appointed National Heritage Secretary, a position which gives her control over the UK Government's Broadcasting Policy. She is married with three children and gained her MSc after graduating at the University of Essex.

Kathryn BOUCHER
Sales Manager at *96.7 BCR* in Belfast.

Simon BOUGARED
News presenter at *BBC Radio Guernsey*.

Frank BOUGH
Former sports presenter on BBC TV, Frank is now presenter of the Friday morning breakfast programme (with co-host Shyama Perera) on *London Newstalk*.

Hilary BOULDING
Hilary is now the Head of music and the arts at *BBC Radio Wales*.

Janet BOULDING
Producer at *BBC Radio GMR* in Manchester.

David BOULTON
David is the host of the mid-morning programme each weekday from 10am until 2pm on *Minster FM* in Yorkshire.

John BOUNDY
Producer of arts programmes on *Radio Four*.

Dickie BOW
Joined *Atlantic 252* in early 1995, and promoted to breakfast show host in May. Currently hosting Saturday afternoon chart show.

Jane BOWDEN
Presenter at *BBC Radio Northamptonshire* and *Radio Oxford* in the 1990s.

Dave BOWEN
Programme Controller at *Devonair Radio* in Exeter, *Plymouth Sound* and also a presenter at *Swansea Sound*.

Gareth BOWEN
Gareth is the Presenter of 'First edition' programme on *BBC Radio Wales*

George BOWIE
Presenter at *Radio Clyde* in Glasgow.

Claire BOWLES
Presenter at *BBC Radio Merseyside*.

Howard BOWLES
Howard is the Manager at *Orchard FM*.

Eric BOWMAN
Assistant editor of News and Current Affairs Department, BBC Radio.

John BOWMAN
Company secretary, Radio Clyde in Glasgow.

Greg BOWN
On - air news journalist at *Orchard FM*.

Nicky BOYD
Presenter of the 'London Today' programme each saturday morning (6 to 10) with Christopher terry on *London News Radio FM*.

Tommy BOYD
Host of afternoon drive time programme on *Talkradio UK* when the station launched and recently moved to lunchtime programme.

Malcolm BOYDEN
Presenter of a mid-morning programme (9 to 11) each weekday on BBC *Radio WM/* CMR.

James BOYLE
Head of Radio, at BBC Scotland, Glasgow.

Kieran BOYLE
Sales Director at *Downtown Radio and Cool FM* in Belfast.

Robin BOYLE
A Folkestone, Kent, man Robin was in the services when he got into radio, with the British Forces Network in Hamburg in 1945. After demobbing, he joined the BBC Home Service as a newsreader, and then to *Radio 2* as a regular programme presenter.

Robin's name is associated with a dozen or more programmes, but he's best known for 'Friday Night is Music Night'.

Paula BOYS-STONES
Began her broadcasting career at *BBC Radio Cumbria* in 1984 and then held production posts at *Radio Derby* and *Radio Shropshire*.

In 1991 she joined *Radio Nottingham* as a radio journalist and is now the station's Assistant Editor.

Cassie BRABAN
Producer at BBC Educational Directorate.

Malcolm BRABENT
Malcolm is a Foreign Correspondent in Athens for *BBC World Service*.

Dickie BRADBEER
Director of *Isle of Wight Radio Ltd*.

Malcolm BRADBURY
Director of *Broadland FM* in Norwich.

Rod BRADBURY
News Editor at *Oasis Radio* in St Albans.

Conor BRADFORD
Host of 'Newsbreak' programme on BBC regional radio In Northern Ireland.

Dave BRADFORD
Weekday presenter at *Ocean FM*.

Earl of BRADFORD
Chairman of *Beacon Radio*.

John BRADFORD
Born on the 18th February, 1945, John was a leading campaigner for local commercial radio and a member of the LRA. In 1974 he bec ame Managing Director of one of the first stations, *Radio Tees* in Stockton.

After five years he moved to become the first managing director of *Mercia Sound* in Coventry and in 1983 moved west to Bristol and a similar role at *Radio West,* the forerunner of the GWR station in the city.

After three years in Bristol, John joined leading accountants KPMG Peat Marwick to be their Head of Media and in 1990 was the first Chief executive of *Jazz FM.* In 1993 he became the Director of the *Radio Academy.*

Michael BRADLEY
Producer of 'Friel's Fancy' on *Radio Ulster.*

Vincent BRADLEY
Host of a weekly concert programme on *BBC Radio Sheffield* in the 1990s.

Sue BRADSHAW
Sales Manager at *Manx Radio* on the Isle of Man.

Charles BRAHAM
Charles is the Chairman and Managing Director at *Swansea Sound.*

Sandra BRAIN
Member of the Luton programme team at *BBC Three Counties Radio.*

Paul BRAITHWAITE
Presents 'lunchtime Show' each weekday on *BBC Radio Cumbria.*

Jakki BRAMBLES
Jakki presented several different programmes for Capital Radio in the 1980s and later joined BBC Radio One where she hosted the 'Drivetime and Lunchtime Shows' on weekdays in the early 1990s.

Harriet BRAND
Director of Talent and Artist relations at MTV.

Tony BRANDON
Born in December 1933 in Dorset, Tony became a cub reporter in Portsmouth and did a variety of different jobs while resting from his early acting career. He passed an audition to appear with the Carroll Levis Show on the Light Programme, and later toured with them.

After touring army camps abroad he got a position at *Radio Luxembourg* in 1966, leaving after a few months for a short stint on the army fort off Whitstable better known to listeners as *Radio City.* He was soon snapped up by *Radio London,* just across the estuary and stayed until it closed on 14th August 1967.

"While Radio Luxembourg gave me my break, I was much happier on Big L, where I had freedom to be creative and have complete control of my own programme," he said recently, in Keith Skues' book "Pop Went The Pirates."

When Big L upped anchor and left for Germany, Birdbrain, as Tony had become known, got into *Radio 1* (Mid-day Spin and Radio One Club) and, a few years later, he moved to BBC Radio 2, where he has hosted several programmes as well as appeared in light drama and appeared in Pantomime with Lulu and Basil Brush.

He recorded several singles, the best undoubtedly being "Candy Kisses" on MGM in 1968, but none charted (undoubtedly because of lack of airplay) and also fronted TV programmes for Southern TV (forerunner of TVS and Meridian). In recent years he's returned to acting, with roles in the stage show 'Run for your Wife' and the TV drama "Miss Marple - Murder at the Vicarage'.

A prolific voice over artiste he also still hosts radio programmes, and is currently at *County Sound* in Guildford.

Ian BRASS
Presents a Saturday evening programme on *BBC Wiltshire Sound.*

Tim BRASSELL
Manager of Press and Public Relations at BBC North in Manchester.

BRASSO
DJ on *Radio Luxembourg* in the early 1980's.

Dave BRAY
Music Presenter at *Great North Radio.*

Mel BRAY
News Editor at *2CR* and *Classic Gold* in Bournemouth.

Andy BREARE
Presenter on *Pirate 102* in Cornwall.

Alisun BRENNAN
Journalist at *BBC Radio Lincolnshire.*

Dave BRENNAN
Presenter of the Jazz programme each Monday evening on *Radio Sheffield*

Paul BRENNAN
Journalist with Network News.

Edward BRETTEN
Presenter of morning programme on *Lincs FM*.

David BREWER
Reporter for BBC News and Current Affairs.

Gordon BREWER
Foreign Correspondent for BBC World Service.

Clive BRIDGES
Director of *Heartland FM* in Scotland.

Colin BRIGGS
Producer and host of the evening Drive Time sequence at *BBC Radio Newcastle*.

David BRIGGS
Deputy programme Director at *Capital Radio*.

Mark BRIGGS
Head of *Capital Radio*'s new production company, selling Capital programmes to radio stations overseas.

John BRIGHT
Managing Editor at *BBC Radio Oxford*.

Tom BRIGHT
Presenter at *The Wave* in Blackpool

Pam BRIGHTON
Drama Producer for BBC Radio, based at *Radio Ulster* in Belfast.

Paul BRIGHTON
Host of the weekday drive time programme at BBC Radio GMR in Manchester.

Martin BRISSAC
Director of Allied Radio Group plc..

Paul BRINKS
Head of A&R and marketing at Polydor Records, Holland for 6 years, then with Van Ende Productions, before moving to become Head of Entertainment at Veronica O.O, Holland's leading independent radio company in Autumn 1993.

Anne BRISTOW
Producer of cinema programmes on *BBC World Service*.

Robin BRITTEN
Head of Planning at *Radio 5 Live*.

Ian BRITTON
Commercial Production Manager at *Great North Radio* and author of a guide on how to use ISDN lines and equipment.

Arthur BROCKLEBANK
Presenter of classical music at *Moray Firth Radio* in Inverness.

John BROCKS
The first Managing Director at Lantern Radio.

Alex BRODIE
Foreign Correspondent for *BBC World Service* based in Jerusalem.

Caroline BRODIE
Administrator of financial affairs and Personnel at BBC Wiltshire Sound.

Graham BRODIE
Supervising Engineer at *BBC Radio Devon and Dorset FM*.

Peter BROMLEY
Journalist of long standing, peter is now a presenter and racing commentator at BBC Radio 5.

Bob BROLLY
Presenter of Irish music Programmes at *Mercia Sound* (Coventry) and Leicester Sound.

Paul BROMLEY
Presenter at *Viking FM* in Hull.

Peter BROMLEY
Racing Correspondent for BBC Sports Unit.

Anthony BROOK
Chairman of *Invicta FM* and *Ocean FM*

Tim BROOKE-TAYLOR
Presenter of "I'm sorry I haven't a clue' on *Radio Four*.

Bruno BROOKES
Born 24th April, 1959, and went to Woolstanton Prep School and Seabridge High School. Began doing discos and working clubs as well as promoting his own gigs at the age of 14 and later worked on a cruise liner.

Like most aspiring DJs, Bruno sent tapes to lots of stations, Radio Stokes Geoff Lawrence wrote back telling him he was too nasal, had no new ideas and sounded monotonous. he persevered with guests pots and eventually got his own programme - the Bruno Brookes express. Johnny Beerling gave him breaks on Radio One in the eighties, initially relieving Mike Reid, and later taking the station's early morning programme and prestigious Sunday chart show.

A relentless worker in clubs, Bruno has stayed loyal to his Staffordshire roots. He is also a presenter on *Sky One* and presents the 'Official UK Top 40' for *BBC Radio 1.*

Hayley BROOKES
One of the presenters at the launch of *Sunset FM*, Manchester.

Neil BROOKES
News Producer at *BBC Radio Derby*.

Adam BROOKS
Foreign Correspondent for *BBC World Service* in Indo-China.

Chris BROOKS
Went to school in Watford and Lengleybury and early career included spells as a postman, roofer and a salesman. His radio career began in hospital radio in Eastbourne and St Albans where he became programme controller. In June 1993 he got his break into big time radio, doing weekend overnights with *Chiltern.*

While doing swing shifts at Chiltern also worked at the *Metro* network and in July 1994 was awarded the regular shift at *Northants FM* and the local chart show each Saturday morning. Chris enjoys the guitar, work, football and people and hates Brussel sprouts and snakes, especially if they're on the same plate!

Fiona BROOKS
Head of News at *Island FM*, Guernsey.

Martin BROOKS
Head of BBC Regional Broadcasting Centre for the North in Leeds.

Peter BROOKS
Managing Editor of *BBC World Service* News.

Roger BROOKS
A native of Rother-ham in Yorkshire, Roger has worked in broadcasting for 20 years. he trained as a journalist in the late 1960s and joined *Radio Hallam* when it

opened in 1974. He progressed through news reading, presentation, documentary production to general management.

Roger joined *Viking Radio* at its launch in 1984 where he was the station's Managing Director and Programme Controller.

While at Viking Roger helped pioneer 'frequency splitting' creating *Viking FM* and *Viking Gold*. When the station merged with Hallam and Pennine, Roger married the stations' five AM transmitters with one programme, *Classic Gold*. Under Roger's leadership, the Yorkshire Radio Network stations generated over 20 million listening hours each week making YRN one of the biggest radio groups at that time.

When YRN was acquired by the Metro Group, Roger switched media to join Yorkshire TV as a regional officer based in Sheffield and he has been involved in production and presenting a wide range of radio and TV programming including news, documentaries and features.

In August 1994 he moved south to join Bournemouth's *Two Counties Radio* which operates *2CR* and *Classic Gold 828AM* as Station Director. Roger likes all types of music and also has a part time job as a vocalist and drummer in a pop band, but that these duties are now very limited (by time and public demand!).

Sue BROOM
Producer at BBC's Arts, Science and Features Department based in London.

Alan BROWN
Managing Director of 'Wireless Workshop'.

Alison BROWN
Head of traffic department of *Invicta FM* and also at *Ocean Sound* in Fareham.

Andy BROWN
Presenter on *Invicta Supergold*.

Ben BROWN
Foreign correspondent in Moscow for the BBC.

Benny BROWN
Born in Texas in 1949, he was educated in the USA and did a degree course in radio and TV at the University of Kansas. He got into radio by spinning discs at a high school hop when only 15 years old and embarked on a career which reads like a world tour of radio. He served in the US Army in Vietnam as a tank commander, and also spent some time on Oahu in Hawaii.

In 1979 Benny joined *Radio Luxembourg*. While there he also worked for *AFN* (just down the road in Frankfurt) and had one of the biggest road shows in Europe in the 1980s. He also won a Billboard 'International Air Personality' award, is a keen kite-flyer and hates the growing lack of

creativity in radio. He left Luxembourg in 1985 and has since appeared on many stations through a US chart countdown syndicated by Unique Productions.

Now living just outside Frankfurt-am-Main he runs his own studio from where he provides in flight programming for airlines and operates sponsored touring shows.

Dave BROWN
Presenter at the launch of *Radio Broadland* in 1984, and in September 1995 he launched another station - *Amber Radio,* where he now presents an afternoon programme.

Ernie BROWN
News Producer at *BBC Radio Cleveland.*

Evelyn BROWN
Began her career as a customer service and administrative assistant in the satellite industry and made 'the big step' via hospital radio. Her first full radio broadcast was at *Radio Tay* on a youth show which led to a weekly album show on *Radio Forth*. She then moved on to *2CR* in Bournemouth hosting a variety of shows before graduating to a daily afternoon programme.

A move back to Scotland brought weekend and evening work at Radio Forth and she now hosts the overnights on the stations *MAX-AM* outlet. In addition to radio, Evelyn also does voice over work, and the highlight of her radio career was an interview with Barbara Cartland, being a finalist in *Atlantic 252*'s 'Search for a DJ' competition. She was also a finalist in BBC Radio Scotland's chart show host competition.

Evelyn's first night working in a night club proved to be her last - while operating the lights the only ones she flashed on and off were over the bar, resulting in spilt drinks everywhere! She loves a challenge, is versatile and likes professionalism, Woody Allen films, Jack Dee and live music, but not baked beans, bad drivers and cooking.

Ian BROWN
Regular commentator and presenter of sports programmes on BBC *Radio Wales.*

Jim BROWN
Head of Sport and Programme Controller at *Great North Radio* in Newcastle.

Julie BROWN
Producer at *BBC Radio Ulster*.

Lee BROWN
One of the presenters who launched *Sunset Radio* in Manchester.

Malcolm BROWN
Station Manager at *Nevis Radio* in Scotland - he also presents a programme each weekday afternoon.

Mick BROWN
Began career working in the records department at Selfridges and then moved to an advertising agency. While there Capital called him and asked him to join them! His first broadcast was reading dedication on the Nicky Horne 'Summer in the City' show. SInce then he's acted as producer of the station's Breakfast Show, Pick of the Pops and produced Chris Tarrant and Kenny Everett.

Mick also has been involved in several TV shows, such as Sidestep, Bux Beat and ITV's Night Network. The highlight of his career was being asked to swap from being a producer to a full time on-air personality at the station, and appearing live on Capital FM in front of 60,000 fans at Cliff Richard's Wembley Show.

He's also well known for his charity work and appeared on 'Top of the Pops' with Pat Sharp as a double act performing the "help a London Child" singles. Four made the charts and one of them, 'I haven't stopped Dancing Yet' made the Top 10. Likes football and music, and hates anyone who is flash.

Paul BROWN
Paul's career began in the army, but he was influenced by the offshore stations to become involved in radio. He was the first programme director at *Radio Victory*, one of the first ILR stations, based in Portsmouth, in the 1970s. He has hosted a variety of programmes himself, including drive-time stints. He then joined the IBA in the 1980s where he was responsible for monitoring ILR stations' programming.

When the Radio Authority took over in 1991, Paul became its deputy Chief Executive. He resigned from the Radio Authority in 1995 and took on the role of Director General of the Association of Independent Radio Companies.

A radio person through and through, Paul is a dial-hopper in his listening and claims that radio is the one area of his life where he enjoys promiscuity.

Paul likes all kinds of music, from Donald Fagin to ZZ Top, via the Spin Doctors and Weber. A keen boater, he believes DAB will be the information highway of the future and hopes radio will be the leading part of it.

John BROWNE
Finance Director at *KCBC*.

Peter BROWNLOW
Company Secretary and a director of 'Investors in Radio' and the Border TV interest stations - *CFM, Century Radio* and *Scot FM*.

Rebecca BROXTON
Reporter at *BBC Wiltshire Sound*

Ken BRUCE
Born in Glasgow on 2nd February, 1951 ijn a nursing home (now a pub) he was educated at Hutchesons Boys School in his native Glasgow and Ken's first job was as an accountant.

His break into radio was via hospital radio, into *Radio Scotland* where he began with a three month contract. His first broadcast was a news bulletin, since when he's fronted programmes such as 'Night Beat', the SRO Road Show and Friday Night is Music Night'.

In the 1980's Ken moved to *Radio 2* where he now hosts a mid-morning programme. He still lives in Scotland with wife Fiona and two sons.

Cousin BRUCIE
Overnight DJ on *Atlantic 252* in 1985. (Not the legendary US jock of the same name).

Alice BRUGGEN
Alice is in charge of administration at Unique Broadcasting's Special Products division.

Nick BRUNGER
Schoolboy experiments in making radio plays and programmes were followed by university radio and finally a chance to 'do it for real'

when he joined the newsroom at *Radio Leicester* and took charge of filing and making the tea!

After a year as a freelance journalist writing for radio, TV and newspapers, including the Nottingham Guardian, Nick joined the BBC in London working on programmes like 'Waggoners Walk', 'Desert Island Discs' and Radio Newsreel'. In 1980 he helped launch *Radio Lincolnshire* as the breakfast show presenter and joined *Radio Nottingham* in 1987.

Nick is now Assistant Editor at *Radio Nottingham*, where, although he doesn't get as much chance to broadcast as he would like, is wheeled out to act as question master in station quizzes form time to time.

Dawn BRYAN
Senior Producer at BBC Radio *GMR*.

Sir Paul BRYAN
MP for Howdenshire and one of the leading MPs who forced through the Sound Broadcasting Act in the early 1970s, which laid the foundation for the UK's ILR network. A director of Granada TV and Manchester's *Piccadilly Radio* for many years, he's now retired and farms just outside Scarborough.

Jason BRYANT
Jason is the Programme Controller at Central Scotland's regional station, *Scot FM*.

Nigel BRYANT
Chief Radio Drama Producer for BBC in the Midlands.

Franco BUCCI
Marketing Manager at *Spectrum International*.

Wolfgang BUCCI
Managing Director at *Spectrum International*.

Martin BUCHANAN
Started his career as a DJ operating a mobile disco when he was only fourteen. He progressed to hospital radio in Eastbourne and then joined *Radio 210* in Reading. For four years he was a presenter on Music Box for a satellite television channel. Until the autumn of 1988 he was broadcasting for *Radio Luxembourg* and he joined *Capital Gold* in 1989.

Richard BUCHANAN
Director of *Radio Forth Group* in Edinburgh.

James BUCKLE
Presenter at *Southern FM*, Brighton.

Paul BUCKLE
Presenter on *Cool FM* in Belfast.

Andy BUCKLEY
Sports Producer at the BBC local station, *GMR*.

Bill BUCKLEY
Presenter on *South Coast Radio*.

Chris BUCKLEY
Presenter on *Key 103* in Manchester.

Martin BUCKLEY
Producer of network radio programmes for the BBC, based in Southampton.

Ben BUDWORTH
Managing Director of *Metro Networks,* the nation-wide traffic news service.

Margaret BUDY
Editor of 'PM' on *BBC Radio Four*.

Michael BUERK
Began his broadcasting career at *BBC Radio Bristol,* where he "gave blood for BBC Local Radio!" He was at the station when it began and developed a nose bleed during a live new programme. Now with BBC TV as a main newsreader on 'The Nine O'clock News'.

Bob BUFTON
Managing Editor of *BBC Radio Devon & Dorset*.

Cheryl BUGGY
Presenter on *South Coast Radio*.

Michael BUKHT
Capital Radio's first Programme Controller, he also worked at stations in the USA and in Kent and is currently in charge of programmes at *Classic FM*.

Clive BULL
Clive hosts a phone-in programme each weekend evening at 10pm on *London Newstalk*.

Judith BUMPUS
Producer of Arts and Science programmes for the BBC based at Broadcasting House.

Carol BUNDOCK

Went to school in Essex and got a BA honours degree from the University of East Anglia in Drama and English. After a careers talk at UEA she went to *Radio Norfolk* and made her first broadcast in January 1990, although she had done some voice over work before that. Since then she's presented drive time and breakfast news and current affairs at radio Norfolk, as well as the mid afternoon sequence until 1994.

Carol has now branched out to include TV news reporting for BBC East and voice overs for documentaries. She lists the highlight of her career as interviewing John MacArthey and Jill Morrell, and giving John Patten a live roasting on air! Her countless verbal blunders are the funniest things, and she likes interviewers who listen. Is a committed bon viveur and cocker spaniel owner!

Colin BUNYON

General programme Producer at *BBC Radio Cleveland* and host of a weekly programme each Sunday afternoon called Vintage Vinyl.

Paul BURBANK

Presenter at *GEM AM* in Nottingham.

Bernadette BURBRIDGE

Presenter at *BBC Radio York* in the mid-eighties. She then moved to Tyne Tees TV in Newcastle, where she now presents 'Shoebox', a religious programme each Sunday.

Colin BURBRIDGE

Member of the North Bedfordshire production team at *BBC Three Counties Radio.*

Kevin BURCH

Assistant editor of *BBC Radio Suffolk*

John BURCH

 A prime organiser of the *Caroline Movement* and one of the station's background helpers in the 1980s. At that time he was an active land-based pirate being frequently heard on several stations in East London and Kent under a pseudonym, Iain Johnston.

In 1992 John was one of the founders of one of the most unique RSL stations, '*Offshore Radio*' which broadcast from a ship anchored off Frinton, Essex, the first station to so transmit legally.

He now operates a radio newsline on 01 426 910390 and pursues his other interests - his career in buses and his family.

William BURDETT-COUTTS

Chairman of *Kiss FM,* Manchester.

Peter BURDIN

Foreign Affairs producer for BBC News and Current Affairs department.

Paul BURELL

Presenter at *Chiltern Supergold* until Summer 1995 when he moved to *Xtra AM* in Birmingham.

Wietske BUREMA

Producer at *BBC Radio Devon and Dorset.*

Gerry BURKE

Born in October 1963 in Helensburgh, the youngest of five children, Gerry was educated in Glasgow and Kirkaldy. He's always worked in broadcasting: and got into the business by working in Hospital Radio Lennox in Alexandria, Scotland when he was just sixteen years old. He spent two years at Clyde Cable Vision and then in 1987 joined *Northsound* in Aberdeen, for three years.

In 1990 Gerry joined *Radio Clyde* where he stayed until he joined *Scot FM* in 1994 and presents the station's afternoon programme.

The man who once cycled around a windswept Peterhead on a tandem in top hat and tails, without raising any money, also works as a continuity announcer at Scottish Television. He's married to Fiona and they had their first child in May 1995.

Gerry likes eating out, his social life and his new mountain bike, but isn't keen on squids with bad manners.

John BURLEY

John is the Chairman of *Island FM*, the ILR station on Guernsey.

Paul BURNETT

Born on the 26th November 1943 in Manchester he attended no less than 12 schools as his family travelled. His radio break was while in the RAF out in Aden, but on hearing about the boom of offshore radio in the mid sixties he bought himself out of the services and took a job at the Top Rank club in Darlington, where he was heard and snapped up by a new station for Yorkshire, *Radio 270*.

Hours before the launch of Radio 270, the station's mast fell into the sea and journalists attending a press reception in Scarborough wrote the station off as a joke - the moral of that story is don't launch on April 1st!

He fronted the breakfast programme on the station for six months, he gained a reputation as the ship's main practical joker, with PD Neddy Noel being his usual victim. One notorious jape was his being seasick during an advert for bacon, on sale at a supermarket owned by the station's managing director Wilf Proudfoot, who recently admitted he was going to fire him but the weather was too rough to get a message out to the ship.

Paul succeeded Noel as operations manager on the ship, but left in April 1967 for a land-based gig at Great Britain's only legal commercial radio station at that time, *Manx Radio*. In 1968 he moved to *Radio Luxembourg*, just in time for the station to drop it's patchwork quilt of sponsored programmes and strip DJs horizontally across each evening. While there he met a local girl Nicole, who became his wife and gave him two sons - and they now live in Berkshire.

Six years later *Radio One* noticed him and gave him a Sunday morning programme; within a year he had a five days a week programme each lunchtime, during which time he got a record made jointly with DLT into the charts (Convoy GB). In the eighties he moved across to *Radio 2*, had a brief flirtation at the dawn of satellite radio on *Radio Nova* and became a star name at London's *Capital Radio*.

One of his best programmes was a double header with legendary US jock, Cousin Brucie and his commentary of the 'Miss World' TV programme from the Albert Hall is well remembered. The highlight of his radio career was a live broadcast from a parachute 600 feet aloft. He continues to present the weekly chart show on *BBC World Service*.

Linda BURNHAM
Sales Supervisor at *Worlds Greatest Music Station* in Peterborough (now Classic Gold).

Chris BURNS
Managing Editor at *BBC Radio Kent* until moving to *Viva 963*, when the London-based women-targeting station launched in 1995.

Greg BURNS
Presenter on the Marcher Group FM stations in North Wales.

Ian BURNS
A director of *Wear FM*, which closed in July 1995.

Iain BURNSIDE
Producer of 'Voices' programmes on BBC *Radio Three*.

Nicki BURRELL
News Producer at *BBC Radio Solent*.

Simon BURRELL
In 1995 he was doing weekend overnight shifts at *Essex FM*.

Alfred BURROWES
Classical Music Presenter on *Downtown Radio* in Belfast.

John BURROWS
Director of *Capital Radio's* Enterprises arm.

Mark BURROWS
Presenter at *GEM AM* in Nottingham, also heard on *Trent FM* and the new Derby based station, *RAM FM*.

Anthony BURTON
Presenter on BBC Radio Three and on the BBC World Service.

Chris BURTON
Presents religious programmes on Sundays at *BBC Radio Cambridgeshire*.

G BURTON
Director of *Leicester Sound FM*.

Gary BURTON
Presenter on the *Trent FM*, Nottingham

Lesley BURTON
Administrator in charge of finance and personnel at *BBC Radio Cornwall*.

Peter BURTON
Peter ran leading computer retail business and he is also a much respected and engineer. He was the Chairman of *Chiltern Radio* from its inception until its take over by the GWR Group in August, 1995.

Sheila BURTON
Director of *Oasis Radio* in St Albans.

Piers BURTON-PAGE
Producer and Presenter on *BBC Radio Three*.

Karl BURTONSHAW
Presenter at *Swansea Sound*.

Dom BUSBY
Dom currently hosts the weekday 'across Midnight' shift (10pm to 2am) on *Minster FM* and on *Yorkshire Coast Radio* in Yorkshire.

Phillipa BUSBY
News reader on the BBC northern local station sustaining service *Night Network*.

Mike BUSHELL
Journalist at *BBC Radio Solent*.

Dave BUSSEY
Producer and presenter of lunchtime weekday programme on *BBC Radio Lincolnshire*.

Mike BUTCHER
Mike is the head of *Coastal Radio*, a new company which is bidding for an ILR licence in Lowestoft.

Tim BUTCHER
Tim is the producer and host of several programmes on *Wiltshire Sound*, including the station's weekend early morning programmes.

Billy BUTLER
Former club DJ of many years standing, he was the resident DJ at the world-famous cavern club from 1964 until 1969. He got into radio in 1971 after being asked to replace Kenny Everett on BBC Radio Merseyside for six weeks. Seven years later he left the BBC for a stint with Liverpool's ILR station, *Radio City* and was voted 'DJ of the Year' two years on the trot, and took the honour again three more times in the early nineties.

In 1984 he returned to *BBC Radio Merseyside* and is still there,m hosting several programmes including a weekday mid-morning programme and an outrageous Sunday quiz show called 'Hold yer Plums'. Billy is now a living legend on Merseyside where his appearances on ILR and BBC over the years have bought laughter to millions and tears to more than a few eyes.

The highlight of Billy's radio career was being honoured by the Variety club of Great Britain for 21 years in local radio, but Billy is just as at home on TV and has appeared on 'Thank your Lucky Stars', 'Fun Factory', 'Whickers World' and 'What the Butler Saw' to name but a few.

Humourous events are part and parcel of Billy's life and he could fill a book with them (and it's time he did!) - he loves his job and life but not people who are narrow-minded musically. His programmes have sold thousands on cassette copies, sent all over the world.

Joe BUTLER
Presenter on *Radio City's* AM service.

Keith BUTLER
Presenter on *Xtra AM* in Birmingham

Tony BUTLER
After school in Wolverhampton, Tony had a period in print journalism with the Evening Mail and Sunday Telegraph before his first radio break - it was in 1963 for the BBC's 'Sport in the Midlands'. He then contributed local and national sports items to the BBC

Sports Unit and in the mid-seventies joined *BRMB* as Sports Editor. Then came a move back to the Corporation when he joined *Radio WM* on the breakfast show, and in the early 90s it was back to the commercial sector and *XTRA AM*, again on the breakfast show.

As well as radio Tony has appeared in audio visual presentations and had three series on BBC TV (Sporting Butler, Boating Butler and Biking Butler). The highlight of his career was interviewing Princess Anne for BRMB and IRN, and he once lost £58,000 worth of BBC camera and sound equipment when he fell into the River Trent while filming 'Boating Butler.' Like chocolate, champagne and football (in that order) and doesn't like snobs and his greyhound losing races.

Stephen BUTT
Senior Producer in charge of weekend output at *BBC Radio Leicester*.

Sanjiv BUTTOO
Freelance presenter of ethnic programmes at *BBC Radio Leeds* and *BBC Radio Lancashire*.

Jeremy BUXTON
After Manchester Grammar School, Jeremy studied Media and French at Leeds University where he got his BA. After some hospital radio and a stint on A Roadwatch (Manchester) Jeremy joined *Signal Radio* in Stoke in december 1989.

He then moved to KFM in Stockport before a move across the Pennines to *BBC Radio Leeds*. After a brief flirtation with *Aire FM* in Leeds, he moved to *The Pulse* in Bradford, and then *Lincs FM* before his most recent move, to BBC Radio Humberside in June 1995 where he currently hosts an afternoon programme.

Jeremy's radio highlight was having his 'Jim'll fix it' broadcast by Gloria Hunniford when he was eleven years old, and he once stumbled through "mist patches" when Dr Spooner struck.

He likes France, cats and dogs and holidays but not mushy peas and people who slack off (so don't do it when he's around - at 6 feet 6 he is one of radio's tallest presenters!)

Roger BUXTON
Sports Producer at *Essex FM* and *Breeze AM* in Southend.

Dave BYERS
Chief Producer of music at *BBC Radio Ulster*.

Mark BYFORD
Controller of Regional Broadcasting for the BBC, based at White City.

Francis BYRNES
Radio producer for BBC Network Radio based at Southampton.

Lucy CACANAS
Producer of 'Midweek' on BBC *Radio Four*.

Thomas CADWALLADR
Producer of Welsh programmes at *Swansea Sound*.

Jim CAINE
Producer of classical music and jazz at *Manx Radio*.

John CAINE
Presenter at *TFM* in Stockton until 1995 when he joined the on-air team at *Heart 100.7* in the Midlands to host a Saturday evening programme, from 6 until 10pm.

Michael CAIRNS
Producer at *BBC Radio Ulster* and *Radio Foyle*.

Tom CAIRNS
Company Secretary at *West Sound* in Ayr and *South West FM* in Dumfries.

Lisa CALENO
Presenter of programmes on *BBC Radio Kent*.

Colin CALEY
Producer at *BBC Radio Devon and Dorset*.

Dave CALLAGHAN
Sports Producer at *BBC Radio Leeds*.

Paul CALLAN
Lunchtime presenter at *Classic FM*.

David CALLISTER
Country Music presenter at *Manx Radio* where he also hosts the station's phone in programme 'The Mannin Line'.

Stefanie CALLISTER
Began her radio career at Craigavon Hospital Radio in Northern Ireland, before being talent spotted in the early 1980's by Chris Carey. He hired her for his Dublin Super Pirates, *Radio Nova* and *Kiss FM*, where she acquired skills as a radio-journalist.

A move back to Belfast and *Downtown Radio* followed, after which she moved sideways to the BBC and began fronting television pieces.

For a while Stephanie was a fashion expert and ran her own boutique in Banbridge for several years. She was the Ulster anchor for BBC TV's 'Children in Need' and then moved to *Sky TV* to host 'International Business Report' in 1989. She now lives in London and is married to TV newscaster Chris Mann. Stefanie's hobbies include cookery, travel and music.

Bob CALVER
Bob is now the Assistant Station Editor at *BBC Radio Shropshire*.

John CALVERT
Creative Manager at *Essex FM* and *Breeze AM* in Southend.

David CAMBURN
Production Editor of *BBC Radio GLR*, .

Douglas CAMERON
Born on the 29th October, 1933, In Newcastle, he was educated at the Edinburgh Academy and became a Chartered Accountant. His first radio broadcast was as a reporter on TV in 1961 and throughout the sixties he appeared on many educational TV programmes.

In the late sixties Douglas joined the 'Today' team on Radio Four and in 1974 teamed up with Bob Holness at *LBC* to co-host their early morning news -wrap - called AM.

Douglas now presents weekday breakfast shows on *Newstalk Radio* in London (from 6 until 10 am) and lives in Middlesex.

Ewen CAMERON
Chairman of *Orchard FM*.

Geoffrey CAMERON
Editor of Current Affairs for *BBC Scotland*

James CAMERON
Jointly presented the breakfast programme on GLR with Janice Long.

Kevin CAMERON
Mid-Afternoon Presenter for *Q96*.

Nancy CAMERON
Director at *Heartland FM*.

Stuart CAMERON
Early morning presenter for *Fox FM*.

Adrian CAMBELL
Member of the news team at *BBC Radio Cornwall*.

David CAMPBELL (1)
Born in Glasgow and educated at Kelvinside Academy, David moved to the USA in the mid seventies where he attended Washington University in St Louis and gained an AB in Communications and Media Management as well as an MBA in Marketing. He worked for several American companies, including Pepsi Cola at their New York HQ where he was the company's youngest marketing manager. In 1984 he returned to Europe to be Pepsi's first Marketing Manager for the UK and oversaw all the Company's Business in the Netherlands.

David joined the Virgin Group in late 1986, just before its public flotation, and worked on most of the group's thirty subsidiaries. By 1991 David was running Virgin's 'Rushes' division, and under his stewardship they won Gold, Silver and Bronze awards at the Cannes Film Festival.

In 1993, he became Chief Executive of *Virgin Radio* and oversaw the launch of the station later that year. He enjoys foreign travel, is a freeman of Glasgow and a licensed helicopter pilot.

David CAMPBELL (2)
The Assistant Editor of *BBC Radio Oxford*.

Dougie CAMPBELL
Mid afternoon presenter for *Q96*.

Duncan CAMPBELL
Well-known crime correspondent of the

'Guardian' newspaper, for frequent appearances on TV and numerous books on secrecy, Duncan's first radio broadcast was in 1973 when he began a career as a reporter and presenter with London news station, *LBC*.

In 1994 he joined *Radio Five Live* where he presents the station's 'Crimedesk'.

Gavin CAMPBELL

Born in Letchworth in Hertfordshire in March 1946, he trained at the Central School of Speech and Drama and worked in theatre before joining the BBC. He worked as a newsreader and an announcer on BBC network radio and also became a producer.

Has also appeared on several TV programmes as a reporter on Nationwide, Breakfast TV and London Plus, as well as being one of the regular presenters on 'That's Life'.

Gordon CAMPBELL

Financial controller at *Orchard FM* .

Joseph CAMPBELL

Managing Director at *West Sound Radio* .

Kenny CAMPBELL

Presenter at *South-West Sound Radio* in Dumfries and at *West Sound* in Ayr.

Martin CAMPBELL

Programme Controller for *County Sound Radio* until 1995 and at *Radio Mercury*.

Nicky CAMPBELL

Born in Edinburgh on 10th April, 1961,he gained a history degree from Aberdeen University and became a DJ and copywriter at Northsound Radio in Aberdeen.. After two years he moved to *Capital Radio* in London, and in 1987 joined *Radio One* as a daytime presenter.

While with Radio One he presented 'Top of the Pops' and 'Video Juke Box', as well as being a script-writer for 'Spitting Image'. In 1988 he married Linda and has now become a better known as the presenter of TV game show 'Wheel of Fortune'. He currently hosts Radio One's afternoon programme on weekdays from 2 until 4pm.

Trish CAMPBELL

Presenter of the weekday 'Daybreak' programme from 5 to 6am each weekday morning on *BBC Radio Gloucestershire*.

Claire CAMPBELL-SMITH

Presenter of religious programmes on *Radio 4*.

Luis CANDAL

Presenter at *Ocean FM*.

Samantha CANN

Samantha is the Head of Programmes at two in-store radio channels delivered by satellite, *Texas FM* and *Asda FM*.

Geoff CANNELL

News Editor at *Manx Radio* and also an accomplished sports commentator.

James CANNON

After a period as a presenter at GWR FM in Bristol, James is now the Station and Programme Organiser at *Galaxy Radio*.

Steve CANNON

Presenter at *Mix 96* in Aylesbury.

Veronica CAPALDI

Country Music Presenter at *Lincs FM*, although she lives in East Yorkshire.

Tony CAPSTICK

Tony is the long-serving mid-afternoon (1 to 4) presenter at *BBC Radio Sheffield* who also had a chart hit with one of his singles in the 1970's parodying a TV commercial.

Chris CAREY

Ballroom DJ experience in 1967 led to a job at post 'Marine Offences Act' *Radio Caroline* later that year, as hi-sould and club jock 'Spangles Muldoon'. After Caroline was towed away he organised one of the first serious'land pirate' stations, *Radio Free London* (along with Peter Mutrtha and Stevie Merike(qv).

In 1970 he reappeared on *Radio North Sea International*, and two years later was instrumental in relaunching *Radio Caroline* where he became station manager. He then established an electronics company in London and returned to his DJ role in 1975 at *Radio Luxembourg*, becoming Manager.

Who's Who in British Radio

By 1980 Carey was to be found in Ireland, establishing unlicensed *Sunshine Radio* with Caroline colleague Robbie Dale (qv) and later his own 'super-pirate' *Radio Nova*, which became the country's most successful radio station. Chris grew this into extra channels and even a TV station at one stage.

On returning to the UK he expanded his electronics company into an international marketer of satellite TV decoders, and in 1987 he launched the first true satellite radio station, calling it *Radio Nova International*. He closed this in 1992 and a year later bought the FM-only ILR station *Buzz FM* in Birmingham.

Some imaginative programming and hiring led to Buzz achieving a cult following in the city in 1993, but Chris decided to pull the plug suddenly, stripping the station of all equipment one afternoon in November 1993.

Always full of innovative ideas, and, unlike most people, brave enough to try them out, Chris will no doubt be back on the radio scene very soon.

Eileen CAREY
Sales Manager at *RTM* in London, she left for a period but has now returned, again in sales.

David CARGILL
David is the Managing Director at *Broadland FM*, the Chairman at *SGR FM* and the Chairman of the Suffolk Radio Group.

Joseph CARLIN
Director of *Q102.9 FM* in Londonderry.

Paul CARLISLE
Chief Engineer at *BBC Radio CWR*.

CARLOS
Carlos is a presenter on *BRMB FM*.

Ian CARLTON
Administration Controller for *Heartland FM*.

Iain CARMICHAEL
Late-show presenter for *BBC Radio Scotland*.

Chris CARNEGY
Managing Director for *Spire FM*.

Liz CARNEY
Producer at *Radio 4* for a programme called 'File on Four'.

Lewis CARNIE
Sales and Marketing Director at *Northsound*.

Danny CARPENTER
Senior Producer at *BBC Radio York*.

Krissie CARPENTER
Educated at Grammar School and college in Northern Ireland, Krissie got into radio by helping her (then) husband Paul at *WABC*, which was one of Ulster's most popular stations in the mid eighties (even though it had no licence).

She was soon presenting her own programmes, both on the Hot Hits outlet and the gold outlet (both powerful FM stations) and stayed there for almost four years until she moved to *GEM AM* in Nottingham.

While there she was one of the station's best-known voices hosting the weekday afternoon programme. In 1995 she left to join *Signal Gold* in Stoke on Trent.

The highlights of Krissie's career were visiting WCBS FM New York in 1994 and also interviewing Al Jarreau. For Krissie, all radio is fun (you can tell just be listening to her on the air!) and she has had many humourous events in her career - she's probably saving them for a book.

Krissie likes genuine people who say exactly what they think, and was recently short-listed for an Oprah Winfrey type programme for TV.

Steve CARPENTER
Mainstream Presenter on *Orchard FM*.

Sue CARPENTER
Presenter of a programme called 'The Morning Report' on *LBC Newstalk*.

Jane CARR
Journalist for *BBC Radio Solent*.

Anna CARRAGHER
Editor of 'Eurofile' on *BBC Radio Four*.

Kathleen CARRAGHER
Producer of a programme called Rafferty on BBC Northern Ireland.

Justin CARRIGAN
Joint Deputy Editor for I .T. N. Radio News

Desmond CARRINGTON
Born on the 23rd May, 1926 in Kent, Desmond was educated at the Bromley Grammar School and his first job was as an office boy in a publishers. He then became an actor before joining the Royal West Kent regiment of the army.

In 1946 he made his first broadcast, opening up *Radio Rangoon* after the Japanese had left and he was then seconded for radio work - in Ceylon his colleagues included David Jacobs.

After demob, the BBC dismissed his audition, so he joined the BBC Rep as an actor, but was soon back presenting programmes on *Radio Luxembourg*. He appeared in the TV drama 'Emergency Ward 10' as Doctor Anderson and his was the face on the Daz commercials on television for most of the 1960's.

In the 1970's he joined *Radio Two*, presenting such programmes as Housewives Choice and 'Album Time' and now has a weekday lunchtime programme on the station.

Julia CARRINGTON
Programme Producer at *BBC Radio Cleveland*.

Paul CARRINGTON
Paul's introduction to radio was in 1982 as a Production Assistant on Timmy Mallett's show at *Piccadilly Radio*, along with Chris Evans and Simon Mayo's producer, Chris Watmough.

Over the next eight and a half years he worked in almost every department at Piccadilly, including Commercial Production, Features and Programmes, and moved down the M6 to Stoke where he joined *Signal Radio*. He presented Signal's Breakfast Programme, winning him a Sony Award in 1993.

Towards the end of 1993 Paul moved to hull and joined *Viking FM*, moving on after nine months to neighbouring *Minster FM* in York, as Programme Controller on Yorkshire Day.

Paul then moved back to the Metro Group to join The Pulse in Bradford where he presented the Breakfast Show once again.

In late Summer 1995 Paul was back with the Metro Group to become Programme Manager at *Great Yorkshire Gold*, based in Sheffield. He's also been hosting the mid-morning show recently, showing some of the younger DJs how radio can be entertaining and fun.

Charles CARROLL
Charles is the host of the 'London Live' programme each weekday at 12.30 on *BBC Radio GLR*.

Malcolm CARROLL
Head of Current Affairs at *Plymouth Sound*.

Alan CARRUTHERS
Programme Manager at *Xtra AM*.

Ford CARRUTHERS
Chairman at *Heartland FM*.

Sarah CARRUTHERS
Station Administrator at *Heartland FM*.

Clare CARSON
Clare is the Head of News at *Classic FM*.

Nicola CARSLAW
Reporter for BBC News and Current Affairs.

Bob CARSWELL
Presenter of Gaelic programmes on *Manx Radio* on the Isle of Man.

Magnus CARTER
Born on the 29th March, 1948 in Sunderland, Magnus attended the Bede Grammar School in the city and became a junior reporter with a

local freelance news agency. After newspapers, he worked in theatre administration for a spell Magnus made his first broadcast on *Radio Clyde*, presenting a programme of classical music.

He then joined *Radio Forth* in Edinburgh, where he worked his way up from being a reporter, through the JLR 1and 2 routes he became duty editor and then senior news producer at the station and finally joined *BBC Radio Scotland.*

In 1979 he returned to independent radio, working for *LBC* in London where he became one of the station's news anchors and most popular presenters. Although he doesn't like London traffic and prefers real ale, he's stayed in the capital and now hosts a weekly programme (Saturdays, 10 until 2pm) on *London Newsradio.*

Tony CARTER
Sales Director at *Eclipse FM*, a cable radio station in Sutton, Surrey.

Richard CARTLEDGE
Richard is the host of the afternoon programme (from 1 until 4pm) each weekday on *BBC Radio Solent.*

Tony CARTLEDGE
Tony was a news reporter at *BBC Radio Humberside,* before joining *Radio Newcastle* where he now hosts the station's flagship weekday breakfast programme.

Mike CARTWRIGHT
Mike joined *Radio Humberside* as the reporter responsible for the Grimsby area and he is now the station's Assistant News Editor.

Dave CASH
Born in 1942 in Bushey, Herts but moved to Vancouver, Canada with his family when aged 7. Dave's first job was at *C-FUN* there and he returned to London in 1964, where Ben Toney(qv), the PD of *Radio London* signed him for a stint on the ship.

The next two and a half years saw him become one of the most popular sixties DJs, part-based on a double headed show with ship-mate Kenny Everett (qv). Left Big L in early 67 to join the *BBC Light Programme*, where he hosted a live band show called 'Monday Monday' and later several programmes on *Radio One* from its launch that September. In 1969 he had regular daily programme 'Cash At Four' with a star studded guest list which included Spike Milligan, John Cleese and Peter Sellers.

In 1969 Dave helped launch international English station, *Radio Monte Carlo* with Kenny Everett and others, "I learned more at Monte Carlo in 6 months than I did in six years elsewhere" he says. The following year saw Dave writing presenting a 26 week series for Harlech TV, where he met his wife, the actress Monica Evans, who had recently returned from the USA where she starred in 'The Odd Couple' on Broadway for two years and appeared in the film with Jack Lemmon and Walter Matheau.

In 1973, Dave was in charge of production and sound at the launch of *Capital Radio* where he stayed for 19 years. He also found time to do programmes for other stations, such as *Radio Luxembourg, Invicta Radio, Radio West*, and for *MTV*. In 1989 he became one of the anchors for the launch of *Capital Gold* where he still hosts the top-rated sunday morning strip.

In 1992 he turned his hand to writing, with a novel based on life around a top London ILR station called *The Rating Game*. He followed this up in 1993 with another radio station saga centred around a mythical pop radio ship, Radio FREE. He now lives in an oast house in Kent and is hard at work on his third book, while also helping organise the *Eclipse FM* application for a new station in south west London.

Mike CASS
Born on the 3rd April, 1974 in Leicester, Mike got into radio by sheer persistence and making

lots of coffee at *Leicester Sound*. He then moved to a job at *Mercia* in Coventry and then on to *MFM* in Wrexham.

The next move in Mike's career was a shift at *Suffolk Group Radio* in Ipswich, from where he moved to the Midlands and in Summer 1995 he joined London's new AC station, *Heart FM* .

The highlight of his radio career was broadcasting from an airship in a gale and hosting an REM concert for syndication to American stations. He loves American radio, good food and music, but not rave music and certainly not Brussel sprouts.

Brian CASSIDY MBE

As well as being a Member of the European Parliament, Brian is a also a director on the board of *2CR* in Bournemouth.

Nigel CASSIDY

Phone-in host on BBC *Radio Five Live* in 1995.

Pauline CAUSEY

Journalist at BBC *Radio Cornwall*.

Lord CHALFONT

Author, broadcaster and journalist. Born Alun Jones in 1919 in South Wales, Lord Chalfont was commissioned into Army in 1939 where he stayed until 1961, when he became defence correspondent for The Times.

He was a government minister in Harold Wilson's cabinets from 1964 to 1970 and then the opposition spokesman on defence. He resigned over Common Market issue and took directorship with IBM's UK arm. A former member of the IBA and the ITC, he chaired the Radio Authority from its inception to the end of 1994. Lord Chalfont's wife Mona is paediatric doctor and he also sits on the board of directors of many companies and a merchant bank.

Bryan CHALKER

Bryan, a very tall, very grey man with a very deep voice, was a commercial artiste and then a policeman for seven years in Portsmouth as well as spending periods as a stage hand in Canada and a freelance journalist. He got into

radio by having a great degree of tenacity and a wide knowledge of country music. His first radio was a 'What's On' spot for Dave Cash on *Capital Radio* and he then secured the afternoon show on *Radio West* in Bristol.

Bryan hosted the Late Show on an FM station in Oman for the last year as well as programmes on Country 1035 in London, and the Europe-wide satellite station *CMR- Country Music Radio*.

As well as radio, Bryan fronted the successful 'New Frontier Band' from 1969 to 1979 and is also the author of several books including 'This is Country Music'(Phoebus) and 'Cook Ups of World War 2' (Redcliffe).

He claims the highlight of his radio career has been getting fired by *Country 1035* for playing a Hank Williams and Lefty Frizell track "a great career move - I haven't looked back since!" That occasion is also the funniest moment he's had on radio "getting fired by *Country 1035* for playing country music, when they didn't recognise it."

Bryan dislikes accountants, traffic wardens, politicians and other liars but loves country music, vintage cars and steam transport.

Judith CHALMERS

Born in Manchester in October 1936, Judith's first radio broadcast was during 'Children's Hour' on the *Home Service* when she was just 13 years old. She spent several years voicing pieces for *Radio Four's* 'Women's Hour' and hosted her own programme on BBC *Radio Two* for a time.

She then moved into television, being an announcer on BBC TV and a commentator on 'Come Dancing' as well as hosting various beauty pageants. In the 1980s, Judith became nationally known as a regular presenter of 'Wish You Were Here', an ITV holiday programme and in 1994 was awarded the OBE, for sices to broadcasting.

Sandra CHALMERS

Sister of Judith(qv) who was a staff announcer at BBC *Radio Four* based in Manchester in the 1970s and moved to London to become a BBC Publicity Officer for *Radio Two*.

Barrie CHAMBERS

Formerly a presenter at *KCBC* in Kettering, responsible for all sports output, he left in 1995 and is currently planning in RSL in Northamptonshire.

Lynn CHAMPION.

A youth worker, originally hired by Radio 1 access programme *Talkabout* producer Sue Davis,as a researcher. Became freelance reporter for Radios 1, 2 and 4. After becoming staff producer at Radio 4, she created WPFM, an imitation of pirate radio.

She left the BBC when Radio One refused to play more dance music and took up a role as music video producer, then was a founder of KISS FM, helping to prepare their application for a licence. Now a senior figure at the London dance music station.

Jane CHANDLER

Jane is a news reporter based in Salisbury for BBC Wiltshire Sound.

Paul CHANTLER

Paul has been a professional journalist and broadcaster for 17 years, starting his career in *Hospital Radio Tunbridge Wells*, and on local newspapers in Kent. He worked as a presenter, journalist and manager at *Invicta Sound* in Kent, *Southern Sound* in Sussex and at *BBC Wiltshire Sound* where his was the voice which launched the station in 198.

Paul joined the *Chiltern Radio Network* in October 1989 as Head of News and he was made Group Programme Director in 1991. As well as being Chief Executive of *Galaxy 101*, the new regional station in the South West, Paul is the Managing Director of

'Network News' which began in 1991 and the co-author of the text-book "Local Radio Journalism" published by Focal Press in 1992.

Dave CHAPMAN

Dave is one of the record librarians at *Community Radio Milton Keynes*.

John CHAPMAN

John is Sales Manager and deputy Sales Director at *Fortune 1458*.

Kit CHAPMAN

Kit is a Director at *Orchard FM*.

Liz CHAPMAN

Liz is a Sales Director at *Great North Radio* and sister station *Metro FM*, both in Newcastle.

Susanne CHARLES

Disc jockey on *Radio Caroline* in the mid 1980s.

Martin CHARMAN

Martin is Chief Engineer for the Golden Rose Radio group of stations (*Jazz FM* and *Viva 963*).

Nigel CHARTERS

Programme Director of *London Newsradio FM*.

Angela CHAUHAN

Host of late night programmes on the new Midlands station, *Radio XL*.

Francis CHEETHAM

Francis is a Director of *Broadland FM*, Norfolk.

Rachel CHESHIRE

Promotions Executive at *Severn Sound*.

Charlie CHESTER

Born on 26th April, 1914, in Eastbourne, he went to school in the town and to the LCC School in Clapham. When he was 17 he formed his own band and made his first broadcast in either August or September in 1937. He soon became on e of the country's best loved comedians with hosting many regular programmes on the *Light Programme* over the last fifty years.

In recent years Charlie has hosted his own 'Sunday Soapbox as well as 'Listen to The Band' on *Radio Two* each Sunday.

A keen painter, he now lives near Herne Bay in Kent and still hosts programmes each Sunday afternoon on *Radio Two*.

Bob CHESWORTH
Engineer-in-Charge at *BBC Radio Lincolnshire*.

Ian CHETWYN
Sales Manager at *Signal Radio* in Cheshire.

Paul CHILVERS
Paul is a programme presenter at *Lincs FM*.

David CHIPP
A Director of *Talkradio UK*.

Sam CHISHOLM
Born in Australia countless years ago, he learend broadcasting in that country's competitive environment and came to the UK in the 1980s to help launch Sky TV. After a successful career in Sky News he left (following a dispute with Chris Mann) and joined *Talkradio UK* in 1995.

He originally hosted a mid-morning programme when the station began and can now be heard each weekday evening from 4 until 7pm.

Mark CHIVERS
Mark is the presenter of the 10 until 2pm slot each weekday at *Fox FM* in Oxford.

Chris CHOI
Presenter at *BBC Radio York* in the 1980s, he is now nationally know for his on-screen work as an investigator on TV consumer programmes.

Danny CHORANJI
Presenter of 'Eastern Beat', an Asian-oriented programme on several BBC East Midlands local stations in the early 1990s.

Rashid CHOUDREY
Director of *Oasis Radio* in St Albans.

Dave CHRISTIAN
After public school at Shoreham and an 18 month spell in the Royal Navy, dave worked at Radon Electronics making mobile disco and PA equipment.

He worked on Worthing Pier for some time and one day in 1968 visited the *Radio Luxembourg* office in London to collect some audience research figures for a these is he was writing. Tony Windsor, then working as a programme assistant, asked him to a voice test and he was asked to go out to the Grand Duchy the following Monday as a newsreader.

John CHRISTIAN
Managing Director of *Radio Mercury* and in 1995 formed a new company, *Phoenix Radio,* to bid for the Mercury Group's Crawley licences.

Mark CHRISTIAN
Mark is the host of the late night programmes at weekends on *Signal Radio*, Cheshire.

Terry CHRISTIAN
Born in Manchester, he has worked at BBC *Radio Derby, Radio Four* (a programme called 'WPFM') and at *Radio One* where he hosted 'Saturday Live' for a while.

Terry has been heard on *Sunset Radio* and *Piccadilly Radio* in Manchester and on Stoke's *Signal Radio* as well as *TFM* in Stockton and *KFM* in Stockport.

Better known as a presenter on Channel Four TV programme 'The Word' until 1995. He hosted a Sunday evening programme in the early days of *Talk Radio UK* but was fired in September 1995 for allowing blasphemous remarks on the air.

Philip CHRYSSIKOS
After school in Chiswick and A-levels at college, Philip became a departmental head at a B & Q superstore and helped out on a market stall. He did some shifts as a hospital radio presenter at the Central Middlesex in London (June 1990) and worked at *Radio Cracker* at Harrow in 1993. After two weeks work experience at *Capital Radio* in the production and presentation department, he became a helper at *Star 106.6* in 1993 and finally got a regular programme with them in May 1994. The highlight of his career was learning to waterski in two months so he could take part in the World Championships in Reading in 1994.

Louise CHURCHILL
One of the first female newsreaders in ILR at *Plymouth Sound*, she took a role in management at the station and is now the chairman.

David CLARGO
David hosts a magazine programme each weekday (from 1.30 to 4.30) on *BBC Radio Oxford*.

Iain CLASPER
Born in Scotland, Iain began his radio career at *Moray Firth Radio* in Inverness before moving south to Dundee and *Radio Tay*. He then moved to Wales where he was a member of the team responsible for the launch of *Touch AM*, and then joined the Metro Group, where he became Sales Director at *Viking FM*.

Alan CLARK
Born in Wales, but educated in South London,he applied for a job on *Radio City* after hearing a plea for more DJs on the air. He was hired by American DJ Rick Michaels (now head of the worldwide radio finance broker, CEA) and served a trial period on the fort for just his expenses.

Eventually he was hired as a full-time DJ and was on the station when the fort was seized by thugs and dockers during a takeover battle in 1966, which led to the station owner, Reg Calvert, being shot dead by a some-time Radio Caroline Executive, Major Oliver Smedley.

Alan hosted many programmes on City and is best remembered for his contributions to the 'Aunty Mabel Hour', a satirical programme which parodied the music and radio business.

"It was 16 months of thrills and spills on City".

says Alan, and when the station was closed down eight months later he joined neighbouring *Radio 390*. Following Radio 390's premature closure he moved to Holland's overseas service, *Radio Nederland*.

Alan spent 6 years with LBC and IRN as a journalist then joined TV companies TVS and more recently Meridian TV, where he is now Parliamentary Correspondent, based in London.

Greg CLARK
Senior news producer at *BBC Radio Solent*.

Jeremy CLARK
Presenter (weekdays) at *Power FM*.

Jerry CLARK
Journalist at BBC *Radio Cornwall*.

Luis CLARK
Presenter at *Metro FM*, Newcastle.

Peter CLARK (1)
DJ on *Radio Caroline* in 1983.

Peter CLARK (2)
Director of *Talkradio UK* and acting Managing Director of the station after John Aumonier left the station in September 1995.

Ray CLARK
Ray had lots of jobs in his youth but always hankered after working on the radio. When the chance of a job on *Radio Caroline* came, he jumped at it and became one of their most popular DJs, broadcasting under the pseudonym Mick Williams.

Ray came ashore in the eighties to join *Invicta Radio* in Kent and the presented shows on their 'Gold' service, *Coast AM*. In 1993 he moved around the Estuary to become breakfast show host at *Breeze AM* in Southend, where he is now one of the station's most popular DJs.

His career highlights include the widely acclaimed tribute to *Radio Caroline* produced by him and aired all day by *Breeze AM* at Easter, 1994, and winning awards in the New York Radio Festival.

Simon CLARK
Sports producer at *BBC Radio Sheffield*.

Al CLARKE
Al is currently the host of the 5 pm to 9pm shift at *Southern Counties Radio*.

Alistair CLARKE
Head of the newsroom in second part of the day at *The Wave* in Blackpool.

Lorna CLARKE
Programme manager of *Kiss FM* in London.

Jaqueline CLARKE
Born in Slough on 13th February 1942, Jaqueline trained at RADA and treaded the boards in the West End for several years before joining the *Radio Two* comedy programmes 'Mike Yarwood', Castles on the Air' and 'Thirty Minutes Worth'.

Nick CLARKE
Presenter at *BBC Radio York* in the 1980s.

Sue CLARKE
Sales Controller at *Southern FM* in Brighton.

Simon CLARKE
Simon was a presenter on *Chiltern FM* until October 1995 when he joined *Radio Aire* in Leeds to host their afternoon programme.

Jeff CLARK-MEADS
Communications Director at the BPI, then European news editor for Billboard Group and Music Week, Jeff is now UK Bureau Chief of *Music and Media.*

Robert CLARKSON
Robert is an Executive at Associated Newspapers' media arm, *Harmsworth Media.*

Glynne CLAY
Chairman of *Red Dragon Radio* in Cardiff.

David CLAYTON
Went to Great Yarmouth Grammar School and became an accountant and a shop manager before getting into radio by making the tea!

His first broadcast was in 1979 on a regional programme for *Radio Four* and the following year he moved to *Radio Norfolk* as a freelance producer and presenter, where he stayed for seven years.

During that time he also appeared on *Anglia Television* as a continuity announcer and on BBC TV's 'Look East' as a presenter.

The funniest moment so far of David's career was looking for naturists in the sand-dunes and trying not to look suspicious - while the highlight was receiving a Sony Award for his mid-morning programme on Radio Norfolk.

In 1987 he moved back to *Radio Four* for four years, and then back to *Radio Norfolk* where he is now the station's Assistant Editor.

John CLAYTON
Born on 27th May, 1965 at Billericay in Essex, John became an accountant with a merchant bank and dabbled in hospital radio. His first broadcast was on *Delta Radio* and *County Sound* in Guildford where he did weekend shifts.

John then moved across to *Essex Radio* to do weekend afternoons and swing cover, and then moved further round the coast to Suffolk group radio doing similar shifts.

In September 1995 he joined *Heart 106.2* in London, the highlight so far of his career.

The funniest event in John's radio work was working with a certain top sports journalist, renowned for his laugh, which one day went on for five minutes! he likes football, music, the theatre and cinema, but not negative people.

Yvonne CLAYTON
Financial controller at *Pirate 102* in Cornwall.

Julian CLEGG
Julian is currently the host of the morning show on *Southern Counties Radio.*

Pete CLEMENTS
Born in Norfolk at a very early age, Pete started playing records on an educational cruise ship. he went to Wolverhampton Polytechnic to study biology, and began doing programmes on *Beacon Radio* in the early 1980s with Mick Wright, eventually taking a full-time job with the station.

In the nineties he has become one of Beacon Radio's leading on-air personalities.

Lucy CLINGAN
Lucy is a Radio Production Assistant at *BBC Radio Berkshire*, now merged with Radio Oxford to form *Radio Thames Valley.*

Nick CLITHEROE
Head of News and Sport at *Plymouth Sound.*

Charles CLIVE-PONSONBY
Director at *Orchard FM.*

Who's Who in British Radio

David CLOAKE
Cloakey's first job was as a test technician for a flight simulation company. He'd already begun his radio career in hospital radio when he was just 12 years old. In 1988 he began working as a technical operator at *Southern Sound*, and then early in 1991, made his first broadcast as a weekend presenter at *Radio Nova*.

Later that year he moved to Chiltern radio as a swing presenter; in April 1992 he took over the Drive Show at *Northants FM* and a few months later moved to *Severn Sound*. After 18 months on the 'Drive Time' programme he got the station's coveted breakfast programme in November 1993 and 18 months later he's still there.

Brian CLOUGH
Presenter of country music programmes on *Great Northern Radio*, based in Newcastle.

Gordon CLOUGH
Presenter for 'Europhile' on *BBC Radio 4*.

Gillian CLYNE
Gillian is the Head of News at *Fortune 1458*, the easy listening station in Manchester.

Graham COATES
Chairman of CD 603 in Gloucester.

Louise COATES
Producer of 'News Quiz of the Year' for *BBC Radio 4*.

Peter COATES
Director of the *Signal Radio Group*.

Elizabeth COBHAM.
The Viscountess is Chairman of *Heart FM* and lives near Stourbridge in the West Midlands.

Joanne COBOURN
Joanne is currently a reporter and also the Head of News at *Mix 96*.

Tim COCKRAM
Tim is the Director of Engineering at *Touch AM* and *Red Dragon Radio* in Cardiff.

Paul COIA
Born in Glasgow on 19th June, 1957, he joined *Radio Clyde* as a DJ on leaving University. While there he also worked as an announcer at Scottish Television which led to his being the first announcer to be heard on Channel Four when it launched in 1982.

Since then he's appeared on dozens of TV programmes including Rab C. Nesbitt and now lives in London with his wife, TV Presenter Debbie Greenwood and their daughter Natalie. Paul likes music, writing, keeping fit and cats. Recently heard presenting programmes on *BBC Radio Two*. Agent: Sara Cameron Management.

Joanne COBURN
Head of News at *Mix 96*, in Aylesbury.

Dave COCHRANE
Head of Music at Moray Firth Radio.

Tim COCKRAM
Director of Touch AM, Cardiff.

Steve COE
Presenter on *Amber Radio* in East Anglia.

Chris COLE
Chris presents a programme on *Eleven Seventy* each Sunday called 'Cross Rhythms'.

Derek COLE
Chief Engineer at *London Newsradio*.

Jenny COLE
Managing Director of the newsgathering operation at BBC World Service; based at Bush House.

Les COLE
A programme producer at *BBC Radio Cleveland*.

Simon COLE
Simon is now a senior executive with *Unique Broadcasting*.

Grant COLEMAN
Grant is a sports producer nd also the presenter of the Saturday afternoon sequence on BBC Radio Solent.

Jonathan COLEMAN
Born in Edinburgh in 1956, he moved to

Australia with his parents while still a child. After a period in advertising and playing keyboards in an R'n'B band, he shot to stardom on Australian TV as half of the due 'Juno and Dano'

Jonathan turned down a role in the TV programme 'Neighbours' because he felt the programme would never take off but later appeared on 'Home and Away' as himself. He hosted radio programmes for one of Sydney's top stations for over a year, and then in 199, returned to the UK and hosted a prime time rock show on the ill-fated BSB's *Power Station.*

Following stints on BBC Radio Four and GLR, he joined *Virgin 1215* when it launched in 1993. After a stint on early evenings he joined Russ Williams for the now popular "Russ and Juno" breakfast show, the station's highest rated programme.

Stuart COLEMAN
Started his broadcasting career in 1976 with Radio One and two years later managed to combine this with *BBC Radio London* where he took over the slot vacated by Charlie Gillett, a hard act to follow,when he moved to *Capital Radio.* Stuart continues continues to broadcast for the *BBC World Service.*

Lloyd COLES
Country and western DJ at *Swansea Sound.*

Ron COLES
Joined the local radio pioneers at *BBC Radio Leicester* (UK's first local station) as freelance broadcaster and reporter just after it opened. After short spells in Current Affairs (network radio) and a stint as an instructor in the Network Training Unit, he returned to local radio to take up the post as Programme Organiser at *Radio Nottingham.*

He was then appointed Manager, *Radio Sheffield* and in 1980 joined *Radio Trent* as Managing Director, launching additional services for Leicester and Derby as well as the first regional Gold 24 hours a day service, *GEM AM.* After a merger with Midland Radio Holdings, Ron became Managing Director of the result - Midlands Radio plc, responsible for seven radio services.

In 1992 Ron started his own consultancy business providing advice on all aspects of radio station management and operation, research into potential acquisitions, assistance with licence applications and training in the UK and abroad.

In 1993 he undertook a major project as Chairman of the Inquiry into the Future of Manx Radio for the Isle of Man Government.

In January 1994 ron accepted a short term contract to manage Leicester Sound for the GWR Group and took up his present duties heading up 'Investors in Radio" in November, 1994.

Ron has been active in the commercial radio industry, he was a member of the Council of the AIRC from 1982 to 1992 and served as Chairman from 1986 - 1987. he also served as chairman of Labour relations and of the Finance committee for four years until 1982. he has recently been appointed to Skillset, the radio training forum. Ron is Chairman of the Radio Academy.

Iain COLHOUN
Presenter at *Q 102.9* in Londonderry.

John COLLARD
John is the Manager of *BBC Radio Stoke*.

Dave COLLINS
After a period at CFM in Carlisle, Dave is now a presenter at *Bay 96.9* in Lancaster.

Mark COLLINS
Station Organiser at *Northants Supergold*.

Martin COLLINS
Born in Kingston in June 1960, Martin attended Norton High in Letchworth and Hitchin College. and a one time car-door riveter, Martin's first DJ work was at Hitchin College supporting visiting bands. He then worked at *Chiltern Radio* for a while, with his first broadcast being a Sunday Afternoon in the mid seventies, before getting a programme at *Capital FM* in April 1989.

Martin loves "having loads of fun" which he believes is an essential qualification to be a good DJ. A keen motorcyclist, he works out regularly and plays volleyball and squash and says the highlight of his career has been meeting Rod Stewart. He hosts Capital FM's late night programme most weekdays and now lives in Northwood (London) with his two children.

Rodney COLLINS

In 1969 Rodney joined the news team at Record Mirror, which was then undoubtedly the best informed and most influential music business weekly. While in charge there, he gave substantial coverage to radio, both the new stations, , and on-air personalities.

In 1970 Rodney joined the ATV Group (workjinmg for Pye records and the Stol Moss Theatre Groups) and a year later was appointed Publicity Officer for *Radio 1* and *Radio 2*.

In the Mid 1970's Rodney joined *Radio Luxembourg* handling PR at the station's London office, and in 1981 they appointed him Director of News programming for RTL in London.

In 1989 he moved to Glasgow as station Manager for *East End Radio*, one of the first 'incremental/community' stations (now called Q-96) and the following year he returned to London to manage RTM Radio in Thamesmead.

Sali COLLINS
Sali is the Editor of *BBC Radio GLR*.

Steve COLLINS
Steve's career began as an accounts clerk at a local authority, but by mid 1977 he had made it onto the air at the *Voice of Peace* off the coast of Israel. From there he moved to *Radio Top Shop* in London, and then to *Red Rose Radio* in Lancashire.

He moved back down to London once again and joined *Capital Radio* and then moved out to Surrey for a gig at *County Sound* in Guildford. Further moves to *Jazz FM*, and then to the Chiltern Group where he began by hosting programmes at the station's *Galaxy* station in Bristol.

Steve then moved to *Oasis Radio* in St Albans where he was station manager and also had a seat on the board. In Autumn 1995 took up a new role at *Key 103* as deputy Programme Director. He likes eating out and being made to laugh and hates insincerity.

Tony COLLINS
Tony joined *Magic 828* and *Radio Aire* in Leeds in October 1995, where he is responsible for press and public affairs.

Steve COLLYER
In the early part of his career, David was a vicar to the Hells Angels and got into radio by various controversial debates in November 1964 Since then he's made many broadcasts on many stations, primarily on *BBC Radio Ulster* and *Radio West Midlands*.

He has also appeared on various religious TV programmes for ATV, the BBC, London Weekend and Ulster TV. The highlight of his radio career was joining *Xtra AM* in April 1993 - he likes Evesham and asparagus, but not singing in public.

Who's Who in British Radio

Michael CONNOLLY
Michael was Chief Executive at the Transworld Radio Group (Piccadilly, Aire and Red Dragon) until its takeover by EMAP in August 1994. He is now head of the Independent Radio Group, a company formed in 1995 to invest in existing and new radio stations.

Paul CONROY
Paul went to Beechen Cliff School in Bath and worked as a disco jock in many nightclubs in the West country and in Yorkshire. He got into radio, he confesses, by bombarding stations with audition tapes and telling lots of of lies! After some hospital radio in Bath, he got his first radio appearance at *Pennine Radio* in West Yorkshire in 1989 when he did a Saturday mid-morning programme and has also broadcast on *SIS Radio* in Brussels.

Paul then did some swing work at *Radio Aire* in Leeds where the highlight of his career came - a party in the park for 60,000 people. He's also presented a late evening show at *Capital Radio 604* in South Africa where he hosted the UK Top 30 every Sunday.

Paul had a late night networked programme at *Horizon Radio* in the Midlands, and is now at the Chiltern network's regional station, *Galaxy 101*. He hates bland radio stations and says the most humourous event was interviewing Mark King of Level 42 after six pints, calling him Elvis and then falling asleep while interviewing him!

Tom CONTI
Presenter on *Classic FM*.

Steve CONWAY
Dublin-born Steve was a computer installer, who was persuaded to present some programmes while out on the *Radio Caroline* ship. He became the station's head of News in 1987 and Programme Controller from 19988 to 1989. In the Nineties he joined satellite station *Euronet* and then established *Line One*, a media news service which gives regularly updated information mainly about radio in the UK (Call 0336 404575 - stories usually updated Monday and Thursday). In 1994 Steve married another former Caroline DJ, Wendy Shepherd. The highlight of his career however was rebuilding Caroline's audience after the ship's mast collapsed in the hurricane of 1987 . He likes sci-fi, the countryside and *Atlantic 252* but not chatty DJs and stations where ego is more important than music.

Harvey COOK
Presents 'Late Night Talk Show' each weekday evening on *BBC Radio Kent*.

Richard COOK
Presenter of 'GLR Jazz' programme in the early 90s

Sarah COOK
Office Manager at *Heart 100.7 FM*, the light-rock regional station in the Midlands.

Sue COOK
Born in in Ruislip on 30th March, 1949, Sue's first broadcasting job was at *Capital Radio* in London. She then joined the BBC and worked at *Radio One* and *Radio Four,* and then moved into Television where she is seen regularly as an anchor host on 'Crimewatch'.

Sue was married to classical guitarist John Williams for a while and has a son called Charlie and a daughter called Megan.

Tim COOK
Programme producer at *BBC Radio Shropshire*.

Tony COOK
Tony hosts the 'Sports Report' programme each Saturday (2 til 6pm) on *London Newsradio*.

Vikki COOK
Vikki is the host of the Sunday Morning sequence on *BBC Radio Bristol*.

Bryce COOKE
DJ on *Piccadilly Gold* in Manchester.

Graham COOKE
Presents the 'Drive Time Programme' on BBC *Radio Kent* with daily news and travel every 15 minutes, daily from Monday to Friday.

Michael COOKE
Breakfast show host on *BBC Radio Sheffield* in the early 1990s.

Who's Who in British Radio

Paul COONEY

Born in 1958, Paul trained as a journalist and joined Glasgow ILR *Radio Clyde* in 1975. Since then he's worked on most aspects of the stations output. He is the proud holder of a 'Radio Journalist of the Year award.

Recently he has been one of the leading sports broadcasters on the station, hosting Clyde's 'Super Scoreboard' as well as co-hosting 'Scotsport' on Scottish television. He has also been handling Clyde's public affairs and in 1995 was appointed to the Board as Director of Public Relations.

Phil COOPE

Presenter / producer at BBC *Radio Berkshire*, he was promoted to be the station's assistant editor.

Chris COOPER

Sports producer at *The Pulse* in Bradford.

Emma COOPER

Journalist with *BBC Wiltshire Sound*.

James COOPER

News and sports reporter at *Radio Aire*.

Jeff COOPER

Presenter at *Hallam FM* in Sheffield.

Karl COOPER

Karl says that listening to Jimmy Young (his Mum's favourite DJ) was what made him want to work as a radio presenter. He joined the staff of *BBC Radio Nottingham* in November 1987 after spending two years as a rookie at the local station in his home town, Leicester.

He is now Radio Nottingham's 'Teatime' presenter, which as a regular technology feature enabling him to combine radio with his other main passion - computers. He lives in Nottingham and says he doesn't want to move, because it's the best city in Britain.

Martin COOPER

News producer at *BBC Radio York*.

Mel COOPER

Presenter at *Classic FM*.

Neil COOPER

Neil is the station Director and Head of Sales at *GWR* (East) FM in Swindon.

Winton COOPER

Afternoon presenter at *Radio Sheffield* in the early 1990s, Winton now hosts the weekday drive programme and Saturday Mornings (9 to 12) on the station.

Jackie COPESTAKE

A reporter at *BBC Radio Solent*.

Mel COPPER

Presenter at *Classic FM*.

Chris COPSEY

After a spell being responsible for outside broadcasts and features, Chris is now Programme Manager at *Southern FM*, Brighton.

Robert CORBERT

Robert is a director at *Radio Wyvern*.

Jim CORBETT

Host of a programme featuring Irish music on Kix 96, the new ILR station in Coventry.

Daragh CORCORAN

Graduated with a communications degree from Dublin City University and began his career in radio reading community announcements on the city's *Northside Community Radio*.

He worked in news and presentation at many Dublin stations, including *Sunshine 101*, before landing the breakfast show at legendary Waterford super-pirate, *ABC Radio*. In the late eighties he moved to *Marcher FM* and then to *Red Rose FM* where he hosted rock programmes and was Head of Music.

He also had to change his name while in Preston: formerly known as "the boy with the beard" he lost it for charity and became a man! He then crossed the Pennines to help launch *Minster FM* in 1992 and now is morning presenter and Head of Music at *Radio Aire FM* in Leeds.

He also has a lot of voice over work and cites helping launch *Minster FM* as one of the highlights of his career. A true radio man through and through, the thing Daragh likes most is the new Optimod processor installed by *Aire FM* in Spring '95!

Who's Who in British Radio

Carlos COREIXAS
Carlos is the studio manager at *World Radio Network*, the international programme consolidation station based in London.

Roger CORKILL
Host of a daily rock music programme on *Manx Radio* on the Isle of Man.

Nikki CORP
Nikki is the Head of Community services, responsible for helplines and other community projects at *Capital Radio*.

Richard CORRIE
A daytime presenter at *CFM* in Carlisle.

Margaret CORRIGAN
Margaret is a Member of the Radio Authority.

Neil COSSAR
Neil is the Programme Controller at the *Signal Radio* outlet in Cheshire and also hosts a late night programme each weekday on the station.

Jenni COSTELLO
An early morning DJ on Saturdays for BBC *Radio One* in the early 1990s, she was one half of the successful breakfast team on *Trent FM* in Nottingham for several years and in 1995 joined *Premier* in London to produce and present the station's Youth and Arts programmes.

Mary COSTELLO
Mary hosted several weekend programmes at *GLR* in the early 1990s and currently presents her own show each saturday evening at 6pm.

John COTTRELL
The Chairman of Radio Wyvern.

Julie COTTRELL
Julie is the Head of News at Wey Valley 102.

Linda COUCH-SMITH
Linda is the Station Director of *Hereward Radio*.

Christine COULETER
Christine is the record librarian at *Downtown Radio* and its FM outlet, *Cool FM* in Belfast.

Annie COULTHARD
Annie produces the 3 to 5 pm Drive Time programme on *BBC Radio Newcastle*.

Charlotte COUNSELL
Presenter at *BBC Radio York* in the 1980s.

Lyn COURTNEY
Head of speech output at *Swansea Sound*.

Dave COUSINS

After a career in newspaper advertising David co-founded the highly successful rock-folk band, The Strawbs, who had chart success in the seventies with numbers such as "Part of the Union" and the excellent "Lay Down".

Throughout the seventies he produced programmes for *Danmarks Radio* (the national service in Denmark) from the BBC Radio One studios. In 1978 he wrote the winning application for *Devonair* and in 1979 became the programme director of *Radio Tees*. He later returned to Devonair as Station Director, becoming Managing Director in 1984.

David was responsible for establishing several ILR stations including *Orchard FM* and *Wessex FM* where he remains a director, as he also is at *Lantern Radio* in Devon. He was also instrumental in the establishment of *Minster FM* in York and is currently working on the launch of *A1FM* in Darlington, another company of which he is a director.

His market research company St David's Research acts for many companies. In 1995 he was contracted as Special Projects Director to CLT UK Radio in London. He currently lives in Chiswick and tours occasionally with the Strawbs in the States, Canada and Italy - a real dynamo of a music radio all-rounder.

Raymond COWAN
Chairman of Q96 in Paisley.

Robert COWAN
Presenter at *Classic FM*.

Jon COWAP
Weekend breakfast presenter on *BBC Radio Humberside* in the eighties, he moved to *Radio York* in 1992.

Charlie COX
MD of *LBC* until the station lost its licence in 1994. Charlie is now the MD of Associated Newspaper's radio arm, Harmsworth Media.

Danny COX
Head of operations at the Colchester station of Suffolk Group Radio.

Malcolm COX
Marketing Director at *Kiss FM*, London.

Gerard COYLE
Worked for several stations, including community stations and BBC locals (such as London station *GLR*) before joining *Premier Radio*, London's new Christian station in early 1995 to host some overnight programmes

Paul COYTE
Born in Romford in 1967, Paul's first job was as a London bus tour guide from where he graduated to the *Virgin Megastore* station. In 1988 he moved to Peterborough and a radio gig at *Hereward Radio* doing a variety of programmes including the station's breakfast show. He then joined *Virgin 1215* and initially hosted overnights, but was soon on an evening slot.

When the *Virgin FM in London* station opened in Spring 1995, Paul began a programme called 'Live in London' with co-presenter Rowland Rivron which features his well known 'little black book' from which he calls famous stars at random and puts them live on air.

He's addicted to Spurs, the Beatles and chocolate and once achieved fame when he played as a guest for Peterborough United in a friendly game against Aston Villa.

Peter CRABTREE
Sports reporter and commentator at *BBC Radio Sheffield* in the eighties and nineties.

Andy CRAIG
Born in Cumbria on 5th December, 1954, Andy gained an honours degree in agriculture at Newcastle University and while in the city hosted 'Simply Soul' on the city's *Metro Radio*. In 1978 he joined Tyne Tees TV and later joined the ill-fated BSB. Now lives in Nottingham - likes old cars and records.

Geoff CRAJO
Host of the Sunday breakfast programme at *BBC Radio Gloucester*.

Andy CRANE
Born in in Morecambe, Lancashire, on 24th February 1964, Andy trained as a Technical Operator at *Piccadilly Radio* and then worked as a presenter at *Capital Radio* in London, before joining BBC Children's TV programme 'Motormouth'.

Bob CRANE
Director of *Downtown Radio* and Cool FM.

Steve CRANE
Director of *Talkradio UK*.

John CRANSTON
John is a news producer at BBC Radio Suffolk.

Paul CRANWELL
Director responsible for local sales at *Trent FM*.

Neil CRASKE
Neil is currently the Head of Music at *Community Radio Milton Keynes*.

Jay CRAWFORD
Got into radio "by luck and bullshit" and made his first broadcast on *Radio Forth*'s first day on-air in January 1975 when he hosted an early evening rock programme. He's presented almost every shift on the station over the last twenty years, although he had a two year 'sabbatical' at neighbouring at *Radio Clyde* in the late 1980's to host their afternoon show.

He's currently head of Music for *Forth FM* and *Max AM*, and hosts the breakfast show and Edinburgh Rock'.

The highlight of Jay's career was hosting the Hogmany Party Night in Princes Street edinburgh with 250,000 guests, as well as interviewing Paul McCartney.

Jay likes Denim shirts, clear skies, black crows and whiskey, but not meat, pollution, ties. Has three sons and a daughter and can be reached at Radio Forth - 0131 556 9255.

Who's Who in British Radio

Gary CRAWLEY
Programmes on GLR in the early 1990s

Vivien CREEGOR
Born in London on 10th April, 1956, Vivien gained a Business Diploma at the City of London Polytechnic and joined the BBC. She worked for several networks and programmes as a production assistant before being heard on *Radio Four* as an announcer and newsreader.

In the early 1980s Vivien moved to Bristol to produce and present a TV programme and in 1984 became co-presenter of 'News After Noon' on BBC1. In 1989 she joined Sky TV and is one of the main anchors on the Sky News network. Now married to David Applebaum, her hobbies include reading, swimming and the cinema.

Chris CRENER
Head of news gathering at *BBC Radio Five.*

Jamie CRICK
Host of Sunday afternoon programme at *Classic FM.*

Chris CRIDDLE
Presenter on *Orchard FM* and *Classic Gold.*

Dave CROFT
Dave is the head of music at *CFM* in Carlisle where he also presents programmes.

Georgie CROOK
Georgie is a radio production assistant at *BBC Wiltshire Sound.*

Adrian CROOKES
Programme Controller at *Hereward Radio.*

Garth CROOKS
Presenter of a sport programme each saturday on *BBC GLR* in London.

Glynn CROPPER
Glynn is the General Manager of Sports Media Broadcasting.

Gavin CROTHERS
Company Secretary and Finance Director at *Downtown Radio* and *Cool FM* in Belfast.

Gary CROWLEY
Presenter of a late night programme each

Thursday and a Sunday lunchtime programme on *BBC Radio GLR* in London.

Ray CROWTHER
Ray was a qualified nurse and a staff nurse from 1981 to 1986, he got into radio, like many, by being in the right place at the right time. He did a year or so in hospital radio and the joined *Signal Radio* in 1987 and has been there ever since. Likes chocolates and hates lumpy custard.

Daragh CROXSON
Head of News for the Suffolk Group Radio stations based in Ipswich.

Brian CULLEN
Presenter at *Marcher Gold.*

Jeff CULLEN
In 1995 he was presenting a late Friday night programme on *Essex FM.*

Mary-Jane CULLEN
Presenter and producer at *BBC Radio Suffolk.*

John CULSHAW
Presenter at The Wave in Blackpool.

Mark CUMMINGS
Presenter of a Saturday morning programme on *BBC Radio Gloucester.*

Simon CUMMINGS
Simon went to school in Somerset and studied Russian language and English law at the University of Surrey, but not exclusively, as he also found time to do shifts on the campus radio station. From there he got a shift at *Radio 210* in Reading - his first programme was in 1981.

In 1983 he moved to *County Sound* and did the afternoon programme until 1991 and then in 1993 moved to *Star FM* where he currently hosts a four hour afternoon slot as well as Sunday breakfasts.

Simon has also done a variety of voice work, ranging from Sony to Eastenders, but the highlight of his career was being lead singer on a charity record (for a dare) with backing vocalists Cliff Richard, Justin Hayward, Alvin Stardust and Rick Wakeman.

Simon's middle name should be tenacity as he once presented his programme from a hospital bed for two weeks while laid up, more painful than humourous. He likes Thai food, Arsenal and table tennis, but hates records with very quiet intros.

[Forthcoming Productions 01 483 894841]

James CURRAN

James is the Head of Music at Central Scotland's regional station, *Scot FM*.

Peter CURRAN

Weekday afternoon programme presenter on BBC Radio GLR.

Tony CURRIE

Radio addiction began at the age of 4 when Tony learned to read with the aid of The Radio Times. When he was 11 he built a studio on the attic and, assisted by friends Steve Wright and Dave Marshall, operated a station every day in the holidays for the benefit of the old people's home next door.

His professional radio debut was on Los Angeles station *KPFK FM,* and a year later he hosted the opening night at *Radio Clyde,* since when he's hosted all types of programmes

ranging from chart countdowns to classical music programmes. He has also presented for long list of stations, including *West Sound, LBC, Blue Danube Radio* (Austria), *Radio Arcs* (in the Alps), *Radio Wales, Lucky Luxembourg, Radio Scotland, Radio Four* and *Classic FM.*

At the launch of *Radio Nova,* Britain's first satellite radio station, in 1986, Tony read the first news bulletin. His name is synonymous with the development of cable broadcasting; he set up *Radio Six,* Europe's first cable radio station, and he was head of the Cable Authority for many years.

Tony has also been involved in TV, as senior announcer at Scottish TV for eleven years and in the early nineties he was the Chief Executive of *Asiavision.* With *Radio Six Ltd* he led a bid for the Central Scotland Regional licence with an all-speech format.

He is now a freelance writer (with a weekly column in the *Radio Magazine,* a monthly radio column in the TES Scottish editions and regular contributions to the RTS journal), a broadcaster (presenting a weekly UK chart programme on *Ukrainian State Radio* as well as regular voice over work on the BBC).

He also works as a consultant and is an active broadcasting historian, with regular work on the subject for the Radio Times.

Francis CURRY

Francis was host of several programmes at Minster FM before moving to *Invicta FM* where he is now head of outside broadcasts, features and information.

Barry CURTIS

Born in Kingston, Jamaica, Barry arrived in the UK in 1961 and studied electronics at college. In 1972 he joined BBC *Radio Birmingham* (now known as *Radio WM*) and hosted the UK's first all-black music show, specialising in soul and reggae.

In 1978 he joined *Beacon Radio,* and stayed for many years, hosting a much respected daily programme showcasing black music. In 1994 he joined *Radio Harmony* in Coventry, which has now been relaunched as KIX 96.

Who's Who in British Radio

Mike CURTISS
Assistant Editor at *BBC Radio Lincolnshire*.

Lainey D
One of the presenters at *Sunset Radio* in Manchester when the station launched.

Carlton DALE
Station Director at *The New Leicester Sound*.

Roger DALLEYWATER
Presenter on BBC *Radio Kent's* 'Time for Jazz' evening show.

Claire DALTON
News Editor at *Hallam FM*, Sheffield.

Darren DALY
Disc jockey at *TFM* in Stockton.

Hitman DAN
Evening DJ at *Atlantic 252* in 1995.

Umit DANDUL
Programme Controller and programme host at *Turkish Radio* in London.

James DANIELS
Presenter at *Ram FM*, Derby.

Siobhan DANIELS
Producer at *BBC Radio Cleveland*.

Graham DANTON
Host of the Sunday afternoon programme from 2 until 5pm on *BBC Radio Devon and Dorset*.

Jon DARCH
Worked at several stations before joining *Minster FM* at its launch in 1992 as General Manager.

John DARIN
Presenter at *Q 103* in Cambridge until 1995 when he moved to on *Great North Radio*.

John DARROCH
Operations controller at *Radio Tay*.

John DASH
Born 6th Apr, 1959, in Cwmbran in South Wales, John studied Mathematical Sciences at the University of Bradford, before joining *Pennine Radio* as a Production Assistant.

Two years later he moved back to South Wales as Daytime Presenter and Sports Editor at *Gwent Broadcasting* in Newport and, after two years there, moved on again, this time to *Two Counties Radio* in Bournemouth.

In May 1987 he returned to South Wales joining *Red Dragon Radio* as presenter and becoming Head of Music, then deputy PC and finally Programme Controller in May 1992.

In January 1995 John moved to the EMAP Group's *Piccadilly Radio* as Head of Music and in May 1995 he was promoted to Program,me Director. John is also a Barker of the Variety Club of Great Britain.

Claire DAVEY
Presents the Sunday request programme on BBC *Radio Nottingham*.

Barry DAVID
Born in Liverpool in November 1955, David wanted to produce records and radio programmes, but he was discouraged from trying to get a job in radio when he left school and told to "get a proper job!"

While working as a plumber he was called in to fix the toilets at *Radio City* in Liverpool and as a result was also asked to voice a new package of idents and jingles for the station's FM and Gold stations.

Since then Barry has recorded over jingle packages for over fifty stations in the UK and Ireland. he's also done presenting and production work on many stations, including *City, Signal, Echo 96, KFM, Marcher* and *BBC Radio Lancashire*. He's currently part of the on-air team at *Jazz FM*, the North West regional station.

He likes painting pictures with sound and collecting radio programmes from around the world as well as photography. As he gets older he finds himself unwinding by listening to speech radio, as music is his work.

Barry wants to encourage a greater appreciation of the value of training in programme presentation and is a member of Equity and the Radio Academy.

Ian DAVIDSON
As well as being the Sales Manager at *Wey Valley Radio* and the host of a jazz and big band music programme there, Ian also is heard on Kent's new local station for Tonbridge, *KFM*.

Bruce DAVIDSON

Bruce joined *Piccadilly Radio* in the mid eighties an engineer and two years later moved to *Metro Radio*. He became the Metro Group's Chief Engineer resigning in October 1995, following the EMAP takeover.

He joined the Minster Group in December as General Manager at its new station in Sunderland - *Sun City*.

Matt DAVIDSON

Presenter of weekends mid-afternoon sports programme on BBC *Radio Kent*.

Anne DAVIES

Producer at *BBC Radio Cleveland*.

Basil DAVIES

Basil hosts a programme called 'Black Mix', mostly dance music, on *BBC Two Counties Radio*.

Bob DAVIES

Sedgeley-born Bob presented *Beacon Radio's* night-time programmes in the eighties.

Eira DAVIES

Presenter at *Marcher Gold* in Wrexham.

Gary DAVIES

Born in Manchester in December 1954 , Gary worked in the sales promotions department of a mail order company, before becoming a discotheque manager in his home town.

Prior to joining *Radio 1* in December 1982, he worked as a disc jockey for commercial radio - presenting a variety of programmes during his three year stay with the station.

Gary is a keen sportsman and plays squash and tennis and enjoys water-skiing.

Gerson DAVIES

Presenter at *Marcher Gold* in Wrexham.

Ian DAVIES

Managing Director *Enterprise Radio* and also a director at *Mix 96*, Aylesbury.

Jon DAVIES

Born on the 5th December, a long time ago, in Cardiff, Jon was a reporter for the Northpix agency in Liverpool before joining the city's ILR station, *Radio City*. He then moved through the industry, being paid by *Capital Radio, LBC* and *IRN, BBC Radio London, Radio One, Radio Five, BBC TV News* in London, *Sky News, ITN Radio* and then *Network News* where he was Managing Director.

Jon then moved back to *Sky News* and then *Radio One* once again before heading up the news operation at *Heart 106.2* at the station's launch in September 1995, which Jon believes is the highlight (so far) of his career.

A true journalist of the old school, he likes tea, cream cakes, food, fine art and rubber, but not small measures, or Guinness or toast.

Paul DAVIES (1)

Began his career as a local newspaper journalist in 1969 in Southport and in 1974 joined Radio City as a journalist. He contributed regularly to IRN on sports news and four years later joined the national news provider for three years. In 1981 he was lured by TVS and after two years joined ITN.

Paul broadcast from inside Romanian radio centre during the revolution there in the late eighties and was also active in the Gulf War and in Bosnia, winning a Gold Nymph Award for his coverage. He was made an OBE in 1993 for his war reporting from war zones.

Paul DAVIES (2)

Managing Director at Medià Sales and Marketing, a radio rep' house in London.

Paul DAVIES (3)

Presenter of a programme of gospel and country music on *Two Counties Radio*.

Peter DAVIES

After a period as a producer at several local radio stations, Peter is now the Managing Editor of BBC Radio WM and WCR.

Sharon DAVIES

Sales director at *Radio 210* in Reading.

Sue DAVIES

Producer / Presenter at *BBC Wiltshire Sound*.

Who's Who in British Radio

Terry DAVIS
Began his radio career on *Radio North Sea International* in 1972 and worked at *Essex Radio* in Southend for many years hosting the afternoon drive programme.

Tom DAVIES
DJ at *TFM* in Stockton.

Everard DAVY
Assistant News Editor at *BBC Radio Sheffield*.

Alison DAWES
News Producer at *BBC Radio Peterborough*.

Andrew DAWSON
(See Andy Archer)

Steve DAWSON
Programme controller and also presenter of some programmes at Classic Gold and Mercia FM in Coventry.

Brian DAY
After working in theatre and starting his own film company and entertainment agency, Brian managed 15 pop groups, published a monthly pop magazine and ran a mobile disco in the late 1960s. He's also promoted wrestling, bingo and dances and compered several national tours with Gary Glitter, The Sweet and other seventies bands.

Appearances on *Radio One Club* and his own show at weekends from 1969 to 1972 led to work at *Plymouth Sound* in 1975, where he remained for eleven years. He also ran a record shop and a novelty emporium at this time.

In 1990 he moved to *Red Dragon Radio* in Cardiff and presented the breakfast show at the launch of *Touch AM*. Later that year he moved to the *GWR Group* and over the next few years presented drive time shows and produced film reviews for the network. In 1994 he moved to the new regional station for the North West, *JFM*, where he hosts daily and weekend programmes.

Graham DAY
Host of the Saturday afternoon sports programme from 2 until 6pm on *BBC Radio Gloucester*.

Martin DAY
Weekend evening programme host at *Essex FM*.

Mike DAY
Host of the weeeknd breakfast programmes on *BBC Radio Humberside*.

Roger DAY
Born in Cheltenham on the 29th March, 1945, Roger worked as an accountant by day and ran a small recording studio by night. He got into radio by collaring a Big L DJ who'd played a request for him and asking for advice.

The tip he got was to look up two Americans, fresh in town that day to plan a new station called *Swinging Radio England*.

They wanted a British voice and Roger's persistence and enthusiasm meant he was one of the first they hired. He soon became one of the most popular DJs on SRE in 1966 and was the only DJ with the station from launch to close-down. He was also heard on sister station *Britain Radio*.

The following year he joined *Radio Caroline* after the Marine Offences Act and became the station's most popular breakfast show host, winning several awards for No 1 DJ over the next few years.

67

In 1968 Roger hosted programmes on *Radio Andorra* as well as *Radio Luxembourg* and in 1970 he became the first DJ on *Radio North Sea*.

The early seventies were spent at UBN and in 1973 he put in a further appearance on *Radio Caroline*, but on tape this time.

In 1974 Roger joined *Piccadilly Radio* in Manchester for the station's launch becoming Head of Music, until 1979 when he moved to become breakfast presenter at BRMB in Birmingham, until 1982 when he joined *Radio West* in Bristol. In 19893 he helped assemble a bid for the Kent ILR franchise and even though unsuccessful, the resulting station, *Invicta Sound*, hired Roger for the afternoon programme when the station launched in October 1984, staying there for eight years. He then moved to *Pirate 102* in Cornwall as a consultant but later returned to Kent for family reasons.

After a period with *Jazz FM* in 1993 he returned to Manchester for another stint at the *Piccadilly Gold* outlet, but returned to Kent once again, to make an unsuccessful bid for the Kent licences at their renewal. He's now working as a consultant for station, specialising in music scheduling, DJ training and application writing.

The highlight of Roger's career was meeting the Beach Boys and his days on Caroline, and the most humorous moment is the BBC telling him he'd never make it in radio. He loves personality radio and honest people, but not bull-shitters and bland radio.

In fact, in 1996 Roger celebrates thirty years almost continuous broadcasting in British commercial radio, possibly the longest-serving DJ never having worked for the BBC.

Kevin DEAKIN
Sales manager at *Viva 963!* and of *Jazz FM* (London).

Andrew DEAN
Formerly sales director at *Radio Mercury* in Crawley, he is the Managing Director of *KFM*, the new ILR station in Tonbridge, Kent.

Jason DEAN
Host of the programme called 'Jaywalk' each weekday from 11 to 2pm on *BBC Radio Stoke*.

Jonathan DEAN
Presenter of a programme each Sunday teatime (4 until 8pm) at *Fortune 1485*, the new easy-listening station in Manchester.

Kelami DEDEZADE
Sales Director at *Turkish Radio* in London.

Alan DEDICOAT
Host of *Radio Two* programmes after midnight early in 1995.

Maurice DEE
Host of an evening phone-in programme on *Talkradio UK* since the station began. Occasionally known as Moz Dee.

Ricky DEE
Presenter at *CFM* in Carlisle.

Robbie DEE
Began his career in hospital radio and doing mobile discos, he got into radio doing holiday reliefs at *Essex Radio* in 1986. He stayed there for five years before moving to Hull's *Viking FM* in 1991, where he served for three years with the Metro Radio Group.

The funniest thing which happened to Robbie was a Phil Collins CD getting stuck while he was sat on the toilet, and he cites the highlight of his career as being a series of "Airchecks with The Boss" (Springsteen). In 1994 he moved back to *Essex FM* where he enjoys both the on air shifts and doing station gigs and other outside broadcasts.

Peter DEELEY
Presenter of Newsday from 4 until 7pm each weekday on *London Newsradio*.

Carole DEENE
Born in Thurnscoe near Rotherham in 1944, Carol had several hits in the early 1960's and was then signed by *Radio Luxembourg* to present a series of programmes.

Frank DELANEY
Born in Ireland in the 1920s, Frank was originally a bank clerk who got into broadcasting

Who's Who in British Radio

in the Summer of 1966 and over the last 30 years has presented a variety of programmes on most BBC networks. In recent years he has been heard on several arts programmes on BBC *Radio Two.*

Mike DELAP
Mike is Head of Development of English language programmes at the BBC World Service.

Marc DE LEUW
Overnight presenter on London Newstalk AM.

Nick DEMUTH
Director of the *Signal Radio* group.

Daryl DENHAM
Presenter of the 'Early Riser' show on BBC Radio Kent every weekday morning.

Stephanie DENHAM
Programme Coordinator at *Radio Wyvern.*

Graham DENE
Graham started his broadcasting career in hospital radio and then joined the BBC as a librarian. He thought he could get friendly with the DJs so they could put in a good word for him, but it turned out he was working in the book library!

Dave Dennis (qv) suggested he join the *United Biscuit Network*, one of the first in-factory cable radio stations, which Graham acknowledges gave me a lot of training and helped him get his first 'big break' at *Radio City* in Liverpool. After a year he moved to *Capital Radio* in London, where he spent seventeen years, originally on late nights and lunches and then on the station's breakfast show. He now presents weekend breakfasts at *Virgin 1215.*

Graham loves football and for many years turned out for the 'Show Biz Eleven' and the one thing he hates most is his alarm clock.

Mark DENNISON
DJ at *Viking FM* in Hull in 1995.

Mark DENTON
Mark is a news producer at *BBC Radio York.*

Sonia DEOL
Weekend programme host at *Radio XL.*

Frank DEPELLETTE
Chief Engineer at London station, *RTM* until 1995 when he left for non-radio work.

Laura DE VERE
Queen of the late night radio scene in the North East when she worked at *Radio Tees* in the late seventies and early eighties, she is now part of the on-air team at *Heart 100.7*, a light-rock regional station in the Midlands she now hosts a similar programme at 10pm each weekday evening.

Robert DEVEREUX
The Chairman of Virgin Communications, the entertainment division of the Virgin Group, which compasses radio and television. A busy man, Robert is also involved in Virgin Travel and retail business .

Candy DEVINE
Born in Autralia and worked for ABCfor two years before joining Dowtown in 1976 . Hosted mornings for many years and is now a part of the furniture! ALso is an accomplished singer and musician(with much film and TV work under her belt) and station ambassador. Candy was once asked by a 4 year old if she was the Pope! She's vice-president of Yoth ACtion and patron of three integrated schools.

Ian DEVINE
Ian is the Programme Organiser at *BBC Radio Leicester*, the UK's first local radio station.

Jenny DEVITT
Born in Bangor, North Wales and educated in Zimbabwe, Somerset and Cambridge, Jenny began her career as a secretary for the World Wildlife Fund in London and also worked at UNESCO for awhile.

Her first broadcast was in 1978 on the *BBC World Service*, about the anti-whaling rally in Trafalgar Square. Since then she's worked on many programmes heard on BBC local radio stations and *Radio Four*, including 'Woman's Hour', 'The Food programme' and 'Today'.

Tony DEWHIRST
Tony was finance Director at the Transworld Group until its take-over by EMAP in August 1994 and is now in a similar role with Independent Radio Group, a new company formed in 1995 to invest ILR stations.

Steve DEWITT
The son of a Nottingham photographer, Steve went to school in Swansea and made his first broadcast on *Swansea Sound* in September

1977. He got that break after the station's Head of Presentation heard him working in a local nightclub as a DJ and was impressed by his knowledge of soul and disco music.

Steve spent several years hosting various programmes on Swansea Sound and in the early 1980's was in charge of the breakfast show.

Paul DEXTER
Born in Los Angeles in 1954, Paul pursued a career as a set and lighting designer and arrived in the UK in 1986 with a reputation gained working with the Carpenters, Ozzy Osbourne and Elton John.

He was involved in the creation of a number of award-winning videos with his work seen on MTV, HBO and Sky TV. In 1992 he founded *Heritage Media* with Toby Horton which supplies radio programmes to radio stations in the UK and in Europe.

Paul is also a director of *A1-FM*, the new licensee of a radio station in Darlington.

Paul DICKEN
The Head of Policy at the British Tourist Authority and also a director of *Premier Radio,* the new Christian station in London.

Clive DICKENS
Head of programming at *Capital Radio.*

Neville DICKENS
Director of *Marcher Coast* and *MFM.*

Ross DICKENSON
Weekday presenter at *The Pulse* in Bradford.

Peter DICKSON
Born in in Belfast in 1957, Peter attended the Royal Academy and Queens University in Belfast where he obtained a BA with Hons in Psychology. While at University he passed a BBC voice audition and his first job was as an announcer at *BBC Radio Ulster.* Since that first broadcast in 1975 (reading the Midnight news bulletin and shipping forecast) he's done television and announcing work at *BBC Radio Two.*

Gerry DIDYMAS
Host of a nostalgia based programme on BBC *Radio Solent* from 1976 until 1994.

Richard DIGANCE
A Londoner, Richard attended college and University in Glasgow before becoming an engineering draughtsman, but his main love was always music. His activities as a folk singer led to his first broadcast, on *BBC Radio One*, and in 1976 his album 'How the West Was Lost' was named 'Album of the year' by Melody Maker magazine.

The success of that album led to lots of radio work, and he became a regular satirical singer on the *Radio Four* programme 'Stop the Week'. In 1979 *Capital Radio* gave him two weekly programmes which ran for years.

Tim DISNEY
DJ at *Trent FM* in 1995.

Leo DIVINE
Born in 1962, Leo worked as a reporter for programmes on *Radio Four* and as an instructor in the BBC Local Radio Training Unit. In 1985 he joined *Radio Leicester* as a presenter, then a producer, Programme Organiser and Assistant Station Editor. While at Leicester he received an award for the best radio documentary of 1990, about preparations for the oberammergau Passion Plays.

In 1995 he moved to BBC *Radio Cornwall* as the station's new Managing Editor.

Dulcie DIXON
Host of a Saturday teatime programme on BBC Radio Leicester.

Eric DIXON
Freelance presenter at *BBC Radio Essex.*

Mike DIXON

Born in London in Summer 1961, Mike was a civil servant and worked in newspapers after leaving school.

He was born interested in radio and in 1987 joined the *Voice of Peace* off Israel, where the highlight of his career came. That was being told by Kenny Page (now at Radio Tay) that he had done a good job standing in for him on the breakfast show.

From the Peace Ship Mike moved back to the UK and worked at *Radio Caroline* and the station's sister station, *Radio 819* a Dutch language station. He also broadcast on *Euronet,* a satellite station, currently off air.

An avid 'clipper nilgiri blue mountain' tea drinker, he abhorrs clone radio stations and DJs, he got married in 1994 and the one thing he'd like most is to remember all the funny jokes he hears. He's better known as 'Coconut' and is now the editor of a radio magazine called 'Playback'.

Phil DIXON
News Editor at *Gem AM* and *Trent FM* in Nottingham.

Maurice DOBSON
After sixteen years in the newspaper industry, Maurice joined Metro Radio in Newcastle in 1980. He was appointed to the Metro Board in 1981 a as Sales and Marketing Director.

Maurice won considerable respect for his blunt 'tell it like it is' sales techniques and in 1994 orchestrated a much acclaimed presentation at the NAB convention in Dallas. In October 1995 when he resigned, just two weeks after EMAP bought the Metro network.

Bill DODD
Freelance presenter and host of a Saturday Morning programme on *BBC Radio Essex.*

Richard DODD
After attending University in the city, Richard first broadcast on *BBC Radio York* in 1984. After three years as a 'do anything' freelance reporter he returned to his native Merseyside to host the 'Night Owl' graveyard shift on *Radio City* while also working at *BBC Radio Shropshire* and *Radio Manchester.*

As the eighties drew to a close he landed a full time position at *BBC Radio Nottingham,* where a two year stint on 'Drive Time' prepared him for the rigours of five years presenting the weekday breakfast sequence on the station, during which period he's been nominated twice for a Sony Award.

Martina DODSON
Station Director at *Capital Radio.*

Tracy DOLLIMORE
Sales controller at *Talkradio UK.*

Lesley DOLPHIN
Lesley is a presenter at *BBC Radio Suffolk.*

Julie DONALDSON
Born in 1970, Julie went to college in Sunderlandand in October 1990 began working at *Wear FM*, the city's community radio station. She combined the roles of record librarian and admin' assistant, and later that year worked on the morning show.

In 1991 she got her own afternoon programme and the following year became the station's first female breakfast show presenter - which many feel helped the station win a Gold Sony Award in 1992 as 'Station of the Year'.

She now works at *7FM,* Tyneside's community station which runs frequent RSLs, where her talents have not gone unnoticed by many in the industry, particularly by Anne Karpf who recently wrote in her radio column in The Guardian "Donaldson ripples with personality. A strong geordie, unaffected and full of vim, she's passionate about music playing a very wide range and meandering exuberantly about their history." The NME have described her shows as "a smorgasbord of indie and dance" while Radio One told her she wasn't experienced enough and was too manic.

Peter DONALDSON
Born in Egypt where his father was stationed in the services, Peter was educated in Cyprus and in Suffolk. His first job was as an actor with the National youth Theatre and then at Sadlers Wells, the Globe Theatre and the New Shakespeare Company. In 1970 he joined *BBC Radio Two* as an announcer and three years later he transferred to *Radio Four .*

Dougie DONNELLY
Born and educated in Glasgow he was educated at the University of Strathclyde. While there he interviewed Radio Clyde's PD Andy Park for a student TV programme, and was asked to send in an audition tape.

Who's Who in British Radio

This led to his presenting a variety of programmes on *Radio Clyde* in the 1970s and early 1980s and in 1982 he was awarded both the 'Radio personality of the Year' and a similar TV honour by the Scottish Broadcasting Awards Dinner. In the 1980's he hosted a weekly TV programme 'Friday Night with Dougie Donnelly' on BBC TV Scotland.

James DONNELLY
James is the Chairman of *Downtown Radio* and *Cool FM* in Belfast.

Ambrose DONOHUE
He's always been involved in music and was asked to do record reviews on 'Country Meets Folk' programme on *BBC Radio Two*. Since then he's worked at *RTE*, the Irish state radio service, *Irish Festival Radio,* and now at *Country Music radio*, the satellite pan European station. As well as radio, Ambrose does lots of live appearances, at concerts, festivals and other venues. The funniest thing he can think of is his ex-wife, while the highlight of his career was joining the first all country music radio station, CMR.

Ed DOOLAN
Australian-born and educated, Ed always wanted to be in radio but his parents insisted he pursue teaching as a career. While travelling in Germany in the Summer of 1970, he heard that *Deutsche Welle* (The German overseas radio service)needed an English voice - and his Australian one was accepted as being close enough!

He hosted a series of programmes for the network and also presented programmes on BFBS. In the mid-seventies he moved to the UK and joined Birmingham's ILR station, *BRMB*, and in 1982 moved across town to BBC Radio Birmingham, which for Ed was the greatest moment of his career.

He made his name as a news reporter and hard hitting journalist at BBC *Radio West Midlands* (as Radio Birmingham became known) in the late 1980s. He once used his phone-in programme to arrange a liaison with a dangerous criminal on the run, who he arrested personally.

Bob DORAN
Bob is the Editor of BBC Radio One's 'Newsbeat' programme.

Stephen DORRELL
Born 25th March 1955 and educated at Uppingham and Brasenose College, Oxford, he was in the RAFVR in the early 1970s and then challenged John Prescott for the safe Labour seat of Hull East for the Conservatives in 1974.

In 1979 he became MP for Loughborough and a PPS, Assistant Government whip, and other political appointments before becoming Minister at the Department of National Heritage, being responsible for the Government's broadcasting policy, until 1995.

Norman DOUGHERTY
Presenter at *Q 102.9* in Londonderry.

Celia DOUGLAS
Member of the Board of *Lincs FM*.

Clive DOUTHWAITE
Sales Director at *Century Radio* in Newcastle.

Tim DOWER
Presenter at *BBC Radio York* in the 1980s.

Terry DOYLE
Educated by the Christian Brothers in Ireland, Terry worked in hotel management until 1987 but still found time to work on a station called *Kingdom 102*. In 1988 he moved to England and took a job with *KCBC* in Kettering.

The funniest thing to happen to Terry so far has been being attacked by 'Mr Blobby' at a Silverstone racetrack roadshow. He has since moved to the Chiltern Group, where he hosts breakfasts on their *Supergold* stations and is also the programme controller at *Northants Radio*.

Eve DRAPER
Senior Producer at *BBC Radio GMR*.

Mickey DREAD
Reggae-oriented presenter at *Radio Aire* in the early 1990s, he is now with the GWR Group.

Fiona DRIVER
Finance Director at *Kiss FM* in London.

Gordon DRUMMOND
Sales director at *Kiss FM* in London.

Jeremy DRY
The son of a well-known boxer in East Yorkshire, Jeremy worked at *BBC Radio Humberside* and then in the late eighties moved to *Radio Hereford and Worcester*. He now hosts late night programmes each weekday on *London Newstalk*.

Patrick DUCKER
Head of the Radio Two music department.

David DUCKWORTH
Orchestrator of the 'AM Stereo' campaign.

Ken DUDENY
Ken hosts a programme each Sunday evening on *BBC WM/WCR*.

Anne DUFFELL
Producer of educational programmes at BBC *Radio Stoke*.

Tessa DUGGLEBY
Assistant Editor at B*BC Radio Devon and Dorset*.

Jim DUNCAN
DJ at *WABC* in the West Midlands.

Richard DUNCAN
Born in 1957, he joined *Red Rose Radio* in Preston in the 1980's and was the station's senior presenter for three years. He then moved to *Radio City* in Liverpool, but returned to *Red Rose Radio* in mid-1995.

John DUNN
Born a Glaswegian in 1934, John attended Christ Church Cathedral Choir School in Cambridge and did a variety of jobs before becoming a studio manager for the BBC. His first broadcast was acting in a play on BFBS while he was doing his National Service (RAF airman) which is where he got the radio bug but when he applied to BFBS they said he lacked experience and suggested the BBC.

After a period as a studio manager he became a staff announcer on all the domestic networks, *Light Home* and *Third* and then chose Radio Two on the national networks' relaunch in 1967. For seven years he presented a breakfast programme on *Radio Two* as well as 'Late Night Extra' for a year. Has since become freelance and still presents programmes on *BBC Radio Two*.

John was awarded 'Radio Personality of the Year' Award by the Radio and television Industries Club in 1984 and in 1986 and in October 1988 he was voted 'Radio Two personality of the year' in the Daily Mail -BBC Awards. In 1994 he picked up a BASCA Gold Award.

He likes skiing and buying good wine, is married with two daughters and lives in Surrey.

Margaret DUNN
Promotions Manager at *Invicta FM*.

Riocjard DUNN
Head of BBC English at the World Service

Al DUNNE
Hosts the Sunday morning breakfast programme on *Atlantic 252*.

David DUNNE
Born on the 14th March, 1962, in Manchester, David got into radio by organising a charity weekend on *Piccadilly Radio*. Following that David spent a year working in the station's promotions department before making his first broadcast, on the station's *Key 103* outlet.

He then became a producer and presenter of features and a jazz show. Later he hosted a dance music programme and then moved to drive-time before becoming Head of Music.

After a two year sabbatical from radio, David then joined *Hereward* and *CNFM* to present a dance show. He moved on to *Kiss 102* in Manchester in September 1994.

As well as radio work he has also worked as a TV researcher and a plugger for a record company as well as handling PR for Manchester festival and the band Simply Red.

For David, the highlight of his career was meeting Ernie Wise clad only in his boxer shorts and interviewing his hero and role model, Sir James Savile OBE. Loves jocking in night clubs but hates wittering radio jocks!

Julian DUNNE
Weekday breakfast host on *BBC Radio Cambridgeshire* in 1995.

David DUNNING
David is now one one the senior producers of news at *BBC Radio Solent*.

Neil DUNWOODIE
Producer at *BBC Radio Berkshire*.

Al DUPREES
DJ at *Viking FM* in the nineties.

Don DURBRIDGE
Born in Glasgow in 1939, Don attended school in London and joined the Jack Hylton Entertainment Organisation as a clerk before working on several local newspapers in the London area.

His first broadcast was on 'The Younger Generation' on the *Light Programme,* after seeing an advert in the 'Radio Times' for teenagers wanting to broadcast.

Don did over 200 programmes before his National Service. He later joined *Radio Two* as an announcer and presented most of the station's programmes, including 'Family Favourites', 'Sport on Two' and 'The Early Show'.

In 1978 he joined *BBC Radio Medway,* which a few years later became *Radio kent* but continued to host a weekly programme on *Radio Two* as well as sports commentaries on BFBS.

Adrian DURHAM
Sports editor at *Q103* in Cambridge.

Mo DUTTA
Mos is the host of Saturday Breakfast Programme each week on BBC *Radio Two*.

Wayne DUTTON
Host of Sunday morning programmes on Signal Radio's Cheshire outlet.

Jo DWYER
Producer with special responsibilities for Devon at *BBC Radio Dorset and Devon*.

Mike DYBLE
Director of *Piccadilly Radio*, Manchester.

Fiona DYE
Producer of the 'Annie Othen Programme' on BBC Radio WM/WCR.

Ian DYER
Engineer at *BBC Wiltshire Sound*.

Peter DYKE
Chairman of *Channel Travel Radio*.

Ann DYSON
Sales Director of West Yorkshire Broadcasting Company Ltd, the operators of *Radio Aire* in Leeds.

Jon EARLY
Operations Manager and the Head of Music at *Mix 96* in Aylesbury, Buckinghamshire.

Rick EASTER
Rick's career began in hospital radio, then a series of RSL exploits and in 1995 he joined *Premier Radio* in London to host the station's drive-time programmes.

Anna EASTMENT
News reporter at *BBC Radio Leicester*.

Phil EASTON
Programme Controller at *Orchard FM*.

John EBDON
A Londoner, John joined RADA and after a bomb blast during WWII was warned that 'bright lights' could irreparably damage his sight, so he changed careers and became a salesman. In 1960 he became a narrator at the London Planetarium and became its director within eight years 'by outliving my friends and outwitting my enemies."

John's first radio broadcast was in 1961 on the Home Service and he's since appeared on several hundred programmes on *Radio Four*.

Mark ECCLESTON
Programme producer at *BBC Radio Newcastle*.

Robb EDEN
Robb started his broadcasting career on *Radio North Sea International* in 1970 and returned to the station the following year as a DJ, later staying with RNI as a station organiser until 1974.

It was at this time he transferred his allegiance to *Radio Caroline* and then, in September 1974, he joined *Radio City* in Liverpool as Head of Commercial Production \ announcer.

Two years later Robb returned to London to take up the post of Promotions Manager with EMI Records. He scored with hits from Natalie Cole, Glenn Campbell, Tavares and Dr Hook amongst others. This in turn, led to his secondment to Holland as Head of Public Relations and Promotions for EMI Europe.

In late 1977 Robb returned to the *Radio Caroline* fold taking the role as Station Manager and as DJ and organiser of the popular, landbased, Caroline Roadshow. In 1978 Robb formed his own consultancy advising on all aspects of music production and as a self-employed writer/creative producer, Robb worked for *Chiltern Radio, Mercia Sound* and *BRMB*, not only writing and producing commercial output but also documentaries and interviews with politicians, artistes, and local personalities. During his time with Chiltern Radio he was also offered the post of Promotions Manager dealin with publicity, public relations, roadshows, merchandise and outside broadcasting

In 1988, having gained knowledge of the satellite broadcast market, he joined with Chris Carey to set up *Radio Nova International* and, as General Manager, developed the sustaining service format which, at that time, was taken by *Northsound Radio, Severn Sound, West Sound* and numerous commercial stations in Ireland, Italy, France and Norway.

He instigated discussions with PPL which brought about the first agreement for unlimited needletime which in turn led to an unlimited needletime agreement between PPL and the AIRC.

Robb is currently Managing Director of FBL limited, a company whose main area of business is in the design and installation of professional broadcast studios throughout the world.

Richard EDGAR

Born in Brighouse, Yorkshire, *in* January 1955 and after a period in the Royal Navy became a meteorologist, firstly on TV, but since 1993, on BBC *Radio Three, Radio Four* and *Five Alive.*

Steve EDGE

Born in Aberystwyth in 1962 he started his own company after leaving school in 1977. Got into radio by "sheer persistence" and made his first broadcast on *Shropshire Sound* in 1984. In early 1993 he helped organise and operate an RSL in Crewe and then in October that year joined *Radio Maldwyn* to host the drivetime programme.

In September 1994 he became one of the station's music coordinators and in June 1995 took over the mid-morning show. As well as radio, Steve has operated his own mobile discotheque since the 1970s and now has a staff of five, but he is sure that joining *Radio Maldwyn* was the highlight of his career.

Steve likes good food, sleeping but hates nagging women and is twice divorced!

Noel EDMONDS

Essex boy Noel was an avid radio listener in the sixties and while at school in Brentwood sent in audition tapes to all the offshore stations. Eventually Tony Windsor heard one, but the station (*Radio 355*, on a ship off Frinton) was closing down they didn't need new DJs!

A year later, TW hired Noel for pre-recorded Decca sponsored shows at *Radio Luxembourg*; they too dried up shortly afterwards, so he went out to the Grand Duchy as a newsreader. His first newscast was almost his last as he collapsed in a fit of laughter mid-sentence, but he was eventually forgiven and eventually heard doing programmes.

After becoming one of 208's favourite voices he left for holiday relief work at *Radio One*, and his first broadcast on the station was 21st July, 1969, the day man first walked on the moon. After a period making trailers he depped for Johnnie Walker on the Saturday afternoon programme and then got his own programme; unfortunately it was Kenny Everett's old slot after he'd been fired: "I was the one who took over from the guy everybody loved."

Who's Who in British Radio

After several years on Radio One's Breakfast programme, Noel moved to television which enables his to spend more time with his first love - helicopters. He had a brief involvement with one of the companies bidding for the UK's INR 2 licence, but they lost out to Virgin. He now runs his own TV Production company and is about to start a new series of prime time 'Houseparty' on BBC 1.

Bruce EDWARDS
Bruce hosted overnight programmes on *Great Yorkshire Gold* in the mid-nineties and then moved to *Fortune 1458* in Manchester to present the 10 to 2am slot.

Carys EDWARDS
Producer at *Radio Devon and Dorset*.

David EDWARDS
Director at *Moray Firth Radio* in Inverness.

Greg EDWARDS
Began his radio career at *Capital Radio* in London in the 1970s, and in the 80's worked briefly at *Radio Nova* in Dublin.
He was also one of the presenters at the launch of *Sunset Radio* in Manchester and now presents a daytime programme on *Jazz FM* in London.

Janice EDWARDS
DJ at *Mercia FM* in Coventry.

Mark EDWARDS
Programme Director at *Sunshine 855*.

Stephen EDWARDS
Newsreader on *Great Yorkshire Gold* based in Sheffield and in 1995 moved to a similar role at *Viking FM* in Hull.

Steve EDWARDS
Presenter of Sunday evening soul music programme on *Radio One*.

Tom EDWARDS
Born in 1945 in Norwich, Tom was educated in the city and then became a stocktaker in the family wholesale business. After a period as a journalist, he also became a Blue Coat at Pontins, which led to his auditioning for a presenters job at the then newly opened Border television. He made his first appearance however on regional news magazine 'About Anglia' and worked for a time as an announcer on Border TV's 'Beat Up The Border'.

He was hired by *Radio City* in 1965, became the programme director, picked up his "Tatty Tom' nickname. and stayed with the station until it closed in 1967. He even moved house to Whitstable in Kent so he could be close to the station (located on a former anti-aircraft fort, eight miles out into the Thames Estuary).

When City was closed down, Tom moved further out to sea, on *Radio Caroline South* where he remained until the Marine Offences Act was introduced. After that he bombarded *Radio One* with tapes until they gave e him the Monday lunchtime 'Midday Spin' programme in 1968 which was al;so carried on radio two.

He became a staff announcer on *Radio Two* and presented many programmes in the seventies and eighties, such as 'Night Ride', 'What's New' and 'Radio One Club'. He also dabbled in television, one of his keen interests and was a regular continuity announced on *Thames TV* for a while.

In the 1980s he moved to Los Angeles to pursue TV and became a host of programmes such as 'Hollywood Stars', 'The Name Game' and 'LA in the Morning', as well as appearances in 'Around the World in 80 days' and 'Face to Face'. He has also presented radio and TV programmes in many other countries, including Germany, France, Antigua and Australia.

In the nineties, Tom returned to his home city of Norwich and has appeared on several local programmes on *BBC Radio Norfolk*. Tom still shudders when he recalls working on the Radio City fort, ninety feet over the Thames Estuary with very shaky catwalks, and says that one of the most exciting moments of his career was meeting Bette Davis.

He is proud of once having to ad-lib before camera for four minutes when a programme feed failed. Likes Italian food and the film industry, but isn't a great fan of the taxman.

Steve EGGINGTON
Managing Editor at *BBC Radio Gloucester*.

John ELEY
Presenter / producer at BBC Radio Suffolk.

Tim ELLINGFORD
Host of the Saturday morning show and a request programme each Sunday lunchtime on *BBC Radio Cleveland.*

Ted ELLIOT
Throughout the seventies, Essex-born Ted worked for a number of record companies and music publishing houses as a plugger, trying to elicit plays for artistes such as ELO and the Bee Gees. His active participation in various escapades resulted in offers from several stations and he has been heard on *Chiltern, Mercia, Extra AM* and Central TV.

Ted is one of the country's busiest voice over artistes. In 1994 he joined the new regional station in the Midlands, *Heart FM* where he hosts the station's morning show, and he's recently had his first book published - called 'An introduction to shaped Picture Discs'.

Janet ELLIS
Born in Kent on 16th September, 1955, Janet went to no less than seven schools (three of the overseas) because her father was an Officer in the Royal Engineers. Trained at the Central School of Speech and Drama and has made several dozen TV appearances, including TV commercials for Daz and four years on Blue Peter. Janet's break into radio came with her own series on *GLR* in London - 'Janet's Bottom'.

Monica ELLIS
Producer for BBC *Radio Devon & Dorset FM.*

Stella ELLIS
Wilf Proudfoot's secretary and main administrator for *Radio 270* in the 1960's, she now lives in Spain.

Steve ELLIS
Station and production manager at *CD603*, the ILR station in Cheltenham.

Stuart ELLIS
Born in Bromsgrove in the West Midlands, and raised in Studley, Stuart sneaked into the back door of *Wyvern Radio* in Worcester while station boss Norman Bilton was guarding the front entrance! That was back in October 1987, and Norman eventually moved him on to *BRMB Birmingham* in 1989 where he stayed for three years. He says that the highlight of his career was working there with Les Ross "you felt as though you were making way for a real radio presenter when he took over your chair." His most amusing moment was managing to get stuck in the lift at BRMB with 'Take That'.

After a brief period working for *Chiltern Radio* he joined Leeds ILR *Radio Aire* in 1993, where he currently presents the station's afternoon programme.

In 1994 he began working as a newsreader for next door YTV's 'Calendar' programme and he also comperes a variety of events.

Dave ENGLAND
Weekday presenter at *Plymouth Sound.*

Phil ENGLAND
Head of promotions and sponsorship at *Signal Radio* in Stoke on Trent.

Steve ENGLAND
The son of variety artistes, Steve fell in love with pirate radio while living in Bristol. He visited the *Radio Caroline* ship twice and on his second visit, while the ship was temporarily in port, began tidying up and was rewarded with a job on overnights. His talents were soon harnessed on prime shows and his skills in production brought the station a new identity.

His production of jingles for a new Dutch station, Radio Mi Amigo led to his joining a belgian ship, *Radio Atlantis*, where he soon became Programme Director. After Atlantis closed Steve returned to the UK and joined *Piccadilly Radio* in Manchester.

He later set up his own jingle and commercial production studios, Alfasound, which is now one of the leading companies in that field.

Jim ENSON
Assistant Editor at *BBC Radio Suffolk.*

Eric EPSON OBE
Eric is a director of *Radio Mercury.*

Who's Who in British Radio

John ESCREET
East Yorkshire -born John worked in pubs and clubs for several years before joining *Viking Radio* in Hull in the mid-eighties. He is one of the area's leading authorities on rock'n'roll and hosted programmes on the station's 'Gold' outlet on the AM Band (one of the first in the country).

He currently freelances around the area and is also the Press and PR man for the coastguard.

Chris EVANS
Began his broadcasting career sorting Timmy Mallett's fan mail at *Piccadilly Radio* in Manchester and later moved to London as a script-writer for Jonathan Ross.

In the mid-eighties he joined the ill-fated BSB satellite network to host programmes on 'The Power Station' and in 1989 *GLR* gave him a weekly Saturday programme 'Round at Chris's' which ran for four years.

In 1992 he was hired to host a weekly programme on *Radio One* and the same year joined Channel Four TV to launch 'The Big Breakfast'. In 19945 he was hired for the Radio One breakfast show.

Gillian EVANS
Sponsorship and Promotions Manager at *Country 1035* in London.

Helen EVANS
A journalist at *BBC Radio Lincolnshire.*

Ken EVANS.
Australian-born Ken worked in commercial radio in Sydney (on 2CH) and came to London to carry out some interviews in 1962. He met fellow countryman Alan Crawford who was running a music publishers and who wanted to start an offshore station.

These two gentlemen organised *Radio Atlanta* and raced Radio Caroline to get on the air first (Caroline won, by two weeks although the stations later merged). Ken became a leading backroom boy organising programming on Atlanta and, after the merger, worked at Caroline House in Chesterfield Gardens in a similar role.

In 1966 he joined *Radio Luxembourg* to produce programmes sponsored by EMI and was responsible for contracting DJs such as David Jacobs, Simon Dee, Tony Blackburn and Alan Freeman to 208. Ken then became Programme Director of the station, a role he held until in 1977, when he left to go into the record industry.

The radio big had bitten however and it wasn't long before she was back in the studio - this time at *BBC Radio Two*, producing the David Jacobs programme each lunchtime

Nick EVANS
Managing Editor of *BBC Radio Wales.*

Penny EVANS
Sales Director at *Q 103* in Cambridge.

Richard EVANS
Richard is a presenter on the 'Newsbeat' programmes on *BBC Radio One.*

Spencer EVANS
Weekday presenter at *Fortune 1458*

Wyn EVANS
Presenter at *Swansea Sound.*

Peter EVERETT
Editor of Network Radio for the BBC in the Midlands and South East, based at Pebble Mill.

John EVINGTON
Born and raised in Cheshire, John studied economics to degree level at the University of Portsmouth and while there helped establish the campus radio station. In 1978 he joined *Piccadilly Radio* gaining expertise as presenter and producer of all daytime sequences including weekday breakfast and sport. In 1980 he oversaw the commission of a new package of station ID jingles.

In 1981 he moved on to a senior presentation position at *Leicester Sound* and presented the breakfast show for 18 months as well as becoming Head of Music. In August 83 he moved to *Signal Radio* in stoke with a similar role and the following year was contracted for a series of early morning programmes on *BBC*

Radio Two. He is now Programme Director of the Signal Group of stations.

Dave EVISON
Sunday afternoon presenter on *Signal Gold.*

Richard EYRE
Born in Yorkshire in 1954, he graduated from Oxford with a degree in Politics, philosophy and economics in 1975 and joined an advertising agency.

After nine years, including a spell at Scottish TV, he moved to an offshoot of Collett Dickinson Pearce as media director in 1984. Two years later Richard became the first media director at Bartle Bogle Hegarty, and oversaw his department double its billings in each of its first four years, reaching £100 million by 1991.

Early in 1992, he became managing director at *Capital Radio* which now employs 450 people and has a £250 million capitalisation. Under

Richard's control, profits last year rose by 59% to £17.9 million.

He is also involved in a growing young church in Croydon, where he lives with his wife and three children. "We're all passionate about music and the house is always full of it, either live or recorded," he says.

Julie FAIR
Sales director at BRMB, Birmingham.

Richard FAIR
Host of community programmes on *BBC Radio GMR* in Manchester.

Paul FAIRBURN
For several years he was Programme Director at *Aire FM* in Leeds and in 1995 moved to Midlands regional station, *Heart FM* in the same role.

Peter FAIRHEAD
Initially a road safety technician and sales representative in Essex, Peter got into radio "by sheer persistence and talent." After that first broadcast (on BBC *Radio Medway* in the early 1970's) he joined Ipswich station *Radio Orwell* and then in the 1980s moved to *Pennine Radio* in West Yorkshire.

A move across the Yorkshire Radio Network to *Viking Gold*, later *Classic Gold*, he is still at the same network which is now known as *Great Yorkshire Gold* and also doing shifts for Manchester station, *Fortune AM.*

As well as radio, Peter has also voiced a railway video (although it was difficult to wear cans and his anorak!) and also many commercials. He's also a country music specialist, but the highlight of Peter's career was a fabulous review on Radio Four's 'Radio programme' special about 'Gold' stations.

Adam FAITH
Adam is a director of *Melody Radio* in London.

Corrine FALLOWS
Presenter at weekends on *Swansea Sound.*

Dave FANNING
Was best known presenter on *Irish RTE 2 FM* for several years and joined *Virgin 1215* at its

launch and now presents a nightly programme.

Michael FANSTONE
Presenter of the early morning show 'Together on Sunday' for *BBC Radio Kent* and a similar programme on *Classic FM*.

Jenny FARISH
Presenter of programmes on *West Sound* in Ayr and on *South West Sound* in Dumfries.

James FARMER
Began his radio career at *Radio Hallam* and then moved to *Invicta FM* in Kent. There he became station director and Group Sales Director before leaving in 1995 to join Metro Networks as Group Sales Director.

Zelda FARR
News producer at *BBC Wiltshire Sound*.

Andy FARRANT
Journalist at *BBC Radio Lincolnshire*.

Chris FARRELL
Born on 15th December, 1970 in Westminster, London, Chris became a stockbroker after leaving school and then a roadie as well as working in a library. He got into radio after listening to 'Timbo' on *Essex Radio* - which he thought sounded more fun and in 1981 he made his first broadcast on *Essex Radio*, aged just 11.

Over the next six years he appeared on lots of other programmes on *BBC Essex* and in 1988 he joined *Radio Wyvern*. After that he spent some time at *MFM/ Marcher Sound* and in 1990 moved to *Chiltern Radio*. After three years at Chiltern, 1993 saw him moving north to *TFM* and *Metro;* just two years later he arrived back in London as a regular weekday jock at London's new AC station, *Heart 106.2*.

The most memorable moment of his career has been working with Erica North, although he once turned up for an interview with Phil Collins 24 hours too early! Likes eating Haagen Dag ice cream in Leicester Square and has a phobia of the Northern Line.

Fiona FARRELL
Travel news presenter at GLR in London.

Dan FARTHING
Former producer and journalist at *Radio Humberside*, Dan is now the Assistant Editor at BBC *Radio York*.

David FARWIG
Presenter at *BBC Radio York* in the 1980s. he is now the Station Manager at *BBC Radio Cornwall*.

John FASHANU
Director of *Kiss FM* in London and also host of the Gladiators on ITV.

Rod FAWCETT
Engineer in charge at *BBC Radio Newcastle*.

Paddy FEENY
Paddy joined the BBC as a studio manager in 1956, working at Bush House. In 1959 he secured a trial run on the 'Sportworld' programme. He has appeared on many programmes on the *Home Service* and *Radio Four*, including 'Top of the Form' and also on several TV programmes.

Paddy was host of Saturday afternoon sports programmes on *BBC World Service*, for 36 years until he retired in August 1995. He continues presenting some programmes for World Service, such as 'Write On' and 'Pick of the Week'.

Nigel FELL
The son a a BBC Studio Manager he was educated at St Hilda's School in Yorkshire and Southend High and made his first broadcast on *Radio City* (the offshore one) in 1965. His next appearance was on *BBC Radio Leeds* in 1969 and in the seventies he presented almost every type of programme imaginable on the station. In the 1980s he was the co-host of a daily programme called 'West Riding'. Nigel likes pubs and beer, and worries about radio station bosses discovering what he's up to.

Ian FENN (*The man they call Mr Comedy*)
Born September 1970 and educated in London, Kent and Guildford, Ian worked at the University of Surrey as a technician until 1991 and was programme controller of the campus radio station for six years.

In 1992 he worked at the Kidbrooke Comedy club in London, and for a publisher in Brighton. He also spent a year as freelance trainer for the Midlands Action Radio Trust and was the producer of the 'Golden Hour of Comedy' at LBC and a freelance contributor to 'Cinema 2' at *Radio Two*.

In 1993 Ian took over from Max Clifford as Head of Media Relations for Scallywag magazine, and then helped produce the award winning play 'Hello?' for *LBC*. He has also been responsible for a variety of other independent productions, notable 'What am I bid?' for *Radio Four* and as a researcher for 'The Comedy Quiz' for *Radio Two*. He spent two years as a freelance reporter for the Steve Jones breakfast show on LBC and hosted programmes on *Croydon FM*, an RSL operation.

For the last year he has been a radio technology demonstrator at the BRIT School in Croydon, a producer and manager at a comedy club and a columnist for an arts magazine.

Ian has an MA in Radio from Goldsmiths College of the University of London, recognised by the NUJ and is being assessed for acceptance by the NCTJ. He was the first mature student without a degree to gain this qualification and received distinctions for his dissertations.

Mike FENNEL
News Editor at *BBC Radio Humberside* in the 1980s.

Stewart FENWICK
Previously with University Radio Aithrey from 1980-'88, he ended with a 24 hour Country Show in May 1988. Currently a Country Music Presenter at *Central FM*.

Alison FERGUSON
Alison mans the information desk at *Moray Firth Radio* in Inverness.

Anne FERGUSON OBE
Director of *Capital Radio*.

George FERGUSON
Afternoon presenter on *Manx Radio*.

Maria FERGUSON
Afternoon presenter on *Wessex FM* in Dorchester.

Kevin FERNIHOUGH
Afternoon presenter from 1 until 4 each weekday on *Signal One* in Stoke.

Kate FERRAND
Producer at *BBC Radio Devon and Dorset*.

Tom FERRIE
Presenter at *South West Sound*.

Andy FERRISS
Presenter at *South Coast Radio*.

John FIELD
Host of a Saturday evening programme on BBC *Radio Three*.

Fred FIELDER
Host of a Sunday programme on *Signal Radio*.

Rob FIELDING
Producer at BBC *Radio Cleveland*.

Peter FIELTER
Sales Director at *KLFM* in Kings Lynn.

Charley FIGGIS
Co-presenter of 'The Breakfast Show' with James Stewitt every weekday on *Radio Kent*.

Lee FINAN
Music Presenter at *Metro FM*.

Jane FINDEN
Sales executive at *Ocean Sound*.

Bruce FINDLAY
Presenter at *Scot FM*.

Richard FINDLAY
Richard Findlay is a graduate of The Royal Scottish Academy of Music & Drama in Glasgow and worked for a time as an actor in theatre, radio and television before being recruited by the BBC and the Ministry of Overseas Development on behalf of the Government of Saudi Arabia to assist in the launch of an English-language radio service for the country.

While in Saudi Arabia, he also launched an

English-language newspaper; both the radio service and newspaper continue to this day. On his return to the UK, he was employed by the COI where he was a member of a small team providing information services overseas under the auspices of the Foreign Office.

He joined *Radio Forth* as Programme Controller in August, 1974 as Programme Controller from *Capital Radio* in London where he had been a duty News Officer. SInce then he's been appointed as Chairman of Radio Tay and is also a director of Moray Firth Radio.

He has served as Chairman of AIRC for two separate terms, chaired a number of it's Council and then Board since 1977, the year in which he has appointed Managing Director of *Radio Forth*.

Elly FIORENTINI
Presenter and producer of an afternoon programme each weekday on *BBC Radio York*.

Carlo FIORENTINO
DJ at *KCBC* in Kettering.

Tony FISH
Managing Editor of *BBC Radio Newcastle*.

Dick FISHER
Born in Birmingham, snooker fan Dick joined *Beacon Radio*. In the nineteen eighties he was breakfast presenter at weekends, as well as hosting the station's weekly request programme. He moved to the company's MOR service WABC in the nineties.

Geoff FITCH
Presenter on *Invicta FM* in Kent.

Wayne FITZGERALD
Presenter at *Hereward Radio* in Peterborough, he left early in 1995 and in the middle of the year was operating an RSL station - *Lite FM*.

Lydia FLACK
Sales Controller at *Horizon Radio*.

Mark FLANAGAN
Managing Director of *Fox FM* in Oxford.

Jackie FLAVELLE
Presenter at *Downtown Radio* in Belfast in 1995.

Lisa FLAVELLE
Head of programmes at 96.7 BCR in Belfast.

Alan FLECKNEY
Presenter on Plymouth Sound's AM station.

John FLEET
Host of a programme of big band music and other old time nostalgia each Sunday lunchtime on *BBC Radio Sheffield*.

Derek FLOOD
Began his radio career on local stations in Ireland and in 1995 joined *Viking FM* in Hull to host a mid-morning show.

John FLORENCE
Host of a phone-in programme called 'Newstalk' on *BBC Radio Leicester*.

Mike FLYNN
Mike got into radio after working in an in-factory cable station in Wrexham in the early 1970s. From there he moved to Liverpool stations *Radio City* and *Radio Merseyside*.

In 1978 Mike joined *BBC Radio Wales* on the day it opened. For many years he presented his own daily programme with music and interviews called 'On The Road'. His interests are flying (he has his own Piper Cherokee) and fast cars.

Shelagh FOGARTY
After school in Liverpool and University in Durham, Shelagh became a Spanish and English teacher in Barcelona. She got into radio via the BBC's local Radio Training course and made her first broadcast from a creaking Humber Bridge in high winds.

From *Radio Humberside* she moved to the warmer climes of *Radio Guernsey*, then *Radio Bristol, Radio Sheffield* and *Radio Merseyside*.

After a brief sojourn to *Radio Four*, she returned to *Radio Merseyside* where she covered the James Bulger Trial. Dislikes "dithering colleagues who get away with too much."

Sean FOGERTY
Producer at *BBC Radio Shropshire*.

Pat FOLEY
Station Manager and Head of Sales at *KCBC*.

Who's Who in British Radio

Bryan FORBES
Director at Capital Radio Group Plc.

David FORBES
Managing Director, Programme Controller and Sales Manager at *Q96* in Paisley, Scotland, where he also presents the station's weekday breakfast show.

Patrick FORBES
Religious producer at BBC *Radio Berkshire*.

Sandy FORBES
Host of a long running nostalgia based programme on *LBC* as well as a four hour Sunday afternoon programme, he is now heard on BBC *Wiltshire Sound*.

Brian FORD
Educated at the Leith Academy, Edinburgh, Brian became an Editorial Assistant with the Scottish Daily Mail and a sound engineer. By way of hospital radio and a great deal of determination he got into radio and made his first broadcast on *Radio Clyde*.

Since then he's also worked for *Radio Forth, Radio City, BBC Radio Scotland* and *Radio 2*.

Brian is currently with *Scot FM* and also does voice over work and television presentation at Scottish TV. Agent - Voicebox, Stockport and Talking Heads , London.

Brian J. FORD
Born on the 13th May 1939 in Wiltshire, he attended Kings School in Peterborough and then the University College at Cardiff, before embarking on a career in science, with the Medical Research Council. He became a lecturer for the FCO and has edited many scientific publications.

His first broadcast, aged 21, was on the old Welsh region of the Home Service, since then he's appeared many times on *Radio Four* and has contributed on scientific matters to 'Woman's Hour' and to Radio One's 'Newsbeat' programme.

Dee FORD
Managing Director at *Red Rose Radio*.

Gerry FORD
Born in County Westmeath, Ireland, in 1943, Gerry was always musically inclined, singing in his local church choir and teaching himself to play the guitar. He worked as a baker and confectioner, first in Edinburgh and later in London. While living in the capital took a part time job as a DJ at the Majestic Ballroom in Finsbury Park, introducing the Beatles on their first London gig. In 1965 he moved back to Edinburgh and became a policeman for eleven years.

When *Radio Clyde* opened he guested on a programme called 'Country Sounds' and was bitten by the radio bug. The following year he persuaded Edinburgh's new station, *Radio Forth*, to let him present a country music programme. In 1976 he was nominated the Top Country DJ by the CMA and the same year he went professional as a singer. The next two years he won further awards from the CMA for his work as a Country Music DJ and joined *BBC Radio Scotland* to present country music there.

In the eighties he moved to national *Radio Two* and has presented a variety of country music programmes.

Julian FORD
Julian is the Information Technology and Telecommunications manager of the BBC Helpline service.

Keith FORDYCE
Born in Lincoln in 1928 he attended Emmanuel College, Cambridge, following which he joined the RAF. While in Hamburg he was seconded to the *British Forces Network* as an announcer, since when he's hosted programmes for *Radio Luxembourg* and the BBC. He was a mainstay of the *BBC Light Programme* in the early 1960s and worked for the BBC for over thirty years, hosting such programmes as 'Sounds of the Sixties' and 'Beat The Record' on *Radio Two*.

In 1964, Rediffusion TV, then holding a London ITV franchise and being responsible for many nationally networked ITV programmes, gave Keith one of the resident presenter jobs on 'Ready Steady Go'.

Vintage aircraft is Keith's main interest and he operates the Torbay Aircraft Museum near Paignton. He likes flying and gardening.

Keith is now hosting a programme each Saturday evening from 10pm until midnight on *BBC Radio Solent.*

Liz FORGAN
Managing Director of Network Radio at the BBC, based at Broadcasting House.

Mark FORREST
A true Yorkshireman, while at Newcastle University, Mark applied for a job at *Metro FM* in the city as a production assistant and two days later became their overnight DJ.

He soon rose to become the station's breakfast programme. He left for a taste of world travel in the early nineteen-nineties, but the station's bosses held the show open for his return.

Among his non radio exploits are motorcycling across Europe (the long way - Norway to Spain) and exploits in the USA.

In 1994 *Virgin 1215* attracted him to their new national network and he now does weekday lunchtime shows there, including the station's 'Crunchie Album Chart Countdown'.

John FOSTER
John was the host of *Great Yorkshire Gold's* early-morning programmes on weekdays until July 1995 when he joined *Sun City FM* in Sunderland at its launch. He now does breakfasts at the station.

Stephen FOSTER
Stephen is a news producer at *Radio Suffolk.*

Steve FOUNTAIN
Afternoon presenter at Great Yorkshire Gold.

Adrian FOX
After a grammar school education, Adrian became a lead guitarist in a band as well as a mobile DJ. he also did some hospital radio and had some bit s and pieces used by *Radio One* in the 'Music Biz' programme. His first broadcast was from the Leigh (Essex) Regatta in 1982 and he was given a regular saturday morning slot a couple of months later. Since

then he's freelanced with both *Essex Radio* and *Essex FM,* and since 1994 has been presenting programs for the company's *Breeze AM* all gold station (currently doing weekend breakfasts).

He also works as a magician, voice-over artiste and a video director. the funniest thing which happened to Adrian is getting covered in soot while doing a live OB from a steam engine, and having to jump over hurdles in a charity event when his dog refused to do so.

Bob FOX
Chief Engineer at *Viking FM* in Hull.

Mary FOX
Mary is the producer responsible for Telford affairs at *BBC Radio Shropshire.*

Neil FOX
After Bath University he did two years in sales and marketing. he sent audition tapes to his local station *Radio Wyvern* who gave him his first programme in September 1985. After 18 months, he got a bigger gig at *Radio Luxembourg,* and soon came to the attention of Richard Park, who gave him a programme at *Capital Radio* in September 1987. He's been there ever since and is well known throughout the UK as the host of the ILR network's Sunday 'Network Chart show', as well as for his TV appearances on Thames, Sky and LWT. A new programme for LWT was scheduled to start in Autumn 1985.

The high-flying Doc Fox loves helicopters, Harley Davidsons and sky-diving, and says that the highlight of his career was being awarded the Sony 'Broadcaster of the Year' award in 1995. Dislikes Anoraks, racism and mooses.

Roy FOX
Director of *Touch AM,* Cardiff.

Alan FRANCE
Alan is a director at *Red Rose Radio.*

Jacqueline FRANCE
Durham reporter for *BBC Radio Newcastle.*

Jennifer FRANCIS
Member of the Radio Authority.

Who's Who in British Radio

Keith FRANCIS
Keith was a presenter on *Severn Sound* and the programme Organiser at *Galaxy Radio* in the early 1990s. In 1994 he joined *11-70* in High Wycombe, as the Managing Director.

Neil FRANCIS
Neil is a presenter at *Invicta FM*.

Roger FRANCIS
Roger was the senior engineer at LBC for many years and in July 1995 joined Clyde Electronics as Head of Business Development.

Stewart FRANCIS.
Managing Director of *Mid Anglia Radio Plc* for twelve years until the network was acquired by GWR Group in 1994. Stewart was also a chairman of the Association of Independent Radio Companies and in 1995 became Chief Executive of a DTI-funded business support network in Peterborough.

Ashley FRANKLIN
A Welshman by birth, Ashley was educated in Nottingham and Birmingham and had a variety of jobs in his early part of his career, including making 'Quavers' for Smith's Crisps. His first broadcast was in 1971 on *BBC Radio Nottingham* after winning the station's DJ contest. He then moved to *BBC Radio Derby,* where he remains to this day. He presented the station's early morning programme in the early 1980s and has since hosted a wide range of programmes.

Mark FRANKLIN
Began working in hospital radio when he was only 11 years old, and from there he got a job with *BBC Wiltshire Sound* in early 1989. This led to work at *BBC Radio Five,* and then *GWR-FM.*

Mark was a 'Top of the Pops' presenter for over two years and also presented the O-Zone on BBC 2 TV. The highlight of his career was getting his first break at the BBC and helping launch the station he now works at, *Galaxy 101* in September 1994.

Peter FRANKLIN
After studying on the post-graduate journalism course at Falmouth, he joined *Ocean Sound*'s Fareham newsroom in mid-1995.

Ken FRANKS
Ken is the Trowbridge News producer for BBC *Wiltshire Sound.*

Lesley FRASER
Educated at the James Gillespie High school For Girls and did a Nursing Diploma at the Queen Margaret College, following which she did twelve years counselling. She then spent five years running her own business, designing wedding dresses and ballgowns before moving into radio by way of working on phone-in problems for young people.

At Christmas 1993 Lesley did her first pieces for radio - a series of video reviews, and the following September 1994 hosted her first overnight music programmes on the new regional station, *SCOT FM.*

Since then she's hosted many programmes and live events and has been fielding calls on the station's 'Open Line' since January 1995.

As well as her radio work Lesley is a Senior Nurse at the Brook Advisory in Edinburgh, and a film critic andAagony Aunt on the 'Lanarkshire Extra' newspaper. She's presented two series of sex education programmes for Grampian Television's 'Living and Growing' She's also a prolific freelance journalist, the coordinator of Max-AM's Help a Child and is a part-time skiing instructor.

Likes horses, men, good food and a gin and tonic, but not tripe, and says the highlight of her career, apart from her first show, was a live broadcast from The Orange Airship over Edinburgh.

Lawrence FRAYNE
Lawrence is the chief engineer at *BRMB* and sister station *Xtra 1152* in Birmingham.

Alan FREEMAN
He worked in Australian radio for several years and came to the UK in early sixties. He joined theBBC and took over the Sunday afternoon chart show 'Pick of The Pops" on the Light

programme, which was continued by *Radio One*.

Alan also spent several spells with *Radio Luxembourg* hosting sponsored record company programmes, and made many TV appearances, both in commercials and as the host of pop music programmes. he was also a regular presenter on BBC 1 TV's 'Top of the Pops' for many years.

Alan, or 'Fluff' as he's known in the industry, moved to *Capital Radio* in the 1990s where his 'Pick of the Pops' is still a very popular programme.

David FREEMAN

Popular programme host at *BBC Radio Oxford* until his afternoon programme was axed (in February 92) and then moved to *Fox FM* in April 1992, where he hosted a weekly blues show and the evening 'Fox Report'.

He now presents a weekday programme on *Jazz FM* in London.

Philip FREEMAN

Host of the 'Traditions' Programme each Monday evening on *Radio Maldwyn*.

Stuart FREEMAN

Born in Blackpool in 1952, after education at the local school and Technical College he worked as an insurance clerk by day and mobile disco jock by night. He guested on a Pop Quiz programme on *BBC Radio Blackburn* and that started his interest in radio.

After a period in hospital radio, he got his first 'real' radio programme - soul music showcase on *Swansea Sound* in 1976. On visits to the USA he broadcast on WMMR in Philadelphia and WNET in Boston.

Stuart then did a variety of programmes including *Swansea Sound*'s breakfast show and in the early 1980s moved to Harlech Television as an announcer and news reader.

Graham FREER

Graham is a presenter at *South Coast Radio*.

Val FRENCH

Val is the News Editor of 'Gold Radio' in Shaftesbury which launched in June, 1995.

Emma FREUD

Great grand-daughter of Sigmund Freud and daughter of former Liberal MP Clement, Emma was raised in Suffolk and London and studied Greek and Drama at Bristol University. After several TV appearances and programmes, such as 'In Bed With Emma Freud' and 'The Big Picture Show', she moved across to Radio, spending eleven months with *Radio One* hosting a lunchtime programme but has now returned to TV and is currently hosting programmes on BBC2.

Jane FRIGGENS

Presenter on *Pirate 102*, Cornwall ILR station.

Raymond FROSTICK

Raymond is the Chairman of *Radio Broadland*.

Trevor FRY

Trevor is a presenter at *Brunel Classic Gold*.

Elizabeth FUNNING

Presenter of religious oriented programmes at *BBC Radio Berkshire* which is now merged with Radio Oxford to form *Radio Thames Valley*.

Barbara GALE

Researcher with *BBC Wiltshire Sound*.

Roger GALE

Born on 20th August, 1943, in Poole, Dorset, Roger earned his place in the history books by becoming the first DJ to become an MP. After being educated at Southbourne Prep' and at the Guildhall School of Music and Drama, Roger became a freelance broadcaster, joining *Radio Caroline South* as a producer and presenter.

He then moved to *Radio Scotland* when the station launched on New Years Eve, 1965 where he became the station's Programme Director. Six months later he moved to Yorkshire to work with another MP with radio connections, Wilf Proudfoot who had just become Managing Director of *Radio 270*.

Roger then moved into the film business for a few years but returned to radio in 1972 when he joined *BBC Radio London* as a freelance news

Who's Who in British Radio

reporter. In 1973 he moved to national radio, being a producer with the *Radio One* 'Newsbeat' programme and also with 'Today' on *Radio Four*. In 1976 he moved to television as a childrens TV producer at Thames TV and then did three years as editor of the company's Teenage Unit.

A conservative since 1964, he stood for the Party in Birmingham in 1982 and the following year was elected as Member of parliament for Thanet North - he has been the area's member ever since. A keen sailor, he also enjoys swimming and canoeing and was a panelist / speaker at the World DJ Convention in 1986. Roger is also am ember of Kent County Cricket Club.

Bert GALLON
Bert is the Chief Engineer of BBC Resources.

Mervyn GAMAGE
After a long BBC career, in the late 1980s Mervyn became the Programme Organiser at *BBC Radio Stoke on Trent*.

He is now the Assistant Editor at the station.

Paul GAMBACINI
New York City born (as long ago as in 1949) Paul was educated at Dartmouth College and then at Oxford University(UK).

A life long radio afficionado, his first radio gig was at *WDCR* in New Hampshire, the Dartmouth College station and he also worked as an Executive Producer at WBZ in Boston.

While at Oxford he was a contributor to 'Rolling Stone' magazine and *Radio One* producer John Walters asked him to do a series of talks.

This evolved into participation in all manner of programmes, including a long running regular strip on *Radio One* and appearances on TV, in particular on the 'Old Grey Whistle Test'. In recent years he has presented a chart countdown programme on *Classic FM* and in October 1995 he joined BBC *Radio Four* as a regular presenter for 'Kaleidoscope' and also as a presenter on *BBC Radio Three*.

His work co-editing of the 'Guinness Book of Hit Singles' is one of his proudest achieve-ments - his most exciting moment was finding it had become the country's best selling book; Paul lives in London.

Norma GAMBLE
Born in Belfast, Norma's first job was as a nurse. After some experience in hospital radio, she joined *Radio Tay* in 1980 and hosted the station's 'Afternoon Affair' programme in the 1980s.

Neil GANDER
Neil is a news producer at *Radio Newcastle*.

Roger GANE
The Executive Director of RAJAR, the industry audience research system jointly owned by the BBC and commercial radio, since its commencement in 1992. Roger ran the JICRAR radio research service in the mid 1970s and developed international TV audience research systems in the 1980s. he is a frequent speaker at international media research conferences.

Carron GARDEN
Carron is a programme producer at BBC Essex.

Graham GARDEN
Born in Aberdeen in 1943 and a member of the Cambridge 'Footlights' revue team, he worked closely with the Goodies' Bill Oddie on various TV programmes and also on two series on *Radio Two*.

Paul GARDENER
Head of Sales at the Essex Radio Group outlet in Harlow, *Ten Seventeen FM*.

Stephen GARDINER
Stephen was the News Controller at *London Newsradio* when the station launched in 1994 and is now the Managing Director of *Reuters Radio News*.

Alistair GARDNER
Director at *Moray Firth Radio* in Inverness.

Barbara GARDNER
Barbara has managed sales teams in the north west for eighteen years now. In the 1970s she woprked in publishing and moved into radio in

1987 when she joined Liverpool station *Radio City* as Head of Local Sales.

Her team substantially increased City's share of advertrising against newspapers and in 1994 she moved to *Piccadilly Radio* in Manchster as Sales Director. She is also a council member of the Manchester Publicity Assocition.

Jim GARDNER

Jim is the chairman of the north east regional station, *Century Radio*.

Kirsty GARDNER

Kirsty is a producer at *BBC Wiltshire Sound*.

Mick GARRETT

Mick is the Company Secretary to the Board of Essex Radio group.

Gill GARSTON

Gill is the News Editor of CFM in Carlisle.

Mike GASTON

Station Manager at *BCR* in Belfast.

Pearly GATES

Born in Tuskegee, Alabama, Pearly's began working when only five years old helping her family on the cotton-fields and by the time she was six she was picking herself "I'm not afraid of hard work - we started at 6am and worked until 5.30 in the evening."

The evenings were spent round the radio and she became Viola Geneva when she appeared at talent shows with her sister Jean.

In the late sixties Pearly came to the UK as one of the Flirtations releasing half a dozen excellent singles, and appearing as an actress on Cliff Richard's TV show.

For several years she toured as a solo performer and after appearing on *Radio Luxembourg* as a guest celebrity DJ she was offered a regular series of programmes on the station in 1979.

John GAUNT

John says he got into radio "quite by luck" in September 1993 at BBC Radio CWR with an early evening one hour programme. He was then moved to mid-mornings at the weekends and since December 1994 has presented the station's Breakfast Show.

John GEAR

Born in Redhill, Surrey, in 1936, his first broadcasting role was as a radio reporter on regional radio Four programmes. He has also hosted 'Music In Question' on *Radio Three* and dislikes pop music.

David GEARY

A Hertfordshire man, David was educated at Cheltenham College and RADA. He first trod the boards at the Criterion Theatre and has played all over the country in rep'.

His first broadcast was on the BBC *Light Programme* and he worked for some time as a freelance for Anglia Television and at *LBC* in London on their 'Artsweek' programme. After many years as an actor, he was invited to join the BBC as a staff announcer on *Radio Two*.

Stuart GEDDES

Stuart is the producer of a programme each weekday at 6pm on *BBC Radio Devon and Dorset*.

Caesar GEEZER

Controversial shock jock at *Talkradio UK* at its launch, he was fired by the station in September 1995 after attracting highest ever number of complaints about the content of his programme.

John GELSON

Born and brought up in the North-East, 30 year old year old John began his journalistic career as a reporter at the Hartlepool Mail. He then worked at the Sunderland Echo, while dabbling in RSL and community stations in the North East.

In 1992 he moved into broadcasting full time as the Sunderland reporter for *BBC Radio Newcastle*. In September 1994, he moved south to *BBC Radio Cleveland* as weekend producer. He produces and presents the station's weekend breakfast output and a weekly sports review, called 'Seven Days'.

Andy GEMMEL-SMITH

Andy's first radio activity was running a pirate station in Kent, for which he was fined £30. He later joined *Radio Atlantis*, a Belgian pirate ship, as engineer where he also presented programmes. Later in the 1970s he joined *Essex Radio* and hosted programmes using the name Andy Anderson. He also worked at the station as an engineer and established a business selling equipment to radio stations.

In 1995 the company of which he's chairman, KFM, launched a new ILR station in kent.

Chad GEORGE
Host of a dance music programme each Saturday evening on *Kix 96*, the new specialist music station in Coventry.

David GEORGE
Presenter at *BBC Radio Cornwall*.

Duncan GEORGE
Duncan is the Sales Director at *Capital Radio*.

Geoff GEORGE
Weekday presenter at *Piccadilly Radio*.

Mike GEORGE
Born in Harrow, Middlesex, Mike was educated at Bushey Grammar School near Watford and became a weather instrument maker. He then spent ten years in the Royal Navy where he made his first broadcast and after coming ashore joined *Radio Wyvern* where he presented an afternoon programme when the station first launched.

Steve GEORGE
Steve left school at 16 and did a variety of jobs for a few years, including a period as a fireman. During the late seventies and early 80s, Steve played National League Division One Volleyball and also played the game international for England.

He was also working in clubs and worked at *RTM Thamesmead* before joining Southend based *Breeze AM* in 1989. Initially on evening shows he's progressed around the station clock on many different slots, but has held the mid-morning slot since 1992, which he recently traded for an afternoon programme.

Steve is completely in love with radio, and says its all wonderful - that could be something to do with the luxurious lifestyle as he lists the most humourous event in his career as having

a body massage live on air at Breeze!

Cathryn GERAGHTY
Cathryn is currently the Head of Human Resources at *Atlantic 252*.

Janet GERSHLICK
Host of weekend evening programmes on *Talkradio UK*.

Cate GIBBERD
Cate is an editorial administrator with the Radio Academy.

Sir Peter GIBBINGS
Born on 25th March, 1929, Sir Peter was educated at Rugby and Wadham College, Oxford. After service with the Queen's Royal Lancers, he was called to the Bar in 1953 and worked as a newspaper executive (with Associated, the Observer and the Guardian) until the 1980s.

In 1984, Sir Peter joined Reuters and later the Press Association, and in 1988 became a director of Anglia Television. A keen skier and tennis player, on 1st January 1995, he took over the role of Chairman of the Radio Authority.

Dave GIBBINS
Dave's first broadcast was in 1974, after acting as a Saturday afternoon receptionist taking calls for *BBC Radio Humberside*'s sports team. He then moved to the county's ILR station, *Viking* where he became Sports Editor. Then followed a period as Sports producer at *TFM* in Stockton, before a move back to *Radio Humberside* in 1988.

Dave has also worked as a narrator for a video production company based in Burton on Trent and as a Rugby League correspondent for *Piccadilly Radio*.

The highlight of Dave's career was commentating on the 1988 FA Trophy Final at Wembley and presenting and commentating the 1992 4th Division play off at Wembley. He once described a goalkeeper as 'Sprouting raddish' and (surprise, surprise) he likes sport and The Arsenal.

Not exactly the world's biggest Spurs or Liverpool fan - Dave is another of those radio presenters whose age always remains the same!

Nicola GIBSON
A senior producer at *Radio Gloucester.*

Pat GIBSON
Pat handles traffic and travel at the *Red Rose Radio* stations in Preston.

Andrew GIDLEY
Born in London in 1954 and educated in Croydon, he worked in public relations before his first radio job, which was commentating on a game between Crystal Place and Hull City for LBC.

Later in 1979 he joined LBC full time and was their tennis correspondent for many years. He left radio to pursue journalism in newspapers

Barrie GIFFARD-TAYLOR
Barrie is the Secretary of the GWR Group.

David GILBANK
David came to the UK from Australia in 1991 after working in radio in Brisbane and New South Wales. He worked in commercial production for the *Metro Radio* group until joining *Piccadilly Radio* in March 1994.

David has won numeorus awards for commercial production and creative writing, both here, and ijn Australia and in the USA.

He has Bachelor of Arts Drama and Bachelor of Business Communications degrees from Queensland University.

He is currently the Creative Services Manager at Piccadilly Radio .

Colin GILBERT
Head of Comedy at *BBC Radio Scotland*

Graham GILBERT
Sales & Managing Director at *Plymouth Sound.*

Roger GILBERT
Managing Director of Associated Newspapers' radio arm, Harmsworth Media.

Ian GILCHRIST
Presenter at *South Coast Radio* in Brighton.

Bill GILES
Born in South Devon in 1939, Bill joined the

Met Office after attending Bristol College of Science and Technology and was sent to observe the effects of the first H-bomb tests.

He moved to the London Weather Centre in 1972 and has since been heard as a regular forecaster on all BBC radio networks, especially on *Radio Four.* He is now the Principal Officer of the Meteorological Office and head of the BBC Weather Centre since 1983. Lives in Oxfordshire and his hobbies are golf, cricket and gardening.

Tony GILHAM
After ten years at BBC *Three Counties Radio,* Tony moved to GWR *Classic Gold* in 1995.

Ian GILL
Presenter of late night programmes on *BBC Radio Cymru.*

Pam GILLARD
Presenter of the Sunday Breakfast programme (6am to 8am) at BBC *Radio Solent.*

Dave GILLBEE
Began his career as Dave MacKaye at *Radio City* off Whitstable in the 1960s, later moving to *Britain Radio* on board the good ship Laissez Faire off Frinton. In the mid-eighties he presented a Sunday afternoon programme at *BBC Radio Essex.*

Peter GILLESPIE
Head of Sales at regional station, *Scot FM.* -

Julia GILLETT
Producer of several programmes for BBC Network Radio, based in Southampton.

Tim GILLETT
Head of News at *Essex Radio* until early 1994.

Tony GILLHAM
Presenter at *Brunel Classic Gold.*

Alan GILLIES
Director at *Moray Firth Radio,* Inverness.

Andy GILLIES
Born just before Christmas 1959 in Perth, he attended Trinity College Glenalmond and Corpus Christie in Cambridge, where he presented some programmes on the campus sta-

Who's Who in British Radio

tion. From Cambridge he landed his first job at *Hereward Radio*, just up the road in Peterborough, where he presented most programmes including a lunchtime news wrap. He became the station's programme controller from 1984 to 1990 and then joined BBC radio Sport as a producer.

The following year he was lured back to the Peterborough station, by now known as Mid Anglia Radio, where he spent three years as Programme Controller for the network. In 1994 he moved back to the BBC for a job as Managing Editor at *BBC Radio Stoke*. The highlight of Andy's career was winning a Silver Sony Award for 'Sport on Four'

Tony GILLINGHAM
Music Presenter at *BBC Three Counties Radio*.

John GILLMORE
Presenter at *Red Rose Gold* in Preston.

H. GILLTRAP
Director of *Mid Anglia Radio Plc*.

Paul GING
Paul is a news reporter at *BBC Radio Solent*.

Nick GIRDLER
Programme presenter of late night programme each weekday on *BBC Radio Solent*.

Justin GLADDIS
Senior journalist at *Isle of Wight Radio*.

Anthony GLADSTONE
Anthony is the Chairman of *Fortune 1458* in Manchester.

Ken GLADSTONE-MILLAR
Ken is a programme presenter at *South Coast Radio* in Brighton.

Fiona GLOVER
The regular host of BBC GLR's weekday breakfast programme.

Richard GODBER
Richard is the Chairman of *Horizon Radio* in Milton Keynes.

Michelle GODDARD
Michelle is secretary to the Manager of the *Radio Two* music department.

Moira GODDARD
A reporter at *BBC Radio Peterborough*.

Johnny GOLD
The Managing Director of Sportsmedia Broadcasting.

Sean GOLDSMITH
Born in 1972, Sean led a pretty uneventful early life until leaving school, and then he did a few years working in various factories and warehouses as well as hospital radio. His break into radio came at *Leicester Sound* making trailers and he joined the station full time in 1992.

For eighteen months he did the evening show and then moved to *Trent FM* in October 1994 to present a similar programme. Like several others he has been attacked by Mr Blobby, and once interviewed Chaka Demus & Pliers and never understood a word they said!. Likes chips and hates mayonaisse, so he's probably never been to Belgium.

Kenneth GOLDSTEIN
Director of *Talkradio UK*.

David GOLDSTONE
David is a director of *Swansea Sound*.

Mark GOODIER
He grew up in North Wales, later moving to Newington in Edinburgh , where he began his career in hospital radio. By the age of 18 , he had his own show on *Radio Forth*, and also worked on *Radio Tay* and *Radio Clyde*, before moving to *Metro Radio* in Newcastle. Despite his meteoric rise Mark says that he never wanted to be a DJ !

He then moved to *Radio One* where he presented several programmes and is currently the permanent host of the station's most listened to programme, the UK Top 40, on Sunday afternoons as well as an evening show each weekday.

Nik GOODMAN
Attended the Merchant Taylors' School in Liverpool and gained a degree in radio produc-

tion from Bournemouth University. He got into radio by answering the phones and pestering people, which got him a Friday evening programme at Liverpool's *City FM*.

For twelve months Nik was a swing jock at Radio City and was then given his own show. the highlight of his career so far has been interviewing Kylie Minogue, although he admits he was drunk at the time. Likes soul music, whisky and curry, but doesn't like the boss in a bad mood!

Ed GOODRIDGE
After several years freelancing as a journalist, joined *Wey Valley Radio* In Alton (Hampshire) to head newsroom operation in 1995.

Haig GORDON
Haig is a presenter on the regional radio station in Central Scotland, *Scot FM*.

James GORDON
Educated at Glasgow University, where he was President of the Union and graduated with an MA Hons degree. In 1965 he joined Scottish Television as Political editor and eight years later became one of the architects of *Radio Clyde*, Scotland's first (land based) commercial radio station.

James was Managing Director at the launch of the station and has overseen its tremendous success and growth into Scottish Radio Holdings Plc. In 1991 he became vice-chairman of *Melody Radio*, the London-based continuous sweet music station.

In 1994 he was awarded a Sony Award for 'Outstanding Services to Radio' and in the same year was made a Commander of the British Empire. In 1994, Jimmy became the Chairman of the AIRC and a Fellow of the Radio Academy.

Peter GORDON
After the usual O levels and A levels, Peter did a degree in politics at Yorks University and then took a job in the city. He got into radio on the campus radio station and also did a few bits and pieces for BBC Radio York. He then went to work at *Delta Radio* as a journalist and

also did a variety of work at neighbouring *County Sound*.

A similar variety of news and music programming at sister station *Radio Mercury* preceded a move to *Star FM* where he became News Editor as well as hosting the station's breakfast show.

He has also been a debate host for cable TV in nearby Windsor and once got stuck a hundred feet down the side of a building while reporting on abseiling.

Steve GORDON
One of *Radio Caroline*'s best known DJs in the late 1970's, he was one of the last voices heard on the air from the station's Mi Amigo ship, being rescued from it minutes before it sank in March 1980.

Sarah GORRELL
Sarah is a presenter on the FM service of *Plymouth Sound*.

Carl GOSS
Producer at John Mountford Studios, the Norwich-based commercial production house.

Phil GOUGH
Currently a journalist at *Network News*.

Madeleine GOULD
Reporter at *BBC Radio Cornwall*.

John GOVIER
Producer at *BBC Radio Devon and Dorset*.

Janey Lee GRACE
Born in Nottingham in the seventies, Janey got a BA in Performance Arts and became a well known 'sexy voice' on *Radio One* programmes of Mark Goodier and Gary Davies and she has also appeared on *GLR, BBC Radio Essex* and the *World Service*.

Now *Virgin 1215*'s only female presenter, she has recently had chart success with "7 Ways to Love" and recorded with Boy George, Kim Wilde and Natalie Cole. Her break into Virgin came with travel spots of the breakfast show, then some overnight work, and more recently the late Sunday evening shift.

Damian GRADY

Commercial production manager at *The Bay*.

Douglas GRAHAM

Vice Chairman at *Moray Firth Radio*.

Lesley GRAHAM

Press officer at Channel Four television, and Chairman of a group bidding for an ILR licence for Cambridge.

Paul GRAHAM

 Educated at Uppingham School and Trinity College, Dublin, Paul worked at British Railways and in a textile factory. He also spent a lot of time pestering the manager of *BBC Radio Leicester*, in fact Graham even made him cry, before he relented and gave him that break into radio in 1969.

Graham finally left Radio Leicester in peace in 1978 and a year later was cruising the North Sea on the offshore *Radio Del Mare*, which gave him his biggest laugh in radio when station owner Gerard van Dam removed his trousers to help paint the station's tender. He then set off on a four year tour of Irish Radio, which saw him hosting programmes at *North West Radio*, *Eastside Radio* and Waterford super-station *South Coast Radio*.

He then decided to move back to England and did a spell at *Sunshine Radio* in the West Midlands before spending a couple of years on *Caroline 558*.

That was one of the highlights of his career so far, and it took three false starts to get there! Paul's world tour then took him on to *RBL*, a local station in Boulogne and then back to London to in-store *Radio HMV*. In 1990 he returned to the air with programmes on *KCBC* in Kettering, and in 1990 moved on to *Mellow 1557* in Frinton, where he now hosts a daily shift.

During the last five years Paul has also freelanced for stations such as *Invicta Supergold, WBMS* in Peterborough and *Radio Nova* and he does quite a lot of voice-over work.

Alan GRANT

News producer at *BBC Radio Humberside* in the 80s and 90s and then moved to Dundee where he is now a reporter for *BBC Radio Scotland*.

Gerry GRANT

Station Manager of *Q 96*, in Paisley.

Glen GRANT

Director at *Moray Firth Radio*.

Lou GRANT

Presenter at *South West Sound* in Dumfries and also at *West Sound* in Ayr.

Peter GRANT

Peter is a presenter at *Hallam FM* in Sheffield.

David GRAVELLS

Director of *Stray FM* in Harrogate, Yorkshire.

Caroline GRAY

A producer at *Radio Devon and Dorset*.

EZEKE GRAY

'The Man Ezeke' presents 'The Sunshine Show' on BBC *Radio One* on Wednesday nights and he also hosts a reggae programme each Sunday evening (8 until 10pm) on *BBC Three Counties Radio*.

He released a record in 1994 called 'Oh Diane' and this was a big hit in Holland in Spring 1995.

Mike GRAY

A Londoner by birth, Mike attended Latymer Upper School in Hammersmith and the Central School of Speech and Drama. He got into radio by answering the telephones at the BBC and did some work as an entertainment reporter at *BBC Radio London*. Mike then became the producer of Robbie Vincent's programme in 1983 and in 1985 moved cross to *BBC Radio Four*, also as a producer.

The following year, Mike moved to the coast and a role as a senior producer at *Radio Solent* and five years later was appointed Programme Editor and the Assistant Editor at BBC *Wiltshire Sound*.

In 1994 he became a reporter at BBC TV in Bristol and in October that year he helped launch *KISS 102*, in Manchester as Programme and News Controller, the highlight of his career.

The most humourous event in his radio career was doing a balloon dance with Tony Blackburn on stage during a Radio London Soul Night Out, and he likes the music Kiss 102 plays and not the music heard elsewhere.

Anna GRAYSON

A fully qualified scientist, Anna is a keen gardener and is currently producing a series on *BBC Radio Two* which looks at the gardens of various celebrities.

Andy GREEN

Andy is a weekend DJ at *Fox FM* in Oxford.

Benny GREEN

Born on the 9th December, 1927 in Leeds, Bennie attended the Marylebone Grammar School in London and was taught to play the saxophone by his father who was a professional musician.

Bennie spent over twenty years gigging with a variety of bands, including Ronnie Scott's and he also wrote a column in the NME in the mid-fifties. As well as columns in newspapers such as the Observer and the Mirror, he has written biographies of P G Wodehouse and Fred Astaire as well as editing books on cricket.

His first broadcast was a talk on jazz music in 1955 and he hosted a record review programme for several years on the *Third Programme*.

His most prolific output has been on *Radio Two* - several dozen different programmes over the last few decades and he's also been heard frequently on *Radio Four* programmes 'Kaleidoscope and 'Stop the Week'.

He also appeared on Michael Aspel's programme on *Capital Radio* to discuss jazz (and other matters!) for many years and was the host of the popular 'Jazz Score' on *Radio Two*

until recently. he now hosts a jazz programme each Sunday afternoon.

Colin GREEN

Host of the 'Green Light' programme each Saturday morning (from 10am to 12 noon) on *BBC Radio Leicester.*

Gary GREEN

Early- morning weekday DJ on *Signal Cheshire* and he also hosts a programme on Sunday evenings on *Signal Gold*.

Liz GREEN

Huddersfield-born Liz went to Loughborough University where she was actively involved in the campus radio station, from where she joined *LBC* as a producer, being responsible for the Michael Aspel show. After a year in London she returned to the North, joining Piccadilly's new FM station, *Key 103*.

After a period in Manchester, Liz returned to Yorkshire and joined *BBC Radio Leeds,* becoming Programme Organiser. Radio Leeds was the first of the BBC local stations to increase its speech content and she was moved into presentation.

Liz's current shift is the 10am to 1pm lunchtime news and talk-oriented slot. As well as her programme she attends a lot of events on behalf of the station and is a well known figure throughout West Yorkshire.

Michael GREEN

Controller of *BBC Radio Four.*

Sarah GREENE

Born in in London, Sarah's birthday is 24th October and she made her first appearances as a child actor and gained a degree in Drama Studies at Hull University.

She has made numerous broadcasts on *Radio One* and *Radio Four*, such as Radio One Club and on Woman's Hour but is best known for her TV appearances on six series of Going Live!'

She won the SOS Best Woman on Television Award three years running. Sarah is addicted to radio, married to Mike Smith (qv) and likes swimming and playing tennis.

Who's Who in British Radio

Kevin GREENING
Hired by *Radio One* in early 1990s he now hosts their Sunday Lunchtime programme.

Neil GREENSLADE
Attended the Grange Comprehensive School where he did some DJing on the school in house radio station, and finally made his first real radio broadcast in May 1988 at *GWR FM*, as the character 'Hungry Howard'. He then moved to *CD 603* and, despite disliking football, Neil has hosted a sports show; he's also broadcast a bungee jump live. Neil once appeared at a GWR roadshow resplendent in a wedding dress and did music reviews for *Wire TV* cable channel in 1994.

Neil is currently at *Galaxy 101* in Bristol where he does overnights and a Sunday evening programme.

John GREENSTREET
Features producer at *Spire FM*.

Carl GREENWOOD
Presenter at *The Bay* in Lancaster.

Debbie GREENWOOD
Born in Liverpool on 16th September, 1959, Debbie gained a BA with honours in French and german and won the 1984 Miss Great Britain beauty contest in 1984. She later became a presenter with *Granada TV* and in 1987 joined BBC *Radio Two*, where she's presented her own programme ever since.

Debbie is married to Paul Coia (qv), they have a daughter called Amelia; she likes writing eating and playing tennis.

Derek GREGORY
Derek is the chief accountant at *Fox FM*.

Hugh GREGORY
Director at *Orchard FM*.

Peter GREIG
Presenter and programme controller on the AM station of *Plymouth Sound*.

Alan GREVESON
Alan is a producer at BBC Radio York, based at the station's Harrogate studio.

James GRICE
Producer at *BBC Radio Devon and Dorset*.

Freda GRIER
Freda is a director of *West Sound* in Ayr.

Andrew GRIFFITHS
DJ at GWR FM (West) in Bristol.

Dewi GRIFFITHS
Presenter of the 'String of Pearls' programme on BBC *Radio Wales*.

Mark GRIFFITHS
Early morn ing presenter on Classic FM.

Peter GRIFFITHS
Producer of various programmes on *BBC Radio Four*.

Sarah GRIFFITHS
Saturday lunchtime presenter at *BBC Radio Sheffield*.

John GRIPTON
Broadcast journalist at BBC Wiltshire Sound.

Simon GROOM
Presenter at *BBC Three Counties Radio*.

Kevin GROVER
Salisbury-based presenter and Producer for *BBC Wiltshire Sound*.

Simon GRUNDY
Born in October 1969, Simon did two weeks work experience at BBC *Radio Lincolnshire* and *Hereward Radio* in his last year at school in Boston, Lincs.. He was by then working at Pilgrim Hospital Radio and he then worked as apart of a voluntary team at *BBC Radio Lincolnshire*.

In 1990 Simon joined Mid Anglia Radio, working as a presenter at both *Hereward Radio* in Peterborough and *CNFM* in Cambridge. Two years later he moved back to Lincolnshire and *Lincs FM*, presenting the Drive Time show from the station's first day until being moved to breakfasts.

In March 1994 he moved north to become breakfast show presenter (weekdays) on C-FM in Carlisle.

Paul GUINERY
Presenter on *BBC Radio 3*.

Who's Who in British Radio

John GUN
Presenter of vintage music programmes on BBC local radio stations in East Anglia.

Ted GUNDRY
Presenter at *BBC Radio Cornwall.*

Les GUNN
Founder of the North East Travel Network.

Nick GURNEY
Studied media and journalism at a college in Letchworth, Herts and by the age of 20 he was a TV rental shop manager. Nick started his broadcasting career in hospital radio then moved to the *Chiltern Network* working in Promotions. His first broadcast was presenting travel shows and show covers in '91.

His biggest break came via *Radio Nova* (satellite radio) which led to full time shows on *QEFM* where he hosted both the late show and breakfast. In February '92 he moved to *Country Music Radio* before joining *Boss 603* in Cheltenham as breakfast/drive presenter and assistant Head of Music. His most humorous event was whilst interviewing the U.S. W.W.F Wrestling Superstars, when one of the opposing tag teams leapt out from behind and attacked him!! Likes pizza and hates anchovy.

Ann HACCIUS
Programme Controller at United Christian Broadcasters, the satellite Christian music station.

Najma HAFEEZ
Non Executive director of *Heart FM.*

Peter HAGAN
Peter was born and educated in Liverpool after which he joined the Wolverhampton Chronicle and then the Shropshire Star. He then moved south to the Plymouth Evening Herald, becoming News Editor before moving to the BBC in 1990 as regional journalist in the city's TV newsroom.

He later became assistant news editor and moved across to *BBC Radio Kent* in a similar role before becoming General Manager at *BBC Radio Jersey and Radio Guernsey.*

In 1994 he became political editor for the BBC

in Plymouth and in February 1995 he was appointed Editor of News and programmes at *BBC Nottingham*, giving him the responsibility of supervising the output of BBC Radio Nottingham and the BBC's 'East Midlands Today' regional TV news magazine. Peter's interests include coaching youth football and walking.

Kenny HAGUE
Presenter at the New Leicester Sound.

Robin HAGUE
News Editor at Brunel Classic gold.

Steve HAIGH
Yeovil producer for BBC Radio Somerset

Max HAILEY
Presenter at *Mix 96* in Aylesbury.

Bobby HAIN
Bobby is Head of Music at *Radio Clyde.*

Tony HALE
Teatime presenter at *Southern Counties Radio.*

Alex HALL
Has been a phone-in host at *Pennine Radio* and then *The Pulse* in Bradford for many years and recently branching out into TV presentation.

Graham HALL
Presenter at *Beacon Radio* in Wolverhampton.

Malcolm HALL
Director of *Channel 103* on Jersey.

Tony HALL
Managing Director of BBC Radio News and Current Affairs.

Jo HALLAM
Journalist at BBC *Radio Cornwall.*

Nigel HALLAM
Journalist at *BBC Radio Lincolnshire*, based in Sleaford.

Richard HALLAM
Sales Director at *RAM FM* in Derby.

Malcolm HALLIDAY
Religious producer at Mercia FM.

Who's Who in British Radio

Jayne HALLIWELL
Secretary to the Marketing Director at *CFM*.

David HAMILTON
Born in Manchester in 1941 he was educated at Glastonbury - the school, not the Festival! His first job was as a scriptwriter for the then holder of the Midlands ITV franchise, ATV. He became well known as a nationally networked continuity announcer in the sixties, and in 1967 released a single called 'A special good night to you' on the Sceptre label.

David joined *Radio One* and hosted a regular afternoon programme there before moving over to *Radio Two*, and then in the nineteen eighties he switched to *Capital Gold*, where he presented the mid morning programme for many years, following Tony Blackburn, just as he'd once done on Radio One.

Like Tony, he also presented some programmes on the short lived W.H. Smith TV channel, *Lifestyle*. He is now presenting programmes at Capital-owned station, *Xtra AM* in Birmingham.

Guy HAMILTON
(see Gerry Zierler)

Mike HAMMOND
Born on 30th September, 1956 in Bridlington, Mike was educated at Headlands School in the town and then in the Army.

His radio career began on *Hospital Radio Devizes* in 1978 and he also did programmes for the hospital radio station in Bridlington.

Mike's first full broadcast was on *Radio Aire* in Leeds. and he also broadcast on the station's AM station *Magic 828*. While at Radio Aire he had the highlight of his career - his first roadshow in front of 10,000 people in Knaresborough Market Square.

It was also at *Radio Aire* that Mike had his most humorous event, when fellow DJ Carl Kingston (qv) wound him up on the phone pretending to be an engineer testing the equipment.

In 1993 Mike moved to Scarborough to help launch *Yorkshire Coast Radio* and was the station's sales manager, - continually breaking revenue sales targets as well as holding down a regular air-shift on the station.

Mike likes sport and music, but not ignorant people. he is an accomplished copywriter, voice-over man and actor - he has also appeared in Pantomime at the Scarborough Spa Theatre for the last two years and describes himself as an all-round ace person (but then, he would say that, wouldn't he!?)

Jim HANCOCK
Born in 1948 in Plymouth, Jim became President of the Students' Union at Manchester University. In that role he was introduced to Philip Birch, who appointed him as his assistant when he launched Manchester's first ILR, *Piccadilly Radio*, in 1974.

He then took a position as Editor of Current Affairs for the station while holding down other positions such as lobby correspondent for IRN and local news reporter for BBC TV in the North West. He is now a political correspondent for the BBC at Westminster.

Tom HAND
Engineering Manager for *Atlantic 252*.

Valerie HANDLEY
Valerie had a varied career (beauty consultant, wine importer and in the social services) before her first job in radio - on reception. Her first broadcast was during a school quiz on *County Sound* in Guildford in 1984. She then became a news assistant and journalist and finally news editor at the station.

Valerie's next step was to become News Manager at *Radio Mercury*, before a move to Slough to be Head of News at *Star 106.6*. She's now been made the station's Managing Director and says that every day of her life in radio has been a highlight.

Valerie likes people but hates rubber gloves which are wet inside!

97

Julia HANKON

Julia is the Drive Time presenter on BBC Radio Newcastle.

Karen HANNAH

Karen has worked at several stations and is now a Senior producer at BBC GMR, Manchester.

Stella HANSEN

Arts programme producer at *BBC Radio Two*.

Jean-Paul HANSFORD

DJ at *Fox FM* in Oxford and then Programme Controller at Fox also until 1995 when he left after predicting the results of a survey, before it was done!

Ali HANSON

Presenter of Bengali programmes each Sunday on *BBC Radio Leeds*.

John HANSON

Religious producer at *Mix 96* in Aylesbury.

Bobbie HANVEY

Presenter on *Downtown Radio* in Belfast.

Michael HAPGOOD

Station Manager at BBC *Radio Bristol*.

Ambrose HARCOURT

After a chemistry degree from University, Ambrose worked in the insurance industry for a while as well as Radio 5, a hospital radio station in Tooting.

His first radio broadcast was for the *BBC World Service*, and he's since been heard on *Radio Luxembourg, BBC Radio London, Radio Five Live* and *Southern FM / Ocean FM*.

Ambrose is well known as 'Mr Lurve" in the South because of the high profile of his 'Heart and Soul' programmes seven days a week on *Southern FM* and *Ocean FM* and also does a lot of commercials, voice overs and fashion shows. Likes music, sport and good wines, but not caravans and people who knock success.

[Agent: John Wilcox 01 81 364 4556].

Giulia HARDING

Producer and host of weekday afternoon programme on *BBC Radio Shropshire*.

John HARDING

Born as long ago as 1961 in Hull, he attended the city's grammar school and then joined central heating manufacturer, Stelrad, for what he describes as his "exciting day-job" where he's now progressed to be a management executive. He got into radio thanks to Alma Cooper, the News Editor at local station *Viking FM* who allowed him to help out with sports inserts for no pay.

John's first broadcast came in October 88, when, knowing little about football, he promoted Lincoln City while reading the results!

John has since hosted several programmes on the many incarnations of Viking's AM service, as well as neighbouring *Lincs FM* and *Yorkshire Coast Radio,* where he was one of the station's founders. John has also found time to take part in various RSL stations in the area and organised the only such station to broadcast in Bridlington, *Quay FM*.

He recently presented the Saturday night 'Great Goldmine Gameshow' on *Great Yorkshire Gold* and is proud of the fact that, despite being one of the cheapest and most willing jocks around, who has a reputation of being prepared to do anything to get an air-shift, he has never had to do overnights!

Philip HARDING

While at York University he persuaded Jimi Hendrix to play for £300 and made a profit of £3,000. Later became a BBC News Trainee and his first broadcast was on *Radio Four*.

He became a newsroom sub-editor and then moved to TV for a variety of jobs, all on current affairs programmes. TV couldn't hold Philip Harding though, and he was soon back in radio as editor of 'Today' on *Radio Four* where the highlight of his career to date was covering the Lockerbie disaster.

Philip was then delegated to lead a research project which resulted in the birth of *Radio*

Who's Who in British Radio

Five Live and he is now the Editor of News Programmes at the network. Likes radio, but not 'twee radio'.

Richard HARDING

Richard's career began on the floating *Voice of Peace* radio station off Israel in 1988 and he also worked on board *Radio Caroline* for a while before moving ashore to present regular shows on the Mid Anglia Group stations, *Hereward FM* and *CNFM*, and for the Suffolk Group stations *Radio Orwell and Saxon FM*.

He has also been heard on other stations, such as *Radio Dan* in Tel Aviv, *OCI* in Marbella, Spain and *Radio Calypso 102* in Malta, doing voice overs.

In 1992 he moved to Paris to present (in French) on Parisian Dance music station *Voltage FM*. He's since moved back to the UK and *BBC Radio Cambridgeshire* and now used his real name - until recently he'd been known as Richard West. Lives in Hertfordshire with girlfriend Laura Raymond of AA Roadwatch fame.

Simon HARDING

Host of afternoon programme on *Kix 96* in Coventry, where he also presents the local chart countdown each Saturday.

Gerard HARDY

Director at *Capital Radio*.

Jason HARDY

Went to Brownhills School in Stoke and the Chesterton High School. Jason got into radio by doing a disco for Signal Radio personality Mel Scholes and his first broadcast was on overnights in August 1993.

The highlight of his career to date was getting a regular evening shift on Signal Radio - he likes swimming, tennis and meeting people but definitely not spiders!

Tom HARDY

Former *Radio Caroline* DJ of the seventies and eighties who worked at various stations in Ireland and in the ILR industry

Harry HARISH

Presents the 'Nawrang' Asian music programmes on *BBC Radio Nottingham*.

Jim HARLAND

Jim was the sports producer at *BBC Radio Newcastle* until the early nineties.

John HARLE

John is a producer at *BBC Radio Newcastle*.

Chris HARMANDE

Chris is Sales Director at *London Greek Radio*.

Diane HARPER

Diane is a reporter at *BBC Essex*.

Stephen HARPER

Company Secretary of *CD 603*, in Cheltenham.

Griff HARRIES

Presenter of classical music at *Swansea Sound*.

Bob HARRIS

His career started in 1968 when he was a founder of "Time Out" magazine . He started broadcasting in 1970 on *Radio One*, on a programme called 'Sounds of the Seventies'.

In 1972, he took over as host on the legendary "Old Grey Whistle Test" on BBC 2, and stayed there for seven years, becoming the most memorable TV presenter of rock music of the decade, Whistle Test took him all over the world interviewing many famous personalities. During the seventies he was also a record producer for both EMI and ATLANTIC.

In 1975 he left *Radio One* to join *Radio Luxembourg,* but by 1981 he was back with the Corporation doing local radio work, especially at GLR and programmes on *Radio 1*.

There followed a period at LBC and BFBS as well as the ill-fated Branson overnight sustaining service for ILR stations called *Radio Radio*. In 1994 he signed up for a series of programmes at GLR and is still there in late 1995, on the air four nights a week, having celebrated a quarter of a century in broadcasting. .

Jeff HARRIS

DJ at *Mercia Classic Gold* in Coventry.

Justine HARRIS

Born in 1969 in London, Justine has a degree in psychology. Before getting into radio she "did anything, from tee-shirt printing in

California, to being a Penthouse agony aunt on an 0898 number."

It was through voice over work that she got her break into radio, with Metro Traffic control and her first broadcast was on *Spectrum Radio* in London in January 1993. She managed to drop a cart on some mysterious button and put the station into delay: "I spent the rest of the show pushing buttons at random, with my voice several seconds behind my mouth . . it's been like that ever since!"

With *Metro Traffic* she was heard on almost every station in the south-east, and she then moved to Southend where she set up the *Essex Radio* Group's traffic unit. As well as that work, Justine also makes corporate videos and does radio and TV voice over work. She likes the idea of watching the sunrise every morning, but hates the reality of it.

Keith HARRIS
Keith is a director at *Swansea Sound*.

Nigel HARRIS
Nigel worked on *Radio Caroline* in both the seventies and eighties, earning much respect for his sheer professionalism. He is now a presenter at *Invicta FM*.

Peter HARRIS
Peter is Company Secretary at *Capital Radio*.

Reginald HARRIS
Non executive director at *Radio Mercury*.

Russell HARRIS
Russell qualified as an engineer before entering broadcasting. He was one of the presenters at the 1988 Radio Show and in1988 his programme on *BBC Radio Humberside* won a Sony Award for Best Children's Radio programme.

He's also hosted phone-ins on *BBC Essex* and *Radio Kent* and then moved to *GMR* in Manchester and became a sports producer and presenter at *Radio Five Alive* while also hosting several programmes on BBC local radio's The Night Network.

As well as radio work he's also appeared on cable TV in Arizona and on several programmes in the UK, including Coronation Street, Brookside and Emmerdale Farm.

Sarah HARRIS
Sarah is a reporter at *BBC Radio Newcastle*, working from the Sunderland newsroom.

Charles HARRISON
Head of Sport at *Metro FM*.

James HARRISON
Producer and presenter at *Wiltshire Sound*.

Roger HARRISON
Roger is deputy Chairman at *Capital Radio*.

Veda HARRISON
Veda's teenage dream of working in radio led her to voluntary work at *BBC Radio Nottingham*. She then completed a London University degree before joining the Scripture Union's Sound and Vision Unit as an assistant producer, and in 1995 joined *Premier Radio* in London as a producer and presenter.

Jason HARROLD
Presenter at *Red Dragon Radio* in Cardiff.

Alison HARTLEY
Programme Assistant at *BBC Essex*.

Andrew HARTLEY
Andrew joined *BBC Radio Newcastle* as a News Editor and is now the stations Assistant Editor.

Victor HARTMAN
Born and raised in Grimsby and a keen radio amateur, Victor operated his own successful mobile discotheque and worked as a resident DJ on North Sea Ferries service between Hull and Rotterdam before joining *Radio Caroline* in the 1980s. He has also taken part in several RSL stations and is a shareholder in a bidder for a licence in Kingston upon Hull.

David HARVEY
Head of News and Talks at *Capital Radio* until 1995 when he decided to work as a freelance once again.

Jeff HARWOOD
Jeff is sales manager at *Lincs FM*.

Vernon HARWOOD

The host of the breakfast show each weekday from 6am to 9am at *BBC Radio Gloucester*.

Paul HASHFIELD

Paul is the managing director of *Lantern Radio* in Devon.

David HATCH

Born on the 7th May, 1939, he was educated at St John's School in Leatherhead and at Queen College in Cambridge where he obtained an MA and appeared with John Cleese, Graham Chapman, Bill Oddie and Tim Brooke-Taylor in the 1963 'Footlights Revue'. He then joined the BBC as an actor and writer, notably in 'I'm Sorry, I'll Read that again' in the sixties.

In 1971 David became an Executive Producer with responsibilities for programme development and by the late seventies had become Network Editor based in Manchester. as well as Head of Radio Light Entertainment.

Two years later he became Controller of *Radio Two* and in 1983 moved to take up a similar role at *Radio Four*. In 1986 and 1987 he was the BBC's Head of programmes, and then became Managing Director of all BBC Radio for six years. In 1993 he received the Radio Academy's Creative Award and the same year was appointed Advisor to the Director General. David retired from the Corporation in 1995.

David is married to Ann and has two sons and a daughter. His recreations include Bruegel jigsaws, his family and laughing.

Roy HAWKES

Technical coordinator at *GMR*, Manchester.

Andy HAWKINS

Commercial Director of CLT with special responsibility for *Atlantic 252*.

Chris HAWKSWORTH

Chris is a presenter *at BBC Radio Leeds*.

Brian HAYES

Born in Australia in December 1937, the son of a gold miner, Brian's first broadcast was reading the local news on station 6KJ in Kalgoorlie, Western Australia. He had been frustrated at his job (as a clerk) so just called the station manager, went in for an audition and got a job!

He came to the UK in the early 1970s and worked at *Capital Radio* producing their phone in programme and then in 1976 moved to LBC , in the days when it broadcast from a site of cupboards just off Fleet Street. For many years he hosted his own daily mid morning programme and won an award for a series of programmes from Belfast. His late night phone-in programme currently goes out on ten BBC local radio stations in the South East.

In 1994 he joined *BBC Radio Five* for a daily programme and also hosts a weekly phone-in on *Radio Two*.

John HAYES

John is the host of a mid morning programme (9 to 11.30) each weekday at *BBC Essex*.

Mike HAYES

Broadcasting career began in the RAF at an Aden Forces Broadcasting station in Aden, which was not part of the UK Forces operation which had separate studios.He later did broadcast for the RAF, on Cyprus.

Six feet tall Mike was first heard by UK listeners on *Radio City* at the end of 1966, but he got worried about some of the less glamourous folk then eying the fort-based stations and so moved up to Yorkshire for a more gentle life. He joined *Radio 270* where he soon became a leading breakfast show presenter, alternating with Paul Burnett.

In early 1967 Mike was promoted to become the station's joint programme manager. When Radio 270 closed in August 1967, he arranged for former colleagues in the RAF to use a rescue helicopter at nearby RAF Leconfield to fly programme tapes out to the ship for the last day as the weather was too rough for a tender.

Mike was better known on the air as 'Mikey Mo' and as a theme tune used 'There's a Rainbow Round my Shoulder". A very proficient and personable DJ, he was one of the first British jocks to sing a theme tune as an intro to his programme - an innovation he'd heard on a tape of a New York station.

A great fan of Nancy Sinatra, rum and coke and lamb chops, Mike left the UK to further his career in German radio, made a fortune there and never came back!

Phillip HAYTON

Phillip joined the offshore station *Radio 270* as a newsreader in 1967 while still at University and after the station closed he went on to the BBC as a journalist.

In 1980s became one of the regular presenters on the BBC 1 TV programme 'The Nine O'Clock News'.

Kate HAYWARD

Kate is a reporter at *BBC Radio Essex*.

Hollywood HAZE

Afternoon jock at *Atlantic 252* in 1985.

Arthur HAZLERIGG

Director at *The New Leicester Sound*.

Bob HAZLEWOOD

Host of a regular folk music programme on *BBC Radio Sheffield*.

Gavin HEALEY

Presenter at *Downtown Radio* in Belfast.

Martyn HEALY

Commercial production manager at *Metro FM*.

Paul HEANEY

Sales Manager of *Atlantic 252*, .

Paul HEINEY

Born in Sheffield in the 1940s, he became a stage sweeper in rep' and a scenery builder after leaving school. He then worked as a lighting technician and joined BBC Television as a trainee assistant film recordist.

In 1971 he joined *Radio Humberside* as a producer, moving to *Radio Four* where he worked on 'Today' and 'Checkpoint', before moving back to television as a 'That's Life' presenter in 1979 and later the 'Food and drink' programme. Paul is married to writer and presenter Libby Purves he has two two children.

Gerald HEDGES

Gerald is the Finance Director and Company Secretary at *Fortune 1458*, as well as Group Finance Director of the Allied Radio Group .

Bill HEINE

Bill hosts a morning programme from 9.30 to 12 noon on *BBC Radio Oxford*.

John HELLINGS

John spent much of his life working in printing and publishing and got into radio by making lots of audition tapes for others at hospital radio and decided to do one himself, which resulted in an interview at a new station, *Radio Wyvern* in Worcestershire. He got his break on the air by sitting in for someone else who preferred to play in a cricket match to doing the programme.

For nearly five years John hosted a jazz programme at *Radio Wyvern* and then freelanced for the BBC, before giving up his daytime job to set up the new Gold service at *Severn Sound* in Gloucester, which is now part of the Supergold network. He also does voice over and production work.

Geoff HEMMING

Presenter at *The Pulse*, in Bradford until 1995 when he joined *Sun City FM* in Sunderland as Programme Controller. He only stayed a short time and left in the Autumn.

James HEMMINGS

DJ at *Fox FM* in Oxford.

Jonathan HEMMINGS

Educated at Kings College of London University, he got in to radio by working at *Hospital Radio Colchester* and sending a demo tape to *Essex Radio*.

Jonathan worked on *Caroline* in Summer 1990 as 'Johnnie Blackburn' and then moved back ashore to *Essex Radio,* freelancing for a couple of years.

Jonathan shocked Mariah Carey by asking her if she married Tommy Mottola to advance her career, while confessing that the highlight of his own career was getting Maria McKee and Rebecca De Ruvo to put their feet behind their head while he interviewed them.

In 1994 Essex gave him a full time job at the station and he now hosts the 'Red Hot Late Show' on the groups FM station.

Who's Who in British Radio

Barbara HENDERSON
Barbara is an Alnwick-based producer for BBC Radio Newcastle.

Kelvin HENDERSON
Host of a programme each tuesday night at 9pm on *BBC Wiltshire Sound*.

Michael HENDERSON
Born in Nottingham in 1942, and better known to Ulster radio listeners as Hendi, Michael made his first radio broadcast on a Radio One Club programme with Tony Brandon after going up to producer Aiden Day (see elsewhere) and just asking him if he could!

He also freelanced for the BBC and appeared on 'Zoom In', on Ulster TV. He later joined *Downtown Radio*, Belfast's first ILR station, and has hosted most programmes, including the coveted breakfast slot.

Neil HENDERSON
Neils career began in hospital radio, and professionally at the BBC on Grandstand as a Scottish football reporter. From TV he moved across to BFBS, Sky and then to Radio Five, before his current roles at *Scot FM* and London News.

Although neil hasn't yet had the highlight of his career, his most humourous moment came during his first TV commentary, when he managed to miss the first goal! He doesn't like bigots, arrogance or programme controllers and is also a full Equity member.

Mike HENFIELD
Mike was Station Controller for the GWR Group, as well as being Station Director of Brunel and *Classic Gold*. In the early 1990s he moved to *Red Rose Radio* to become Managing Director, and in 1994 joined the new regional station in Lancashire, *Jazz FM*, as Programme Controller.

Andy HENLY
Andy is a presenter at *Brunel Classic Gold* .

Nick HENNEGAN
Born on the 14th August in Birmingham he attended Wheeler's Lane School in the city and his first job was in the police force. From there he moved to London to become a social worker which led to his pursuing a career in broadcasting.

His first broadcast was just before Christmas 1981 on BRMB, back in Birmingham, and he hosted the station's 'Morning Call' and 'Whaddyawant' for some years, as well as 'Romantics' - a programme of love songs.

Frank HENNESSY
Presenter at *CBC* in Cardiff in the early 1980's and now the host of a lunchtime programme on *BBC Radio Wales* six days a week. His 11 to 1.00 programme on Sunday lunchtimes is one of the the most listened to on Radio Wales.

Mike HENRY
Head of Commercial production at Londonderry station, *Q102.9*.

Stuart and Ollie HENRY
Born in Edinburgh on 24th February, 1942, his first job was as an actor with BBC radio, following which he joined a rep' company. he decided to move into pirate radio when it was all happening in the sixties, but couldn't settle to life on board *Radio Scotland*'s pitching rolling former lightship anchored off Ayr, Scotland, so became one of the first to pre-record his programmes from the station's studio in Glasgow.

His career in radio spans some twenty years. While on Radio Scotland, David Jacobs heard him and introduced him to his agent Bunny Lewis, who quickly arranged for stuart to get one of the first programmes on *Radio One* when it opened. Stuart quickly made Sunday morning's his own; however the BBC didn't understand Stuart's then developing illness, multiple sclerosis, which occasionally impaired his speech and didn't renew his contract.

When his contract ended with Radio One Stuart was thinking of giving up radio altogether. Instead, he accepted Luxembourg's offer and joined in May 1975. Stuart met Ollie when he was travelling from gig to gig. She was a well-known model, but gave up her career to share in Stuart's work.

When she joined Luxembourg, she became the first women newsreader in British radio and co-hosted his programmes with him until he gave up regular programmes in the 1980s. They now live in Luxembourg.

John HENTY

Born in Croydon in 1936, he worked initially in PR with BEA and then at station KIST in Santa Barbara, California. On returning to the UK he did some work in hospital radio, and joined *BBC Radio Brighton* when it launched in February 1968, where he presented local radio's first travel programme 'Travel Bag'. John ran a museum on Hastings Pier for some years and has now retired to concentrate on his family and other interests.

David HEPWORTH

Presenter of a programme at 4pm each Sunday afternoon on *GLR*.

Vince HERBERT

Vince is the programme controller of South London station *Choice FM*.

Johnny HERO

Presenter at *Downtown Radio* in Belfast.

Raymond HERVOE

Programme Controller of *Nevis Radio*, Scotland.

Angela HESLOP

After gaining a degree in drama and media studies at Leeds, Angela worked in London for the British Theatre Association. She got into radio after returning to Liverpool to get married and was working part time for a local youth theatre project; she saw a job advertised for a receptionist at *Radio Merseyside*. Her first broadcast on the station was reviewing a play for the breakfast show and reading the religious news.

After a period as a receptionist she became an education secretary and the radio production assistant. Now a fully fledged producer, she presents a weekly arts programme ('Artwaves' and various other material for many other programmes at Radio Merseyside).

The highlight of Angela's career was interviewing Sir Derek Jacob, an actor whom she'd admired for many years while the funniest event involved someone wheeling a supermarket trolley past her during a live broadcast, and yelling about the price of peas.

Peter HETHERINGTON

Nostalgia presenter on *Great North Radio*.

Ivan HEWETT

Presenter on *BBC Radio 3*.

Dave HICKMAN

Dave is the presenter of the 8pm to midnight slot each weekday evening on *Heart 100.7* .

Katie HICKMAN

Kate is a news reporter at *Radio Leicester*.

Nicky HICKMAN

Financial Controller at *Premier Radio* .

Stuart HICKMAN

Presenter at *Beacon Radio*.

Jim HICKS

Jim was the information and OB officer at *Ocean Sound* and also worked at *Southern Sound* in Brighton. In mid 1995 he joined *Radio Aire* in Leeds as Programme Director.

Robin HICKS

Born on 6th December 1942 in Purley, he went to school in Essex and College of Agriculture in Devon. His first job was as a farm labourer and shepherd and he came into radio as a reporter in 1968.

Robin joined the BBC and was responsible for many farming oriented programmes on *Radio Four* for many years until becoming Head of Network Radio in Bristol.

Chris HILL

Presenter at *Red Dragon Radio* in Cardiff.

Dominic HILL

Dominic is a presenter on *Invicta FM* in Kent.

Jane HILL

Born in 1964, Jane has been in radio for nine years and made it through to the semi-finals of the TV quiz 'Mastermind'. Until recently she was the News Manager at *Invicta FM* in Kent and recently joined *Lincs FM* as Programme Controller.

Mike HILL
News producer at *BBC Radio Humberside* in the 1980s.

Peter HILL
Peter is a director of *Radio Wyvern.*

Roy HILL
Roy is now a news producer with responsibilities for South Cheshire at *BBC Radio Stoke on Trent.*

Stephen HILL
A director at *Fox FM* in Oxford.

Beverly HILLS
Host of the Saturday afternoon stretch on *Atlantic 252.*

John HILLS
While working as a volunteer teacher on the Pacific island of Tarawa, he was suddenly drafted in to run the island's very primitive radio station and his first broadcast was in a tin hut with chickens clucking around his feet!

Returning to the UK he was a producer at *BBC Radio Blackburn* from 1970 to 1975 and then spent five years as a regional producer at the *BBC Norwich* outpost , before going freelance for another ten years, notably as the producer of 'Does he take Sugar?'. Since 1992 he's been the host of 'Norfolk Tonight' for the BBC and he also does media training and makes company 'in house' tapes.

Elisa HILTON
Elisa joined *Minster FM* in 1994 and hosted the late night programmes until Autumn 1995 when she left to join *Aire FM* in nearby Leeds.

James HILTON
One of the presenters at the 1993 launch of *Yorkshire Coast Radio* in Scarborough, he moved to *The Wave* in Blackpool six months later.

Richard HILTON
Treasurer of the Community Radio Association.

Geoffrey HINDS
Geoffrey is a director at *Downtown Radio.*

Frazer HINES
Born in Horsforth near Leeds, he trained as a dancer and appeared in half a dozen films and countless TV series, most notably as Joe Sugden in Emmerdale Farm. For the last few years he's been a regular weekend presenter on *BBC Radio York*, where he usually co-hosts programmes with his wife, Olympic champion water-skier, Liz Hobbs.

Philip HINTON
Managing Director at *Essex Radio* from the late 1980s until early 1995.

Dave HISKETT
Dave worked as a production projectionist at the EMI film dubbing theatre in London, and then as a VTR operator for Rank studios. In May 1988 he answered an advert for presenters for the satellite station *Radio Nova* and has since worked at *Radio Mercury, County Sound, Essex Radio, A Roadwatch* and the now defunct *Airport Information Radio* where he once hiccoughed his way through a live read sequence!

He currently presents the weekdays and Saturday early evening show on *Breeze AM* in Southend and also a Sunday afternoon show on *Mercury Extra AM* in Crawley, as well as holding down a Friday morning spot at *Channel Radio* on the M20 in Kent.

David likes chocolate fudge cake and riding, as well as good feedback from listeners and hates people yelling at him during live reads.

Lesley HITCHEN
Lesley was a broadcast journalist at *BBC Radio Berkshire*, which recently merged with Radio Oxford to form Radio Thames Valley.

Bob HOAD
Station Director of *Southern Sound* in Brighton.

Peter HOARE
Documentary producer at *BBC Radio Four.*

Peter HOBDAY
Born on 16th February in Dudley in the West Midlands, Peter attended St Chad's College in Wolverhampton and then Leicester University. After National service in Paris he joined the BBC and was first heard on the *Home Service* in 1957.

Work on the *World Service* followed but he is better known in the UK for his work on *Radio Four*, which has included being the resident presenter of 'The Financial World Tonight' and 'World At One' as well as 'Today'.

Chris HODDER
News producer at *BBC Radio Newcastle*.

Shaun HODGETTS
Shaun is the News Editor for *GWR FM* East.

Ann HODGSON
Born on the 14th March in Harpenden, she was discovered at a party in Dubai and became a newsreader before progressing to host an instrumental programme. Ann then hosted a classical music programme twice a week and a year later was offered a mid-morning magazine programme.

She now hosts weekday late evening programmes on *Great Yorkshire Gold*, as well as doing voice overs for video and audio tapes for Linguaphone. Ann also runs a pub in her spare time.

Charles HODKINSON
Mid-morning presenter at *BBC Radio Lincolnshire*.

Paul HOGAN
DJ at *Viking FM* in Hull.

Keith HOLDEN
For six years until 1985, Keith worked for Mecca Leisure as a DJ, as well as satisfying an urge he'd got from Radio Luxembourg DJs in the seventies to get into radio, by broadcasting on south London pirate *TKO* - it stood for "total knock out". He bombarded stations with demo tapes and finally got a gig with *Marcher Sound* in Wrexham on the late show from where he progressed to drive time shifts and sports.

Between 1991 and 1993 he did programmes on various satellite stations in addition to his Marcher shows and in 1993 joined *Essex FM* where he's remained to this day. He's also working on a project for a TV series based on "lurve" and claims to have been the first to break the news of Margaret Thatcher's resig-

nation and announce the outbreak of the Gulf War on his late night programme.

Keith likes not only David Letterman Show, but writing articles about radio people, but not people who won't smile, or say please and thank you.

Carole HOLDER
Director of Signal Group of stations.

Noddy HOLDER
West Midland's singer and guitarist Noddy played in several bands before forming Slade in 1969 - their first two singles were sadly under-rated (and ignored by radio programmers) but they topped most European singles charts for the next five years and then spent another five years enjoying great success on the festival and stadium circuit.

In 1974 Noddy starred in a film about a fictitious band called Flame, in which they visited Tommy Vance playing a DJ on a pirate station on the old Radio City fort during an armed raid - a set-up for TV publicity. Noddy has always been interested in radio and took little persuading to host his own radio programmes. He's still heard on certain select stations - including Piccadilly in Manchester.

Russell HOLDING
Russell is programme controller at *Eclipse*, the cable station in Sutton, Surrey.

Geoffrey HOLLIMAN
Geoffrey's career in broadcasting began with Southern TV, then Yorkshire Tyne Tees (both in sales). After a period in poster advertising, in August 1984 he joined *Radio Clyde* and five years later was appointed the company's Sales and Marketing Director. He is now S& M Director for the entire Scottish Radio Holdings Group and also the chairman of the Marketing Society in Scotland.

Andy HOLLINS
Presenter at Viking Radio in the mid-1980s, he moved to Radio Tees. He is now a presenter at *Power FM* in Hampshire.

Paul HOLLINS
Presenter at *Piccadilly Radio*, Manchester.

Who's Who in British Radio

Mike HOLLIS

Mike Hollis must be one of the fittest DJs in radio! Every day he goes jogging, swimming, plays football, cricket or squash. He used to run a mobile disco whilst working in a solicitors' office, and then as a salesman. After he had a serious road accident he had to give up his job because the doctors advised him that he shouldn't drive again for another year, so then he turned to full time dee-jaying.

Mike's radio career began at Birmingham Hospital Broadcasting Network (BHBN) in the mid seventies, followed by a year at *BBC Radio Birmingham*. He then moved across town to *BRMB* for five years before joining *Radio Luxembourg* in July 1982. While there he presented 208's early evening shows and the major weekly chart show and returned to Britain's Second City in 1993. It was in the Grand Duchy that Mike experienced the highest and lowest points of his career: "Joining the Great 208 was terrific, but seeing it close totally heartbreaking."

In September 1993, he joined the city's all gold station, *Xtra AM* and remains one of their most popular on air voices. A strong West Bromwich Albion supporter, Mike also likes lager, chips, Coronation Street and women, and doesn't like know it all DJs and two-faced politicians - or people who smoke in restaurants.

Patricia HOLLIS

Patricia is a director of *Broadland FM*.

Phil HOLMES

Phil drives the afternoon programme (from 2 until 6pm) each weekday, as well as the breakfast programme (from 6 until 10am) each saturday and Sunday on *Minster FM* in York.

Peter HOLMES

Programme Controller at *Essex FM*.

Bob HOLNESS

Born a Scorpio in South Africa many years ago, he went to Ashford Grammar School in Kent and Maidstone college of Art. He went back to South Africa to work in printing, but discovered he liked acting and then went into South African radio as an actor in a serial in the fifties.

On returning to the UK in the early sixties, he first worked in TV on Junior 'Criss Cross Quiz' and 'World In Action' for Granada TV. He presented some programmes for *Radio One* in its early years, including Housewives Choice and Mid-day Spin and then moved to *LBC* in the seventies to co-present the station's highest rated programme 'AM' with Douglas Cameron.

While on LBC, Bob won the Variety Club's 'ILR Personality of the year Award' for his work on the station's breakfast programme. Now better known for his presentation of 'Blockbusters' TV quiz series, which is now seen daily on *Sky One*, and on the ITV network and a prime time Saturday evening programme offering the largest ever prize on UK broadcasting - a house.

Bob is still a keen radio man and is also heard each week on *Radio Two*. He has two daughters who are both pop singers and likes gardening and music.

Penelope HOLTON

Penelope was Head of Promotions and Press Relations for the Chiltern Group of stations until 1994 when she was appointed Chief Executive of Severn Sound.

Tom HOOPER

Began his radio career at *Trent FM* in Nottingham and then moved to *KCBC* in Kettering. In 1995 Tom joined the *Radio Magazine*, the industry's only weekly publication, where he is now Editorial Assistant.

Chris HOPKINS

Was originally a sales and marketing manager and an electronics engineer and then got into radio by organising a 'Flying Eye' traffic watch aircraft for *2CR-FM* .

When 2CR later required a presenter Chris presented his first programme from an aircraft doing a 'Flying Eye' travel report. he has been heard on the sister station, *Classic Gold 828*.

As well as presenting, Chris spent 2 years as Promotions and Sponsorship Manager, presented breakfast, morning, afternoons, drive-time and evening shows as well as being Sports Editor. The highlight of his radio career was working in Florida and France and meeting Linda Lusardi.

Anne HOPPER

One of the true characters of local radio, Anne initially worked in radio as a secretary and general assistant at *BBC Radio Cumbria*, Anne's first broadcast came in September 1992 when someone fell ill. Radio is her life (which she thinks is very sad at her age!) and the highlight of her career was broadcasting from a lifeboat and a hot air balloon in the same week - "it was hilarious" she recalls.

Anne likes people who talk to her, and dislikes those who run away when they see her coming. She was once described by a listener as an elderly John Noakes - those who saw the early 'Blue Peter ' programmes will understand.

Matt HOPPER

Born in Hertfordshire in the fifties, Mark went to Portsmouth Polytechnic and then had a variety of jobs including a spell on some local pirate stations, but knew he wanted to be in big time radio. Eventually he was accepted by *Radio Victory*, the ILR station in Portsmouth, where he presented their 'Morning Call' programme each weekday morning for several years in the early eighties.

Matt once cited meeting Mick Jagger as the most exciting moment of his career. When *Ocean Sound* took over the franchise he moved there and is still one of the area's most popular DJS.

Tony HORDER

Tony is one of the weekday DJs at *Ram FM*.

Nicky HORNE

He joined *Capital Radio* in September 1973 and has since been involved in numerous programmes including the award-winning "Your Mother Wouldn't Like It" programme. Nicky presents the evening sports magazine programme "Sportswire" with Mark Webster for Wire TV.

In 1992 he joined *Classic FM* and presented an educational programme each Sunday afternoon.

Nicky is currently hosting an afternoon programme on *Virgin 1215*.

Tony HORNE

Presenter at *GWR FM East* in Swindon.

Guy HORNSBY

Born on 24th March, 1958, in Twickenham, Guy was a computer programmer with Honda UK before his radio career.

He got into radio by answering the phones at BBC Radio London and in January 1974 joined them as a Station Assistant.. By 1980 he'd become a producer, handling the award winning Robbie Vincent phone-in programme and then from 1981 to 1985 he produced the Tony Blackburn daily strip on the station. During that time he was presenter of BBC TV's 'Saturday superstore' for a while.

After working for the *World Service*, Guy joined *Ocean Sound* in 1986 as breakfast Presenter and was programme manager there from 1989 to 1990. In 1990 he was made Group Programme Controller of *Southern Radio* group - he stayed there until 1994, during which time he also worked as a continuity announcer at TVS, based in nearby Southampton.

In 1994 Guy moved north to Manchester and joined *KISS FM 102* as Managing Director.

The highlight of Guy's radio career was teaching Prince Charles to jock at the opening of Ocean Sound (in October 1986). His most humorous moment was being rushed to hospital after a bulk-eraser exploded during his breakfast programme (maybe there's a limit just how much old material anything can take?).

Guy likes good radio, good friends and good food, but not bad radio, stuffy people and all the many 'isms'.

Linda HORSWELL

Linda is currently the Sales Manager at the two *Plymouth Sound* stations.

Toby HORTON

Born on 18th February, 1947 in London Toby was educated at Westminster School and at Christ Church College, Oxford. He worked for many years in the world of merchant banking and arrived in the radio business in 1979 he was head-hunted by *Radio Tees* after they'd advertised in The Economist for a Managing Director.

Toby's first broadcast was on Radio Tees in the 'North East Business News' programme and he was part of the team which engineered the station's rescue in the 1980s by its merger with neighbouring Metro Radio to form the Metro Group.

In 1991 Toby returned to broadcasting as a founder of the *Minster* radio company which successfully bid for the York licence, the highlight of his career. In 1992 he arranged Minster's buy out of *Yorkshire Coast Radio* and subsequent successful application for the Scarborough licence.

In 1995 he resigned from the boards of Minster and YCR to concentrate on the group's new acquisition, *Sun City* in Sunderland, where he is Deputy Chairman.

Toby is also Managing Director of *Heritage Media*, the UK's major supplier of classic and nostalgic speech radio programmes to stations all over the UK. He is also Chairman of *Baltic Radio Group plc*. He finds every day in the radio industry humourous - cites his favourite people as The Radio Authority and claims to dislike grovelling! Enough Said.

John HOSKEN

Born in 1937 in Cornwall, John was educated in Truro and joined a local newspaper after leaving school. Following National Service in the RAF he joined the Daily Herald newspaper and made his first broadcast in 1966 on the Home Service.

Since then he's hosted many programmes on *Radio Four*, including 'World at One' and 'International Assignment' and has also appeared as a contributor on many programmes on *Radio Two*.

David HOULT

A Birmingham boy by birth, David attended Redditch High School, Manchester University and the Manchester School of Music before becoming a musician and music teacher.

His first broadcast was in 1975 and in the 1980's he presented programmes on *Radio Three*, such as 'Music for Pleasure'.

Fred HOUSEGO

Former taxi driver Fred shot to national fame when he won 'Mastermind' in the seventies following which he became a TV presenter on Thames TV. He now hosts a Saturday evening programme called 'Laugh-In' on *London Newsradio FM*.

Kevin HOWARD

Kevin is currently the Programme Controller and also a DJ at *Marcher Gold*.

Margaret HOWARD

A Surrey girl, Margaret was educated in various convents and at Indiana University in the USA. On leaving University she asked the BBC for a job as an announcer, but accepted a position in the Corporation as a clerk and messenger.

Her first broadcast was ringing a bicycle bell on a children's programme on the *Home Service*, but as a presenter she hosted 'Forces Favourites', Listeners' Choice and 'The World this Weekend' on *Radio Two* and *Radio Four*. She also worked extensively on the *World Service* and in 1982 hosted the first international phone-in on the service.

In 1974 she took over the 'Pick of the Week' programmes on *Radio Four* and hosted the programme for almost twenty years; she joined *Classic FM* in 1993.

Mel HOWARD

Canadian born Mel first saw light of day in 1941 and arrived on these hallowed shores in the early sixties. He worked at EMI Records factory in Hayes for a while and, after a trip back to Canada when he worked on local stations in Winnipeg, returned to the UK in 1965 and joined *Radio Caroline*.

The following year Mel moved north of the border to *Radio Scotland* where he became a regular DJ based on the ship off Ayr.

After Radio Scotland closed Mel didn't like the look of Radio one, it didn't bob around as much as his two previous stations, so he caught a plane home and has since been hosting a regular TV series as well as radio work.

Chris HOWE
Host of an angling programme on BBC Radio Northamptonshire.

Richard HOWE
Richard is a producer and presenter at BBC *Radio Devon and Dorset.*

Jeremy HOWELL
Reporter at BBC *Radio Solent.*

Jude HOWELLS
After many years as a producer with the BBC Radio Features Department and a period at the BBC's Continuing Education Department, (when she was known as Judith Howells) Jude is now the Assistant Editor (Programmes) at BBC GLR.

Railton HOWES
Presenter of programmes and features on fishing at *BBC Radio Newcastle.*

Ivan HOWLETT
Ivan was once the Editor of the Local Radio Programme Department at Broadcasting House and he's now the Managing Editor at BBC *Radio Suffolk.*

Kevin HOWLETT
Producer of documentaries on music business history on *BBC Radio One* in the 1990s.

Andy HUDSON
Andy is a director at Unique Broadcasting's Special Projects Division.

Jerry HUDSON
Jerry is the Chairman of *Eclipse FM* in Sutton, Surrey.

John HUDSON
John is the Finance Director of *Eleven Seventy.*

Matt HUDSON
News Editor at *CNFM* in Cambridge.

Ednyfed HUDSON-DAVIES
Ednyfed is the Chairman of *Lincs FM.*

John HUESTON
Presenter at *Downtown Radio* in Belfast .

Kevin HUFFER
Radio career began in hospital radio, then RSLs and in 1995 he joined *Wey Valley Radio* in Alton (Hampshire) to host an afternoon drive time programme.

Chris HUGHES
Chris is the Station Director at *Trent FM* and *GEM AM* in Nottingham.

Daniel HUGHES
Daniel is the Director of Operations at World Radio network, the international radio consolidation broadcaster.

Donny HUGHES
Educated at George Herriot's school in the Scottish capital and then worked for British Gas for a while while working as a part time DJ in a nightclub. When they sponsored a weekly dance music show in September 1987, Donny was asked to host it and two years later he became a full time presenter on *Radio Forth's* Drive Time show.

In February 1990, the station split its AM and FM frequencies and Donny found himself at the helm of many programmes, including breakfast, afternoon and evenings.

In September 1992 he moved to *Max-AM* to present "Drive Time with Donny", and then in May 1994 he became the station's Music Coordinator - although he still hosts the station's Drive Time programme.

He's also appeared in a TV commercial as a featured actor and the highlight of his radio career was broadcasting live from Hollyrood Park during Fringe Sunday at the Edinburgh Festival and a live programme from Seaworld in Florida. Another memorable event was being driven around a stage of the Scottish Rally by top driver Malcolm Wilson - Donny loves cars and driving, but isn't too fond of bad drivers and ignorant people.

Who's Who in British Radio

Franklin HUGHES
Managing Director of *Choice FM*'s Birmingham station until September 1995, when he left following a major disagreement with the Board.

Gerry HUGHES
Gerry is a producer and presenter at *BBC Wiltshire Sound*.

Graham HUGHES
Born in Shrewsbury in 1953, he worked as a teacher in the USA for a while before his first radio job, on hospital radio in 1976. He joined *Severn Sound*, Gloucester's ILR, in early 1981 and then moved a few miles north to *Radio Wyvern* to present a daily afternoon programme. After getting married he moved across to the BBC where he is now a producer at *BBC Radio Shropshire*.

Henry HUGHES
Engineer in charge at *BBC Radio Shropshire*.

Ian HUGHES
A Londoner by birth, Ian was at one stage a motor technician and a windsurfing instructor, but his first radio job was at *Radio Tees* where he presented a variety of programmes, including a spell as Head of Children's Programmes. He came a close second in the awards for best children's programmes.

Nick HULL
Born on the day after Boxing Day in 1960, Nick's career began as an engineering technician and he cut his radio teeth on hospital radio before moving into the business full-time at the tender age of 19.

In Summer 1980 he sailed the Mediterranean with the *Voice of Peace,* and then flew back to Ireland and *KCR FM* where he was a presenter, reporter, commercial producer and eventually Programme Controller.

In 1983 he returned to the UK and a job at *Radio Wyvern* (ILR in Worcester) where he moved from presentation to News Reporter (but still dabbling in Commercial Production).

In September 1995, Nick moved to Pebble Mill to become a senior sports producer at the

BBC before moving on the Yorkshire stations (*Radio Leeds and Radio Humberside*).

In 1986 Nick joined BBC Radio Nottingham as sports reporter and programme presenter and the following year moved back to Yorkshire once again and a similar role at *BBC Radio Humberside*.

A year later he was on the move again, this time to *Marcher Sound* in Wrexham, and six months later his love affair with the city with which he shares a name lured him back to a job at *Viking Radio* as Deputy News Editor. He frequently presented programmes over the next five years at the station, leaving only for a better position as News Editor at one of the south's main ILR stations, *Essex Radio*.

Nick is a true radio all-rounder having been involved in advertising copywriting, voice-over work and presenting outside broadcasts and promotions.

Chris HULME
Station engineer at *BBC Radio Sheffield*.

Gloria HUNNIFORD
Born in Portadown Co Armagh on 10th April, 1940, she started singing at the age of nine and starred on many TV programmes in Ireland. She became a radio presenter in Canada in 1959 and on returning to Europe joined the BBC as a production assistant, while continuing her singing career.

After releasing a record she was given some interviewing work on *Radio Ulster* and eventually was given the station's breakfast programme as well as 'A Taste of Hunni'.

In 1981 she was invited to fill in for Jimmy Young as a holiday relief following which *Radio Two* gave her her own daily programme. She also hosted some programmes for the *BBC World Service* including 'Album Time' and the following year was one of the hosts for the 'Royal Variety Performance'.

After Eamonn Andrews confronted her with the Red Book for TIYL, she was made the Variety Club's 'Radio Personality of the Year' in 1983. Since then she's presented her own afternoon programme on *Radio Two* and lives in Kent with her daughters.

Who's Who in British Radio

Jon HUNT
Jon is the host of a Saturday morning programme from 9am to 1pm on *Southern Counties Radio*.

Justin HUNT
John is the Head of Consumer and Public Relations at *Capital Radio*.

Nigel HUNT
Installer and maintenance engineer with radio equipment suppliers, Eastern Electronics.

Geoff HUNTER
Chairman of *Oasis Radio* in St Albans.

Neil HUNTER
neil is the Marketing Manager of *Metro FM* and *Great North Radio*.

Tom HUNTER
Managing Director of regional, Scot FM.

Shane HUNTLEY
Very experienced radio host with an international pedigree, Shane's world tour of stations has included sojourns in New Zealand and Hong Kong, and in 1994 he was programme producer at *Island Sound* on Gozo, Malta. In 1995 he returned to the UK to join *Premier Radio*, London's new Christian radio station, where he now is a host of the station's flagship breakfast programme.

Mike HURLEY
Mike joined *Pennine Radio* as a DJ in the seventies, and then later moved to BBC *Radio Humberside* where he has presented a weekly Saturday morning show ever since.

His is a well-known voice on many radio stations all over the world, as he is a prolific voice-over artiste able to quickly turn around a variety of voices - the best known of which (Bill Bore) was used to lead the Radio Advertising Bureau's campaign in early 1995.

Phil HURLEY
Sales director at *Mercia Sound* in Coventry for several years. In 1995 he joined the city's new specialist music station, *Kix 96* in a similar role.

Mark HURRELL
Born 31st July 1954 in Poole, Dorset, Mark attended Kings College in Taunton and a French University before working in the petroleum industry for while. He did some promotions work for CBS and spent six months as a tour manager for EMI cassettes as well as hospital radio work at *Radio Wey* in Surrey and in 1976 went out to Israel to join the *Voice of Peace* offshore radio station.

In 1978 Mark joined the BBC as a travelling station assistant, working at a dozen BBC local stations, including *BBC Radio Derby*.

In 1980 he did a week at *Radio One* and then joined new ILR station *Centre Sound* in Leicester. He is now a senior producer at *BBC Radio Gloucester*.

Mike HURRY
News Editor at *Moray Firth Radio*.

Chris HURST
Sales Manager at *Signal One*, Stoke on Trent.

Dominic HURST
News Journalist at *BBC Radio Berkshire*.

Christine HUSSEY
Journalist at *BBC Radio Cornwall*.

Kenny HUTCHISON
Kenny is a presenter at *Scot FM*.

John HUTSON
John is the host of a programme of classic rock each Sunday on *BBC Radio Gloucester*.

Paul HUTTON
Reporter at Network News.

Margaret HYDE
Margaret was the station manager of *BBC Radio Cambridgeshire* and in 1994 she joined *BBC Essex* as Managing Editor.

Stephanie HYNER
Stephanie is a news producer at *BBC Radio York*.

Jack HYWELL-DAVIES
From 1987 to 1994 Jack scripted and presented the *BBC Radio Four* Sunday morning programme, 'Morning Has Broken' which was one of the BBC's most popular religious programmes with a regular audience of 350,000.

In 1995 he transferred the programme across to London's new all Christian music station, *Premier Radio,* where he also has a Wednesday evening programme.

Tony INCHLEY
Programme controller at new Midlands station, *Radio XL* and much involved in the planning stages, he resigned just two weeks after the station launched in May 1995.

Lord INGLEWOOD
Born in 1951 and educated at Eton and Trinity College, Cambridge, he also attended the Cumbria College of Agriculture and was called to the Bar, Lincoln's Inn in 1975. In 1989 he became MEP for Cumbria and Lancashire North and in 1993 was appointed Deputy Lieutenant for Cumbria.

In July 1995 he was appointed Parliamentary Under-Secretary to the Department of National Heritage, the Government department responsible for setting broadcasting policy in the UK.

Tom INGRAM
A former rock'n'roll club DJ and promoter, Tom got into radio by doing some programme son pirate stations in the 1980s - his first broadcast was with *Skyline Radio* in 1984. In 1986 he did the first of some occasional programmes for Radio One and got some promotional work at BBC Radio GLR.

He took part in several RSL broadcasts, including *Raiders FM and* now hosts a rock'n'roll show on CMR- Country Music Radio.

AS well as radio, Tom also promotes concerts and supplies fifties paraphernalia as well as working as a film extra. The highlight of his career was a one hour rock'n'roll show on Radio One, following which the BBC switchboard lit up with fans wanting a regular programme.

Tom's most humourous event was his part in the film 'Quadrophenia' (he's the one whose finger Sting shuts in the cigarette case). Tom is wild about Michelle Pfeifer, French food and rock'n'roll, but not sixties music, football or programmers who think there is no demand for his favourite music.
CALL- Rock'n'roll Weekends 0181663 6355.

John INVERDALE
In the 1980s John was a presenter on *BBC Radio Two*. When *Radio Five* took over most radio sport activities, John joined them and now hosts a drive time programme each weekday

Ian IRVINE
Ian is the Chairman of Capital Radio Group Plc.

Felicity IRWIN
felicity is the Chairman of *2CR* in Bournemouth.

Keith ISAAC
Keith is the Finance Director and also the Chairman of *Wey Valley 102* in Alton.

Mark JACKS
Born on the 10th November, 1960 in Newcastle-upon-Tyne, David's first broadcast was on the *Voice of Nigeria* short wave station. After beginning as a continuity announcer he graduated into journalism with several BBC and ILR local stations and is now "blissfully employed" at Kiss 102 in Manchester "until the world discovers I'm more talented than Chris Evans."

"Every day's a highlight - that's why we call it showbiz" claims news-reader Mark although admits that once in a moment of panic he forgot Dame Kiri Te Kanama's name and called her Dame Edna!

Andy JACKSON
Born in London, Andy attended Dulwich College and got into radio helping out with several London pirate station, notably *Horizon, Solar* the UK's first soul station, *Radio Invicta* in 1978. In 1988 he became a swing jock at *Essex Radio* and then in 1990 moved to *KCBC* in Kettering to do the late show and some weekend shifts.

The following year Andy moved back to *Essex Radio*, first on overnights, then late show and in 1994, to host the lunchtime programme on the group's FM station. He also works as an AA Roadwatch reporter and freelance voice over artiste. Andy now hosts the weekend evening programmes on *Essex FM*.

Gerry JACKSON
Gerry is a producer at *BBC Radio Newcastle*.

Nick JACKSON
Born in 1952 in Tanzania, Nick went to school in Bolton, Lancs and his first job was as a trainee accountant. . In August 1975 he joined Portsmouth ILR station *Radio Victory* after meeting Dave Symonds at a DJ convention. After several years in Portsmouth he moved to *BBC Radio Two* as a newsreader and later as a presenter of weekly programmes.

Neil JACKSON
Presenter at *Beacon Radio* in Wolverhampton.

Robert JACKSON
Sports reporter and commentator at *BBC Radio Sheffield* in the eighties and nineties.

Steve JACKSON
Weekday DJ on *Kiss FM* in Lodnon.

Sue JACKSON
Sue is a presenter on *Isle of Wight Radio*.

Tim JACKSON
Tim was one of the first Yorkshiremen to become involved in radio and in 1966 joined the Board of R*adio 270*. He and the station's Managing Director, Wilf Proudfoot, bought a piece of land in Scarborough for building a transmitter station once licences became available - they sold it just a year before the licence was offered.

In the 1970s he was a major investor in *Radio Tees*, the station in Stockton and with MD Toby Horton was one of the team which engineered the merger with *Metro Radio* in the early 1980s.

Tim was one of the founders of Yorkshire Coast Radio, the Scarborough licensee and is a director of the station.

Blair JACOBS
Blair is a presenter at *BBC Radio Solent*.

Clive JACOBS
Born in 1939 in London, Clive did his National Service in the Royal Navy and enjoyed it so much he signed on for an extra five years in the Fleet Air Arm.

After leaving the services he had a brief period in corsetry and bras at Marks and Spencer and then auditioned for the BBC. They hired him as a reporter on regional radio and he became a features reporter for the *Radio Four* programme 'The World Tonight'.

Since those days Clive has worked on most major *Radio Four* programmes, including 'Going Places', 'Woman's Hour' and 'Today'. Clive is based in Southampton.

David JACOBS
Born in South London in 1926, David's first broadcast was in 1944 whilst he was still with the Royal Navy. He became an announcer with *BFBS* and joined the BBC in a similar role after the war.

He's since hosted many programmes on the *BBC Light Programme* and as well as being the chairman of 'Juke Box Jury' he was one of the first hosts of 'Top of the Pops.

David recalls fondly the time he was sacked by the BBC for laughing while reading a news bulletin and one of his most exciting moments was introducing Judy Garland at a Variety Club lunch.

His radio work continued into the nineteen eighties, hosting a regular daily programme on *Radio Two*, and in 1984 he received a Sony Award for his outstanding contribution to radio. He'd previously won the both the Variety Club's Radio and TV Personality of the Year awards in 1960 and 1975.

Currently presenting programmes on *Radio Two* and Sky Television's Travel station, he is also a director of *Kingston FM*, a would-be station operator in South West London. He is till on air each week at Radio Two.

Gary JACOBS
One of the first presenters on *Talkradio UK*.

Mike JACOBS
Mike is the Company Secretary of *Eleven Seventy* in High Wycombe.

Sanjay JAGATIA
Host of late night programmes on *Radio XL*.

Laraine JALILI

Laraine is the Group Sales Manager at the Invicta stations in Kent.

Bob JAMES

He built his own studio and transmitter while only 12 years old and has been at it ever since! In 1983 he invested in a course at the National Broadcasting School and has worked at *Radio Victory*, and *Southern Sound* in Brighton.

He's worked as an engineer and air personality, and also had a stretch at *Radio Mercury* in Crawley before returning to *Southern Sound* as chief engineer and afternoon host.

His most hilarious event was broadcasting from a bath-tub while sailing down the river - it sank live on air!   Bob likes rock music but hates being late for anything. Bob is a total workaholic, but with six children, and a thirst for large motorbikes, he has to be.

Caren JAMES

Born in 1963, Caren was a successful business-woman before her first broadcast, which was on *Wear FM* in Sunderland in 1989 as a newsreader. She also hosted several pro-

grammes at the station, including the station's breakfast show before moving to the Metro Group's *TFM* station in Stockton where she hosted the 'Bacardi Club Chart' and 'Lovelinks' programme.

Then came the highlight of Caren's career, a move to the GWR Network and *Trent FM's* Breakfast Show, and the moment she feels most proud of is being part of a Sony Award winning station. Caren is of slim build, has a Lamda certificate and specialises as a presenter of audio and audio visual productions

The funniest moment for Caren so far was getting covered in shaving foam and toilet paper at a station roadshow; she likes David Duchovny (from the X files programme) and hates any woman who gets to him first!

Ian JAMES

Ian is a presenter with *MFM* in Wrexham.

Kenni JAMES

Presenter and Programme Director at *The Bay*.

Marilyn JAMES

Marilyn is the Sales Manager at *Radio Ceredigion* in Wales.

Mo JAMES

Mo is the presenter of the Saturday and Sunday morning breakfast programmes on *BBC Radio Leeds*.

Neale JAMES

Presenter of overnight programmes and 'Rockline' phone-in programme on *BBC Radio One* in the 1990s and currently is still presenting programmes there.

Nicky JAMES (1)

When *Capital Radio* launched in 1973 he joined them as a senior programmer, and in 1990 returned to the BBC as Head of the Transcription Service. In 1993 he returned 'down under' and is now a senior executive at the ABC Radio headquarters in Sydney.

Nicky JAMES (2)

Nicky enjoyed his years at boarding school, but not his first job in advertising, so Nicky then ran a wine bar and also had a hot dog van for while before getting a break into radio

Who's Who in British Radio

courtesy of Ed Doolan at *Radio WM* in 1982. He spent a couple of years doing programmes for a pirate soul station in the Midlands and then in 1990 joined *Buzz FM* in Birmingham as co-host of the breakfast show.

Moving on to the satellite station *QEFM*, Nicky presented a daily 'arts' show for a year before moving to Gloucester's *Severn Sound* to present their 'Overdrive' programme. At a disco someone asked him for 'Sex', and never heaving heard the Paul Young track, Nicky, innocent as he is (?) misunderstood so he hit him with a 12 incher!

In 1994 he joined the new regional station in the Midlands, *Heart FM* where he presents the late night love songs programme. He also does presentation work in discos and has his own promotions company called 'Classique Promotions'.

Paul JAMES
Currently hosts breakfast and request show on *BBC Radio Kent* as well as programmes on *Ocean Sound*.

Peter JAMES
Born in New Zealand where he worked on the NZBC networks for four years, he arrived in the UK in January 1965 and joined *Radio Caroline*. Later that year he became an announcer on *Radio 390* in its second week on the air and became Chief Announcer very quickly.

The following year he too over as Programme Director, based at the station's Pimlico headquarters, and began production of a TV series called 'Seeing and Doing'. In 1967 he joined the BBC, as producer of the *Radio One / Radio Two* programme Housewives Choice. He also produced 'Midday Spin' on *Radio One* and 'What's New' on *Radio Two*.

Richard JAMES
Richard was a leading presenter at *Pennine Radio* in Bradford in the late 1980s. He now does the breakfast show at *Radio Aire* in Leeds.

Terry JAMES
Presenter at *Q103* in Cambridge.

Tony JAMES
Presenter on *Pirate 102* in Cornwall.

Trevor JAMES
Programme Controller at *CNFM*.

Vic JAMES
Miss James hosts the breakfast programme each weekday on *10-17* in Harlow.

Derek JAMESON
Born on November 29th in 1929, Derek was brought up in a foster home in London's East End and evacuated to Bishop's Stortford during the war. He started work as a messenger at Reuters when he was 14 and became a trainee reporter two years later. In 1960 he moved into newspapers and became a picture editor at the Sunday Mirror and broke the circulation records of the Daily Mirror when he became Northern Editor in the 1970s.

In 1978 he took over as Editor of the Daily Express and launched their Daily Star the following year.

In 1981 he gave up newspaper editing to become a TV commentator and soon got a name for his forthright and irrevernt approach on chat shows and current affairs programmes. Rupert Murdoch lured him back to Fleet Street in 1982 as Editor of the News of the World, but two years later he returned to broadcasting, becoming a household name on TVAM and hosting a BBC TV Programme 'Do They Mean Us?'

His break into radio was in 1985 on Radio Four's 'Colour Supplement' programme and the following year he took over the Breakfast Programme on *Radio Two*.

After six years of early starts he was given his own late night programme in January 1992, which he now hosts with his wife Ellen.

Derek was named 'Radio Personality of the Year' in 1987 by both SOny and the TV & radio Industries Club and also voted BBC Radio Personality of the Year in 1988.

He and Ellen live in Brighton and his interests include opera, music and reading. Since April 1995, his Radio Two programme has been produced by Unique Broadcasting and transmitted from Scotland.

Ellen JAMESON

Ellen was born in Galsgow in October 1949 and spent her early years globe-trotting as her father was in the RAF - she attended no less than 22 schools all over the UK and in Singapore and Germany.

Ellen's broadcasting career began in 1966 with *Radio Scotland* (the one on board a ship off Ayr). When Radio Scotland was closed down she moved to London to write for pop magazines and after writing a book about David Essex she also made an appearance in his film 'That'll be the Day'. She then joined 'The People' and 'Women's Own', and finally met and fell in love with larger-than-life Fleet Street character, Derek Jameson.

When Derek left Fkleet Street for showbiz, she became his manager and now plays a full part co-hosting the late night Jameson chat show on *Radio Two* four nights a week.

Geraldine JAMESON

Weekend presenter at *Manx Radio,*.

Sue JAMESON

Born on the 3rd July in Sydney, Australia, she attended Surbiton High School and Liverpool University, during which time she worked as a volunteer at *BBC Radio Merseyside*. It was there she made her first broadcast, on a student programme called 'Precinct'. On graduating Sue joined Liverpool ILR station *Radio City* and in 1980 moved to LBC in London where she became Arts Correspondent to IRN.

David JAMIESON

David keeps his age a secret but is proud of attending Daniel Stewart's College and the Heriot Watt University, both in Edinburgh. His first job was selling space in a magazine and he also worked at the University while working in hospital radio.

In 1969 he guested on a *Radio One* programme and then joined *BBC Radio Leicester* where he presented a breakfast programme. After a move to *BRMB* hosting late night shows he relocated to Scotland and *Radio Clyde* and in the early 1980's moved south again to Coventry for a Head of Music role at *Mercia Sound*.

Finally, in 1995 he joined Heart FM, the regional light rock station in the Midlands, where he now hosts a programme from 2 until 6pm each Sunday afternoon. David is a keen record collector and computer enthusiast.

Anton JARVIS

Anton is a news producer currently working at *BBC Essex*.

John JASON

Presenter at *Touch AM* in Cardiff.

Johnny JASON

Born in London as Rudiger van Etzdorf, Johnny worked in radio in Australia in the early seventies and on his return to the UK joined *Radio Caroline* in Summer 1973. He stayed with the station until 1975, when its accidental drift into UK waters led to his arrest for illegal broadcasting. Johnny then came ashore and joined Metropolitan Radio (as *Metro FM* was called then!) for a while, hosting several programmes.

Maurice JAY

Head of Music at *BCR* in Belfast.

Martyn JEANES

One of the on-air presenters at *Heart FM*, the regional light-rock station in the Midlands.

John JEFFERSON

John was a producer at *BBC Radio Humberside* in the 1980s. He then moved to *BBC Radio Leeds* where he is now the station's Managing Editor.

Peter JEFFERSON

Born on the 12th May in London, Peter attended prep school in Walton on Thames and grammar school in nearby Shepperton. After working in an estate agents office for a while he joined the BBC as a tape Library Clerk in the Overseas Service and then became a studio manager.

His first broadcast was on the *BBC World Service* where he became the regular host of 'From our Own Correspondent'. He also worked at *Radio Two* hosting 'Nightride' for several years. and in the mid seventies moved to 1974 as a staff announcer and newsreader.

Peter doesn't like people who panic, and once continued reading the news on the World Service while two colleagues ripped his script up (noisily) and poured cold water on his head from a tea-pot!

David JEFFREY

David is the Chairman of *Gold Radio*, which launched in Shaftesbury in June 1995.

Bill JENKYNS

Bill is a senior producer at *BBC Radio York*.

David JENSEN

Born in Victoria, BC on 4th July 1950, David's first job was as presenter at *CJOV* in 1967 while studying classical music in high school. The following year he came to Europe and joined *Radio Luxembourg*, where his colleagues christened him 'Kid Jensen'. He stayed there for seven happy years.

In 1975 he moved to Nottingham ILR station *Radio Trent* and was snapped up by *Radio one* the following year. Apart from a brief interlude in 1981, he spent another seven years at Radio One, hosting a variety of programmes, before being lured to *Capital Radio* in 1984.

David's also done numerous one-off projects for various stations, as well as appearing on both ITV and BBC television. Pop Quest, Top of the Pops, Nationwide The Roxy (where he was associate producer) are just a few of countless programmes he's appeared on.

Kid lists the highlight of his career as winning five Sony Awards and a Tric Award. In 1984, he was Melody Maker's 'DJ of the year' in a readers poll and he also won two 'Spotlight' awards in 1970 and 1971. He likes most sports, especially soccer and baseball, and the only thing he really dislikes is London traffic.

In 1975 he married Icelandic air stewardess Gudrun and they have three children. Available for live PAs through John Miles (01 275 854675 and for voice over work through Hobson's agency (01 81 995 3628).

Bob JOBBINS

Bob is the Editor of News and Current Affairs at the *BBC World Service*.

Adrian JOHN

Born in London in 1954 his first job was working as a mobile disco DJ and, in 1972 worked as a resident DJ on board the QE2. He barraged *Radio One* with audition tapes and joined the network in the late 70's as a stand-by DJ. In the early 1980s he was given station's early morning shows and later weekend breakfasts and later joined *Radio Kent*, his local radio station.

A keen camcorder enthusiast he enjoys playing keyboards. In August 1995 Adrian moved to Newcastle and joined *Great North Radio* to host the station's mid-morning show.

Kevin JOHNS

Currently a daily presenter for *Swansea Sound* doing various morning and childrens shows. Recently presented three live radio shows from Universal Studios, Florida.

Also presented shows in his time at *BBC Radio Wales* and *BBC Radio 5*. Also co-starred in pantomimes in Port Talbot and Porthcawl.

Adrian JOHNSON

Presents 'The Late Show' on weekdays for *BBC Radio Kent* which includes lively topical debates on the days news.

Colin JOHNSON

An accomplished journalist with spells at several BBC local stations including *Radio Humberside*, Colin now runs the newsroom at Radio Kent.

Dave JOHNSON

Afternoon presenter on *Signal Gold*.

David JOHNSON

Presenter at *Cool FM* in Belfast in 1995.

Duncan JOHNSON

Born in Toronto in 1938, he got into radio in 1960 at a station in Saskatchewan and soon after moved to a radio and TV combo in Alberta. The local climate proved too cold, so he moved out to Bermuda in the middle of the Atlantic Ocean, where he worked with Willy Walker and Mike Lennox, later shipmates on Radio London.

From Bermuda Duncan came to the UK, and after a period using his excellent dulcet tones on commercials, he joined *Radio London* just a few weeks after it launched. In June 1966 he visited the *Radio City* complex on Shivering Sands to prepare for a new station to transmit beautiful music, just hours before City boss Reg Calvert was shot dead over the deal.

In October 1967 Duncan joined *Radio One* as the host of 'Crack the Clue'.

The following year he released a single ("Big Architect in the Sky" on the Spark label) and got married, then in 1970 he returned to the air on board the Swiss-owned pirate ship, Radio Nordsee International. That led to a move into the music business as label manager and song plugger for Mickie Most's new label, RAK Records. He also made EMI a fortune by signing up the Simon Park Orchestra's theme tune for the van der Walk TV series , 'Eye Level' which got to number one in 1972, and the following year he joined *Radio Luxembourg* with old Big L ship-mate, Alan Keen (qv).

After over 2 years with Lucky Luxembourg, he moved across Mayfair to Euston Tower and a presenter's role at *Capital Radio*. He stayed for eight years fronting programmes such as 'Afternoon Delight' and then joined the new Kent ILR *Invicta Radio* at its launch (Autumn 1984). After four years Duncan moved back into the advertising business as a Finance controller at David Knight Advertising.

Gary JOHNSON

For many years he worked in sales at *LBC*, ill fated London commercial talk station. When that station lost its licence in Autumn 93, he moved to *Melody Radio*, the London all music station, to head their sales office.

Gloria JOHNSON

Born in Birkenhead, Goria attended Eastfield School in White City - a popular suburb of West Hull. She had lots of different jobs and interesting experiences before joining BBC *Radio Humberside* to answer the telephones. Eventually she was promoted to be the station's chief receptionist and after seeing Mike Hurley (qv) go through so many of the young girl reporters she decided shoe could put up a better fight and match his diatribe.

After a short trial she became his regular reporter, out and about the county of Humberside, the foil for his merciless teasing which she does admirably and so wins the respect of the station's listeners.

In addition to her Saturday morning forays, Gloria has also hosted a weekly "Songs from the Shows' nostalgia programme on which she's interviewed many stars, from Terry Wogan to Alf Garnett, Anthony Newley to Jackie Collins, but never unfortunately her idol of many years - James Cagney.

She has also done many vox-pops and interviews on Radio Humberside - her easy manner, accomplished wit and genuine liking for people gives her a natural charm which endears her to all kinds of people.

Gloria is also responsible for organising the station's 'Helpline' service which, under her guiding hand, has found bed-legs, lost relatives and all manner of furry and fluffy creatures, as well as solved a whole mountain of problems for the station's listeners.

Away from the microphone, Gloria likes nothing better than sat in her wellies on the riverbank fishing; no shrinking violet she'll happily upturn cowpats for bait but admits to also liking a nice Catherine Cookson or a good murder/mystery story.

Juliet JOHNSON

Juliet is a senior producer at *BBC Radio Oxford*.

Mic JOHNSON

Mic worked for the BBC until he joined Newcastle station Metropolitan Radio in 1974. In 1978 he was appointed to the Board and was Programme Director until September 1995.

Mitch JOHNSON

Born in August 1964, Mitch claims he broke into radio by getting a job selling fridges! he worked at a pirate station in London called Radio Shoestring and then blagged a job at the Virgin Megastore. Finally he got some overnight work at *Capital Radio* as well as some voice over work for TV game shows.

Who's Who in British Radio

After touring various far Eastern countries, Mitch got a job at the British Forces station in Hong Kong where he stayed for over two years doing the afternoon show. In 1993 he returned to the UK to join *Virgin Radio* and he has also done voice over work for BBC TV and some cable channels. He currently hosts the weekend 6pm to 10 pm slot at *Virgin 1215*.

Richard JOHNSON
Station Manager of *Channel 103* on Jersey.

Simon JOHNSON
A presenter on *Orchard FM*.

David JOHNSTON
David is the News editor and is also responsible for political programmes on *Forth FM* and its sister station, *Max AM*.

Alaine JOHNSTONE
Alaine is the Promotion Manager at *Scot FM*.

Adrian JONES
Adrian is a DJ at *Marcher Coast*.

Adrienne JONES
Religious Presenter at *BBC Radio Lincolnshire* where she presents Morningsong' (9am) and 'Evensong' (7pm) each Sunday.

Cathy JONES
News reporter at Mix 96, Aylesbury.

Chris JONES
Producer and presenter at *BBC Radio Lincolnshire*, responsible for the weekday morning programme and 'Replay' each Sunday afternoon.

Claire JONES
Claire is an Editor at BBC GLR in London.

David JONES
A director of the *Signal Radio* group.

Debi JONES
Educated at the 'Waterloo Park School for Fallen Hussies' Debi began work as a computer installer and also had a spell in offshore oil sales before bluffing her way in to *Radio Merseyside* in 1985. She did various link ups, including several with Tommy Vance, and

with *BFBS* stations in Gibraltar and Belize.

Further radio work soon followed, including *Radio Five Live* and Liverpool's *Radio City Gold*. She's also done daytime TV for two years, plus Brookside and Coronation Street, but her most memorable appearance was a live broadcast from London Zoo when, while holding a lima on a lead, it wound twice round her neck almost strangling her and then relieved itself all over her shoes.

Debi likes food wine and humour, hates rudeness and is represented by Paul Vaughan Management, Tel 01 905 64061.

Eifion JONES
Bilingual presenter at *CBC*, Cardiff in the 80's.

Elinor JONES
Elinor is a DJ at *Marcher Gold* in Wrexham.

Faith JONES
News reporter at Network News.

Gethyn JONES
Born on 7th May 1952 in Reading, he was educated at Portsmouth Grammar School and in Gosport. His first broadcast was in 1972 on *BBC Radio Solent* after becoming a record librarian where he remained for most of the seventies and eighties, contributing to *Radio Two* programmes also.

Glyn JONES
Glyn joined *BBC Radio York* as a News Reporter in 1983, and then moved across to Look North regional TV output while producing segments for 'Woman's Hour' on *Radio Four*.

In 1992 he moved to London to become Chief Instructor at BBC Radio Training Unit and in January 1994 was appointed Special Assistant to Liz Forgan, MD of BBC Network Radio.

In September 1995 he took up a post as Managing editor of the BBC's Digital Audio Broadcasting (DAB) service.

Jane JONES
Jane is a presenter at *Classic FM*.

Jeff JONES
Saturday night DJ on *Moray Firth Radio*.

Keri JONES

Educated at Wolfreton School near Hull, 'Kezza' (as he is widely known) took a Politics degree at Leicester University and got into radio by sending a hospital radio tape to *Radio Humberside*. His first broadcast was at *Radio Aire* in Leeds in January 1987, followed by *Viking* (Hull) and *Pennine Radio* (Bradford), before leaving YRN to join *Leicester Sound* and *Mercia,* where he stayed until 1993.

In 1993 came the highlight of Keri's career so far, getting a job at *Devonair Radio* and the saddest occasion for him was being on air and hearing the station was to lose its licence. He moved on to be programme manager at *Mix 96* in 1994, then to *Trent FM* and now currently broadcasting on *Oasis Radio*.

Kevin JONES

After Drummond High School, Kevin became a record shop manager, a rigger and then a postman. He got into radio through working with Tom Wilson as a production assistant and made his first broadcast in August 1994 on 'Steppin' Out 2' on *Radio Forth*.

He also works as a club DJ and writes and produces music too. The man who once fell asleep on the turntables and didn't notice when the music stopped loves an 'up for it' crowd and positive people.

Leighton JONES

Currently a presenter at *Swansea Sound.*

Mark JONES

Born in Old Trafford, Manchester, he went to Chetham's Hospital School and then became an assistant Bank Manager before appearing at live gigs and in various clubs in the Manchester area. His first broadcast was on 4th April, 1975, on *BBC Radio Manchester,* and since then his radio career has been long, distinguished and usually underpaid.

He was the host of several programmes on Liverpool ILR *Radio City* since the late 1970s including the 'Hit The Road' programme each weekday and Saturday Breakfast Programme. He was nominated for Sony Awards several times and stayed at City for 17 years. In 1995 he was lured by a fabulous salary to work at *Great Yorkshire Gold*.

As well as radio Mark has also made numerous TV appearances, including a live OB from Gdansk, Poland, where he hosted the Sopot Music Festival with a TV audience of 350 million.

The highlight of Mark's career was leaving the bank to work in radio full-time, since when it's been highlights all the way. The most humorous part of Mark's life is opening his pay-packet, it's also the saddest. He likes rock and hates musicals and is managed by Allan James of James McGRATH MANAGEMENT 01 71 495 1733.

Neil JONES

Neil was the Sales Manager at *Red Dragon Radio* in Cardiff until the takeover by EMAP in August 1994 and is now a partner in the Independent Radio Group investment .

Paul JONES

After a singing career as lead vocalist with the sixties RnB band 'Manfred Mann', Paul pursued a career in acting and as a solo artiste. He joined the BBC to host specialist music programmes on *Radio Two* in the seventies and scan still be heard there today on occasional programmes.

He also began hosting programmes on the London jazz station now known as *JFM*, and in 1995 joined the new Christian station *Premier Radio* to present a gospel music programme each Tuesday evening.

Peter JONES

Born in Wem in Shropshire he went to the local Grammar School and got his first job in rep' in nearby Wolverhampton.

His first broadcast was made in 1938 from Birmingham, since when he's been a question master, panelist, comedian and narrator on a variety of programmes including 'Hitch-hikers Guide to the Galaxy' , 'Twenty Questions' and 'Just a Minute'. Peter doesn't like recorded music in shops, is married to Jeri Sauvinet and lives in London.

Who's Who in British Radio

Ray JONES
Religious programmes producer at *BBC Wiltshire Sound*.

Rob JONES
Born on the last day in April, 1955 in Liverpool, Rob was educated at Liverpool College and became a trainee accountant, but opted for a career in radio instead. P.D. Gillian Reynolds gave him a programme on *Radio City* on condition he complete his courses at night school (which he didn't!) and he hosted all kinds of programmes at the station.

He later moved to *Radio Luxembourg* where he hosted the station's Early Show, staying with the station until the 1980s when he moved back to the UK, taking on a senior role at *Radio Radio* in 1987.

Sandi JONES
Sandi presents the weekday drive programme (from 4 until 7pm) on *BBC Radio Solent*.

Steve JONES
Born in in Crewe on 7th June 1945, Steve trained as a teacher and worked as a professional musician and ice-cream salesman before joining *Radio Clyde* as a DJ when the station opened in 1973.

He stayed for five years and in 1977 won a Sony Award as 'Scottish Radio Personality of the Year' and the following year left Glasgow for a higher profile role at LBC in London. In 1989 Steve was named by the Variety Club as 'Independent Radio Personality of the Year.'

He's also appeared on several TV programmes, particularly in his other role as a stand -up comic, and also as the host of 'The Pyramid Game' as well as broadcasting on BBC Radio two. Steve lives in London and has three sons.

Tom L JONES
Welsh language presenter at *Swansea Sound*.

Vicky JONES
Vicky is a researcher at *BBC Three Counties Radio*.

Wendy JONES
Born on the 26th September in 1949, in Loughborough, Leicestershire, Wendy went to the local girl's school and then Hull University. AFter a short period as a barmaid she worked as a reporter on the Slough Observer and just about to move to another job in journalism when she read an article about BBC local radio.

She joined *BBC Radio Carlisle* (now known as Radio Cumbria) and made her first broadcast in July 1974.

After two years presenting a variety of news and current affairs programmes and features she moved to *BBC Radio Oxford* for three years and then joined *Radio Four* to work on the 'Today ' programme as a co-presenter with Brian Redhead and John Timpson. In the early 1980s she began producing pieces for 'The World This Weekend' and in 1986 was appointed the BBC's Education Correspondent.

Although a very proficient broadcaster Wendy was never happy self-driving: "At Radio Carlisle I used to break out in a cold sweat when I had to take us out of Radio Two, read the news and go back into Radio Four, without the help of an engineer. Her hobbies are her family and gardening and she's married to a chemical engineer and has two children.

Wynfford JONES
Managing director at *Radio Ceredigion*.

Colin JONNER
Morning show host on *Q96* in Paisley.

Kenny JORDAN
Presents late night Saturday night and Sunday afternoon soul programmes on *Kix 96*, the specialist music station in Coventry.

Marguerita JORDAN
Presenter at *BRMB FM*.

Paul JORDAN
Paul is the Head of Programmes and Presentation at the Red Rose Radio Group's FM outlet, *Rock FM*.

Steve JORDAN

After attending Wolfreton School near Hull, Steve became a postman for nine years while training in hospital radio at Goole and doing various RSLs in East Yorkshire, including *Cod City FM, Radio Cracker* and *Universal.* In September 1993 he made his first full time broadcast on *Lincs FM*, where he now hosts the station's breakfast programme as well as other work as a club DJ.

The highlight of Steve's career so far was getting the breakfast show at *Lincs FM*, and he shudders when he recalls interviewing a lady in a supermarket in Scunthorpe, and asking her when her baby was due - she wasn't even pregnant!. Likes TV, sports and quizzes, but hates marzipan.

John JOSEPHS

John joined *Metropolitan Radio* when the Newcastle-based company was formed in 1974.

He stayed with the station as Finance Director (he is a chartered accountant) and was part of the team which grew it from being a 'close to bankrupt' single station, to a publicly-quoted success story of five major stations by the early nineties. John was appointed Managing Director in 1993 and resigned in September 1995, following the take-over by the EMAP Group.

Just a month later he led the MBO of *The Pulse* in Bradford and is now the new Company's Chief executive.

Roger JUMMERSKILL

After school Roger did a variety of jobs before becoming a journalist and joined BBC *Radio Merseyside* from a local newspaper. His first broadcast was from a public phonebox and half way through it a woman knocked on the door saying she had to make an urgent call!

In his radio career, Roger has been a newsreader on the old *Radio Five Live* and a breakfast presenter and presenter of late night discussion programmes on *BBC Radio Merseyside*.

John JUNKIN

A trained actor, John was 'resting' when the opportunity of a job as a DJ on *Radio Atlanta* came up in 1964. He also hosted programmes for *Radio Caroline*, but then left to pursue a career in acting and has appeared since in dozens of rep' plays as well as on TV. He still has radio connections, having appeared on hundreds of programmes on *Radio Two,* such as the 'Hello Cheeky' series.

Adrian JUSTE

Born on 21st April 1947 in Kirby Muxloe, Leicestershire, Adrian attended Guthlaxton Grammar School in Wigston. His first job as a car mechanic earned him one and seven an hour and he left it after eight weeks to become a shoe salesman. In 1969 came his first broadcast, on *BBC Radio Leicester*.

Five years later he joined one of the new ILR stations, *BRMB* in Birmingham, where he hosted the station's breakfast programme for almost a year. "I'm not very good at that time of day and it almost killed me, so they put me on weekends, which is when I began inserting comedy clips into my show."

Three years later Adrian was asked to make programme trails for *Radio One* and the following April got his first outlet on the station - a Saturday morning programme.

The new nineties Radio One stopped carrying his programmes in 1993, since when Adrian has been running his own 'Show to Go' production company from his home in Garrard's Cross

Kevin KANE

Kevin is programme manager of FM services at *Gemini Radio* in Exeter.

Russ KANE

Born in London on 15th October, 1962, Russ joined *Capital FM* in 1984 after being persuaded to have a go at traffic broadcasts from the station's Flying Eye - despite his dislike of early morning sand flying!

Now a long established traffic commentator, he combined that early morning role with a hectic schedule as an award-winning scriptwriter (he's won 15 international awards) and director of TV and films. Russ is married with two children and lives in Hendon.

John KANEEN

Folk music presenter on *Manx Radio.*

Paul KAVANAGH

Born in 1968, Paul joined *Atlantic 252* when the station opened in 1989 and has been involved in all aspects of the station's operation since, designing and developing the station's output. In 1992 he became Programme and then General Manager and in 1995 he was appointed to the Board of the station.

Brian KAY

Born in May, 1944, Brian attended Kings College Cambridge and joined the Westminster Abbey Choir in 1968. The same year he joined the Kins Singers as bass and made his first broadcast that year.

In 1981 he made his first announcements as a broadcaster and now hosts specialist music programmes on both *BBC Radio 3* and *Radio Four.*

Jon KAYE

Born in 1955 in North London, Jon joined Border TV's London sales office in 1972 and then joined the IBA's radio division two years later, where he supervised programme standards of the new ILR stations, and administered the paperwork relating to royalty agreements.

He also produced tapes about the new ILR stations and in 1976 joined *BBC Radio London* as a freelance broadcaster, and the following year he moved to *Radio Merseyside.* There he was initially a presenter and then producer for nine years, moving back to the south east for attachments at *Radio London* in 1987 and *Radio Sussex* until October 1988.

Jon then took a permanent producers job at the new BBC station, *Wiltshire Sound* and in May 1990 moved back to the commercial sector as Head of Presentation at London multilingual station *Spectrum International.* while

at spectrum he did voice overs for *London Weekend Television,* and in 1993 moved to *BBC Essex* as senior producer.

In mid-1993, Jon decided to become a freelance broadcaster on *Classic FM, LBC* and in September 1994 joined London's new talk station, LNR, where he is a writer and presenter of daily news and feature programmes.

Michael KAYE

Michael began his broadcasting career with *Radio Hong Kong* in 1964 where he became head of current affairs. Michael developed the organisation's new TV unit from 1969 to 1972 and then returned to the UK and the BBC Current Affairs department of the *World Service.*

He then became the first 'Editor' of *BBC 648* (a tri-lingual service for North-West Europe), consultant to the Russian Service, the Polish Service and the deputy head of the French and Portugese services. Since 1988 he has been actively involved in developing the BBC's commercial activities as well as his duties as Head of the German Programmes on the *BBC World Service.*

Michael is the author of *Making Radio,* a highly regarded broadcasters' training manual, and has a first class honours degree from the University of London.

Michael still broadcasts (in English), acts as consultant to other BBC services and teaches radio production techniques.

Steve KAYE

Born on 31st October 1955 in Hampstead, his first job was in sales administration at Border television. In June 1976, after some time in hospital radio, he made his first broadcast on *BBC Radio London* and has since presented a variety of different programmes on the station.

He then moved to *BBC Radio Merseyside* and presented and produced his own afternoon programme on the station for some time. His programmes were nominated twice for awards and the height of his career was meeting Prince Charles in 1992.

Martin KAYNE

Born Andy Cadier in 1943 at Gravesend, Martin went to St Edmonds College in Herftfordshire. In 1959 he joined the RAF and did some work in his off-duty hours for *BFBS*.

On returning to England in 1965 he discharged himself from the RAF (it cost him £200, a small fortune in the sixties!) and sent out audition tapes to get a job in radio. A favourable response from *Radio Essex* saw him heading out to sea in January 1966 where he not only learned the rudiments of broadcasting - he also had to feed half a dozen others on the station's tiny ex-naval fort, twenty miles from Southend.

The following year Martin moved to the slightly plusher *Radio 355* on the ship 'Laissez Faire', but that closed a few months later, forcing Martin to venture towards the Isle of Man, where *Radio Caroline North* rode at anchor.

Martin stayed with Caroline until the ship was towed away in 1968 for non-payment of bills and, after a few years working in night clubs, he joined *Radio North Sea* in the early 1970s. By now married to heather, he left the life on the ocean wave for a career as a caterer nearer home. He now writes a regular page in the enthusiasts monthly, Short Wave Magazine.

Shabana KAZMI

Host of Hindi and Urdu programmes on new Midlands station, *Radio XL*.

Brendan KEARNEY

Until 1994 was a presenter at *Great North Radio*, and since 1995 is a member of the on-air team at *Heart 100.7*, a light rock station in the Midlands.

Kevin KEATINGS

DJ on *Radio City* in the 1980's.

Steve KEEGAN

Steve is the traffic manager at *Melody Radio* in London.

Alan KEEN

Alan held a variety of jobs before getting into radio - he worked in the editorial department of the Daily Telegraph, as an assistant in the

gallery at the House of Commons and as a time and motions man in the RAF! He then spent sixteen years in advertising, mainly with the Daily Mirror, and in 1964 joined Radlon Sales, the company launching *Radio London*.

He was a senior sales executive with Big L and in January 1966 he was appointed to the Board. Later that year he also became Programme Director of the station with first Tony WIndsor and then Ed Stewart as his assistants..

After Radio London closed in 1967, Alan then moved to *Radio Luxembourg,* succeeding Geoffrey Everitt as General Manager.

Mark KEEN

Mark began his radio career on *Mercia FM* in Coventry. In 1995 he moved to become the breakfast DJ at *Kix 96*, Coventry's specialist music station, which launched in mid-1995.

Nicky KEIG-SHEVLIN

Presenter at *Southern FM* in Brighton.

John KEIGHREN

John is the news and sports producer at the Signal Radio Group in Cheshire and he also hosts the *Signal Cheshire* Saturday afternoon sports programme.

Alan KEITH

Born in October 1908 in London, Alan was educated at RADA and trod the boards for some years until his first broadcast in 1935, which was compering a variety show from the St George's Hall.

Since then he's appeared on the *Home Service* and *Light Programme,* and also on *Radio Four*. He has presented 'Your Hundred Best Tunes' for decades - currently on *Radio Two* each Sunday evening.

Randall KEHRIG

Sales Director at *Riviera Radio*, Monte Carlo

Who's Who in British Radio

Alan KEITH

Presenter on *BBC Radio 2*.

Al KELLY

"Wild" Al Kelly was the original overnight talk show host on *Talkradio UK* when the station first launched.

Eamonn KELLY

Eamonn was the manager of a record shop in Kelo, Dublin, next door to *Q102*, and was asked to deputise for a DJ one day who hadn't turned up. From there he moved to super-station ERI in Cork and then to the UK where he joined *Radio Broadland* in Norwich. After a while it was off to Kent and *Radio Invicta* and then, in September 1995, to his current home, *Capital Gold* in London.

He's also co-presented the morning programme on WMKR (K106) in Baltimore, Maryland, and reported live from New York, as well as pursued a career as a song-writer. Likes foreign food, sunshine and good radio.

Henry KELLY

Born in Ireland on 17th April 1946, Henry gained a BA Hons in English language and Literature at University College Dublin and became a newspaper reporter for eight years.

In 1976 he joined BBC *Radio Four* and then moved over to TV where he presented three series of 'Game for a Laugh' as well as 'Going for Gold' and The Big Decision. He's continued his radio work hosting 'Midweek' and The World Tonight' on *Radio Four* and in 1993 joined *Classic FM* where he presents a daily programme.

As well as broadcasting, Henry is still a prolific writer and his book 'How Stormont Fell' is regarded as a first rate primer on the Northern ireland political situation. He is married to Marjorie and they have one daughter, called Siobhan.

Jim KELLY

Presenter and the Head of Commercial Production at *BCR*, Belfast.

Liz KELLY

Sales Manager at *Moray Firth Radio*.

Martin KELNER

Educated at Stand Grammar School in Manchester, Martin trained at the Strathclyde University in Glasgow as a journalist. His first radio broadcast was on *Radio Hong Kong* on assignment for the COI in 1975. On returning to the UK he joined *Radio Hallam* in Sheffield and then moved up the M1 to *Radio Aire*. His next move was shorter, neighbouring Bradford and *Pennine Radio*, from where he joined *BBC Radio Two*.

As well as radio, Martin also keeps his journalistic talents well honed with regular pieces in 'The Independent' newspaper, The Daily Mail and its Sunday sister and is available as a strip-pogram (or as a 'radiogram'). The highlight of his radio career was his first national programme, which went out at 4 am, but only just because he overslept, making it to the studio with just two minutes to spare!

The funniest event in his radio career was trying to an interview with Dennis 'Blackbeard' Bovell in his hotel room while being invited to share his two feet long 'cigarette'. Martin likes all the usual things such as sex, food, drink and poetry, and dislikes racism, bigotry, raw onions and mini-cabs.

He is well known in the North East for his programmes on *Radio Leeds*, especially the late night weekend shows which are taken by most local radio stations in the north. On that programme he is complemented (though rarely complimented) by a posse of side-kicks ranging from the ubiquitous New York cabbie to a raving and lewd Frenchman called Edward.

Martin also hosts a Saturday afternoon programme on *BBC Radio Two*.

Marianne KEMP

Marianne is a Radio Production Assistant at *BBC Wiltshire Sound*.

Mike KEMP

News producer at *BBC Radio York*.

Claire KENDAL

Producer at *BBC Radio Cleveland*.

Neil KENLOCK

Sales Director at *Choice FM*.

Who's Who in British Radio

Chris KENNEDY

After a period on various radio station in Ireland, Chris joined *Radio Caroline* in the 1980s - making it a family affair as his brother, Steve Conway, also worked there. Chris is still one of the station's most popular DJs and was heard on its recent broadcasts to Essex and London.

Kris KENNEDY Jnr.

Presenter at *BRMB* in the 1980's.

Marcia KENNEDY

Marcia was the Head of Sales at *TFM* in Stockton and in mid-1995 moved to the new station in Darlington, *A1 Radio*.

Paul KENNEDY

Presenter at *Downtown Radio* in Belfast.

Phil KENNEDY

Presenter on *BBC GLR* in London hosting the station's 'early show (from 5am to 7am) most weekdays.

Robert KENNEDY

Bob has a wealth of experience in the radio industry. In the mid-seventies he was Managing Director of *Broadcast Marketing Services.* He then assembled the highest bid for the UK's first national commercial radio licence - '*Showtime FM*' (they were unable to raise sufficient funding so the licence went to Classic FM by default).

Bob now works at *Middle East Broadcasting*, a radio and TV company based in West London.

Roger KENNEDY

Roger is the Programme Controller at *Wessex FM* in Dorchester.

Ryan KENNEDY

Ryan is a producer and presenter of programmes at *BBC Wiltshire Sound*.

Sarah KENNEDY

Born in Wallington in Surrey on the 8th July 1950, Sarah was educated at the Notre Dame Convent in Lingfield. Her early career included periods teaching English, peeling potatoes, selling raffle tickets and a post as a matron at a boys prep' school. Sarah's radio career began in Singapore- a roundtable discussion on cystitis for the forces and their families. She later worked on *BFBS* stations in Germany before joining the BBC and working on *Radio London* and on national network programmes.

Radio Two then hired her, initially as a news reader and continuity announcer, and she then became a holiday relief for the 'Family Favourites' programme. She also sat in for John Dunn on his (again, *Radio Two*) programme for some time but then moved to Southern TV and on to LWT where she became a national figure as a co-presenter of 'Game for a Laugh'.

Sarah is far too young to have experienced the highlight of her career yet and likes tennis, running and staying in bed, but not people with no sense of humour. Currently the host of the weekday early evening slot (6 to 7.30) on *Radio Two*.

John KENNET

Charity Coordinator at *Radio Tay*.

John KENNING

John worked in a variety of business in London and was responsible for helping launch the *Laser 558* project in 1983. Later that year he funded his own land-pirate station in South West London, called *Radio Sovereign*, which was the UK's first ever 'all-gold' station.

It built up a large audience, prompting the DTI to close it the following year. john then went to Italy to restart the station there.

Alec KENNY

Sales Director at *Talkradio UK*.

Robert KENNY

Presenter at *Trent FM* in Nottingham

Samantha KENNY

Presenter at *Fortune 1458* in Manchester where she hosts the afternoon slot from 1pm until 4pm each weekday.

Who's Who in British Radio

Cindy KENT
Cindy was once the lead singer with the sixties folk band 'The Settlers' and was invited to host programmes on Sheffield ILR station *Radio Hallam* at the knee of Keith Skues.

After leaving Radio Hallam, Cindy moved to London's *Capital Radio* where she was religious producer for ten years and then moved to *Trans World Radio*. In 1995 she joined London station *Premier Radio* to be the host of the station's afternoon programme.

Nick KENYON
Nick is the Controller of *BBC Radio Three*.

David KERMODE
David is the presenter of the 'First Edition' programme each weekend evening (8 until 11pm) on *London Newsradio FM*.

Mark KERMODE
Co-host of the 'Cling Film' programme on *Radio One* with Wendy Lloyd.

Paul KERRIAGE
Paul is the General Manager and also the Sales Director at *Country 1035* in London.

Peter KERRIDGE
Station Manager at Harlow's ILR station, *Ten-17* since the station launched and also responsible for religious output at Essex Radio .

Gerry KERSEY
Presenter on *Great Yorkshire Gold*.

Andy KERSHAW
In the 1980's Andy hosted several programmes, including a weekday evening show, on *BBC Radio 1*, as well as 'Arts' programmes on *Radio Four*. He now hosts a programme each Sunday evening on *One FM*.

Phil KERSWELL
Senior producer at *BBC Radio Gloucester*.

Richard KEYS
Born in Coventry on 23rd April, 1957, Richard was a journalist in Wolverhampton before joining *Radio City* in Liverpool. He became a sports journalist too and moved across to *Piccadilly Radio* in Manchester for a time where he became deputy newsroom /sports editor.

Richard then joined TV-AM as a sports reporter and hosted several sport-oriented streams for the channel before joining BSB and more recently Sky TV. He now lives in Berkshire with his most cherished possessions - his family and his golf clubs!

Hugh KEYTE
Continuity presenter on *BBC Radio 3*.

Tahir KHAN
Operations Manager at *Sunrise Radio*, the Asian station in Bradford.

Jay KHERA
Jay is the Head of Sales at *Sabras Sound*, the new Asian station in Leicester.

Mike KIDDEY
Host of the lunchtime show on BBC *GMR*.

Lucy KILKENNY
Lucy is a reporter at *BBC Radio Newcastle*.

Dave KILNER
Dave is a DJ at *Hallam FM*.

Alan KING
Alan worked at the *Voice of Peace* and various other stations in the seventies. In the eighties he worked at *LBC* as a news presenter and also set up his own programme consultancy. He is now a regular anchorman on *Sky News*.

Andy KING
Presenter on *Oasis Radio* in St Albans.

Anna KING
Anna is the presenter of the 'Drive Time' (4 to 7pm) programme on *BBC Radio Gloucester*.

Dave KING
Dave is the Programme Controller of *KLFM*.

Gary KING
Born on the 4th August, 1963 at Stevenage, Gary attended the Mountview Drama School and worked as an actor for three years. He made his first broadcast at *Radio Top Shop*, Oxford Circus, at the knee of Howard Rose (qv) and in 1988 joined *Radio Luxembourg*.

After a period with the *Radio Radio* sustaining service, Gary joined *Atlantic 252* and then in

1990 did a series of relief shifts at *Radio One,* including the station's breakfast show and Steve Wright's programme, which he regards as the highlight of his career . . so far!

In 1993 he moved to *Virgin 1215* and in September 1995 joined London's first AC station, *Heart 106.2.*

As well as radio, Gary also writes non-fiction and TV comedy and does voice-overs for radio and TV. He once did a 'chaariddy' abseil during which he had an attack of 'disco leg' which was witnessed by over 200 people; a good job Gary likes humour, as well as food, the countryside and daydreaming, but not early starts, narrow minds and dogma.

Graham KING
Graham is the host of a Sunday afternoon programme on *BBC Radio Lincolnshire.*

Jason KING
Currently a DJ on *WABC*, in Wolverhampton.

Jonathan KING
After a Europe-wide hit in 1965 with "Everyone's Gone to the Moon" Jonathan's pop career flagged a little. He made his debut broadcast on *Radio London* (Big L) in April 1967 when he spent several days on board the ship, hosting programmes and procrastinating on the state of radio in the UK.

In the seventies and eighties Jonathan appeared on several ILR stations and on radio one for ad-hoc programmes, and is now better known for his record productions and plethora of pseudonyms such as 'The Piglets', 'The Weathermen' and 'Sacharin'. He's had many outings into the charts under such names, and his own.

Jonathan has appeared on many stations and, as well as being pretty open with his opinions, he is also an excellent raconteur and has hosted his own programmes on *Radio One* and *Capital Radio.* In 1995 he was hired by *Talkradio UK* to host a morning show and currently is heard each weekday.

Laurence KING
Presenter on *Ocean FM* and on *Southern FM.*

Lorne KING
Born on 1st February, 1943 in Alberta, Canada, he sang opera while still at school and began his radio career at CKSA at the age of 19. After moving to CKRD he was also hosting TV programmes and a few years later he set forth for the UK. He joined *Big L* (Radio London) in February 1967, Ed Stewart's first signing for the station but returned to Canada after just four months.

Ray KING
Host of weekday programmes (from 10am to 2pm) on *Signal Radio* in Cheshire.

Ross KING
Born as Derek King on 21st February, 1964, he got into radio via a hospital radio station when he was just 15 years old. He later joined *Radio Clyde* as one of the country's youngest daytime DJs. Ross then moved into TV and has appeared on a variety of programmes including three series of Quiz Night, two series of Young Krypton factor, and had his own series. He recently hosted GMTV programmes with Anthea Turner.

In 1994 Ross joined *Radio Five* and has presented several sports programmes,. He's also hosted his own programme on *Capital Radio* and the Eurochart Show on many ILR stations.

Ross lives in Broadmarston in Warwickshire where he stores his collection of James Bond memorabilia.

Steve KING
Steve's career began at *Viking Radio* as a DJ in the 1980s and he became PC at *Hallam FM.*

Carl KINGSTON

Born in East Yorkshire and schooled at Hornsea, Carl's first radio broadcast was in 1974 on BBC Radio Humberside and has since included work for *Radio Mi Amigo, Radio caroline, Norwegian State Radio, The Voice of Peace,* and Vienna's *Blue Danube Radio.*

Carl has also worked on *Viking Radio* in Hull, KSMJ in Sacramento as well as WSFW in Senecca Falls, New York. He was one of the regular DJs on *The Superstation*, the Richard Branson / YRN overnight sustaining service aired by some ILR stations in the late 1980s, and the following year to *Radio Aire,* the Leeds ILR station, where he's remained since, doing almost every programme on the schedule.

As a well as radio presentation, Carl is a full Equity member, as well as a prolific voiceover artiste being heard on commercials on radio and TV stations all over the UK. As an actor he has also been seen on programmes such as *General Hospital* and *Coronation Street.*

He has gained a wealth of experience in the music industry and is currently involved in record promotion, public relations and agency management.   Contact Carl on 0113 268 7886

Bob KINGSLEY
After a period with *Scot FM* Bob travelled south to join *Gold Radio* in Shaftesbury as senior presenter when the station opened in June 1995.

Mike KINNAIRD
Mike is a News reporter for *BBC Radio Lincolnshire* and is based in Skegness.

Janet KIPLING
Janet is a news reporter and programme presenter at *BBC Radio Devon and Cornwall.*

Andy KIRK
Andy began his radio career on *Radio 270* off the Yorkshire Coast in the 1960s and moved to *Pennine Radio* in Bradford in 1975.

Cathy KIRK
Cathy is now the Local Sales Manager for Radio Forth stations in Edinburgh.

Roger KIRK
Roger began his radio career on *Radio 270* off the Yorkshire Coast in 1966. In the 1970's he joined *Pennine Radio* in Bradford.

David KIRKWOOD
David is a senior producer responsible for 'social' matters at *BBC Radio Leicester.*

Adam KIRTLEY
Presenter at *BBC Radio Cambridgeshire.*

Steve KNIBBS
Presenter of an afternoon programme from 1pm until 4pm on *BBC Radio Gloucester.*

Alan KNIGHT
Alan is the Sales Director at *Galaxy Radio.*

Andy KNIGHT
Dj at *Ocean Sound* and *Southern FM.*

Alan KNIGHT
Sales Director at *Severn Sound*

June KNOX-MAWER
Born on the 10th May 1930 in Wrexham, June was a reporter on a local newspaper and also freelanced for the Guardian and women's magazines for a while. She made her first broadcast in 1958 on BBC Television talking about travelling in India.

June then moved to the *Fiji Broadcasting Corporation,* doing every kind of job imaginable, including teaching English and voicing commercials. In 1970 she returned to the UK and from 1971 to 1975 presented the afternoon programme on *BBC Radio Merseyside.*

In the early 1980s, June produced pieces for 'Women Hour' on *Radio Four* and occasionally hosted the 'Pick of the Week' programme, also on *Radio Four,* before becoming a regular host on 'Weekend'.

Richard KNIGHT
Richard is the PR Executive at *Atlantic 252.*

Anne KOCH
Anne is currently the Editor of 'The World Tonight' late night news programme each weekday on *BBC Radio Four.*

Geeta KOHLI
Company Secretary of Sunrise Radio Group.

Suman KOHLI
Head of Sales at the *Sunrise Group.*

Don KOTAK
Managing Director an programme controller of *Sabras Sound.*

Who's Who in British Radio

Alix KROEGER
Radio production assistant at *BBC Radio Berkshire*.

Andrea KUHN
News Editor at *RAM FM* in Derbyshire.

Jeremy KYLE
A presenter on *Orchard FM*.

Steve KYTE
Steve began his radio career at *Radio West,* the original ILR station in Bristol. He then moved to *LBC*, the news station in London and joined the BBC. He has been at *Radio Five* since the station launched and currently is Editor of the Radio Five morning show 'The Magazine'.

Alistair LACK .
Alistair is the Head of English programmes at the *BBC World Service*.

Steven LADNER
Senior presenter at *Island FM* on Guernsey.

Daniel LAK
BBC Correspondent in Islamabad, Pakistan.

Mark LAMARR
Mark currently hosts a programme on *BBC GLR* each Sunday lunchtime from 10 until 1pm.

Alan LAMBOURN
Alan is a presenter on *South Coast Radio.*

Peter LANDALE
Peter is the Chairman of *Solway Sound,* which is bidding for the Dumfries local radio licence. He is also the head of a local publishing firm.

Grainne LANDOWSKI
Born on 17th April, 1970, at Carshalton in Surrey, Grainne got into radio in May 1989 on the campus radio station at University of Exeter.

From being a DJ Grainne was soon programme controller and after graduating joined Ocean's *Power FM* as a technical operator, progressing to the heady heights of the station's 'Graveyard Shift'.

After a period hosting Power FM's Late Show, Grainne moved to *Kiss 102* in Manchester to host drive time programmes.

A self proclaimed "total radio purist," the highlight of Graine's career was winning an award for 'Best Radio Programme' from the Institute for the Study of Drug Dependence, and he once bet a fellow jock to do ten minutes of their programme totally naked. Likes being on every guest list going, but not doing the breakfast shift on New Year's Day!

Martin LANE
Engineer at *BBC Radio Leicester.*

Peter LANGFORD
Peter is the Chief Engineer at *Leicester Sound.*

Julie LANGTRY-LANGTON
After a period as head of news at *Hereward Radio*, Julie has now moved to a similar position at the *New Leicester Sound.*

Roy LARMOUR
Born in June 1955 in Belfast, he attended Newtownbread School and became a solicitors clerk before pursuing journalism at the Belfast Telegraph.

After a period in acting, during which he made his first broadcast in a *Radio Four* drama production and gained his first presentation experience on Belfast's ILR station, *Downtown Radio*, producing arts features.

Roy later joined *BBC Radio Ulster* to host an early morning show. He has also been heard on *Radio Three* and on BBC TV in Ulster.

Donna LARSEN
Donna is co-host of the breakfast show and main host of a one hour lunchtime news wrap at BBC Radio Humberside.

Giles LATCHAM
Producer at *BBC Radio Shropshire.*

Brian LATEWOOD .
Head of news at 96.7 *BCR* in Belfast.

Richard LAVELLE
Richard is a presenter at *Brunel Classic Gold.*

Philip LAVEN.

As the BBC's Controller of Engineering Policy, his responsibilities include examining the strategic implications of new broadcasting technologies, liaison with Government, commissioning engineering R&D and advising on technical standards.

Philip has played a leading role in the development of the BBC's policy on digital transmission of both DAB and digital television.

Philip sits on a variety of industry and other committees, including the EBU's Technical Committee, Digital Audio Visual council and the Joint Frequency Management Committee which manages the spectrum for UK broadcasters.

In the 1994 New Year's Honours List he was awarded an OBE for "services to broadcast engineering."

Peter LAVEROCK

News producer at *BBC Radio Suffolk.*

Miriam LAVERY

Director of *Downtown Radio* and *Cool FM.*

Alison LAW

Alison worked as a freelance presenter at *Ocean, Power FM* and *South Coast Radio* and joined the group full time in 1995.

Richard LAWLEY

Managing Director of *Pirate 102* in Cornwall.

Sue LAWLEY

Born in in Dudley, Warwickshire, on 14th July 1946, Sue graduated from Bristol University and became a journalist for three years on regional newspapers. She then joined the BBC in Plymouth as a reporter and programme presenter.

Sue has appeared on many factual programmes over the last two decades and became a regular long term stand-in for Terry Wogan on his thrice weekly series, as well as a newsreader on national bulletins.

In 1992 she took over the long-running 'Desert Island Discs' on *Radio Four* and has a son and a daughter.

Bob LAWRENCE

After school Bob did a year at Goldsmith's Art College in London, and after a flirtation with hospital radio and the London pirate scene (with stations such as *London Music Radio*) popped up on *Radio Caroline* in the 1970s. He became one of the station's most popular DJs there, and was variously known as RICHARD THOMPSON and also as BUSBY.

After his Caroline phase, Bob worked at *Greenwich Sound*, a cable community station in London, and then moved to *BRMB* in Birmingham. A short move up the road to Wolverhampton's *Beacon Radio ensured in the early 1980s, and* when the station split its AM and FM services, Bob became programme manager of the easy listening station, WABC, as well as a close involvement in sales.

The highlight of his career so far was interviewing Keith Richards, and the funniest thing he remembers was an (ex) programme controller at BRMB playing in the Queen's Speech - backwards!

Bob switched to *Buzz FM* in Birmingham for a while, and then returned to *BRMB FM,* and then to sister station *XTRA AM,* the Capital group's 'gold' outlet in the Midlands. he likes intelligent radio presenters gut doesn't like DJs with nothing to say, but who are 'tight' and play lots of sweepers and jingles.

Chris LAWRENCE

Host of a Sunday afternoon programme on *BBC Radio Cleveland.*

Diane LAWRENCE

Essex born Diane was a DJ on *Radio Caroline* in the mid 1980s.

Eric LAWRENCE

Eric joined Metro Radio Group as Financial Controller in 1988 and was appointed to the board in 1992. He is a chartered accountant and the Finance Director of the *Metro Radio Group.*

Gavin LAWRENCE

Announcer and programme manager on *Channel Travel Radio.*

Sarah LAWRENSON
Sarah is the programme controller at *CMR*.

Stan LAUNDON
Born on 15th June in Hartlepool he attended a local school and became an apprentice engineer and then the full time secretary of Joe Brown's Fan Club, around the time he was enjoying major hits.

Stan's first broadcast was on *Radio Two* and *Radio Durham* in a country music programme and he later joined *Radio Middlesborough*, which has since became *Radio Cleveland*. He hosted many programmes on the station in the seventies and eighties, including the station's 'AM 194' breakfast programme.

Graham LEACH
Graham was the BBC Correspondent in Brussel s in the late 1980s and in 1994 joined *London Newsradio FM*, where he now is the presenter of the breakfast programme, 'London Today', each weekday and 'Backbencher' on Sunday afternoons.

Timothy LEADBEATER
Director at *Signal Radio*.

Paul LEAPER
Paul is in charge of promotions at *BBC GLR*.

Paul LECKIE
Paul is a DJ at *MFM* in Wrexham.

Graham LEDGER
Born on 7th February 1955 in Littlehampton, after private tuition in speech and drama he qualified as a Licentiate of the Trinity College, London and worked for his father before a period in summer seasons and pantomimes with the Black and White Minstrel Show, and as a mobile disco DJ.

He tried to get in to broadcasting for several years, unsuccessfully, until his tape to the *Voice of Peace* off Israel brought a favourable response from PD Crispian St John (see Howard Rose, qv).

Armed with the mandatory experience, Graham then got a position at *Radio 210* in Reading, producing weekend breakfast shows, country music programmes and ethnic programming.

Graham added substantially to his ILR experience over the years and is now Programme Controller of *TFM* in Stockton. Ever the showman, Graham recently took up fire-eating in aid of charity and now does a superb 'volcano'!

Mark LEDSOM
Morning presenter at *Nevis Radio*.

Chris LEE
Born on 19th November 1952 in Manchester, Chris was educated in Cheltenham and became a social worker in 1975 and then worked as a kindergarten teacher, a gardener and decorator, before working in a record shop.

He made his first broadcast as a film critic on *Severn Sound* in 1980, having been a founder member of Cotswold Hospital radio and later produced outside broadcasts for the station. Chris devise the station's '388 Tonight' programme (a reference to its AM wavelength) and moved to *BBC Radio Merseyside* to host the station's breakfast programme in the early 1980s.

Dave LEE
Dave is currently the Head of Music at *Minster FM* in York he also presents the 'Juke Box' programme each weekday evening, from 7pm until 10pm.

Jeff LEE
Station Director at *Radio 210* in Reading.

Matthew LEE
Chief Engineer at *The Wave*, Blackpool.

Paul LEE
Presenter of the weekday evening rock music programme on *Essex Radio* in the 1980's

Who's Who in British Radio

John LEECH

A one time trainee health inspector and record shop manager, John also worked for a while as a clerk at the BBC. He did some hospital radio for the Metropolitan Hospital Network, and made his first broadcast in 1984 with *Capital Radio*, doing the pre-dawn shift and running the station's library. John then moved on to Essex Radio where he now presents the weekday evening programme.

John has won many awards, the latest being "Best Soul and Dance Show in the World" at the New York Festival in 1985, which he regards as the highlight of his career so far. He likes chocolate, his cat and 'Have I got news for you, but dislikes garlic, plastic girls and shopping.

David LEES

Formerly a sales executive at *Metro Radio*, he moved to a similar position at *Talkradio UK* in July 1995.

Ian LEES

Presenter of classical and Scottish music programmes at *Radio Tay* in Dundee.

Stephen LEFEVRE

Born in 1957 in County Antrim he attended Grammar School in Larne and the University of Ulster at Coleraine in County Londonderry. His first job was as a management trainee and he also managed a shop for Visionshire for a while.

In 1979 he made his first broadcast on a local radio station and joined the BBC in 1981. He's since presented the 'Early Show' on *Radio Ulster* and became a staff announcer and newsreader. He is now a presenter at *BBC Radio Leeds*.

Jim LEFTWICH

Chairman of *Eleven Seventy* in High Wycombe.

Justin LEIGH

Presenter at *BBC Radio Cornwall*.

William LEITCH

William began his broadcasting career in Ulster, supplying programmes to overseas stations. before moving on to report for an evening programme at *Downtown Radio* and launching with the newly formed *BCR* in 1990, where he ran two programmes. He had the distinction of being the first person to leave the new station of his own volition.

He joined the BBC in the summer of 1990 earning one of that year's coveted 24 places on the local radio trainee reporter's scheme. Placements included *BBC Northampton, BBC Somerset Sound* and *BBC Radio Cleveland*. And it's in Cleveland that William has stayed working for four years as a news reporter and then producer.

Since the summer of 1994 he's been presenting "William Leitch in the Afternoon", trying to increase and develop magazine programme journalism beyond simply sifting through press releases. he confesses to being "interested in everything" with a particular obsession about the County Durham puma!

Terry LENNAINE

After attending various schools Terry became a musician and an actor. He filled in as a night club DJ before getting his first radio show on *BBC Radio Merseyside* in April 1973. he stayed with the BBC until 1988 before moving across town to *Radio City*, where he's remained ever since.

The funniest thing which happened to Terry was, after dedicating 'The Last Waltz' to a listener, being told she had both her legs amputated. Among his favourite things are his wife, cats and dogs, and he hates smoking and drunks.

Andre LEON

Host of a Sunday programme on *Classic FM*.

Roy LEONARD

Born on the 25th April 1948 in Bedford, Roy's s first job was as an apprentice draughtsman and made his first broadcast in 1966 on an RAF camp station.

Following that he did some hospital radio and then community radio, finally appearing on the ether in 1972, courtesy of *BBC Radio Medway*.

Roy worked at *Chiltern Radio* for a while as a freelance presenter hosting the station's weekly chart show as well as other weekend output.

Roy then joined *Radio Wyvern*, where he helped launch the station in 1982.

Later in the eighties he moved to *Metro Radio* in Newcastle and was the Head of Programming when the station launched its *Great North Radio* AM service.

After a period running Metro's Hull outlet, *Viking FM,* he moved back north to *Wear FM* in Sunderland to become Station Manager, leaving in 1995.

Caroline LEOPARD
News reporter at *BBC Radio Jersey.* She also appears on local TV opt-out programmes.

Kathy LEPPARD
Kathy is a staff member at the Radio Academy.

Alex LESTER
Began his radio career at *Radio Aire* in Leeds and then moved to BBC local radio a few years later. Alex was the breakfast programme presenter at *BBC Essex* when it launched on Bonfire Night, 1986.

He has also been heard on *BBC Radio Two* in recent years hosting overnight programmes, from 3am to 6am.

Julia LETTS
Julia is a news producer at *BBC Essex.*

Matthew LEVINGTON
After working for BUPA for three years as Sales Development Manager, Matthew joined *Piccadilly Radio* in 1993 as a Promotions Executive, with special responsibilities for outside events.

In 1994 he was promoted to his current position as Head of Promotions, looking after all revenue generating promotions.

Charles LEVISON
Charles was the second in command at *Virgin Radio* when the company won the 'ILR 2' licence in 1992 and he is now a non-executive director of the Chrysalis group, operators of *Heart FM.*

Charles LEVITT
News Producer at *BBC Radio Humberside* from the early 1980s to the present day.

Harry LEVY
Harry is a director of *Essex Radio* in Southend.

Peter LEVY
Born on the 5th September 1955 in Farnborough, Kent, Peter was educated at Hammersmith College of Further Education and Mountview Theatre School as a teenager Peter was seen as an actor in many series including Dixon of Dock Green, Man about the House and Comedy Playhouse.

Out of curiosity he applied for a job with *Pennine Radio*, got it and never looked back since his first programme, on 20th September in 1975. His own show was heard on Bradford's *Pennine Radio* for four and a half years, then he hosted 'City Extra' on Liverpool ILR *Radio City*.

After two years on Merseyside, Peter went back across the Pennines to join *Radio Aire* in in Leeds for its launch in 1981. Peter stayed with *Radio Aire* for 6 years presenting the popular morning show.

In 1987 Peter joined the BBC in Leeds, since then he has hosted the PETER LEVY SHOW on the station ever since, five days a week and, more recently, on Sunday mornings too.

Peter is THE regular face of TV news for BBC 1 Television in the North of England presenting around 10 bulletins a day and also hosting the lunchtime edition of Look North.

Peter has also hosted the annual TV appeal CHILDREN IN NEED for the BBC. He's also been in pantomime in Bradford with Su Pollard and has narrated numerous stage shows.

Peter loves gliding, badminton and walking on the moors close to his Yorkshire home.

Martin LEWES

Although born in Australia, Martin was brought up in Devon and trained as a journalist in the Midlands. He left newspapers to freelance in radio and TV.

Martyn worked as a radio journalist for *BBC Radio Cumbria* for seven years and now has what he is certain is the best job in radio - running the district office in Kendal: "I get paid to drive around beautiful countryside talking to interesting people!"

Martyn likes variety and hates routine.

A D F LEWIS

Chairman of *Northsound Radio*, Aberdeen.

Anthony LEWIS

Anthony is the News Editor at *Channel 103*.

Bruce LEWIS

Bruce was the first Managing Director of *Metropolitan Radio* in Newcastle.

James LEWIS

Soul music DJ at *Swansea Sound*.

Jane LEWIS

Jane was a broadcast journalist at *BBC Radio Berkshire*, which is now merged with Radio Oxford to form *BBC Radio Thames Valley*.

Johnny LEWIS

Born in Essex on Christmas Day in 1958, Johnny became a pig farmer on leaving school and got into radio while working as a seaman delivering supplies to *Radio Caroline*. He ended up working on the Mi Amigo and by 1978 was presenting programmes on the station under the name Steven Bishop.

When the ship sank in 1980 Johnny went to the *Voice of Peace* for nine months and then went off to Dublin in 1981 to work at Dublin super-pirates *Sunshine Radio* and the legendary *Radio Nova*. In 1983 he became senior DJ at *ABC Radio,* one of the country's biggest private stations, in Waterford.

In 1984 he was hired for the Laser Project and his was one of the key voices on the ship's first test transmissions. Later that year he joined *Radio Caroline* once again and stayed with the station for several years, eventually joining shore based *Radio Wyvern* in Herefordshire staying under Norman Bilton's control for fifteen months. He then joined *Invicta Radio* in Kent where he now hosts the station's breakfast show, 6 until 10 am each weekday morning.

As well as radio, Johnny also appears on screen for Kent Police and spends all his spare time raising funds for the RNLI. The biggest kick of his career was knowing that his father had heard his first broadcast on Caroline, and being involved in the start up of *Mellow 1557* in Frinton.

The funniest event in Johnny's career is one which has gone down in offshore radio history and involves his having a full sack of flour dumped over his head while on the air on Christmas Day, 1979.

He likes a good curry, golf and boats (good and bad ones!) but not the law which outlaws radio ships. Johnny's biggest aim is to put the fun back into radio.

Always available for good causes and fun ideas - Tel 01 04 615196.

Judith LEY
Presents late night programmes at the weekend on *Manx Radio.*

Alan LEYSON
Alan is a director of Lincs FM.

Lady LIGGINS OBE
Chairman of *Mercia FM* in Coventry.

John LIGHTFOOT
John is regional controller of BBC Resources.

Rohan LIGHTFOOT
Traffic manager at *Scot FM.*

John LILLEY
Initially a print journalist, John joined the BBC in 1973 and worked as a reporter for BBC *Radio Nottingham*. In 1980 he was appointed News Editor at *Radio Lincolnshire,* being there for the launch of the station in November that year. He stayed there for four years before moving to Devon, spending eight years there as Programme Editor and Acting Manager.

John also managed *BBC Wiltshire Sound* for a spell and worked as a journalist with regional television. In 1993 he joined *BBC Radio Humberside* as Managing Editor.

Dave LINCOLN
Born in 1953, Dave's radio career began in 1974 at the launch of *Radio City* in Liverpool where he was one of the station's most popular presenters.

In 1979 he became Head of Music at Radio City and in 1987 moved up the M6 to Preston to become Programme Organiser at *Red Rose Radio.* Within a year he was promoted to the role of Managing Director.

While at Red Rose he was responsible for the birth of *Red Rose Gold* and *Rock FM*, recognised as one of the most successful frequency splits to date.

In 1991 Dave returned to *Radio City*, this time as Managing Director, and turned City into a market leader and launching *City Gold* on its AM frequency.

In August 1994 he moved to Manchester, becoming Managing Director of *Key FM* and *Piccadilly Gold* and he is also a member of the AIRC Programming Committee.

Debbie LINDLEY
Presenter at *The Pulse* in Bradford.

Francis LINE
Born on the 22nd February, 1940, she attended James Allen's Girls School and then joined the BBC in 1957 as a clerk and typist. Until 1967 she worked as a secretary in both TV and radio and then became one of *Radio Two's* first producers in 1967.

Six years later, Francis became a senior producer and in 1979 was appointed as Chief Assistant at *Radio Two*. In 1983 she moved to *Radio Four* in a similar role, but after two years returned to radio two as head of *Radio Two's* music department. Frances was appointed Network Controller of *Radio Two* in 1990, a role she held until December 1995.

Her recreations include Sussex, the theatre and taking happy snaps and she is also a Member of the Council of the Radio Academy.

Judi LINES
Presenter on *Great North Radio*.

Magnus LINKLATER
Host of the 'Eye to Eye' programme each Sunday morning on *BBC Radio Scotland.*

Stuart LINNELL MBE

Stuart joined *BBC Radio Birmingham* as a freelance broadcaster in 1970, and four years later moved to Sheffield's *Radio Hallam* as sports editor, a seat he occupied for six years. In 1980 he moved to Coventry station *Mercia Sound* in a similar role and also hosted the station's weekday afternoon programme.

In 1983 Mercia appointed him programme controller, and in 1986 he became Managing Director of Midlands Community Radio and Programme Controller of *Mercia Sound,* roles he was to keep for the next eight years.

In 1991 Stuart was also made MD and programme controller of *Leicester Sound,* and in early 1994 he became acting station director of *RAM FM,* the new GWR station in Derby.

In 1995 he was appointed Executive Director of *Sports Radio UK,* the arm of GWR which provides sporting programme to BBC and ILR stations, and which also operates RSL stations for sporting venues and events.

In addition to managing Mercia, one of the country's most innovative stations, Stuart has been involved in a variety of independent programmes, many of which have won awards and he's been adopted as the house commentator by Coventry City, presenting many videos about the club's success.

In 1990 Stuart received a Gold Medal at the International Radio Festival in New York for Mercia's programme format - the following year the station won two silver medals and there were more awards in subsequent years. In the 1995 New Year Honours List, Stuart received the MBE for his services to radio broadcasting.

Ann LINSCOTT

Director of *Signal Radio* group.

Paul LINSCOTT

Paul is the Chief Engineer at *Radio Wyvern.*

Brian LISTER

Born on the 9th March, 1951 in Ilford, Brian attended Abbs Cross Technical High School in Hornchurch, Essex. After setting up a hospital radio service in Romford, he became manager at University Radio Essex while studying for his BA (Hons) in Telecommunications. He trained with the *BBC* as a radio studio manager, working at Broadcasting House and with the Overseas Services at Bush House.

In 1974 Brian joined *Metropolitan Radio* in Newcastle, where he became Assistant programme Controller.

With the acquisition of *Radio Tees* in 1986, Brian was appointed Programme Director. He later became General Manager of the group's Stockton station, which he successfully relaunched as *TFM.*

From 1985 to 1995 he was also a director of Sunderland Community Radio, which operated the *Wear FM* outlet in Britain's newest city.

He has also worked as a consultant to a number of radio groups and is a visiting lecturer in radio production at Sunderland University. He was a part of the *A1FM* consortium which won the Darlington ILR licence in 1995 and recently moved to harrogate where he is now the Managing Director at *Stray FM.*

His hobbies include flying - he gained his private pilots licence in 1993 - and he is a member of the Radio Academy.

Avtar LIT

Chairman of the *Sunrise Radio Group.*

Lester LITTELBANK

Presenter on *BBC Radio Cambridgeshire.*

Pat LITTLE

Presenter at *Great North Radio* and News Coordinator for the *Metro FM* and GNR stations.

Gareth LITTLER

Gareth is managing director of *United Christian Broadcasters*, which transmits a round-the-clock Christian music programme on Astra.

Trevor LITTLECHILD

Host of *BBC Radio Cambridgeshire* Sunday request programme and also programmes about vintage music.

David LLOYD

David attended Rushcliffe Comprehensive School and then worked for Lloyds Bank (he stresses it's not his family business!)

He got into radio via the shed at the bottom of his garden and hospital radio, with his first broadcast being a week before Christmas 1977.

By 1980 he was hosting the afternoon show at *Radio Trent* and, after a period on the morning shift he moved across to *Leicester Sound* in 1987. While there he won a Sony Award in 1988, did a morning programme and took up the reins as Programme Controller.

In 1991 he moved to Lincoln for the opening of *Lincs FM*, the highlight of his career.

He hosted Sunday morning programmes and became the station's Programme Controller until Summer 1995, when the Radio Authority announced he was to become their new Head of Programming and Advertising from Autumn 1995.

Geoff LLOYD

Host of a weekday evening programme (7 to 10pm) on *Signal Radio* in Cheshire.

Geraint LLOYD

Geraint is the Programme Controller at *Radio Ceredigion*.

Polly LLOYD

Polly hosts a consumer oriented programme each weekday morning from 9 until 121 noon on *BBC Radio Gloucester*.

Steve LLOYD

DJ at *Swansea Sound*.

Sian LLOYD

Born in Maesteg, Mid Glamorgan, on 3rd July 1958, Sian joined *CBC*, Cardiff's ILR station as a trainee journalist.

She later presented programmes, notably an evening rock music programme, before joining BBC TV in Wales in 1981. In the late eighties she moved to ITV and currently fronts networked weather forecasts.

Tim LLOYD

Tim was a very popular presenter on BBC Radio Kent and on Essex Radio in the 1980's, where he was better known as 'Timbo'.

Tony LLOYD

Tonyu is the Presenter of several weekday programmes on *Chiltern Gold* and *Oasis in St Albans*.

Wendy LLOYD

Currently a presenter at *Virgin 1215*.

Aled LLOYD-DAVIES

Aled is a DJ on *Marcher Gold* in Wrexham.

Norman LLOYD - EDWARDS

Norman was the Chairman of *Galaxy Radio*.

Bob LLOYD-SMITH
Bob is the Station Manager at *Radio Jersey*.

Vicky LOCKLIN
Presenter at *Hallam FM* in Sheffield.

Tony LOCKWOOD
Tony is a sports specialist and hosts two programmes each week on *London Newstalk AM* - including the Friday evening 'Ahead of the Game' programme.

Tom LODGE
Tom is the grandson of the man who first demonstrated radio in public (Professor Oliver Lodge - at Liverpool in 1894, and three years before Marconi came to England). He left England aged four end went to Virginia in the USA - by 17 he was a cowhand on a ranch and two years later took part in an Arctic Expedition before joining the Canadian Broadcasting Corporation.

In 1964 he visited England and was snapped up by *Radio Caroline*.

He had the honour of broadcasting live from the ship as she sailed around the British coast to the Isle of Man, where he stayed until the following year when Caroline called him to the south ship to help fight off the new Radio London. Tom's innovative new programming boosted Caroline's standing in the sixties and in 1968 he joined BBC *Radio One* for a year.

Wanderlust took over Tom's life again and he moved back to Canada where he hosted a rock show on *CHLO*, Toronto, and he also established a training course (still running) for engineers and producers.

There followed periods in India and Calgary, as well as Canada and California, until 1995 saw Tom return to England to help *Radio Caroline* with an RSL operation off Clacton, and again in London in the Autumn.

A prolific writer, Tom is currently writing a new book on his views of British radio and a screenplay of his works.

Simon LOGAN

Born on 24th June, 1968 in Chester, Simon worked in clubs as a DJ and compere and also did theatrical work. He's appeared on TV as well as pantomime.

His break into radio came in October 1993 when he joined Hull station *Viking FM*, hosting an evening programme. Three months later he was moved to breakfasts.

The highlight of Simon's career was getting a Sony Award in 1994 in the 'Best Newcomer' category. Humourous events for Simon occur every morning - he likes honest people, cats (his own is called Mostyn and has become something of a cult hero) cooking and swimming, but he hates noisy pubs and heavy dance music.

Glenn LONDON
Head of Sales at *Isle of Wight Radio*.

Heather LONG
Heather is a programme producer and also presents some programmes on *BBC Radio Devon and Dorset*.

Jackie LONG
Jackie was a member of the newsteam at *BBC Radio Bedfordshire* in the early 1990s.

Janice LONG
Janice is the sister of Keith Chegwin and she joined *BBC Radio One* in the mid seventies, hosting some daytime programmes for several years.

In the mid 1980s Janice worked briefly for 'Radio Radio', the overnight sustaining service. She joined *GLR* in the late 1980s where she hosted the weekday breakfast programme with James Cameron.

Who's Who in British Radio

She recently moved back to Liverpool and has been organising Crash FM, an RSL station, to prepare for a bid for a permanent licence for a rock station on Merseyside.

Kirstie LONG
Kirstie is a weekday programme presenter at *Invicta FM* in Kent.

Mike LONGLEY
Mike is a DJ at *Touch AM* in Cardiff.

Dave LONGMAN
Dave was a journalsist at recor Mirror in the 1970s, and he later joined the *Radio Advertrising Bureau* as Head of Communications. In late 1995 he left to join advertising agency McCann Erickson.

Adrian LOVE
In the early 1990s, Adrian was a DJ on County Sound's *First Gold* station. Adrian is now a presenter on *South Coast Radio*.

Captain LOVE
One of the Captain's first jobs was working as a Butlins Redcoat and as a training PE teacher. he then moved to the Channel Islands and worked at a local radio station, then moved back to the UK in 1979 and a job at *Beacon Radio* before moving on to *Capital Radio*.

Jim LOVE
Jim hosts a jazz music programme once a week at *Moray Firth Radio* in Inverness.

Malcolm LOVE
Malcolm is a senior producer for BBC Network Radio, based at the Southampton studio centre.

David LOVELL
David is the Financial controller at *Q103* in Cambridge and also the Station Manager of *KLFM* in Kings Lynn.

David LOW
Host of programmes on nostalgia on BBC local stations in the west; based at *Radio Devon*.

Sally LOW
Sally is the DJ of a Sunday evening programme (6 until 10pm) at *Heart 100.7* in the Midlands.

Stu LOWE
Breakfast DJ on *Manx Radio*.

Mike LOWES
Mike is a sports reporter and producer at BBC *Radio Newcastle*.

Charlie LOWNDES
Charklie is head of the *British Forces Broadcasting Service,* based in London.

Jeremy LOYD
Director of *Fox FM* in Oxford.

David LUCAS
David's career began at *Capital Radio* as a producer at the time of the station's launch in 1973, from where he moved to *Swansea Sound* becoming the station's Programme Controller.

After several successful years in Swansea, he moved along the coast to an appointment as Chief Executive of Cardiff Broadcasting, which became known as CBC.

David was then involved in the launch of *Ocean Sound*, which replaced *Radio Victory* in Portsmouth. After successfully establishing the Ocean operation, David moved to set up *County Sound* in Guildford.

In the 1990's he became an independent consultant, working on the Eurotunnel project and in September 1995 took up a new role as Chief Executive of *Essex Radio* in Southend.

Jon LUCAS
Born in May 1956 in London, Jon's first broadcast was on hospital radio and then on a college station. He is currently the breakfast show presenter at *RTM* in south London where he is also Programme Manager.

The highlight of his radio career is still on its way and the strangest thing which happened was being told George McCrae was dead just after he'd interviewed him!

Likes a pint, but not people who say "can't".

Who's Who in British Radio

Richard LUCAS

Born in London. Richard was educated at Sheffield University and at the University of Florence.

He joined the BBC as a News Trainee in 1970 and after a spell in the radio newsroom he moved to *BBC Radio Solent,* where he became News Editor in 1975.

From Southampton, he moved to the Regional Parliamentary Unit (in 1978) and after a year he was appointed Chief Parliamentary Journalist.

As head of the unit he developed the first fully bi-media department and in the 1983 General Election he was the BBC's Chief Political Correspondent.

In 1984 he retuned to local radio as Programme Organiser at *Radio Lincolnshire,* and two years later headed the team which set up *BBC Essex.* In 1992 he launched a regional television political programme and then returned to *BBC Essex* as Managing Editor.

In January 1995 he moved to Nottingham as Head of Local Programmes in the East Midlands, responsible for the output of *Radios Nottingham, Leicester, Derby and Lincolnshire.*

Sarah LUCAS

Sunday morning presenter on *Classic FM.*

Dave LUCK

Presenter at *2CR* in Bournmouth.

Shirley LUDFORD

Shirley presents a programme each Sunday evening at 7pm on *BBC Wiltshire Sound.*

Diana LUKE

Canadian born Diana was invited to become the first female presenter on *Viking Radio.* She then moved on to the ill-fated Branson overnight service *Radio Radio,* and following this she had a stretch on *Radio Mercury.* Then followed a period at BBC GLR in London, where she hosted a weekday afternoon programme, before joining London's new station aimed at women, *Viva 963,* in 1995 as Head of Music and the station's afternoon presenter.

Simon LUMSDEN

Simon got into radio when he moved to Malta and worked in a small station there. His first broadcast was on a childrens radio show on *Radio Forth* in the 1970's. He is currently anchorman for *Scot FM*'s daily news magazine "The Scot Report" . Previously worked on *Virgin Radio, Network News Supergold , Radio Maldwyn* and *Calypso 102* in Malta.

Robin LUSTIG

Robin is currently one of the main presenters on the BBC Radio Four programme 'The World Tonight'

MICK LUVZIT

Born on the 24th February, 1944 in Canada, Mick wrote lots of songs and appeared as acon cert violinst when he was just 14 years old. He carved quite a career as an actor, singer and TV interviewer in California, and was DJ on several Canadfian stations - CKY in Winnipeg and then moving on to other stations, including hot rocking at the time!) CHUM in Toronto.

Mickfirst hit the UK in 1965. He joined *Radio Caroline* immediately and headed out to the North ship off the Isle of Man, and quickly became the station's most popular DJ, attracting over 1,000 fan letters in his first week on the station.

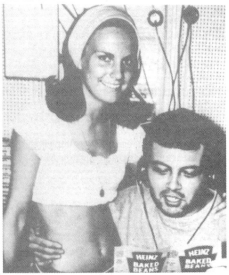

Among his fans was the sister of another Caroline DJ, Ray Teret (qv). She met Ray on several occasions and eventually agreed to marry him. The occasion was very special as it was witnessed by around four million listeners - it took place live on-air on the Caroline North ship, with Dutch Captain Martin Gripps officiating. It's the only wedding ever to have taken place on a radio ship and one of the few broadcast weddings in the world.

Unfortunately, they divorced in the 1970s and Mick went back to Canada.

Chris LYDDON
Senior Producer at *BBC Radio Cornwall.*

Sue LYNAS
Chief Publicity Officer at *BBC Radio Bristol.*

Tony LYMAN
He currently hosts the lunchtime strip at *GEM AM* in the East Midlands.

Lisa LYNCH
Having grown up and attended University in Nottingham, it was only natural that Lisa would start her radio career there too. In 1991 she joined *BBC Radio Nottingham* and since then has proved that adaptability is her middle name; she hosts the lunchtime programme as well as being a frequent weather presenter on local TV.

Hazel LYNES
Hazel is a director of *Fortune 1458*, the new easy-listening station in Manchester.

Desmond LYNHAM
Desmond's first broadcasting job was at *BBC Radio Brighton* as a sport commentator and general newshound. Now at BBC TV as a sports presenter.

Stewart LYTHE
Director of Engineering at the Red Rose Group and also a member of the Board of Directors.

Neil MACADMAM
Neil is the Sales Director of *Radio Mercury.*

Tonya MACARI

Tonya attended George Watson's College in Edinburgh after graduating in law and business studies from three Scottish Universities. She also acted in a professional comedy revue for four years and 'dabbled' in singing for a while but then entered the 'Have A Go' day promotion at *Capital Radio* - who suggested she 'go for it!"

Her first broadcast was on Northsound Radio in Aberdeen in 1989 when she shivered her way through a Saturday morning breakfast programme in the arctic wastelands of a very severe Aberdonian winter.

After two years there she moved to the sunnier climes of the South Africa's Wild Coast and the hot AM station Capital Radio in Durban.

Back to the UK and, after a short period at *BBC Radio Cambridgeshire*, she moved to CD 603 in Gloucester before joining *BBC Radio Gloucester* for a year.

Tonya is also an accomplished music and features writer as well as being a lecturer in business law. The highlight of her radio career was being told that her 20 minute chat with Gloria Estafan was off due to flu. Resolving to never play her records again, poor Tony had to eat humble pie next day when Gloria sent her a personal note apologising.

She also did a spoof 'Madonna Live from LA' link up in 1980 and fooled the station's own newsroom, management and the tabloids who all fell for her 'Madge' accent. Likes chocolate, Brookside and the Scottish Rugby team, and among her pet hates are the Angling Times and having to put the bins out twice a week.

Paddy MACDEE
Paddy is the presenter of the weekday afternoon programme on *BBC Radio Newcastle.*

Who's Who in British Radio

Bill MACDONALD

After university Bill joined *A.C. Nielsen*, a leading market research company in Oxford and was later relocated to New York. After returning to London in the late sixties he helped assemble one of the major bids for the first ILR contract, by the inelegantly named (his words) *London News Consortium*.

When LBC pipped them to the post, Bill brought his Yorkshire Television group and United Newspapers together to bid for the Sheffield / South Yorkshire ILR franchise which became *Radio Hallam*. Bill was appointed Managing Director before the station's launch in 1974 and remained at the helm until 1990.

The station was undoubtedly one of the UK's leading ILR operations, attracting many major radio 'names' to work within its portals, a splendid achievement given Sheffield's rather unattractive 'run down' image at the time, at least as perceived by the London agencies.

Hallam was an instant success with its listeners, but also found time to win awards, the most notable being for a drama-documentary series "Dying for a Drink", master-minded by Ralph Bernard.

Bill MacDonald joined the council of ILR's trade association, AIRC, chairing various committees before becoming chairman of the Association in 1988.

He oversaw expansion of Hallam to become one of the first major groups, the *Yorkshire Radio Network*. YRN was one of the first to split AM from FM services, rolling out its dual operation on Humberside in 1988 after a six month test to the full network of 13 transmitters.

Bill left the network after the take-over by Metro in 1990 and is now Chairman of *Audionics*, a leading audio equipment manufacturer, based in Sheffield. He is also a director of Sheffield International Venues Ltd, which operates the Sheffield Arena, the Don Valley Stadium and the Ponds Forge Leisure Centre, also of the Weston Park Hospital Trust.

Elvey MACDONALD

The Chairman of *Radio Ceredigion*.

Katie MACDONALD

News reporter at *Moray Firth Radio*.

NIEL MACDONALD

Engineer at *Radio Hallam* until 1990 and then in a similar role at *Red Rose Radio* in Preston. In 1994, joined the *BBC*, working in television in London and in 1995 he joined Molinaire Studios in a new department which provides facilities for the American *Sci-Fi TV* channel, which launched in November, 1995.

Spence MACDONALD

Former breakfast presenter at *Signal One* in Stoke, he is now working as a presenter at *Bay 96* in Lancaster.

Trevor MACDONALD

Well known ITN newscaster and journalist, Trevor joined *Talkradio UK* in September, 1995 to host a Sunday morning programme.

Keith MACDOUGALL

A Journalist at *BBC Radio Lincolnshire*.

Peter MACFARLANE

Senior Producer at *Spire FM*

Barry MACHIN

Managing Director (and also Company Secretary) of Signal group of stations.

Gerald MACINTYRE

Director of *Nevis Radio* in Scotland.

Dougie MACK

Presenter at OceanFM and Southern Sound.

Linsey MACK

Secretary to the MD of BBC Network Radio.

Phil MACKENZIE

Host of the 'Overnight' shift from 2am until 6am on *Minster FM* in York and *Yorkshire Coast Radio* in Scarborough and Whitby.

Bob MACKIE

Born Bob McWilliam on 3rd September, , 1950 in Glasgow, Bob started his career in newspaper sales and marketing with the *Scottish Daily Express* and then local and regional newspapers.

He was a hospital radio stalwart in Paisley and with Tony Currie's Radio Six.

Bob joined *Radio Clyde* in 1978 as part of the 'Clyde Guide' promotional journal team but returned to newspapers after a year. He was an unstilting campaigner for local radio in the Paisley area and coordinated the successful application for *Q96 FM*, which launched in September 1992. He became the station's programme controller and a director, resigning to pursue the Central Scotland regional licence with Tony Currie's *Radio Six*.

Recently, he's been broadcasting on Glasgow *Country Radio 105* (an RSL) and is Features Editor and Sales Executive with the fortnightly radio magazine *AM/FM,* as well as being involved with the BBC Radio Helpline.

The highlight of Bob's career so far was getting Q96 on the air and the most humours event he can recall is meeting Ronan O'Rahilly on the Mi Amigo in 1972. Bob is married with two cats and has a penchant for adult contemporary music, italian food and real ale, but doesn't like dance music, Indian food or fizzy keg beer.

Don MACLEAN
Presenter of the Sunday morning breakfast programme on *BBC Radio 2.*

Gary MACLEAN
Presenter on *Brunel Classic Gold.*

Ken MACLEOD
Ken presents country music programmes on *Radio Tay.*

Tracey MACLEOD
Born in Ipswich, Suffolk, in 1960, she gained a BA(Hons) in English from Durham University and became a journalist for various magazines and a TV researcher before joining *BBC GLR,* where she's hosted a programme since 1991.

Bobi MACLENNAN
After attending Inverness High School, he wandered past *Moray Firth Radio* and noticed the front door was open, so got straight in and made his first broadcast in February 1982.

Two years later he was out in the Gulf for a couple of years, working at *Radio Bahrain* and *Radio Dubai,* before returning to the UK in 1987 and a gig at *Essex Radio.*

The following year, Bob returned to Inverness and *Moray Firth Radio* but wanderlust soon took over once again, and he embarked on a world tour which took in *Radio Monte Carlo,* an FM station in Texas and then an American news station before returning to *Moray Firth Radio* once again in 1992.

In 1994 he did some voice over work for Unique Broadcasting and in 1995 joined Scotland's first regional station, *SCOT-FM.*

"Wee Fat Bob" as he's better known once did a breakfast show naked, for the sake of an interview with a nudist - who showed up wearing a suit! He also got his cat Harvey measured up for a suit 'live' on the air.

Helen MACPHERSON
Presenter of weekly country music programme on *Moray Firth Radio.*

Ian MACPHERSON
Financial controller and Company Secretary at *Talkradio UK.*

Christine MACWILLIAM
Director of *Moray Firth Radio.*

Christine MADDEN
Christine is the press and promotions manager at *KISS FM* in London.

Helen MADDEN
Helen presents a programme on *BBC Radio Five* called 'Education Matters' on Wednesday lunchtimes.

Steve MADDEN
Steve hosts a programme in the early hours of the morning on *BBC Radio Two.*

Julie MADDOCKS
Presents mid-morning show on *BBC Radio Kent* and is also heard reading traffic announcements on *Channel Travel Radio.*

Diana MADILL

After school at Portadown College, Diana went to Edinburgh University and made her first broadcast at St Vincents Hospital Radio in Dublin. She got into radio by knocking on lots of doors and spent some time as a reporter in BBC local radio before working on the 'Today' programme on *Radio Four*. She now presents 'The Magazine' programme at *Radio Five*.

As well as radio, Diana is frequently seen as a TV news reporter on both BBC channels and also hosts the 'Summer Holiday' programme on BBC 1. Her most humourous event in radio was taking part in a mock phone-in with 'Spitting Image' characters for 'Children in Need' which fits well with her liking for intelligent debate with humour; Diana can't stand pretentiousness, pettiness, arrogance and liars.

In the 1995 Sony Awards she received a Gold Award for best response to a news event, and a silver award for best phone-in. [Agent Jo Gurnett 01 71 736 7828].

Euan MAHEY

Head of News at *Island FM* on Guernsey.

Gerald MAIN

Phone-in host on *BBC Radio Cambridgeshire's* Sunday schedules.

Tim MAITLAND

Tim was the senior Sports Producer at *Viking FM* from where he went to the BBC World Service and then to *Virgin 1215*.

Graham MAJIN

Graham is now the Assistant Editor at *BBC Radio Kent*, based in the Medway towns.

David MAKER

David became the Chairman and Chief Executive of the Golden Rose Group, which includes *Jazz FM* and *Viva 963*, resigning in September, 1995, to pursue other interests.

Derek MAKIN

Presenter at *TFM* in Stockton.

Bob MALCOLM

After being educated at the Royal High School in Edinburgh, Bob had a string of record shops and was a mobile discotheque operator. he got into radio by way of a quiz on the radio - the prize was a one hour broadcast. His first broadcast was at *Radio Forth* one Monday night in July 1975 following which he hosted two shows a week until being asked to present breakfasts in 1980.

Bob then moved to the mid-morning shift (and became known as 'Bob in the Morning') and is now heard seven days a week on MAx AM. The highlight of his radio career was winning a Sony Award in 1994 as part of the Max AM Breakfast Crew - he likes trout-fishing, football and his family, but not politics.

AGENT Events Organisation 01 968 660218.

Robin MALCOLM

Robin was the Editor of *LBC*'s AM station and Assistant Editor at *LRN* in the late 1980s. he is now the Programme Controller at *London Newsradio FM*.

Caroline MALLETT

In September 1995, Caroline joined the Board of *Minster FM* in York.

Michael MALLETT

Devon-born Michael has had a very long career managing very successful businesses, including a period as a director of the Girobank, and he has also stood three times as prospective Conservative Member of Parliament.

After becoming the chairman of *Radio Hallam*, he oversaw its expansion to acquire *Viking Radio* in Hull and *Pennine Radio* in Bradford in the 1980s, to form the *Yorkshire Radio Network*.

After YRN was bought by the Metro Group in the early 1990s, he bought a YRN subsidiary cable station in Singapore back from them which he's continued to run, along with other ventures in industry.

He is particularly excited about one venture - a CD-ROM company based in the Manchester area, which is backed by Sheffield -based Yorkshire Venture Capital, of which he is a director.

In 1992 Michael led the highest cash bid (by INBC) for the INR2 licence, and later that year took over the *Baltic Radio* project. In 1995 he joined the Board of a company to bid for the Yorkshire regional licence. Michael is also a Master Cutler and a keen horse rider.

Timmy MALLET

Born in Marple, Cheshire, on the 18th october, 1955, Tim got a history degree at Warwick University and went to work at BBC Radiio Oxford in 1977. Four years later one of his highly amusing audiotion tapes won him a contract with *Radio Luxembourg* and the following year he joined *Piccadilly Radio* in Manchester.

In 1984 he won a Sony for 'Local Radio personality of the Year' and in 1986 picked up another for 'Best Music programme'.

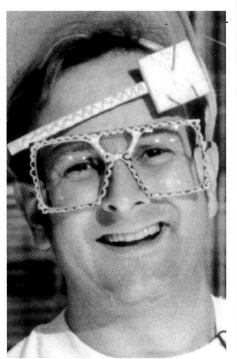

Timmy has appeared on many TV programmes, mostly children-oriented such as 'Utterly Brilliant' and 'Wide-Awake Club', where his zany choice of spectacle frames made him instantly recognisable and his huge foam mallet became a much copied trademark.

In 1991 Timmy was named 'Childrens TV Personality of the Year' by the TV Times magazine.

For several years he presented the Network Chart show and he's also been heard on KIMN in Denver, Co and on 2SM in Sydney, Australia. He al;so had two books published: 'How to Be Utterly Brilliant' and 'The Utterly Brilliant History of the World'.

In 1990 he released a single called "Bombalurina" which reached No 1 in the UK and his was the voice behind 'Del Costa' who had a hit with "Hot Hot Hot" in 1992. Timmy now lives near Slough with his wife Lynda and son Billy.

Tony MALLION

A former paper boy turned newsroom editor, Tony got into radio "because they were desperate!" He was a founder member of the *Radio Broadland* group and his was the first voice on air, reading the 6am news bulletin, when the station launched on october the first, 1984.

Since then he's been a news producer, programme maker, mid-morning phone in host and news editor - and he finds time to compere the "Miss Lowestoft" pageant each year.

The highlight of his career was reporting live from the Gulf in the run up to the war, and the most humourous, was a transmission from a trapeze forty feet above a circus ring. A keen Archers fan, Tony hates smoking and is currently news Editor at BBC *Radio Norfolk*.

Maggie MALTBY

Maggie is a journalist at *BBC Radio Lincolnshire*.

Janice MANDY

Sales Manager at *The Wave*.

Who's Who in British Radio

Alan MANN
Presenter of a programme each Saturday and Sunday afternoon on *Classic FM*.

Chris MANN
Chris was one of the main anchors at Sky News when the channel launched in 1989 and in 1994 joined *Scot FM*, the regional station in central Scotland. In 1995 he moved back to London where he currently hosts weekend breakfast programmes at *London News Radio*.

Terry MANN
Terry was the Head of Programmes at *Wey Valley Radio* in Alton, until June 1995 when he became Managing Director of *Swansea Sound*.

David MANSFIELD
David's broadcasting career began with Thames TV where he was deputy Director of Sales and Marketing. In January 1993 he joined *Capital Radio* as Group Commercial Director and is a full board member, being involved in all its subsidiaries, including *BRMB* and *Southern Sound* in Brighton. In that role, he is responsible for all the group's income, airtime, sponsorship, commercial production and other business ventures as well as overseeing all station advertising, concert promotion and concerts.

Michael MAPPIN
Evening presenter on *Classic FM*.

Simon MARLOW
Head of Music at *Radio 210* in Reading.

Bev MARKS
RDS Project Manager at the BBC from 1986 to 1990, and since then on the VG Broadcast team, helping launch RDS at many stations in many countries. A member of the RDS experts group and recently contributed a section on the subject to the Audio Engineers' Handbook.

[E-Mail 100024.2374@compuserve.com]

Andy MARRIOTT
Presenter at *GEM AM* in Nottingham.

Kate MARRIOTT
Kate is Company Secretary at *Melody Radio*.

Pauline MARSDEN
Presenter at *Radio City*, Liverpool.

Greg MARSDON
Greg is a presenter at *Brunel Classic Gold*.

Andy MARSH
Lincolnshire lad Andy went to school in Grimsby and University in Leeds to take a degree course in communications and media. While on that he did a student attachment at Hull station *Viking Radio* and a week at *Radio One*, which we still considers to be one of the best moments in his radio career.

Andy's first on-air broadcast was some sports bits on *Radio Aire* in Leeds. He finally graduated to a full programme, on *Viking Radio* in September 1989, and, after a period with *Classic Gold*, he moved to *Hallam FM*.

In 1992 he returned to his native Lincolnshire where he joined *Lincs FM* and is still there, enjoying music and vegetarian food as well as going for a bop!

Barrie MARSH
Barrie is deputy Chairman at *Radio City*.

Mike MARSH
A presenter on *Orchard FM*

Pat MARSH
Born on Christmas Eve, 1957 and educated at Wilson's Grammar School in London, Pat's first job was with the Columbia Film Company and then as a DJ on a cruise ship.

He then set up a business supplying several stores in London's West end with programming and became a freelance broadcaster with BBC Radio Kent in 1986

After a few month's standing in for other presenters, he was given the Saturday breakfast show, which he hosted for seven years, adding several weekday strips to his roster of work, ranging from late night phone-ins to the 'Mid Morning Muddle'.

In 1993 Pat moved to *Capital Gold* in London, and in 1994 it was off to Birmingham to become Programme Controller at Capital's new station, *Xtra AM*, where he is often heard on various shifts.

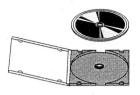

Pat has also made the transition from sound to vision working firstly as a warm-up man for live TV shows at Pebble Mill TV Centre in Birmingham and more recently presenting corporate videos. He currently presents the station's 'Laughternoon Show' each weekday.

Peter MARSH

Peter is a director of *Radio Wyvern.*

Steve MARSH

After a period operating roadshows in mainland Europe, Steve did some hospital radio in Northampton and in 1982 made his first broadcast on Peterborough's *Hereward Radio.*

Two years later he moved to the station's Northampton outlet, and after two years moved on again to *Northants Radio* doing breakfast and mid-morning shifts.

After three years at Northants, he joined the *Chiltern Radio Network* to host breakfasts, and in 1992 was made Controller of *Supergold* in addition to his duties fronting a lunchtime programme.

As well as radio, Steve also finds time for work as an actor and appearing in commercial videos, as well as appearing with the Barron Knights as their own pet DJ!

The highlight of his career was appearing at the Royal Albert Hall for the "Worlds Greatest Music Show' with Kenny Everett and Tony Blackburn, and the funniest event was corpsing in a pantomime after Prince mixed up his lines.

Steve likes beer and cheese, but not smelly people, greens or Radio One. He made some scathing comments on the future of AM at the 1995 Commercial Radio Conference in Dublin and advocates 'Gold' stations receiving FM frequencies automatically.

Andrew MARSHALL

Andrew is now the programme manager at *Talkradio UK.*

Dougie MARSHALL

Dougie joined *Downtown Radio* in the 1980s and presented weekday afternoon programmes.

Hamish MARSHALL

Hamish is a producer and presenter at BBC *Radio Devon and Dorset.*

Steve MARSHALL

Steve found a radio documentary LP in Virgin, and hearing it fired his interest in radio. In the mid seventies he was a well known voice on *Radio Invicta,* London's supreme soul pirate, where he gained a good knowledge of broadcasting.

In 1980 he did a six month stint on the *Voice of Peace,* probably the best training ground in European radio, under the hand of Crispian St John (aka Howard Rose) Johnny Lewis and Top Dutch TV jock, Kas Collins.

In 1981 he returned to Ireland and *Southside Radio* in Dublin.

The following year he got a job at the more upmarket *ERI* in Cork where he became Head of Music and instigated format clocks, on air slogans and supervised and scripted a full jingle package from PAMS.

Then followed five years with *Coast 103* and *Atlantic Sound,* where he hosted a daily lunchtime programme and drive time, becoming the programme controller. 1989 to 1991 was spent at *Riverside 101,* in Ulster, where he was programme controller, bringing formats and an air of general professionalism to the station which research showed had a reach of 60% in its 200,000 TSA. The station was eventually licensed as *Q102,* and many of Steve's edicts are still in force.

By 1991, Steve decided it was time to move on to the UK and he joined *Sunshine Radio* in Shropshire, again presenting a highly regarded drive-time programme.

Steve then spent two years at *Mellow 1557* in Frinton on weekends, being responsible for the excellent 'Jukebox Memories' programme with Ray Anderson. In 1994 came his most recent move - back to London and to *Spectrum International* where he is co-presenter of the station's Irish programme.

Mervyn MARSHALLSAY
Mervyn is the station engineer at *Brunel Classic Gold* and *GWR FM* in Swindon.

Brian MARTIN
Brian is a DJ at *Invicta Supergold*.

George MARTIN
Legendary EMI and AIR Studios producer who is chairman of Chrysalis's London station, *Heart 106.2FM*.

Greg MARTIN
Presenter at *Red Dragon Radio* in Cardiff.

John MARTIN
Managing Director of *Northsound* at Aberdeen.

Jose MARTIN
Director of Information at RNE, Spain.

Julian MARTIN
Sales Controller at *KISS FM* in Manchester.

Neil MARTIN
Promotion Manager at *Ocean FM*.

Phil MARTIN
After graduating from University he joined Lintas, a leading London advertising agency as a Unilever graduate. After his flatmates introduced him to an American DJ on *Radio England*, he spent a brief spell on the ship and ended up as PD of *Britain Radio*.

Sandy MARTIN
Sandy is a club DJ and hosts dance music programmes on *GWR FM*.

Stephen MARTIN
A former journalist, Stephen is now the Assistant Editor at *BBC Radio Suffolk*

Steve MARTIN

Steve was a programme presenter and the Features Producer at *Metro FM* until 1992 he moved to Bradford to be Programme Manager at *The Pulse* and led the station's successful reapplication for its licence in 1994.

In November 1995 Steve orchestrated and helped lead a successful management buy-out bid for the station from EMAP. It is believed to be the first MBO in UK commercial radio .

Mike MARWICK
Programme Director at *Q 96* in Paisley.

Maggie MASH
Presenter on *BBC Radio Humberside* in the late 1980s, she then moved to Leeds and a similar role at *Radio Aire* where she was often heard denouncing "nasty pop music" on the air. In the mid eighties she moved to Yorkshire Television where she is still a continuity announcer.

Steven MASKREY
Steven is Managing Director of *Fortune 1458*.

Colin MASON
Clin was Programme Director at *Swansea Sound* and then moved to *Chiltern Radio* where he became group Managing Director. In 1995, following the hostile takeover of the group he resigned and joined *Choice FM* in Birmingham where he is now Operations Director.

David MASON
David is the traffic manager at *London Newsradio FM*.

Steve MASSAM
Career began in night clubs in the Hull area in the 1970s, and joined *Radio Humberside* as a part time presenter and then became full time producer in the 1980s. By mid nineties was co-hosting the stations 9-11 weekday morning programme.

Guy MASTERMAN
Consultant who assisted in the launch of *Channel Travel Radio*.

Peter MASTERSON
Chairman of the *Red Rose Radio Group*.

George MATHESON
George is the Editor at *Reuters Radio News*.

Susie MATHIS
Presenter on *Piccadilly Gold*.

Bryan MATTHEW

Born in Coventry in 1928 and attended RADA then straight into the Army. He later played in rep' and made his first broadcast with *BFN* in Hamburg. He later did some programmes for *Radio Nederland*, the Dutch overseas service based in Hilversum and then moved to *Radio Luxembourg*.

In 1954 Bryan moved on to the BBC where he's remained since. In the since the fifties he has presented programmes such as 'Saturday Club', 'Late Night Extra' and 'Easy Beat' and now in the nineties presents 'Round Midnight' several nights a week as well as the popular 'Sounds of The Sixties' each Saturday morning on BBC Radio Two.

Neil MATTHEW

Presenter at *Essex Radio* for some years and now operating RSL stations in Billericay and Brentwood.

Danny MATTHEWS

DJ on *Key 103* in Manchester in 1995.

David MATTHEWS

Chief Engineer at *BBC Radio Humberside* in the eighties and nineties.

Lisa MATTHEWS

DJ at *Swansea Sound* in 1995.

Mark MATTHEWS

In the mid 1980's he was a weekday presenter at radio tees in Stockton. Became the Head of programmes (AM AND FM) at *Red Rose Radio* (Preston) in 1995.

Peter MATTHEWS

Born in Lancashire of Scottish parents, Peter's first radio was on hospital radio prior to getting a contract for the lunchtime programme at *Radio Tees* in the early eighties.

Roger MATTHEWS

London born Roger joined *Radio Caroline* in 1976 and became Programme Organiser on the ship for several years.

Adrian MAUGHAN

Presenter at *FOX FM* in Oxford.

Simon MAUNDER

Simon is the deputy chairman of *Lantern Radio* in Devon.

John MAXFIELD

Managing Director and in charge of programming at the new ILR station in Tonbridge, *KFM*.

Bennett MAXWELL

Former assistant Head and Chief Instructor of BBC Radio Training, he has produced many documentaries, talks and features for Radios 3 and 4, the Open University and BBC 2

Bennett has been a visiting professor at the Department of Communication of George Washington University and has taught professional broadcasters in Germany, Holland, Nigeria and Hong Kong and has run the Morley College Radio courses since their inception. Currently a tutor of the 'Instant Radio' courses.

Douglas MAY

Director at the Signal Radio Group.

John MAY

Director at *Talkradio UK*.

Steve MAYELL

Steve, a former radio salesman and actor in China's largest soap opera, is now Head of Sponsorship at *Piccadilly Radio*.

Helen MAYHEW

Daytime presenter on Jazz FM, London.

Simon MAYO

Simon's first radio programme was at the age of eight, with his sister doing jingles on the xylophone, but it was heard only by his family. His first real radio job was on a trainee scheme at *BBC Radio Sussex*, before moving full time to *Radio Nottingham*.

Simon joined *Radio One* in May 1986 and he currently hosts a morning programme on the station. Simon and his wife Hilary live in North London and he also hosts BBC'S game show 'Confessions' on Saturday nights.

Suzy MAYZELL

Born in the late fifties, Suzy's 14 years experience in the USA include working in two of the most competitive radio markets in the world, Chicago and San Fransisco. In the latter city she was vice-President of Programming at Adult Contemporary station, KOIT, an FM/FM combo'. Under her guidance the station became no 1 in the market for 25-44 year olds. She's now programme Director at *Virgin Radio*.

Dennis McCARTHEY MBE

Born in 1933, Dennis was schooled in London and Nottingham and his first broadcast was a report from Crufts in 1968; some years later he presented the TV coverage and got its highest ever audience of 8.5 million.

Dennis's radio expertise is astonishing - he's reported for a variety of talk programmes, including 1400 interviews for the 'Today' programme on *Radio Four,* 1500 inserts and features for *BBC World Service* and 1600 items for the *BFBS.*

Dennis has also written and presented several dozen programmes and features for television. and in the 1980s produced and presented an afternoon programme at *BBC Radio Nottingham.* Later this was networked over BBC local *Radios Derby, Leicester and Lincolnshire.*

His awards include an MBE, a Sony Award for 'Best Outside Broadcast' and he was nominated for 'Radio Personality of the Year' - obviously not by a woman as he is on record as saying one of his pet hates is female broadcasters!

His current work includes a two and a half hour programme each weekday on the four BBC stations in the East Midlands and looking after his top winning kennel of Afghan Hounds and English Toy Terriers.

Douglas McARTHUR

Managing Director of the Radio Advertising Bureau, based in London.

Gordon McARTHUR

Before getting into radio, Gordon worked on North Sea trawlers for a while and underwent management training and then went into press journalism. He joined an applicant group to bid for the *West Sound* station in Ayr and was a duty editor when the station launched. While at *West Sound* he's had many interesting experiences and, although he thinks the highlight of his career has yet to come, he well recalls a live news OB being interrupted by a very angry ram.

Two year after the station launched, Gordon became the station's Head of News, a role he filled for six years before taking up the reins as Programme Controller in 1989, a job he is in today, in addition to his consultancy work for Radio Kilmarnock Football Club.

Neil McCAFFERTY

Neil is a journalist at *Radio Lincolnshire.*

Heather McCARTHY

Heather is a reporter at BBC *Radio Solent.*

Liam McCARTHY

Born in Leicester in 1956, Liam joined *BBC Radio Leicester* on leaving school. He later became Programme Assistant, Sports Producer and the station's breakfast presenter.

After a spell at the BBC's local radio training unit in London, he returned to *Radio Leicester* as programme organiser in 1988. Two years later he took up the post of Senior Instructor at BBC Radio Training before moving back north to *Radio Sheffield* as Assistant Station Editor.

He has also worked on a journalism project in Africa. In July 1995 he was appointed Managing Editor at *Radio Leicester.*

Scottie McCLUE

Gained his BA at Glasgow University and got into radio by telephoning the station concerned, *Centresound FM,* in Summer 19884. He then moved to *Red Rose Radio* in Preston and finally his current station, *Scot FM*. Scottie also does commercial voice-overs and works in the theatre, and in film and TV.

Who's Who in British Radio

He has been a newscaster and announcer at Border, Grampian and Scottish TV and claims a radio record by attracting 500,000 calls in one week. He likes a permanently full switchboard and dislikes callers who agree with him.

AGENT: Bill McMurdo 01 698 813951.

Tich McCOOEY
Tich is the current breakfast presenter at *Moray Firth Radio* in Inverness.

Judie McCOURT
Judie is a presenter at *TFM* in Stockton.

Gavin McCOY
Presenter on *Great North Radio*.

Bob McCREADIE
Bob is a presenter at *Orchard FM* in Taunton.

Brian McCUSKER
Brian is the chief engineer at *Downtown Radio* and *Cool FM* in Belfast.

Linda McDERMOT
Merseyside born, Linda is an experienced broadcaster and journalist who began her career in newspapers and has ten press awards under her belt. She presents a three-hour magazine programme each weekday on *BBC Radio Merseyside* and also hosts a late night chat show live from Manchester for *BBC Radio Five Live*. She hasn't given up writing and still pens columns for the Liverpool Post and several women's magazines. Travel is one of her special interests; she's visited most of Europe and North America and reported on the European Parliament from Strasbourg for a time.

A fitness enthusiast, Linda has run both the London and New York marathons and she's also good at running for buses! Hers is the voice on many commercial video travel guides and documentaries for BBC Television, particularly educational programmes.

Stuart McDILL
News and Current Affairs presenter at *BBC Radio Cambridgeshire*.

Toni McDONALD
Presenter at *BRMB* in Birmingham.

Graham McGARRY
Graham is the Sports Editor at *BBC Radio Stoke*.

Ward McGAUGHRIN
Producer at *Radio Tay*.

Terry McGEADIE
Terry is a presenter on *Scot FM*.

Kieran McGEARY
Kieran is a reporter at *BBC Radio Solent*.

Hal McGHIE
A Director of *South West Sound*, Dumfries.

Derek McGILL
Derek joined *BBC Radio Humberside* as a news reporter in 1988 and is now the station's Daytime Editor.

Ian McGREGOR
Currently hosts Saturday mid-morning show on *BBC Radio Kent*.

Murray McGREGGOR
News journalist at *Moray Firth Radio*.

Carol McGRIFFEN
Host of a 'Juke Box Jury' style programme each Friday on *Talkradio UK*.

Craig McKAY
Born in Guiseley, West Yorkshire, on 21st June, 1973, Craig entered broadcasting in 1984 and a few years later joined 'Emmerdale Farm'. While there he appeared with his real life sister, Glenda McKay, probably the only time that's happened in television soaps.

He currently presents weekend programmes on *Beacon Radio* in the West Midlands.

Katie McKAY
Katie is a new reporter at *BBC Essex*.

Jackie McKENNA
Director of *Nevis Radio* in Scotland.

Paul McKENNA
Essex-boy Paul began his radio career at *The*

Voice of Peace and signed up with *Radio Caroline* on his return to the UK. After a period in ILR he moved to *Capital Radio* and then found fame (and much fortune) from his hobby of hypnotherapy.

In 1994 his TV programme achieved Top Ten ratings, he's made several sell-out tours of the UK and looks set for even bigger success now his TV show is seen all over Europe.

Alistair McKENZIE
A programme presenter at *Classic FM*.

Gary McKENZIE
Host of 'Sunday Club' on BBC *Radio Scotland*.

Mark McKENZIE
Mark worked for the Bank of Scotland for 4 years and then got into hospital radio. He started an H.N.C in radio broadcasting, but three months into the first term he was offered a job doing 5 overnights a week and had to abandon it.

After working in hospital radio in January '87, Mark joined *MAX AM* and *Radio Forth FM* in 1990 where he presented overnight programmes for a year.

While at Radio Forth he presented dinner shows plus 'Billboard' weekly hour-long magazine programmes with local information and famous guests. In his spare time Mark is the P.A announcer at Tynecastle and Hearts F.C.

Tony McKENZIE
A presenter on *Radio Caroline* until 1985 he joined *Radio Nova* in Dublin the following year as programme controller. Following this he had a spell with *Radio Nova International*, the UK's first satellite radio station based in Camberley .

He then moved to *Radio City* in Liverpool where he is now the station's Programme Controller. Tony likes nothing better than a non stop drive on the M6/M1 but he hates bad drivers .

Rod McKENZIE
Rod is a presenter of *Radio One's* 'Newsbeat'.

Francis McLAUGHLIN
Francis is the Managing Director of *Q 102.9* in Londonderry.

Sophie McLAUGHLIN
Sophie is the Marketing Manager at *Radio One*.

Robert McLAUGHLIN
Chairman of *BCR 96.7* in Belfast.

Bobi McLENNAN
Presenter at *Scot FM*.

Ken McLEOD
Presenter of a weekly country music programme at *Radio Tay*.

Rory McLEOD
Rory was the Managing Director of *Southern Sound* until the station was bought by Capital.

He is now a Director of *Orchard FM* in Taunton and Managing Director of *London News Radio*.

Andy McLUSKEY
Andy is a DJ at *Invicta FM*.

Roy McMILLAN
Weekend DJ at *Manx Radio*, Isle of Man.

Harry McNAB
Chairman of *Q-96* in Paisley.

Liam McNALLY
Liam is a presenter of Irish music programmes on *BBC Three Counties Radio*.

Gordon McNAMEE
Gordon was one of the founders of *Kiss FM*, the London dance station, which obtained a licence in the early 1990s - he is now the station's Managing Director and is also a director of EMAP Radio.

Martin McNICHOLAS
Martin is a DJ at *MFM* in Wrexham.

Peter McPARTLAND
Managing Director of *Radio Aire* in Leeds.

Hugh McPHERSON
Hugh is a presenter at *Classic FM*.

Who's Who in British Radio

Gordon McRAE
Head of Newsroom at *Severn Sound*.

Bobby McVAY
DJ at *Red Dragon Radio* in Cardiff.

Dave McVITTIE
Dave is the Managing Director of Point Promotions, the company which organises the annual equipment show SBES and also a writer.

Bob McWILLIAM
Programme Controller of *Q-96* in Paisley, he also assisted with assembling a recent application for a licence for Solway.

Grant McWILLIAM
Head of Telecommunications in the engineering department at *BBC Radio Scotland*.

Ross McWILLIAM
Presenter at *BBC Radio York* in the mid eighties.

Iain MEADOWS
Producer of youth programmes at *Spire FM*.

Mick MEADOWS
Mick is a programme assistant at *BBC Radio Peterborough*.

Peter MEADOWS
First a communications consultant, Peter is also a founder of the 'Spring Harvest' - the world's largest annual inter-church event. In 1994 he joined London's new Christian radio station, *Premier Radio* where he is now Chief Executive.

Samantha MEAH
Presenter of a weekday evening shift at the launch of *Talkradio UK*.

Henry MEAKIN
Born on the 2nd January, 1944, Henry was educated at Plumtree School in Rhodesia. He was an executive director of Pensord Press Ltd until 1974 and has been the Chairman of Aspen Communications since 1979.
In the early 1980s he was a founder of *Wiltshire Sound* (the original Swindon fran-

chisee) and has been the Chairman of the *GWR Group Plc* since the mid eighties. Henry was the original Chairman of *Classic FM* (from 1991 to 1993).

Evelyn MEARS
Evelyn is a director of *Radio Wyvern*.

Brian MEASURES
Presenter on *Plymouth Sound*'s AM service.

Dominic MEDLEY
News producer at *BBC Wiltshire Sound*.

Liz MEECH
Producer at *BBC Radio Humberside* in the 1980s, she is now Education correspondent and producer for *BBC North* based in Leeds.

Sir James MELLON
Chairman of RTM, in London.

Mark MENDOZA
Host of the overnight programme on Mondays at *London Newstalk*.

Derek MEREDITH
Managing executive of *Channel Travel Radio*.

Stevie MERIKE
Born a Londoner on 23rd October, 1945, Stevie attended the Royal Naval School in Malta and then joined the RAF! He then worked in discotheques in the south east and recorded a version of Lady Jane as Tony Merrick, which got to number 49 in 1966, and the following year joined ship-based *Radio Scotland* as a DJ.

After that station closed, Stevie moved to *Radio Caroline* where he hosted the station's breakfast programme and the afternoon show for a few months. Following that, Stevie moved on to *Radio One*, where he also did the breakfast programme for two months while Tony Blackburn holidayed. In 1971, he joined *Radio North Sea International* and became the station's Head of Programmes with Alan West - they also produced a series of very entertaining double-header shows, tapes of which still change hands for extraordinary sums in the die-hard Anorak community.

He then moved back ashore to the BBC and a stint as senior producer at BBC *Radio Sussex*, then on to LBC, Manchester's *Piccadilly Radio* and *Pennine Radio* in Bradford.

Steve's success at Pennine Radio led to a TV series, 'Pop Quest' in 1976 on nearby Yorkshire Television, and he then moved on to *Radio Trent* in Nottingham. While there he began lecturing in radio studies at the nearby South Notts College and supervised a variety of similar courses in Leicester.

He suddenly quit the UK for Australia, and worked at ABC regional stations in Brisbane for a year before returning to the UK and a regular strip at *BBC Radio Leeds*.

In 1995 he moved to *GEM AM* in the East Midlands where he currently presents a weekday afternoon programme.

Paul MEWIES
A director of *Marcher Coast.*

Sir Peter MICHAEL
Born on 17th June, 1938, he went to school in Croydon and obtained a BSc at the University of London. He was the chairman of a micro computer company until 1985 and of Quantel, inventors of the 'Paintbox' signal processor for television and video.

Sir Peter made his first millions by selling UEI to Carlton, and then revived Cray Electronics, making a further £20 millions. In 1993 he took over the chairmanship of *Classic FM* and immediately initiated the station's expansion into Europe, with networks of transmitters in Holland and Finland.

Tony MICHAELIDES
Presenter at Piccadilly's FM service - *Key 103.*

Gordon MIDDLEMISS
Director at *Moray Firth Radio* in Inverness.

Peter MILBURN
Managing Director at *Red Dragon Radio.*

Andy MILES
Afternoon presenter at *Swansea Sound.*

James MILES
BBC Foreign Correspondent in Hong Kong.

Phil MILES
Born in Newport (the one in Gwent) in 1953, he ran a mobile disco and worked in clubs before doing some hospital radio work and finally getting into radio when *CBC,* the community station for Cardiff opened in 1980. He then presented a series of programmes, including two years of breakfasts, before moving to *County Sound* in Guildford to host their breakfast show and the station's Chart Show.

Grant MILLARD
Chairman of *Central FM.*

Andy MILLER
Presenter at *Trent FM* in Nottingham.

David MILLER
News Editor at *BBC Radio York* in the mid eighties, no longer working in radio.

Heather MILLER
Reporter at *BBC Radio Newcastle.*

Nick MILLER
Original overnight presenter at *Talkradio UK.*

Robin MILLER
Chief Executive of *EMAP Group.*

Sarah MILLER
Sarah is the producer of the 'Paddy MacDee Programme' on weekday afternoons on BBC Radio Newcastle.

Bob MILLS
Host of a late night programme each Sunday on *BBC GLR.*

Chris MILLS
Presenter and producer at *BBC Radio Bristol.*

Julie MILLS
Presenter of the Saturday morning breakfast programme on *BBC Radio Sheffield.*

Scot MILLS
Presenter at *Heart 106.2* in London.

Who's Who in British Radio

Alasdair MILNE
Alasdair joined the BBC in 1954 almost by chance. He completed his degree in Modern Languages at Oxford and applied for several jobs, including a well known advertising agency. His wife Sheila sent him to the BBC to be a General Trainee, despite his knowing nothing about broadcasting, just before ITV started.

Alasdair later became involved in applications for the northern ITV licences, but returned to the BBC as controller of Scottish radio and TV. He later became Director General and was asked to resign by the Governors in January 1987.

Sandy MILNE
After a period as the assistant editor of news in the BBC TV newsroom in Bristol, Sandy is now the Managing Editor at *BBC Wiltshire Sound*.

Karl MIOSGA
A former BBC executive, Karl is now the Managing Director of *World Radio Network,* an international programme consolidator based in London whose output is heard around the world by satellite and cable.

Andy MITCHELL
Head of News on the a.m. part of the day at *The Wave* in Blackpool.

Deborah MITCHELL
A news producer at *BBC Radio Shropshire*.

Ken MITCHELL
Head of News at *Scot FM*.

Kersti MITCHELL
Kersti is now the Bradford Producer for BBC *Radio Leeds*.

Mark MITCHELL
Presenter of weekday evening programmes (6 to 9pm) on *Signal Gold* in Staffordshire.

Martin MITCHELL
An ordained Baptist Minister, Martin worked at Leicester Sound and *Gem AM* before joining *Premier Radio* in London in 1995 to host the station's Late Night Show.

Pete MITCHELL
Peter is a presenter at Piccadilly's FM service, *Key 103*.

Steve MITCHELL
Steve is Editor of radio news at the BBC.

Warren MITCHELL
Finance Director and also the Company Secretary at *Moray Firth Radio* in Inverness.

Jim MOIR
Jim joined the BBC in the early 1960s, as a production trainee in television. His first radio work was with the old *Light Programme*, which he acknowledges as his favourite network. He rose to become Deputy Director of Corporate Affairs at the BBC in 1993 and in January 1996 he takes up a new position as Controller of *Radio Two*.

Andy MOLLET
After getting a First Class Honours degree at Leicester University, he qualified as a chartered accountant with KPMG. He later joined Virgin Radio, where he is now the station's Finance Director, and responsible for all administrative aspects of the station's operation.

Rob MOLLOY
Director of *Stray FM*, Harrogate.

Andy MONAGHAN
Andy is responsible for the religious programming at *Forth FM* and its sister station, *Max AM*.

Owen MONEY
Host of a mid morning weekday programme on *BBC Radio Wales*.

Karen MONGER
Karen is a senior producer at Radio Four, currently responsible for items and features on the 'PM' programme.

Dave MONK
Freelance presenter (weekday lunchtimes, 11 to 2) on *BBC Essex*.

Jackie MONKMAN

Jersey-born and educated in Essex, Jackie's first job was as a reporter on a local newspaper in the Channel Islands. She later worked for the London Evening News and the national Daily Mail.

Jackie's first broadcast was at *Radio Solent* (Southampton) in 1981 from where she moved on to join the team (of four) who launched *BBC Radio Jersey* the following year.

Martin MONTAGUE

Technical operator at *BBC Radio York,*

Claire MONTGOMERY

Currently a news reporter at *BBC Radio York.*

Sue MONTGOMERY

Producer at *BBC Radio Devon and Dorset.*

Eric MOONMAN

Chairman of the *Essex Radio* Group of stations.

Angus MOORAT

Angus is the Managing Director of *Network News*, part of the Chiltern Group.

Andrew MOORE

Born on the 12th June, 1975 in Scarborough, Andrew attended Lady Lumley's School in Pickering and says he got into radio by a generous helping of good luck and quite a lot of persistence!

He started as a YTS receptionist at *Yorkshire Coast Radio* in Scarborough and progressed to driving music and adverts on the air, writing listing columns and assembling promotional display ad's. In 1995 he was promoted to become production assistant, acting as a technical operator and having to step in when presenters are 'indisposed'.

The highlight of Andy's career so far was YCR's winning a bronze Sony Award in 1995. He likes well-produced music and radio, plus liberal dashes of fine wine and good company - but not patronising DJ-talk and PRS monitoring days.

Chris MOORE (1)

The first ever programme controller at *Radio Caroline* in 1964, he later moved to California and wrote several interesting books, one of which, 'Rock The Boat', became a best seller.

Chris MOORE (2)

Presenter at *Red Dragon Radio* in Cardiff.

Jeff MOORE

Jeff is a DJ at *Power FM*.

Peter MOORE

A long-term *Radio Caroline* supporter, Peter got involved in the station in the mid eighties when supplyiong fuel injectors for generators and soon become deeply engrossed in it's activities.

Within a short time he was acting as station manager and has continued to do so since the ship ran aground on the Goodwin Sands in the early 1990s. Under his care, the ship is being slowly renovated and has recently been the focus of some RSL stations.

Robert MOORE

Chairman of *Northants Supergold* until 1995.

Warren MOORE

Warren began his radio career at *Minster FM* hosting the station's early evening programmes. His enthusiastic and manic style won him many admirers and he was soon snapped up for huge sujms opf money by neighbouring big city operatoir, *Aire FM* who wisely gave him a more prominent role, where he continues to amass big audiences.

Gary MORAN

Gary was the news editor at *GEM AM* in Derby in the early 1990s but seems to have left radio.

Judy MORAN

Judy is a senior producer at *BBC Radio Leeds*.

Johnny MORAN

Australian born and schooled he began his radio career at *Radio 3AW* in Melbourne and came to the UK after hearing of the success of the pirate ships.

His first role in Britiain was hosting programmes at *Radio Luxembourg*, and then a series of sponsored shows on *Big L- Radio London*, although he turned down a regular job on the ship and later joined the BBC instead, fronting the excellent and sadly missed 'Scene and Heard' in the early years of *Radio One*.

In the seventies Johnny joined Sheffield's new station, *Radio Hallam*, where he became a local hero, often appearing on Yorkshire television.

His was the first programme on Hallam, and his fondest memory of the station was an April Fools day hoax arranged by colleagues Roger Moffat and Keith Skues that he was to ride a horse in the Grand National called 'Hallam Rock'.

Alan MORGAN

Host of a programme each Saturday lunchtime (12 to 2pm) on *BBC Radio Gloucester*.

Bob MORGAN

Presenter on *Amber Radio*, the SRG's new 'gold' station launched in September, 1995.

John MORGAN

see entry for John Myers, below.

Mike MORGAN

Mike is a sales manager at *Radio Wyvern*.

Peter MORGAN

Peter is a DJ at *MFM* in Wrexham.

Vic MORGAN

Presenter of a Friday evening programme on at BBC Radio Devon and Dorset.

Willy MORGAN

Producer and presenter of programmes at *Chiltern Supergold* for many years, he became programme controller in 1995.

Hugh MORGAN-WILLIAMS

Hugh is Chairman of a leading radio equipment supplier, Canford Audio, which supplies radio stations all over the world.

Hugh was one of the founders of *Minster FM* and he is now the Chairman of subsidiary station *Sun City* in Sunderland.

Michael MORIARTY

Born on the 3rd July, 1930, Michael was educated at Reading and at St John's College in Oxford and has spent his entire career in the Home Office. He headed the H.O. Broadcasting Department for three years in the 1980s and in 1991 became a Member of the *Radio Authority,* of which he is now deputy chairman.

Jonathan MORRELL

Born in Sheffield in 1970, Jonathan grew up in Cornwall and his first job was at the local BBC station, *Radio Cornwall*. In 1988 he left the country for a degree course at the Sunderland Polytechnic. While there he freelanced for *BBC Radio Newcastle* and also the city's ILR station *Metro FM.* as well as a period as an in-vision announcer at *Tyne Tees Television*.

After completing his studies, Jonathan presented the breakfast show on *Radio Newcastle* and was nominated for a Sony Award in 1992 for the best speech based breakfast programme.

In April 1993 he joined Cornish station *Pirate 102* hosting the station's breakfast show, but five months later he moved back to *Radio Newcastle*. He's since moved south to *Radio Cleveland* where he now hosts lunchtime and afternoon drive-time news programmes as well as a request programme each Sunday lunchtime.

Bill MORRIS

Bill's career includes a period in the Radio Magazine Production department, during which he was a senior producer for many of the 'Action Specials' on *Radio One* in the 1980s. He is now the Head of the *Radio Two* music department.

Chris MORRIS

Programmes on GLR in early 1990s.

Craig MORRIS

Presenter at *Q103* in Cambridge.

Who's Who in British Radio

Doug MORRIS
News producer at *BBC Radio Newcastle*.

Guy MORRIS
Warwickshire born (in 1956) and schooled in Cheshire, Guy got into radio through work installing sound an d light equipment in clubs and pub.

InJuly 1975, his demo tape was accepted by *Radio Trent*, the new ILR station in Nottingham.

Guy then advanced to *BRMB*, and later on to *Radio Victory*, where he hosted the stations Drive-Time shift and chart show in the early 1980s. More recently he's been heard on the new *Leicester Sound* FM, now a part of GWR network.

Honor MORRIS
Hosted a weekend breakfast programme at *Radio Humberside* in the 1980s.

Peter MORRIS
Presenter at BBC Radio Berkshire.

Tim MORRIS
Tim is the deputy Chairman of *Heart FM*.

Richard MORRIS-ADAMS
Chairman of *Mix 96* in Aylesbury.

Charles MORRISEY
The Chief Editor of IRN until September 1995, he then moved to the Press Association.

Bob MORRISON
Head of News at *Radio 210* in Reading.

Mandy MORTON
Weekend presenter at *BBC Radio Cambridgeshire*.

John MOSS
Presenter on *Manx Radio*, Isle of Man.

Paul MOULTON
Weekend DJ at Manx Radio.

Douglas MOUNCE
Douglas is the host of weekday (9-12noon) programme on *BBC Radio Devon and Dorset*.

Jonathan MOUNCEY
Director at *Radio City*, Liverpool.

Stuart MOUNTAIN
Host of weekend breakfast programmes on BBC *Radio Humberside*.

William MOWAT
William is the chairman of *West Sound* in Ayr.

Bob MOWER
Bob is a DJ at *Invicta Supergold*.

Chris MOYLES
Leeds-born Chris began his radio career at Radio Aire and in 1994 moved to *Signal Radio* in Cheshire where he now hosts evening programmes (7 to 10pm weekdays) on the network's 'Gold' station.

Andy MUIR
As well as being Head of Music at *Eleven Seventy* in High Wycombe, Andy also hosts the station's sports programmes.

Frank MUIR
Born in Broadstairs, Kent, on 5th February 1920-, the story of Frank's broadcasting career would fill this book (indeed, he's written several himself and his biography, Call My Bluff, is much recommended).

Among his radio successes has been My Word and My Music, both regular jewels in the *Light Programme* and then *Radio Two* schedules since the 1960s. he's also appeared on over a dozen Tv programmes and is well known for his role as a panelist on several panel shows, resplendent in his pink bow tie.

He was the assistant Head of Comedy at the BBC for three years and Head of Light Entertainment at LWT after that. Enjoys collecting books and staring into space.

Michelle MULLANE
A music presenter at *Metro FM*.

Liz MULLEN
Freelance presenter currently hosting weekend breakfasts at *BBC Essex*.

Alan MULLETT
Wolverhampton-born Managing Director of *Beacon Radio* since the eighties.

Geoff MULLIN
Geoff is the Head of Music at *Melody Radio.*

Tracey MULLINS
Press and information officer at the *Radio Authority* since its inception.

Donnie MUNRO
Morning presenter at *Scot FM.*

Anna MURBY
In September 1995 Anna took over as presenter of the pre-breakfast programme at BBC *Radio Northamptonshire.*

Judi MURDEN
Presenter / Producer at *BBC Radio Humberside* in early eighties. After a few years break she returned to the station in 1994 to co-present the station's weekday morning programme.

Rob MURDOCH
Controller of Personnel at the BBC's Resources division.

Catherine MURPHY
Catherine left UMIST with a degree in management science and further qualifications in marketing and advertising. She worked in research and marketing at Reed Business Publishing and for Tyne Tees TV in London, from where she moved back to Manchester and *Piccadilly Radio* as Research Manager in January, 1992.

She took up her present role as Research and Marketing Manager in September 1994 which added responsibility for marketing the station to advertisers.

Mark MURPHY
Presenter / producer at *BBC Radio Suffolk.*

Ginny MURFIN
The wife of famous music producer, Muff Murfin, Ginny is Managing Director of *KIX 96* in Coventry. Prior to that she was the driving force behind *Buzz FM* until it failed to have its licence renewed by the Radio Authority.

Brendan MURPHY
Programme Controller at Heartland FM.

Alex MURRAY
Director of *Melody Radio* in London

David MURRAY
Sales Manager at *London News Radio.*

Derek MURRAY
Currently Head of Commercial Production at *Radio Forth.*

Jennie MURRAY
Presenter of 'Woman's Hour' in the 1990s.

John MURRAY
SPorts editor at BBC Radio Cleveland.

Ken MURRAY
Programme Director at *RTM Thamesmead.*

Pete MURRAY

Born in 1928, Pet was trained at RADA with his first appearance being in 'Miss Marigold' at a theatre in Kew. His first radio broadcast was in the BBC's overseas services during the war, but his real fame came when he took a temporary three month contract at *Radio Luxembourg* after the war and stayed for five and a half years!

After some success as a serious TV actor, he returned to BBC radio to host a variety of programmes, including much of the Corporations diet of pop music on the *Light Programme* in the sixties, before landing his own 'Open House' programme on *Radio Two* in 1969, a programme which ran until 1980.

While there he was awarded the MBE and wrote a hilarious autobiography which suggests he often forgets his trousers. In 1981 Pete returned to late night radio for the station and later moved across London to LBC for a similar programme.

Who's Who in British Radio

Peter MURTHA

A native of South London, Peter became embroiled in the London pirate scene in the 1960s, building equipment for stations such as *Radio Free London*.

He joined Swiss owned pop-ship *Radio North Sea International* as engineer in 1970, where he became known as 'Chicago'. Two years later he joined neighbouring competitor *Radio Caroline* as engineer and stayed with the station until the early 1990s.

It's widely acknowledged that, without Peter's input and assistance, the station would have closed many years before.

Peter has singlehandedly operated the ship on several occasions and has performed near miracles on the station's technical equipment. In 1981 he moved to Dallas, Texas, and worked for a transmitter supply company but returned to help build the new Caroline ship, the Ross Revenge, in the early 80's.

He was responsible for relaunching Carol;ine and keeping the ship on air during the station's rennaissance in the 1980s and bravely defended it against armed Dutch policemen who boarded in 1989, closing the ships two stations down and stealing vital equipment. Peter had Caroline back on the air in weeks, after some smart improvisation. He was not on board when the Ross Revenge drifted onto the Goodwin Sands in the early 90's.

Peter is now working as an electronics engineer in London but still finds time to assist with various radio projects from time to time. He recently worked with former Caroline shipmate Paul Rusling to build a new antenna system for Radio Veronica in Holland.

He lives in Margate with the Caroline ship's dog Raffles, and his girl-friend - whose name you can probably guess!

'Big' Jim MURPHY

Texan-born, Jim's always lived by the water and would have us believe he could surf before he could walk. He worked at several stations in the USA and was a respected country jock and PD when he came to the UK to promote a record by pole-squatting until it charted.

Jim joined *Radio Caroline North* where he instigated the 'Midnight Surf Party' as well as a weekly country programme which he handed over to Don Allen when he married an English girl and returned to the USA.

James MURPHY

A former Metropolitan policeman of some 28 years standing, Jim was disabled out of the force when a gun went off near his head at Euston station and he then found work in the solicitors department of the DTI in the early 1980's.

His link to radio came about with his being appointed by the DTI Solicitor's Deepartment to investigate the resurgence of offshore radio in the mid-eighties, for a possible case against any UK links of Radio caroline and Laser.

He became the butt of many japes and on-air references, particularly by *Laser 558*, who parodied his activities on the air quite cruelly, turning him into a minor celebrity. In 1989 he helped mastermind a raid on the Radio Caroline ship and later retired, having failed to close the station.

Dereck MUTTER

Host of a weekly rock show each Friday evening on *Eleven Seventy* in High Wycombe.

Dave MYATT

Programme Manager and host of some programmes on *Beacon Radio* in Wolverhampton.

John MYATT

A director at *Radio Broadland*.

Barbara MYERS

Leeds born and schooled in Lincolnshire and Nottinghamshire, she funded her own Honours Degree at Sussex University. Her first broadcast was in a quiz when she was twelve, which she won.

Barbara then offered stories to *BBC Radio Brighton* and worked there as a freelance producer after graduation, and then spent many years as a reporter and producer for *Radio Four* (mainly on World at One and PM).

She also presented some medical and science programmes for World Service and BBC TV. Still with World Service, Barabara is now the producer of the popular daily current affairs programme 'Outlook'.

Diane MYERS
Presenter at *BBC Radio York* in the mid 80's.

John MYERS
Cumbrian born in 1959, John got into radio with the BBC and then joined *Red Rose Radio* in Preston and *Radio Tees*. In 1985 John spent three years at Border Television in carlisle before returning to *Red Rose Radio* where he launched *Red Rose Gold* and *Rock FM*. he progressed to become Programme Director and achieved the highest ever figures for the Lancashire station.

In 1993 John moved up the M6 to *CFM* in Carlisle as Managing Director, moving the station into profit after 14 weeks and achieving a 45% reach.

John is now Managing Director at *Century Radio,* the first regional station in the North east, he still presents a daily breakfast show under the name 'John Morgan' and has taken that station into profit after just one year on air. Century is the most popular of the five regional stations launched recently.

Graham MYTTON
Head of Audience Research and Listener Correspondence at the BBC World Service.

Roy NAISMITH
Finance Director at *Ocean Sound.*

Andy NASH
Worked on local newspapers in Cambridge before joining the *Chiltern Network* as a technical operator.

His first broadcast came in January 1990 with Chiltern on overnights from where he moved to *Viking FM* in Hull and also presented TV shows at the Meadowhall shopping centre. By 1995 he was hosting the afternoon programme each weekday on *Trent FM.*

In June 95 he added to his working week with an additional Sunday evening programme at *Ocean FM* in Hampshire to his list of work experience. Likes burgers, TV and sleeping and hates being blamed everytime equipment gets broken!

Dave NASH
Editor with special responsibilities for Goole and district at *BBC Radio Humberside.*

Mike NAYLOR
Mike is currently the afternoon presenter (2 to 5pm) on *BBC Radio Shropshire.*

Balvinder NAZRAN
Head of sales at *Sunrise Radio* in Bradford.

Graham NEALE
Presenter of a daily rock music programme at *Radio Trent* in the 1980s.

Chris NEEDS
Chris is a DJ at *Touch AM* in Cardiff.

Richard NEIL
Engineer at BBC *Radio Cambridgeshire.*

Gilbert NESBITT
Gilbert is a director of *Downtown Radio*

Martin NEVILLE
Martin is the Chairman of *Severn Sound.*

Tracey NEWBERRY
Sales Controller at *Northants Supergold.*

Gary NEWBON
Teatime programme presenter at *Talkradio UK* when it launched.

Julie NEWING
A broadcast journalist at *BBC Wiltshire Sound.*

Mark NEWMAN
Afternoon presenter on the FM service of *Plymouth Sound.*

Pauline NEWMAN
A Radio Production assistant at BBC *Radio Berkshire*, which recently merged with radio Oxford to form *Radio Thames Valley.*

1969 saw Annie hosting a variety of programmes for the network for twenty years, in particular, a Sunday evening request programme immediately after the Chart Show, which seemed to be aimed purely at students.

She presented the Who's live radio concert from Canada in 1982 and wrote a good story of life on the radio called 'Chase the Fade'. Now married to Binky Baker, who makes rude records and appears on various TV programmes.

Anne was heard on *Radio One* in 1994 hosting the 'Chill Out Zone' - a graveyard shift at 2 am on Sunday mornings and also presenter of a night-time show. She currently hosts overnights each Saturday at the station.

NINO

Educated in Bristol, Nino worked in clubs before taking a course in broadcasting at *UBN* and was asked to stay on. He did a one off broadcast on *Radio Luxembourg* in 1979 as Disco DJ of the Year and then had a stint at *Radio Victory*.

He then moved to *Radio 210* for three shows and off up the M4 for a longer stay at Bristol's *Radio West*. Three years starring on the breakfast show later and Nino was off to the newly launched *Invicta Sound* in Kent.

He then had a stint at Cambridge ILR station *CNFM* followed by a move to his current station, *Galaxy 101*.

As well as radio, Nino is well known to TV viewers through his appearances on Thames TV's 'Splash', Granada's 'Get Fresh', and the 'Music Box' programmes on Superchannel. he also presents 'The American High' for LWT and has been a reporter and presenter on LWT's 'London Tonight'. He's currently seen on *UK Living* and the host of the 'New Mr and Mrs Show'.

Nino loves personality fun radio and dislikes the programme controllers who believe that US format work in the UK - he hates bland radio.

Tony Fox Artistes tel 0171 602 8822.

Bob NOAKES

Worked as an engineer with the BBC and then joined *Radio Caroline* in 1973 in a similar role. Moving across the sea to the Mebo 2, he became a regular DJ too for a while and left to write a book about his time on the Caroline ship (called the Last of The Pirates - see bibliography). He currently lives and works in Amsterdam.

Ian NOAKES

DJ on *Mix 96* in Aylesbury in 1995.

Kara NOBLE

Born on the 13th July, 1958 in London, Kara worked as a waitress and ran the Songbird Singing Telegram Company until one fateful day in 1986 "someone spotted my voice" and she found herself on Chris Tarrant's Breakfast programme on Capital FM, reading the weather and other urgent information.

Over the ensuing ten years, Kara became something of a morning institution in London and has also done many TV appearances and voice-overs. The highlight of her career so far though was certainly interviewing Robin Williams.

In 1995 she was head-hunted to become the co-host of the morning programme 'Breakfast with Lee and Kara' on London's new AC station, *Heart 106.2 FM*.

Kara likes Jules Holland, but not traffic wardens and the funniest event of her career was reading the weather clad in a wet-suit!

Roy NOBLE

Host of the most listened-to programme on *BBC Radio Wales*.

Katie NOON

News and features producer at *BBC Radio Humberside* in the early 1990s.

Bob NORMAN

Director of *Signal Radio* in Cheshire.

Duncan NEWMARCH
Duncan is a DJ at *Lincs FM*.

Eric NG
Being educated in Hong Kong and the UK, Eric is bilingual in Cantonese and English. he joined London station *Spectrum Radio* in 1992 to host the station's Chinese programmes and has been there ever since.

In 1995 he organised the Chinese New Year celebrations in Colindale as well as a Hong Kong -London teleconference in 1993. A keen snooker fan Eric also likes swimming and watching films on TV, but hates receiving strange telephone calls. Agent: Skyview 0171 434 2835.

Adrian NICHOLAS
Born in March 1960 Adrian joined *Capital FM* in 1987 and has now appeared on almost every show on both Capital stations. He is known as the master of the outside broadcast and something of a dare devil, having broadcast while wing walking, in a freefall from 13,000 feet, prop riding, powerboating and driving a racing car at 200 miles an hour.

Adrian is a fully qualified cave driver, which is billed as "the most dangerous sport in the world" and has a cave named after him in Florida. He is a qualified aerobatic pilot, flies helicopters and fast jets and also an expert skydiver, racing driver, rally driver, barefoot waterskier, snowmonoboarder, sky surfer . . . and he's single.

Sir David NICHOLAS
Sir David, born on 25th January 1930, was educated at the University College of Wales in Aberyswyth and worked as a journalist, beginning with the Wakefield Express, then the Yorkshire Post, the Daily Telegraph and the Observer, before joining ITN.

He became an editor and then Chairman and Chief executive of ITN as well as a board member of Channel 4 and is now the Chairman of *Talkradio UK*.

Jeremy NICHOLAS
Jeremy has a programme each Friday morning and hosts the Saturday sports programmes on BBC GLR.

Emma NICHOLLS
Emma is a DJ on *GWR FM* in Bristol.

Ian NICHOLSON
Ian is a senior producer at *BBC Radio Oxford*.

Colin NICOL
Born in Perth, Australia in December, 1944, his first job in radio was at local station 6PM, and then 6KY where he became programme director. After moving to London he joined *Radio Atlanta* where he became the station's first DJ on the air.

Colin hosted the station's Breakfast Show until it was taken over by *Radio Caroline* and then presented a variety of shows on Caroline South, and left after she began broadcasting from the Swedish *Radio Syd* ship.

A few months later Colin, whose surname is, rarely, an anagram of his Christian name, joined *Radio England* and *Britain Radio* and later *Radio Luxembourg* where he joined the station's permanent staff.

A few years later Colin joined the BBC as staff announcer on continuity and news bulletins on *Radio One* and *Radio Two*, and then after a few years with *BFBS* in Malta and Gibraltar he moved back to Australia where he now manages shopping precincts.

Anne NIGHTINGALE
Born on April Fools Day in Middlesex, she did a journalism course at the London Polytechnic and worked on the 'Brighton and Hove Gazette' and the Daily Express. While at the latter she often derided *Radio One* for not having any female DJs, so eventually they invited her to try her hand!

Since that first broadcast in 1969 she's penned a rock music column in Cosmopolitan and freelanced for programmes as diverse as 'Woman's Hour' and Today.

Humphrey NORRINGTON

Formerly the vice-chairman of Barclays Bank Plc, Humphrey joined the Board of Directors of *Premier Radio* in London in 1995.

John NORRINGTON

Born on 4th October, 1940 in Berkhampstead and his first radio work was in the late 1980s when he worked on the Broadcasting Bill, which was the enabling legislation for the Radio Authority and the basis of all current stations' licences.

John then worked on the conversion of the old IBA franchises into Radio Authority licences and, since May 1990, he has been the Secretary of the Radio Authority. This is the only post specified in the Broadcasting Act and probably the Authority's most important position.

The highlights of his career are too many and varied to list, but he particularly enjoyed being involved with so many dedicated and enthusiastic people at all levels.

The most humourous event of John's radio career was observing the House of Lords attempts to define 'pop music' (for the purpose of INR licences). John likes investigative journalism, but, oddly, hates bureaucracy.

James NORTON

Chief Executive of the *Radiocommunications Agency,* the DTI subsidiary which oversees all technical aspects of radio broadcasting.

Simon NORTON

Simon is now the host of various late night programmes at weekends on *Signal Radio*, in Cheshire.

Charles NOVE

A Londoner he was educated in Glasgow and worked in an electronics factory prior to his first public appearance in 1976 on the Glasgow Hospital Radio service. From there he moved to *Radio Scotland* where he hosted 'Nightbeat' and the weekly 'Scottish Chart Show'. In the early eighties he moved back to London to present programmes on *Radio Two*.

Howard NURSE

Howard obtained a BA(Hons) in Human geography at the University of Sheffield and an NCTJ certificate before setting up his own press agency in Scarborough in 1988, supplying news and sports stories to various media, with specialist coverage of Scarborough FC games to ILR stations throughout the UK.

He joined *Yorkshire Coast Radio* in 1994 and hosts a three hour lunchtime programme as well as the position of head of News and Sport at the station. A keen sportsman he is now divorced and lives in Filey.

John O'BRIEN

John was the chairman of the Granada Group's commercial and overseas division for several years, he then moved to Millwards Shoes Ltd and in 1994 joined *Premier Radio* in London where he is now the company's Chairman.

Mike O'BRIEN

Sales Director at *Gemini Radio* in Exeter.

Estelle O'CONNELL

Estelle is the promotion manager and head of press relations at *Galaxy Radio* in the south West.

Bart O'DONNELL

Bart is the Head of Sales, Sponsorship and Marketing at *Q102.9* in Londonderry.

Conal O'DONNELL

Conal is the producer responsible for Ed Doolan's programmes on BBC Radio WM/CWR.

Mark O'DONNELL

Mark is a news reporter for *BBC Radio Solent*.

Nikki O'DONNELL

Nikki is a senior producer and also the breakfast show each weekday at *BBC Radio Solent*.

Liam O'DONOGHUE

Despite graduating in sociology, Liam did a variety of manual work before becoming a journalist. After four years of newspapers he joined Liverpool's *Radio City* in 1987 and his first broadcast was from a protest outside the Conservative Party conference. In less than eighteen months he became the station's Political Editor and, later in 1989 was voted North West Radio Journalist of the year.

In June 1993 was made Chief Reporter and Documentary maker at City, but he's not totally serious and fondly remembers the morning he sang 'Secret Love' live on the station's breakfast show! Likes good food, good films , good soccer and good (non radio word) and doesn't like racism, violence, intolerance and greed.

In 1995 he won a SONY award for Best Documentary for a programme he produced about the CSA, and he has two nominations for the New York Radio Awards this year.

Robert O'DOWD

Enterprise Director at *Classic FM*.

Donnach O'DRISCOLL

After education in Dublin and New York, Donnach worked in Washington as a merchant banker, before joining *CLT*. He is now the company's international Chief Executive and the deputy chairman of Atlantic 252.

Patrick O'HAGAN

Broadcast Journalist with *BBC Radio Berkshire*, now merged with Radio Oxford to form *Radio Thames Valley*.

John O'HARA

Went to school and college in Dublin and became an insurance claims inspector. He got into radio by helping make the coffee at a Dublin pirate station in the school holidays in August 1976 - they let him on their air at *Radio Dublin* (still on the air and still a pirate) and he was shaking so much he broke a stylus!

In 1982 he stepped up the radio ladder to the high power super-pirates and spent a year at Q-102, two years at Radio Nova, and a similar period at sister station *Energy 103*. These were high power unlicensed stations run by Chris Carey (qv) with massive audiences.

In 1987 he moved across town to *Capital 104* and then to *Radio City,* followed by a year at the short lived Irish national commercial station, *Century Radio* in 1993.

In 1994 he came across to the UK and joined *Radio City* in Liverpool, for whom he hosted a 57 hour marathon broadcast from the window of Marks and Spencer to raise funds for charity.

John likes Guinness, sailing, Goldie Hawn and Coronation Street, but is definitely not into rain, bean curd and new age travellers. John is now Head of Music for Radio City's AM service.

Ronan O'RAHILLY

After a chequered school career in Ireland, Ronan arrived in London in the early 1960s and, after studying acting, he worked in the music business, running several RnB clubs in Lodnon and promoting bands such as the Rolling Stones and singers such as Georgie Fame.

When he couldn't get Georgie Fame's records played on either the BBC (who didn't play tracks by unknown artistes) or Radio Luxembourg (who only played 'paid' or sponsored records by major record companies) he decided to start his own radio station - which is why *Radio Caroline* was begun.

The idea was copied from Radio Veronica, then broadcasting from a lightship off the Dutch coast, which Ronan heard a girl enthusing about at a party.

Despite coming from a rich family (they run a shipping line and owned a former British Railways ferry port) Ronan wanted to make it on his own, so borrowed £50 from a bank to buy a suit with which to impress backers; they were duly impressed, gave him the money to start *Radio Caroline* and the rest is pure modern history which changed radio forever!

He was joint managing Director during the station's halcyon days and has been the organisation's figurehead since.

In 1967 three of the Beatles wanted him to manage them after Brian Epstein died, but Ronan wanted to pursue his film-making career. 'Girl of A Motorcycle' starring Marrianne Faithful was one of his best known works.

Another huge success for Ronan was being asked by Caroline's arch-rival, *Radio Luxembourg*, to consult on the revamping of their French service. Ronan sent them one of his most popular DJs , Emperor Rosko, who built a self drive studio and boosted audiences by a factor of three.

A quiet spoken man who keeps a very low profile and likes nothing more than to chat and talk the night away, Ronan's influence has spread far and wide in the London music business these last thirty five years. He's settled down recently with a wife but can still be found in the smartest watering holes in South Kensington.

Prof J A O'REILLY
Director of *Downtown Radio* in Belfast.

Paul O'REILLY
After being educated at St Michael's School in Garston, Paul became a semi-pro footballer with Aylesbury United. He got into radio by working in hospital radio and then joined *Chiltern Radio* for his first broadcast on May Day, 1985. During that time he also worked with DLT for a year and also conducted Eric Morecambe's final interview before he died.

Paul owns a construction company and as well as liking cricket, football and his wife is also a keen strain-spotter. After spending the last ten years at Chiltern Paul is looking forward to the next ten.

Rick O'SHEA
Mid-day presenter on *Atlantic 252* in 1995.

Mark OATEN
A director at *Oasis Radio* in St Albans.

Steve OATES
Managing Director at *Wessex FM*, Dorchester.

John OGDEN
John's career began as the News Editor at *TFM* in Stockton in the late 1980s. He is now the Assistant Editor at *BBC Radio Cleveland*.

James OLD
Producer at *BBC Radio Devon and Dorset*.

Andrew OLDHAM
Sales Director of Media Sales and Marketing at *Capital Radio*.

Sally OLDHAM
In the late 1980s Sally was Sales Director at *Radio 210* in Reading. She then moved to be station director at *Ocean, Power FM* and *South Coast Radio* and also a director of *Mix 96*, Aylesbury. In 1994 she joined *Fox FM* as Managing Director, but resigned in 1995.

Eleanor OLDROYD
After reading modern languages at Cambridge University, where she also edited the sports pages of the campus newspaper, Eleanor did work experience at *Radio Wyvern* in Worcester for the princely sum of a fiver a day!

Who's Who in British Radio

Her first broadcast was reading a sports bulletin at Wyvern, but over the next two years she hosted a variety of programmes at the station including weekend request programmes. In 1986 she left Wyvern to join *BBC Radio Shropshire* hosting sports and news programmes, and in 1988 was signed by *Radio One* for 'Newsbeat'.

In 1991 she transferred to the BBC's radio sport section as a reporter and presenter, and has appeared on many other shows on *Radio Five*, and more recently *Five Alive*. The highlight of Eleanor's career was interviewing Linford Christie after we won the Gold Medal in the 100 metres at the Barcelona Olympics, and she's pleased at meeting many sporting heroes.

One of her fondest memories is of post match interviews with the Telford Tigers Ice Hockey team in the dressing rooms! She likes most sports, especially cricket and soccer, but only as a spectator, but hates working 9 to 5 and travelling in the rush hour.

Richard OLIFF
Richard is a DJ at *KCBC* in Kettering.

David OLIVER
Born in 1974, he ran the campus radio station at Southampton University and in 1985 went to Gibraltar to launch a cross-border station.

Chris OPPERMAN
Presenter and Producer at BBC *Radio Suffolk*.

Steve ORCHARD
Programme Director at the GWR Group.

Mick ORD
Educated at SFX College in Liverpool, De Salle Grammar and Nottingham University, he was a volunteer helper at CBC in Cardiff before enrolling on a course at the London College of Printing in 1983. He did a couple of years as a freelance reporter before joining *BBC Radio Merseyside* in 1985. A year later he was made Producer and three years later became the station's News editor.

In 1993 he took up TV production roles from BBC Manchester and also became Assistant Managing Editor of *Radio Merseyside* at the same time. A half hour documentary from Crossmaglen in 1991 was the highlight (so far) of Mick's career - he likes football (a keen Everton supporter) as well as reading and keep-fit, but isn't the biggest supporter of either Liverpool or Manchester United!

Andrea ORMSBY
Andrea is a Dorset based producer at BBC *Radio Devon and Dorset*.

Sandy ORR
Sandy is chairman of the *Radio Forth* Group.

Annie OTHEN
Host of the weekday afternoons programme (2 until 4pm) on *BBC Radio WM/CWR*.

Mark OVENDEN
Born on 20th June, 196, in London, Mark attended Barnhill Comprehensive in Hayes and Cowes High School. His first radio work was in a hospital station on the Isle of Wight in 1977 and in 1980 he was first heard on BBC *Radio Solent*.

He had his own programme at Southampton University's station *Radio Glen* for the next four years and worked as a freelance station assistant at Radio Solent.

In 1987 Mark joined *Ocean Sound* as a journalist and three years later moved to *Radio Five* as a reporter.

In 1992 he established a production company, 'Outspoken Productions' which has produced many programmes for *Radio One* including two 1 week series of 'Dance Energy' and excellent documentaries such as 'Lost in Music' and 1FM's coverage of 'Pride 94'.

As well as radio work Mark has also edited a magazine called 'Due South' and been a researcher for *Gaytime TV* and was a Gay Men's Publicity Officer for Manchester City Council.

Who's Who in British Radio

The highlight of Mark's radio career so far was hanging from a helicopter over the Scilly Isles reporting on a Seacat crossing, and getting One FM to cover the 'Gaypride' celebrations. Other memorable occasions have been tripping over a mike lead and stopping a live broadcast. He likes clubbing, comedy and cult TV, not mention cakes, but not homophobia, hospitals, hates and, er, . . hesitations!

Chris OVEREND

Appointed the Marketing and Promotions Manager at *Great Yorkshire Gold* and *Hallam FM* in September, 1995.

Bill OVERTON

Breakfast presenter at *BBC GLR* until 1995 when he joined *Viva 963,* a London based station aimed at women.

Ashley OWEN

Ashley is the host of the 'Hits Not Homework' programme on *Radio Maldwyn.*

Glyn OWEN

Sales Director at *Signal Radio Group.*

Henry OWEN

Programme Controller at *Atlantic 252* in 1985.

Jeff OWEN

Jeff is Nottingham born and bred, and very proud of it. He was educated in Chilwell and then onto Nottingham University for a chemistry and physics degree.

He says he works in radio "because it's easier than pouring chemicals from one tube to another....and it doesn't burn when you spill it."

Jeff used to run the university radio station when he was a student and he presented late night rock shows on *BBC Radio Nottingham* at the same time.

He then spent a period at *Radio Leeds* (mid morning/lunchtime/breakfast) was followed by a journalism training course, then some time in the newsroom before moving back to Radio Nottingham.

He has a Sony Radio Award for the best sequence programme beating Kenny Everett and John Dunn but could use another one now "because bookends usually come in pair!"

Johnny OWEN

Host of lunchtime programme each weekday on *Signal Radio* in Cheshire.

Mike OWEN

Formerly the programme controller of BRMB, Mike is mow the Operations Manager at *Xtra AM* in the Midlands.

Sue OWEN

News Editor at *Heart 100.7.*

John OWENS

Financial controller at *Radio Wyvern.*

Paul OWENS

Paul has worked at many radio stations over the last quarter of a century, including *Radio One, Radio Two, BBC Radio London, Pennine Radio* in Bradford, *Devonair* and *County Sound.*

In 1994 Paul joined *Star FM* in Slough and is now Head of Music at UK Radio Developments and also Programme Controller at *Star FM.*

Barry OWLER

Head of Music at *Q102.9* in Londonderry.

Dianne OXBERRY

Weather and travel presenter on 'Simon Mayos' Breakfast Show' for BBC *Radio One.*

(The ranking) Miss P

Involved in several land-based pirates in London in the 1980s, as a result of which she was hired by *Radio One* to add credibility to its reggae programme.

After a spell presenting this every Sunday night she moved to *GLR* for a similar Friday evening show.

Me Mark PAGE

Born in 1958 in Middlesborough, he joined a local hospital radio channel when only 14 and made his air debut on a *Radio Clyde* sports programme the following year. By the time he was 16 he had his own programme on *Radio Tees* and presented the breakfast show there for many years, possibly the UK's youngest breakfast show jock, a gig he held down for six years. His wacky zany style was years ahead of other more recent UK practitioners and tapes of his broadcasts are still eagerly swapped by anoraks and historians!

Eventually Mark was snapped up by *BBC Radio One* where he spent four years on a regular Friday afternoon slot, weekend shows and countless 'fill-ins'.

Mark wanted more radio so it was back north to Middlesborough and *BBC Radio Cleveland* where he hosted the station's breakfast . .

programme while doing a weekly prerecorded programme on *Radio Luxembourg*, as well as weekends at *Radio Clyde*. *The Luxembourg programme ran for five years* culminating in a New York Radio Festival Award.

While at Radio Clyde (a three year stint) he won a 'Radio Personality of the Year Award in the New York Festival. Two years later he picked up another Gold medal for the best comedy show for a BFBS special. he has broadcast world wide to the forces for over ten years and now transmits the programme live from his home in Stockton over ISDN lines.

During a two year stint on *Radio Aire* in Leeds in the early nineties, he picked up the industry's top award, the 1992 Sony Gold, for Britain's Best Breakfast Show, before then it was split into a number of different categories. He currently hosts programmes on BBC *Radio Cleveland, Newcastle* and the Night Network (Northern BBC station link-ups), in addition to being a much in-demand voice for commercials.

In 1995 Mark formulated Trak Broadcasting's bid for the Darlington ILR licence and he's currently consulting on several radio projects.

Nick PAGE

Nick worked at *BBC Radio Two* and *LBC* in London in presentation before joining *Premier Radio* in London in 1995.

Tim PAGE

Journalist at *Network News* in Dunstable.

Brian PAIGE

Presenter at *South West Sound* in Dumfries and also on *West Sound* in Ayr.

Colin PALMER

Colin is the Head of News and Sport at *Mercia*.

Dick PALMER

Born in Wimbledon on 29th March, 1943, Dick's family moved to Kent when he was nine and he was educated at a variety of boarding schools.

Coming from a family of sea-farers, Dick took an engineering apprenticeship after school and worked in racing car design for a time. A highly skilled motor engineer, Dick joined *Radio Essex* in 1966 and by the time the station changed into *'Britain's Better Music Station* he'd become programme Director, a role he combined with as Fort Captain.

After legislation closed most offshore stations, Dick joined Pink Floyd as the band's road manager and in 1969 took a 20,000 overland trip into the Far East on behalf of the British Museum and Kew Gardens.

In the early 1970's he joined *Radio Caroline* and as well as duties as captain of the ship, was also heard on the air most evenings playing his own quite eclectic choice of music and making wry observations about the future of the world if the ship's complement of young disc jockeys continued to eat confectionery! He gave much solid advice to his ship-mates and listeners alike and many of his predictions, greeted with much derision in the 70's have, unfortunately, come true.

Over ensuing years he became involved in other ship-born ventures and later joined the Omani Navy where he became a Lieutenant Commander and his engineering skills brought him untold rewards. Sufficient anyway to buy a palatial mansion in Sussex and indulge his cravings for rave music and other delights in various clubs in the Brighton area.

Kevin PALMER

Born on 28th October, 1967, in Birkenhead, Kevin got into radio by reading the obituaries and pig prices on a local station in Ireland. This led to work at *Radio City* in Liverpool and then at *Radio West* in Ireland once again.

After a period in France at *Contact 94* Kevin headed in the direction of home again, and took a position at *Marcher Sound* in Wrexham.

From there it was a return to the Emerald Isle and the plum role as Breakfast show host on *Atlantic 252*. He stayed there until until May 1995 when he left to join the new Chrysalis station in London, *Heart FM*.

Being at the birth of Heart was one of the highlights of Kevin's career and he fondly recalls "driving up the Thames being the 1995 University boat race in a floating Ford Fiesta". Kevin rather likes not having to work for a living and hates the thought of having to get a real job - he's available now for Panto (Oh, no he isn't) "Oh Yes I am! Call me at Heart FM on 0171 470 1046".

Liz PALMER

Liz is the Head of Marketing and special events at *Capital Radio*.

Richard PALMER

The Chairman of *Radio 210* in Reading.

Barry PALSER

Presenter at *BBC Radio Cambridgeshire*.

John PANTENNY

Sales Director at *2CR*, Bournmouth.

Steve PANTON

Steve is now the Managing editor of *BBC GLR* in London.

Denise PAPE

The Financial Manager at *CFM*, Carlisle.

Andy PARK

The first programme controller at *Radio Clyde*.

Richard PARK

Born in Kircaldy on the 10th March 1948, Richard attended local high school and Edinburgh University before joining his local paper 'Fife News' as a journalist.

In 1966 he joined the *Radio Scotland* ship anchored near Ayr and on his weeks ashore went gigging with The Who and The Move, playing Motown and Stax sets between their performances.

In 1969 he got some work with the BBC on the Radio One Club but in those days the BBC didn't hire people outside their own London 'clique' so Richard set up one of the first hospital radio stations in Kircaldy.

He also opened a seafood bar on the seafront in Kircaldy and practiced hard for the launch of ILR. This was rewarded with a gig at Scotland's first commercial station, *Radio Clyde* which launched in 1973, and after two weeks he had taken control of the station's play list.

He presented many weekday shows on the station as well as sports programmes on Saturdays and by 1981 had become the station's Head of Music and Sport.

Richard spent fourteen years at Radio Clyde, during which the station achieved a 64% reach figure in Glasgow (still a record) and in 1983 he won the Sony 'Personality of the Year' award. He topped that the following year by winning a 'World Sports Personality of the year' award in New York, and in 1987 he moved to Capital Radio in London.

Under his experienced hand, the station split programming and successfully applied for its licence to be renewed. he soon became programme controller and then was given a seat on the board.

The awards continued to shower on Richard: in 1992 he won a Premio Ondas Trophy for innovation in radio programming and he now has control of the output at all 12 stations in the Capital Group - including *BRMB, Xtra AM, Invicta FM* and *Supergold* in Kent, *Southern FM, South Cost Radio, Ocean Sound* and *Power FM* in Hampshire.

Richard is resolute in what he wants and has tremendous focus; he is a total radio man, and listens around the clock. He credits his time on board *Radio Scotland* as a great training ground "Fantastic training, working with DJs from all over the world with wildly varying lifestyles and ailments!"

Stan PARK
Managing Director at Independent Radio Sales.

Barrie PARKER
Sports journalist at *BBC Radio York*.

Dave PARKES
Presenter at *WABC*, in Wolverhampton.

Steve PARKES
After a period involved in RSL's in East Yorkshire and running the campus radio station at the University of Hull, Steve joined BBC *Radio Humberside* in 1995.

After the usual induction of presenting traffic news, etc, he is now presenting a variety of programmes as holiday relief. He recently began presenting the station's 'Morningtide' programme.

Chris PARKIN
Chris is a director at *Stray FM*, Harrogate.

Simon PARKIN
Born in Manchester on 11th April, 1967, Simon worked in local theatre and got into radio by making background tapes for local radio stations.

He joined *Radio Tees* in Stockton in 1987 and also did some freelance work at *Radio Humberside,* before moving to BBC TV to present Childrens Television and a host of other programmes. In the nineties he did more radio - several programmes on *BBC Radio Five* ('Take Five' and 'Parkin's Summer madness').

Ian PARKINSON

Ian is one of the regular presenters of Newsbeat on *Radio One.*

Michael PARKINSON

Born in Cudworth near Barnsley in 19835, Michael was a newspaper journalist for many years an d achieved fame as a documentary presenter an chat show host on television before moving into radio.

He joined *LBC* to host his own programme in the 1980s and replaced the late Roy Plomley on radio's longest running programme, 'Desert island Discs' on *Radio Four.*

Steven PARKINSON

Programme Controller of *Great Yorkshire Gold* until 1995, when he became Head of Marketing and Promotions at the station.

Darren PARKS

Presenter on *Power FM* in Hampshire.

Ushar PARMAR

Chairman and Chief Executive at *Sunrise Radio.*

Samantha PARR

Samantha is the Head of Promotion and Press Relations at *Beacon Radio.*

Matthew PARROTT

Presenter at *BBC Radio Berkshire.*

Andy PARRY

Presenter at *MFM* in Wrexham.

Chris PARRY

Chris arrived in England from New Zealand aged 20 and played in a band in the UK and in Europe, especially Denmark, for a couple of years before studying marketing.

In 1975 he became the top student in the south east in the Institute of Marketing examinations and joined Polygram. The next few years were spent in marketing and the Artistes and Repertoire departments and in 1978 he set up his own music publishers and record label.

Breaking The Cure in the USA taught Chris a great deal about radio and in the early nineties he became involved with a group who'd run an RSL at the Reading Festival and who wanted to run a rock-oriented station in London. Chris has provided the marketing and corporate expertise for what has become XFM, an organisation strongly supported by the music industry and hopeful of winning a London licence in 1996.

Nicholas PARSONS

Lincolnshire-born actor/presenter with a long pedigree of appearances on stage, in films and on the small screen. He produced a drama series for *Radio Four* called 'The Radio Deceiver' and is the regular host of the *Radio Two* panel game 'Just a Minute'.

Charlie PARTRIDGE

Popular presenter at *BBC Radio Humberside* in the 1980s, where he hosted the afternoon weekday programme. He moved to take a senior production role at *BBC Radio Essex,* where he currently still hosts some programmes. In 1994 he was promoted to be the station's Assistant Editor.

Kevin PASHBY

Kevin is the Head of News at *KCBC*, the ILR station in Kettering.

Richie PASK

Richie trained as a graphic artist before a flirtation with pirate radio led him to a job at BRMB in Birmingham. He then moved to the city's BBC outlet, *Radio WM*, and then to the more avant-garde but short-lived *Buzz FM.*

When that station folded Richie was snapped up by Stoke radio group *Signal*. He now presents overnights on *Signal Cheshire* and a Sunday afternoon programme on *Signal One*. He confesses to liking sport and ten pin bowling, but not smoking.

Martin PASKIN

Martin is the Engineer in charge at *BBC Radio Berkshire*.

Graham PASS

Popular mid-morning phone-in and entertainment presenter at *BBC Radio Essex* in the 1980s, he is thought to be no longer in radio.

Erkan PASTIRMACIOGIU

Chairman and also the Managing Director of *Turkish Radio* in North London.

Joe PATRICKS

Presenter at *Piccadilly Gold*.

Jessica PATTEN

Jessica is the producer of the mid morning show (hosted by Malcolm Boyden) on BBC Radio WM and WCR in the Midlands.

Craig PATTISON

Host of weekend afternoon programmes on *Signal Radio*'s Cheshire outlet.

Tony PAUL

Born in London and studied electronics at the Royal Aircraft Establishment at Farnborough, before moving to Toronto, Canada. There he worked in advertising and returned to the UK in 1974 and worked in nightclubs for a while.

In 1978 he bought a record shop and, after three years selling sounds, decided to go back into playing them, so joined *Beacon Radio* where he remained for most of the eighties.

Dixie PEACH

Dixie is a former night club and gigging band singer who joined Radio Caroline in 1983. After six months he was hired by *Radio One* and hosted weekend dance-oriented programmes for a while. He was last heard of in a pantomime in East Midlands.

Steve PEACOCK

News journalist based at the Wyvern newsroom of *BBC Hereford and Worcester*.

Dave PEARCE

David hosted and produced a weekend evening programme on BBC GLR for several years and moved to *Radio One* when GLR's MD (Matthew Bannister) took over the network. Dave is currently hosting the early morning show, from 4 to 6 am weekdays.

Howard PEARCE

His radio career began at Portsmouth ILR station *Radio Victory* in 1976 as a disco presenter before presenting programmes seven days a week. He then moved to *Radio 210* in Reading and from there, on to *Radio Luxembourg* for two years. Moving further afield he went to Austria's *Blue Danube Radio* and did some TV work for the ORF.

In 1981, Howard returned to *Radio 210* as Head of Music, and also found time to hold down the breakfast show. In 1984 he joined *Radio Two* for a series of early morning shows, and the following year syndicated his "The Hawk" weekly pop magazine to ILR stations in the south.

He moved into syndicated programming with his own company called 'Pearce Productions' and found time for presentation work with *Southern Radio, World Service, Radio Five, BSB* and *Sky TV* as well as *Chiltern Radio*.

On New Year's Day, 1993, Howard joined *Meridian TV* but returned to radio a few months later when he joined *Virgin 1215*, where he is still doing weekend overnights, as well as managing to grace the screens of *Sky Sports*.

Jonathan PEARCE

Born in Plymouth two days before Christmas 1959, Jonathan hoped to have a career as a professional footballer and trained with Bristol City but had to give that up after breaking his leg in his teens.

His sports broadcasting career began in 1980 as a football reporter at *BBC Radio Bristol* and in 1987 he moved to *Capital Gold* to set up the station's sports facility.

Who's Who in British Radio

The following year Jonathan was instrumental in launching Capital's full sports department, where he and his team have won numerous awards including Gold Medals at the New York Radio Festival and several Sony Awards.

John PEARSON

Began his career as a graduate trainee for the Thompson regional newspaper group and joined *Radio Luxembourg* in 1979 as a Sales Executive. The following year he moved to *Capital Radio* and four years later was appointed Head of Sales.

In 1987, John moved back into the world of print, but two years later he returned to radio, as sales Controller at *LBC*, then London's news station. He was appointed Director before leaving to join *Virgin Radio*. In 1994 he was appointed to the Virgin Board and was made Managing Director of Virgin Radio's new *London FM* station in March 1995.

Ashley PEATFIELD

After a period as Acting News Editor at BBC *Radio Leeds* in the early 1990s, Ashley is now the station's Assistant Editor.

Mike PECK

Mike is the training coordinator at Community Radio Milton Keynes.

Roger PECK

Roger is the chairman of *Isle of Wight Radio*.

Andy PEEBLES

Born in 1948 in North London, he went to Bishop Stortford College and left to work in catering, despite living in a flat occupied by the late Paul Kaye of *Radio London* fame who was a great influence.

From 1967 to 1972 Andy worked in discotheques and then moved to Manchester to take up a compere role at the Hardrock concert venue.

Later that year he said his first words on the *Radio Cavell*, the hospital station in Oldham and the following year *BBC Radio Manchester* gave him a weekly programme.

While there he was approached by *Radio One* where he hosted several programmes on the network and for the *World Service*.

Andy compered the Elton John concert live from Moscow in 1980. Later moved to GLR for a weekday late evening show and was recently presenting the mid morning programme on *BBC Radio Lancashire*.

David PEEL

David was a journalist for seven years and a stringer for the BBC before getting into radio at BBC *Radio Middlesborough*, now *Radio Cleveland* in 1974. Since then his career has seen him working as a producer at BBC Radio Cleveland, a regional *TV journalist for the BBC in Bristol* and then promotion to News Editor at *Radio Lancashire*.

He then picked up further experience as News Editor at *Radio Newcastle,* and *Radio York*, before returning to *Radio Cleveland* in 1993 to be the station's Managing Editor.

In addition to that, David also trains journalists and the highlight of his career was winning a silver Sony Award for his coverage of riots in Newcastle.

John PEEL

Cheshire born John Ravenscroft went to school in North Wales and Shrewsbury and after National Service embarked on a four year stay in the USA.

When the Beatles phenomena broke in 1964, he was purloined by KLIF, the legendary station owned by Gordon McLendon in Dallas.

John's unconventional music choice resulted in a quick move to KOWA in Oklahoma, where he picked up a wife and moved on quickly to San Bernadino .

On rturning to the UK in 1967 he got a gig at (offshore) *Radio London* where the overnight shift allowed him a pretty free choice in music - "the perfumed garden' became well known as the most avante garde radio in 1967.

When *Radio London* closed he moved on to *BBC Radio One*, as one of the co-hosts of Top Gear, eventually hosting the programme alone.

For the next quarter of a century he clocked up a variety of programmes, each renowned for their musical content (invariably unknown music, much of which was to remain so but some of which later became widely acclaimed).

A laconic sense of humour, an ear for adventurous musicians and a love of football sums up John Peel, named 'Broadcaster of the Year' in the 1993 Sony Awards.

Julia PEET
Julia is a producer and also presents programmes on *BBC Radio Dorset and Devon*.

Chris PEGG
Weekday presenter at *Mercia FM* in Coventry.

Rob PENDRY
Head of Music at *Swansea Sound*.

Simon PENFOLD
Engineer at *BBC Radio Stoke on Trent*..

Steve PENK
Began his career in commercial production at Manchester ILR *Piccadilly Radio* in the early 1980s. He then hosted several programmes and eventually fronted the station's breakfast show on its FM service, *Key 103*.

He is undoubtedly the city's best known programme host and the station has sold over 20,000 copies of a cassette of excerpts from his programme while station bosses cite his programmes as a major contribution to the station's success.

Clare PENKITH
Producer of the 'Coming Home' drive time programme on BBC Radio WM//WCR in the Midlands.

Dean PEPPAL
After a period at *Hallam FM*, during which he became the station's General Manager, Dean is now the breakfast DJ on *BBC Radio Sheffield*.

Eugene PERERA
Marketing Director of *Kiss FM* in Manchester

Shyama PERERA
Shyama is the co-host of the Friday morning breakfast show on *London Newstalk*.

John PERKINS
Managing Director of Independent Radio News.

June PERKINS
Manager of the financial section of BBC Radio in East Anglia, based in Norwich.

Bruce PERRETT
Bruce is the Chief Engineer of *Mercia FM* and its sister station *Classic Gold* in Coventry.

Roberto PERRONE
Presenter of Italian Music programme on BBC 2 Counties Radio.

Mark PERROW
Programme host at BBC *Radio York* in the 1980s, thought to be no longer in radio.

Ian PERRY
Weekday Presenter at *Beacon Radio*.

Peter PERRY
Peter was the Sales Director of Radio Mercury for many years and in the 1990s took over as Managing Director (after John Aumonier left). He is also a board member of the *Fortune 1458* easy-listening station in Manchester.

Harry PERRYMAN
Harry is the coordinator of community information at CRMK in Milton Keynes.

Ambreen PERVEZ
Ambreen produces and presents the 'Junction 774' programme for Asian listeners each Sunday evening at 1900 on *BBC Radio Leeds*.

Geoff PETERS
Sports reporter at *BBC Radio Leicester*.

John PETERS
Born in February 1970 he went to school in Northamptonshire and studied politics and drama. After work experience at BBC *Radio Northampton* he moved to the Chiltern Group, hosting the breakfast show at *Horizon FM* from September 1991 to the end of that year.

John then moved to Lancashire to join *Radio Wave* in Morecambe where he did the afternoon show until March 1993, when he moved back to the Midlands and *Severn Sound* where he presented the station's mid-morning show. In 1995 he is back in the east Midlands hosting breakfasts at *GEM AM*.

John likes George Michael and spending time with a loved one, and dislikes fox-hunting. His ambition is to write songs which will strike a chord with the public.

Tony PETERS
Information Officer at *Cheltenham 603*.

Sally PETERSON
Sally is the host of weekday overnight programmes on *Classic FM*.

Paul PHEAR
Born in Devon on 24th July, 1961, Paul worked as a photographer, a manager of a record shop and at the world's biggest magic trick factory, before getting into radio at *Plymouth Sound* in 1983.

Paul then moved to *Radio West* in Bristol (*GWR*) and *Chiltern Radio* in Dunstable. While there he hosted the station's breakfast show for three years and moved to *Capital FM* in 1991 where he currently hosts the station's weekend breakfast programme.

During his career Paul has interviewed Robert Maxwell, Jeffrey Archer and Basil Brush and he feels that "a good DJ makes the listener feel that he is a person they would actually enjoy chatting to."

Paul now lives in Leighton Buzzard with his wife and daughter.

Andrew PHILLIPS
Programme Controller at *Radio 210*.

Chris PHILLIPS (1)
Presenter at *BBC Radio Berkshire* and in 1995 at *Kiss FM* in London where he hosts the afternoon programme each weekday as well as 'Kiss Classics' every Sunday morning.

Chris PHILLIPS (2)
Chris is a weekday DJ on *Kiss FM* in London.

Ian PHILLIPS
Senior producer at *BBC Radio Devon*.

Peter PHILLIPS
Peter joined *Radio Caroline* in 1984 and became one of the station's most proficient presenters. The following year he became the station's Chief Programmer and in the late 1980s came ashore to join *Breeze AM* in Southend where he hosted weekday drive time programmes.

In 1985 he moved to *BBC Radio Kent* to host their breakfast programme.

Roger PHILLIPS
A graduate of Cambridge, Roger became an actor, a cabbie and a media researcher before getting into radio by way of a play on Radio Merseyside. On the day of an interview he was asked to read the 6pm news bulletin on the station. In 1978 he became a producer at Merseyside, and then spent the whole of the 1980s hosting the station's mid-day phone-in. The funniest moment for Roger came when one of his callers did a strip on the air - she was 83 years old at the time!

In 1990, Roger moved across town to *Radio City* to present a phone-in and current affairs programme in the evenings, which he did for two years.

He then was lured back to *Radio Merseyside* in 1992 and can't now see himself ever leaving. His main love is the city and people of Liverpool, and he hates sporting fanaticism, and London.

Shirley PHILLIPS
Promotions Executive at *Northants Supergold*.

Steve PHILLIPS
Born in Hull "in the fifties" Steve worked in various night clubs in East Yorkshire before joining *Radio Caroline* at Christmas 1983. While there Steve hosted a variety of programmes and appeared on Anglia TV coverage of the station's relaunch.

He then returned to Hull and joined *Viking Radio* and then moved even further north to Metro and their *Great North Radio* outlet.

In 1994 he joined *Century Radio*, the regional station in the North East. Steve is married to Sharon and has two daughters.

WIlliam PHILLIPS
Chairman of *Moray Firth Radio*.

Robert PHILLIS
Born on the 3rd December, 1945, Bob attended the John Ruskin Grammar School and then Nottingham University. He was a lecturer for a while, at Edinburgh University and then at the Scottish Business School, before joining the Sun printing company.

In 1979 he joined the ITV Publications company and then in 1981 moved to Central television. He was a director of ITN for five years in the eighties and of Zenith Productions and a member of the ITV Programmiong Committee. In 1987 he joined Carlton as Group MD and was Chief executive of ITN from 1991 to 1993.

In 1993 he joined the BBC as deputy Director General (and Managing Director of the BBC World Service until 1995).

Colin PHILPOTT
Managing Editor of *BBC GMR*.

Ian PICKERING
Finance Director at *CRMK* in Milton Keynes.

Liz PICKERING
Liz is the secretary at *CRMK* in Milton Keynes.

John PICKFORD
John trained as a journalist with Thompson Regional Newspapers an d after four years in the local press he joined *Piccadilly Radio* as a repoprter in November 1979.

He became the station's sports editor in 1983 and was made Head of News and Sport in 1986. he was the first reporter on the scene of the Moss Side riots and led the team reporting on major stories such as the Tenerife Air Disaste and the IRA bombings in Manchester for which they won a Sony Award in 1993. he also directed the team on coverage of the Warrington bombing which won a Sony Award in 1994.

John PIERCE
John is a producer and presenter at Radio Devon and Dorset.

Nick PIERCEY
By the early 1990s Nick had become the senior presenter at *TFM* in Stockton and in 1994 he moved to become part of the on-air team (currently hosting drive-time programmes from 4 until 8 pm each weekday) at *Heart 100.7* in the Midlands.

Danny PIETRONI
Danny is a presenter at Piccadilly Radio's *Key 103 FM* outlet.

Danny PIKE
Music presenter at *Southern Sound*, Brighton also responsible for music playlists.

Chris PILLING
Presenter at *The Wave*, Blackpool.

Tom PINDAR
Born on the 30th January 1928, Tom was educated at Scarborough High School and at Leeds Technical College. he joined his family's printing firm in 1949, since when he's held various positions, and of which he's now chairman. Tom also sits on the board of the Scarborough Building Society and is the Chairman of *Yorkshire Coast Radio,* the ILR station in Scarborough.

Tom enjoys the theatre, hill-walking, swimming and gardening and was received an OBE in 1986.

Simon PIPE
Simon is the producer responsible for daytime features at *BBC Two Counties Radio*.

Cameron PIRIE
Head of Marketing at *Scot FM*.

Stella PIRIE
Head of Finance at *Trent FM*, Nottingham.

Aredi PITSIAELI
AreUi is the Community Unit Director at *Premier Radio*, the new Christian radio station in London.

Sam PLANK

Sam presents a mid-morning programme, from 9 until 11 am each weekday, on *BBC Radio Stoke on Trent*.

James PLANT

James is the Finance Director and Company Secretary of *Beacon Radio* in Wolverhampton.

John PLATT

John is the producer of the 'Network Gold' programme which he also presents, each Saturday evening on BBC Radio WM/.CWR.

Martin PLENDERLEITH

Presenter of Radio Humberside's flagship 'Morningtide' breakfast programme in late eighties and nineties. He moved to a late afternoon shift in 1995.

Robert POCOCK

The Finance Director of *Lantern Radio* in Devon.

Cess PODD

Cess hosts a four hour programme at 6pm each saturday evening on *BBC Radio Leeds*.

Sarah POLGLASE

Sarah is personal assistant to the Chief Executive at *Premier Radio*, London's new Christian radio station.

Vivien POLLARD

Director of *Touch AM* and *Red Dragon FM*.

Phillip POLLOCK

Phillip is a Director of Lincs FM.

Andrew POPPERWELL

Andrew is the co-author of 'Making Radio' and was until recently the Training and development Manager of the *BBC World Service*.

Andrew is also a leading science reporter and scriptwriter and has taught the Morley College Radio Courses for the past ten years.

Sheila PORRITT

Managing Director of *Melody Radio* (London-wide background music station).

Dave PORTER

Music presenter on *Great North Radio*.

Richard PORTER

Presenter on Invicta FM in Kent.

Rowland POTTER

Rowland is Local Sales Manager of *Country 1035* in London.

Peter POULTON

Peter is the Sales Director at *Hereward Radio*, Peterborough.

Adrian POWELL

Sunday morning presenter on *Signal Radio* in Stoke on Trent.

Bill POWELL

Presenter at *Touch AM* in South Wales.

Gill POWELL

Producer and presenter of agriculture and environmental programmes for *Radio Four* at BBC Radio in the Midlands.

John POWELL

Currently a weather presenter at *Swansea Sound*.

Mike POWELL

Mike wears a variety of hats, including Chief Executive of *The Eagle*, the new ILR station in Guildhall, he is the Managing Director of *Infinity Radio* and UK Radio Developments and also a Director of *FOX FM* in Oxford.

Peter POWELL

Worked at *BBC Radio Birmingham*, *Radio Luxembourg* and *Radio One* in the 1980s and is now married to Anthea Turner.

Brendan POWER

Irish born Brendan worked as a pool attendant, manager of groups and a night club DJ in Hull before his break onto radio. He sent tapes to every station he could hear and eventually was hired by *Radio 270* in Bridlington Bay just before Christmas 1966.

After the MoA closed the ship down he went to *Radio Antilles* in the Caribbean from where he sent dozens of audition tapes. he landed a gig at BRMB doing commercial production for the rest of the 1970s.

Who's Who in British Radio

Charlie POWER
Presenter at *Red Dragon FM* in Cardiff.

Steve POWER
Steve began his career at *Southern Radio* in Brighton as a presenter and is now the station and programme organiser at *Horizon Radio* in Milton Keynes.

Thomas PRAGG
Managing Director of *Moray Firth Radio* in Inverness and also Chief Executive of AIRC.

Bob PREEDY
Bob has had a long career in BBC and Independent Television and Independent Radio since 1970. Has been a programme producer and presenter on local radio since 1975.

Bob has broadcast on virtually every radio station in Yorkshire and the North East, including *Pennine Radio*, the first Bradford licensee, where he presented a daytime programme from 1975 to 1982.

He is currently a continuity announcer and promotions producer at Yorkshire Television, and also producer and presenters of regular networked programmes on *BBC Radios York, Leeds, Cumbria, Newcastle and Humberside*

Among his business interests are his work as a prolific author and publisher of nine books about local entertainment history. Bob operates a well known Yorkshire cinema and previously operated another in another part of Yorkshire for eight years. He can currently be heard on a chain of BBC local radio stations in the north with a networked country music programme.

D. PRENDEGAST
A Director of *Trent FM*.

Howard PRESSMAN
Presenter at *Hallam FM* in Sheffield.

Jim PRESTON
Sales Director at *Signal Radio* in Stoke.

David PREVER
Breakfast presenter at *Heart 106.2* in London.

Arthur PRICE
Director of *TalkRadio* UK.

Miss B PRICE
Director of *Mercia Radio* in Coventry.

Chris PRICE
Presenter of late night programmes each Saturday on *Manx Radio*, Isle of Man.

Pete PRICE
Originally a comic, he once won the 'New Faces' TV talent competition and has worked at dozens of clubs and halls all over the country. Pete became one of the first freelance presenters on BBC local radio when he joined *Radio Merseyside* in the mid 1970s and also appeared on the Radio One Club programmes.

Pete is a familiar face to TV viewers, having made 35 appearances including Brookside and he also appeared in the film 'No Surrender'. As a comic his life is full of hilarity. He's also been heard on BBC World Service and is now at Liverpool's *Radio City Gold*.

Peter PRICE
Chairman of Minster Sound Plc, the owner of *Minster FM* (York)*Yorkshire Coast Radio* (Scarborough) and *Wear FM* (Sunderland), from 1993 to 1995.

Roger PRICE
Chief Engineer at *Isle of White Radio*.

Simon PRIESTLEY
House Manager and station engineer at *Pennine Radio*, and then at *The Pulse* in Bradford.

Steve PRIESTLEY
Presenter at *BRMB* in Birmingham.

Tony PRINCE
An Oldham, Lancs, boy, Tony attended art school before becoming an apprentice jockey at Middleham in Yorkshire, where he shared a bedroom with another apprentice, Willy Carson, later to achieve racing fame as the Queen's own jockey.

While on holiday at Butlin's Tony was chatting to the drummer of the camp's resident band, Ringo Starr, who was so impressed with his knowledge of current pop music that he advised him to enter the weekly talent competition.

His rendition of "Mean Woman Blues" (backed by Ringo's group, Rory Storm's Hurricanes) won second prize, and he temporarily joined a Manchester band called The Jasons.

After a period singing solo Tony joined the Top Rank dance hall chain fronting a 15 piece band where first tried his hand as platter spinner when the regular jock didn't turn up.

Moving to Bristol he had to give up singing when the Musicians Union cancelled his membership as they objected to the use of recorded music and couldn't have one of their members moonlighting as a DJ!

Tony then moved to TWW, the forerunner of Harlech TV, as assistant to Kent Walton who also had a part-time job, as a boxing commentator as well as being the producer of 'Disc a Go Go'. Tony Blackburn appeared one week to plug one of his singles and enthused about his wonderful new job at *Radio Caroline*. After 'Discs a Go Go' was eclipsed by 'Ready Stead Go', Tony moved on to the good ship Caroline for two years where he became a huge star in the North and then to *Radio Luxembourg* where he helped launch the new 'live DJs' format.

A key team member until 1976 when the London office called him back to Hertford Street (then Luxy's London office), Tony proposed to his wife Christine over the air and their two children, Danny and Gabrielle were born in the Grand Duchy. Tony steered Luxembourg for seven years from his London desk, before setting up the DMC organisation in the eighties. The DMC empire includes record production and the club jock's leading magazine 'Mix Mag'.

In 1992 he was lured back to radio and a daily programme on *Capital Gold*. When Capital bought *BRMB* the following year Tony was brought in to front the station's flagship breakfast show. In 1994 he launched a magazine called 'Gold' to cash in on the nostalgia boom. Among his greatest achievements he lists meeting Elvis twice and introducing him on stage in Las Vegas, as well as singing with Paul MacCartney at the annual Buddy Holly lunch Maccers gives.

Keith PRINGLE

Keith started in the radio business in 1980 as a technical operator at *Metro Radio*. In 1984 he joined *Capital Radio* and in 1985 became a producer. He started by co-producing the 'Early Show' with Ric Blaxhill (now producer of TOTP). Keith was then was promoted to Senior Producer to take care of the 'Chris Tarrant Breakfast Show'

In 1990 Keith joined *Piccadilly Radio* as Head of Music. He was part of the team responsible for turning round the station's fortunes doubling the station's share of audience. In 1994 he became Group Head of Music for all EMAP 's radio interests.

In February 1995 Keith was appointed Programme Director of *Heart 106.2*, London's adult contemporary station owned by the Chrysalis group, which launched on the 5th September, 1995.

Neil PRINGLE

Neil hosts the late night show, from 9pm tom 1am each weekday on *Southern Counties Radio*.

Melvin PRIOR

Melvin is a general programme producer at *BBC Radio Lincolnshire* where he is responsible for the weekday breakfast programmes and a Sunday morning show.

Rt Hon. Lord PRIOR
Chairman of East Anglia Radio Group.

John PROBYN
Marketing Manager at *BRMB*.

Darren PROCTOR

Tony grew up in Stoke-on-Trent, and got a job as a resident DJ and a presenter on *Signal Radio*. There he had a regular weekend breakfast show. He also got a job with *Radio City* in Liverpool doing a drive-time show. He likes sports, but hates early mornings !

Gary PROLE

Presenter at *Mix 96* in Aylesbury.

Jim PROUDFOOT

Sports commentator at *Capital Gold* in 1995.

Wilf PROUDFOOT

One of the founding fathers of British commercial radio, Wilf was Managing Director of *Radio 270*, a regional offshore radio station based off the Yorkshire coast in the 1960s.

He had already served one term as a conservative MP in the early 1960s and was one of the leading figures in his community, heading up the family supermarket empire. In 1970 he was again elected as an MP and brought his tremendous experience to the Sound Broadcasting committee on which he sat. While in Parliament, he was a key member of the team which drafted the 1972 legislation, The Sound Broadcasting Act, which permitted commercial radio in the UK.

A firm advocate of local radio, Wilf was an adviser in the early days of *Yorkshire Coast Radio* and now spends his time running one of the UK's leading colleges of hypnosis and psychotherapy in Scarborough.

W PRYCE-GRIFFITHS

Director of Marcher Radio Group.

Mark PRYKE

Head of Presentation at *SGR FM* in Ipswich.

Spencer PRYOR

Born on 6th March, 1957, on the Island of Jersey, Spencer was a TV News Journalist with Channel TV from 1986 and also broadcast on hospital radio in jersey. He made his first 'ether' broadcast on *BBC Radio Jersey* and took part in several RSLs before moving to Scotland in 1992.

Spencer worked in sales at *Q96* in Paisley and then returned to University to do an M.Sc. in Broadcast Media Management with a thesis on "The Economics of Satellite Delivered Programming to UK Commercial Radio Stations".

Spencer was involved in a cross-country radio application for Central Scotland.

He also works as a consultant for Radio Authority applications and contributes to programmes on BBC Radio, BBC TV and Scottish TV. The Highlight of his career is "Yet to come" and he dislikes voice mailboxes and people who can't make decisions.

This year he was the Grand Finalist on Channel Four TV's 'Fifteen To One' Quiz Show and in April became Editor of the magazine AM/FM.

Katie PUCKRIK

A former singer and dancer (with Michael Clark and Co and on the Pet Shop Boys World Tour), Katie got into radio via her television work. Her first radio broadcast was the 'Fashion Icons' series for *BBC Radio Five* in 1992 and since 1993 she has been a regular contributor on the Mark Radcliffe Show on *Radio One*.

She's also hosted several other programmes, including the Guardian Guide for Independent Radio and the 'Entertainment Superhighway' for *Radio Five* in 1995.

One of the highlights was driving a tank for th *Radio Four* programme 'Going Places' and shopping in Miss Selfridge with Christian Lacroix.

Her break into TV came with 'The Word' since when she's been seen on several programmes, including 'Four goes to Glastonbury' and 'The Sunday Show'. She also presented 'Woodstock' and 'Access all Areas' for MTV in the USA. Likes genuine people but not jobs which start too early in the morning.

Janet PUGH
Janet is a reporter at *BBC Radio Essex*.

Robin PULFORD
Born in Cottingham near Hull he was educated the local Grammar School and his first job was as an apprentice cameraman for the BBC (at Lime Grove). He moved into general production and his first radio role proper was doing local opt-outs in Aberdeen (1964).

He joined Radio Humberside in the 70's and hos its programmes for many years.

A train fanatic, he left Humberside to work as Press Officer for London's Docklands Light Railway, but hankers after his home county and a job in radio once again.

Mrs L PULLAR
Managing Director at *RTM Radio* .

Nicole PULLMAN
News Editor at *BRMB*.

Prof. J Howard PURNELL
Vice-chairman at *Swansea Sound.*

Jonathan PYLE
Since June 1995, Jonathan has been the Sales Manager at *Gold Radio* in Shaftesbury.

Bernie QUAYLE
Music Presenter at *Manx Radio.*

Robert QUAYLE
Chairman of *Manx Radio.*

Liam QUIGLEY
Born on 19th September, 1964 in Clonmell in Ireland, Liam joined *CBC* in his home town after leaving school in 1981. he then moved up the ladder of Irish stations, through *Big L* in Limerick the following year, to the even bigger *ERI* in Cork in 1983.

A couple of years later and he was with the Dublin 'super-pirate' *Energy 103* (sister station of Radio Nova).

In 1988 Liam moved to the UK's first satellite station, *Radio Nova*, based in Camberley in Surrey and later that year joined the ILR network in Southend - *Essex Radio*. After an all too brief period at *Viking FM* in Hull in 1989, he moved back to Ireland to join the country's new national commercial station, *Century Radio* and then two years later joined one of the big new Dublin FM station - *Classic Hits 98.*

Liam acknowledges his time in Dublin, where he was the capital's number one drive time jock as one of the highlights of his radio career - the other was being a part of London's first Adult Contemporary station.

In 1995 Liam moved back to the UK and a regular weekday programme on the new Chrysalis station in London, *Heart 106.2*. He likes all forms of communication, but hates isolation and negativity.

John QUINN
Head of Sales at *Virgin 1215.*

Paddy QUINN
Paddy hosts the overnight programmes on *Atlantic 252.*

Peter QUINN
Peter began his career at *Radio Caroline* in 1983 and is now a presenter at *Southern FM.*

Claire QUINTIN.
Regional VP of *CNN Radio.*

Alan QUIRK
News presenter at *Manx Radio.*

Sue RABIE
Sue is the Secretary to the Managing Editor at *BBC Radio Humberside.*

Mark RADCLIFFE

Mark works from the BBC's Manchester studio centre and presented the 'Pop Quiz' series on *Radio One* in the late 1980s. In the early 1990s he also producing an arts programme on *Radio Two* as well as hosting a programme called 'Hit The North' on *Radio Five*.

He has recently been hosting late night programmes on *Radio One*.

John RADFORD

John presents the breakfast programme each weekday morning on *BBC Two Counties Radio*.

Chris RADLEY

Presenter at *Mercia Radio* in Coventry.

Anna RAEBURN

Weekday 'Agony Aunt' programme presenter at *TalkRadio UK*.

Farid RAJA

Farid presents programmes in Urdu and Punjabi each Sunday evening on *BBC Radio Leeds*.

Danny RAMPLING

Danny is the hot jock fronting the 'Lovegroove Party' programme on *Radio One* each Saturday evening.

Chris RAMSDEN

A former radio journalist, Chris became News Editor at BBC Radio Stoke on Trent in the 1980s. In 1993 he was made Assistant editor of the station.

Robert RAMSEY

Head of Community Affairs at *BRMB*.

Steve RANDALL

Born in 1970 in Kent, Steve went to school in Oxfordshire and worked at Hospital Radio Oxford from 1984 to 1986. In 1987 he joined *Metro FM* for their North East Nightshift programmes and graduated through afternoon drive to breakfast.

He also hosted the station's local chart show for several years, a shift he's recent taken on once again after two years on breakfasts.

He's currently based at *TFM* in Stockton, where he produces and presents the station's Breakfast Show each weekday and Sunday.

As well as radio work, Steve has worked at many live events, from pubs and clubs to concert halls and stadia. His voice over skills are in demand for other Metro Group stations and also Border Television. He also writes commercials and comedy sketches. In 1990 he was a finalist in the Sony Awards for Best Local DJ and he is a full Equity member.

Ross RANDELL

(See Alan West)

Adam RAPHAEL

News Manager at *CBS Radio* in London.

Mike RAVEN

The son of two actors, Austin Fairman and Hilda Moore, Mike was born Churton Fairman in London on 15th November, 1924. After private school and a spell at Oxford, Mike saw active service in the Second World War as an infantry lieutenant.

He then became a ballet dancer, conjuror, actor and TV executive before deciding to embark on a career in radio. He always held very clear opinions on how radio should sound, but before puttin g these into practice, he got some broadcast training, courtesy of the organisation he was later to challenge.

Mike's break into radio came with a series of talks on the Home Service's 'Woman's Hour', and then to one of the first offshore radio ships, *Radio Atlanta*. He then moved to the (slightly) more stable environment of the Thames fort-based stations, firstly with the short lived *KING RADIO*, where he presented the station's breakfast show jointly with his wife Mandy.

When it became *Radio 390* he was made Programme Controller and he left the station in late 1966, following a serialised feature about it in the News of The World.

When *Radio One* opened he was hired to produce and present a weekly RnB programme, which he did until 1971, leaving only to pursue a career as record producer. His Mike Raven Blues sampler is now a collectors item. In the 1970's he bought a farm and a hotel in devon, and appeared no less than four horror films. In 1995 Mike enjoys life to the full with his family at his farmhouse on Bodmin Moor.

Nick RAWLINS
Account Executive at *Lincs FM*.

Liz RAY
Liz worked on various magazine programmes at *BBC Radio Four*. She left in 1994 to freelance as a radio and print journalist and recently worked on Woman's Hour and the Jimmy Young Show for *Radio Two*. In 1995 she joined *Premier Radio*, the new Christian radio station in London, as a producer and presenter.

Robin RAY
After being educated at Highgate and RADA, Robin became an actor and in 1960 he married Susan Stranks, a well-known TV presenter and long-time campaigner for childrens radio.

Robin's acting career includes many stage and TV roles but he also finds time for a wide range of radio work, including acting as a music consultant to *Classic FM*, which he's done since before the station launched.

Robert RAYNE
Robert is a director of Golden Rose Communications, the parent company of *Jazz FM* and *Viva 963!*

Claire RAYNER
Born a Londoner in January 1931, Claire trained as a nurse and midwife before deciding to become a broadcaster. She is the author of more than 70 books on medical matters. As well as television, she has appeared on several heavyweight radio programmes , including 'Woman's Hour', Today', on *Radio Four* and the 'Michael Aspel Show' on *Capital Radio*. Her hobbies are swimming, cooking and giving parties.

Debbie RAYNER
Executive at ITN Radio.

Patrick RAYNER
Drama producer at *BBC Radio Scotland*.

Quentin RAYNER
Presenter at *BBC Radio York* in the 1980s, no longer in radio.

Rev. Ernest REA
Reverend Rea is the producer of religious programmes for *BBC Radio Two*.

Mike READ
Mike has worked for many radio stations, such as *Radio 210, Radio Luxembourg , Radio One* and *Capital Radio*. The highlight of his radio career was 6 years on the Radio 1 breakfast show and hosting 'Top of the Pops, as well as the legendary 'Pop Quiz' TV show.

He presented programmes on *Capital Gold* until September 1995 but has now left the station.

Tom READ
Head of the BBC Monitoring operation at Caversham Park near Reading.

Mike READER
Director of *Isle of Wight Radio*.

Jane RECK
Jane is a broadcast journalist with BBC *Wiltshire Sound*.

Lawrence REED
Journalist at *BBC Radio Cornwall*.

Nigel A REED
Head of Sales at *Minster FM*.

Stuart REED
Chief Executive at *Northants Radio*.

Vernon REES-DAVIES
Vice-chairman of *Swansea Sound*.

Carol REEVE
Director of *Essex Radio Group*.

James H REEVE
Presenter at *Hallam FM*.

Nigel REEVE
Sales Executive at *Classic FM*

David REICH
Chairman of IRS until June 1995.

Andrew REID
Member of the Radio Authority.

Frances REID
Senior producer of daytime programmes at *BBC Two Counties Radio*.

Ian REID
Finance Director at Clyde Electronics.

Tracey REID
Head of Human Resources at *Capital Radio*.

Ian F REILLY
Sales Director at *TFM* in Stockton now moved to Radio Tay.

Bill RENNELS
Bill hosts a programme on *BBC Radio Oxford* each weekday evening called 'Harmony Hour'.

Rosalind RENSHAW
Presenter at *BBC Radio Berkshire*.

Shirley RENWICK
News Editor at *Q 96*.

Michael REUPKE
Member of the Radio Authority.

John REVELL
John began his broadcasting career on BBC local radio in the north of England, working as everything from a messenger to peak-time DJ.

Nine years ago he wrote to Richard Branson with the suggestion that Virgin Megastores run their own in-house radio channel, tailoring the music it played to suit the stores' knowledge-able customers. Branson not only liked the idea but invited John to set the operation in motion.

That done, John spent some time with the Virgin satellite programme syndication ser-vice, *Radio Radio*, before returning to the BBC to help launch *GLR*.

In 1993 he left to join Channel Four TV's 'The Big Breakfast' and later returned to Virgin as joint Programme Director.

Sarah REVELL
Promotion Executive at *Horizon Radio*.

John REYNOLDS
John is the Chief engineer at BBC Radio kent.

John REYNOLDS (2)
John is the presenter and producer of the weekday afternoon programme (2.30 until 5pm) on BBC Radio Devon and Dorset.

Richard REYNOLDS
Richard is the breakfast presenter from 6 until 10am each weekday morning on *Minster FM* in York.

Jenny RHODES
Sales Director at *Channel 103*.

Stephen RHODES
Stephen's father was a dentist and in July 1986 he joined *Beacon Radio* on a 3 month contract, and stayed for several years hosting such pro-grammes as 'Talk of The Midlands". He then joined *BBC Radio Shropshire* where he now presents a double-header weekday lunchtime programme.

In Summer 1995 he stood in for Ed Doolan on *Radio WM* and has also recently been doing some TV weork at Pebble Mill.

Craig RICH
Craig is the presenter and producer of a Saturday morning programme on *BBC Radio Devon and Dorset*.

Wendy RICHARD
Born in Middlesborough when it was still part of Yorkshire, she was trained as an actress at the Italia Conti Stage Academy and has appeared in dozens of TV programmes, cur-rently celebrating ten years as Pauline Fowler in Eastenders.

She's also appeared in several films, including several 'Carry on' releases and topped the UK singles charts in 1962 with Mike Sarne.

Wendy has acted in several radio plays, in radio comedy and as a reader of short stories. She recently hosted the 'Ken Bruce Show' on *Radio Two* as a holiday relief.

Dave RICHARDS
News reporter at *The Bay* in the 1990s.

Glynn RICHARDS
Glyn joined *Radio Caroline* in the 1980s and hosted many programmes including the weekend breakfast programmes. He now lives in East Kent and has been involved in several RSLs.

Jonathan RICHARDS
News presenter at *Capital Radio* in 1995 and also a general magazine programme presenter at *BBC Radio Berkshire*.

Nan RICHARDS
Advertising Sales Executive at *CNN Radio*.

Nick RICHARDS
Presenter of afternoon show at *Q 96*, Paisley.

Tony RICHARDS
Presenter at *WABC* in Wolverhampton.

Alan RICHARDSON
Sales Director at *Signal Radio* in Cheshire.

Colin RICHARDSON
Colin's broadcasting career began at the bottom of a Ministry of Defence sick-bag - it was an assignment with the RAF Falcons and one of the crew had to take over his commentary! After completing the BBC Journalist training course,

Colin joined *Radio Devon* and rose through the ranks in the newsroom to his current role as host of an all-talk breakfast show at *BBC Radio Cleveland*. The tough political interviews are Colin's favourite "It's not very often politicians squirm, but when they do you know you must be getting something right."

Phil RICHARDSON
Sales Director of *Leicester Sound*.

Simon RICHARDSON
News reporter at *Manx Radio*.

Suzi RICHARDSON
Head of Music and librarian at *Manx Radio*. Suzi also finds time to host some programmes on the station, generally mid-morning shifts.

Zita RICHARDSON
Zita is the Sales Director of *Radio City*.

Steve RICHES
Evening programme host on *BBC Radio Cambridgeshire* and also hosts a Sunday morning programme on *BBC Radio Northampton*. In 1995 he was heard presenting programmes each weekday evening on *BBC Radio Essex*.

Howie RICHIE
Howie hosts programmes on *Power FM* in Hampshire.

Jane RIDDLE
PA to Managing Director at *Lincs FM*.

Mike RIDDOCH
Head of Music at *Clyde 2*.

Sarah RIDLEY
Sarah is responsible for administration, financial matters and personnel affairs at *BBC Radio GLR* in London.

Maggie RIGBY
Commercial production manager at the capital stations south of London, from *Power* and *Ocean* in the west to *Invicta FM* in the East.

Ben RIGDEN
News Editor at *Capital Radio*

Phil RILEY
Formerly the MD at *Radio Aire*, in 1984 moved to the Midlands to become Managing Director of the regional light rock station, *Heart 100.7*.

Angela RIPPON
After a successful career reading news (and appearing on the Morecambe and Wise programme!) on TV, she moved to *Classic FM*.

Tommy RIVERS
American-born Tommy came to the UK to join *Laser 558*, one of the most successful ever

offshore radio ships, in 1985, and then joined an American news agency's London office before *Virgin 1215* in 1993.

Rowland RIVRON
Born on 28th September, 1958, Rowland had a quiet childhood and his first job was as a professional jazz drummer for ten years. he worked with flat-mate Rik Mayall on the comedy circuit and formed the duo 'Raw Sex'.

His first broadcasting role was fronting LWT's 'Bunker Show', an irreverent chat show. Jonathan Ross invited him to appear on 'The Last Report" where his 'Dr Scrot' character achieved national notoriety. Virgin hired him for their new London FM service in 1985.

Paul ROBBINS
Chief Engineer at *Radio 210,*Reading.

Andy ROBERTS
Head of Music and DJ at *Red Rose Radio*.

Dave ROBERTS
Soccer commentator at *Capital Gold* in 1995.

Graham ROBERTS
Presenter of programmes on *Manx Radio*, including classical music on Sundays.

Mike ROBERTS
Mid morning DJ at *Kix96* in Coventry.

Miles ROBERTS
Chief Executive at *Orchard FM*.

Nancy ROBERTS
Sunday lunchtime presenter at *TalkRadio UK*.

Phil ROBERTS
Programme controller at *MFM* in Wrexham.

Alistair ROBERTSON
Chief Engineer at *Signal Radio Group*.

James Irvine ROBERTSON
Produces a book show on *Heartland FM*.

David ROBEY
David began his career as a journalist, working in newspapers and commercial radio before joining the BBC. In 1990 he became Programme Organiser at *BBC Radio Leicester* and in 1995 was appointed Managing Editor of *BBC Three Counties Radio* on the station's 10th anniversary.

Paul ROBEY
Programme controller at GEM AM.

Anne ROBINSON
Born in Liverpool, Anne has had her own programme on *BBC Radio Two*. She has a daughter called Emma and also appears on TV programmes such as Points of View.

Barry ROBINSON

Ran the largest mobile disco in Yorkshire before radio debut with BBC *Radio Humberside* in 1970s. After setting up various businesses, returned to broadcasting to help found *Yorkshire Coast Radio*, where he is still both a director and the host of 'Inside Out' weekly strip where his well-known catchphrase "Hello there!, I'm Barry Robinson" is used regularly.

Barry has also been a regular presenter on other stations, too numerous (and embarrassing!) to list. Barry cites a show from the Palace of Westminster with Scarborough MP John Sykes as his most memorable moment, and shudders when he recalls an OB with Britain's youngest pilot who landed sideways because she couldn't see over the nose of the plane!

Despite running his own restaurant in Scarborough (The Coffee Bean) Barry says he hates greasy food cooked by bossy women, but loves boats and 4 wheel drive cars.

An accomplished photographer, Barry is also involved in various other radio projects, and bidding for other licences.

Available for any type of events, from judging Karaoke to the opening of an envelope
- call 01723 354175 for a price list!

Brian ROBINSON
Brian is a producer and also presents some programmes at *BBC Radio Suffolk*.

Dave ROBINSON
Folk music presenter at *Swansea Sound*.

Don ROBINSON
Scarborough entertainment-magnate Don Robinson was involved in a plan to buy a Swedish radio station and bring it to the UK in 1964, and eventually organised a new syndicate which became *Radio 270*. He gave many of today's DJ stars, for example, Paul Burnett, their first break into radio and also hired the first pirate radio DJ to become an MP - Roger Gale.

Don later became involved in many other leisure and media ventures and currently operates attractions in London and a casino in Bulgaria.

Jeremy ROBINSON
Jeremy is the Station Manager at *BBC Radio Leicester*.

Les ROBINSON
Head of BBC Network Radio, based in Manchester.

Neil ROBINSON
Formerly Chief Executive and Chairman of Metro Radio Group, joined the group when it began as Metropolitan Radio in 1974.

Paul ROBINSON
Paul's radio career began in 1978 when Dave Cousins (qv) hired him to present the drive time programme on *Radio Tees*. He was then promoted to the mid-morning call-in programme, which he fronted for four years.

In 1983 he moved south once again, joining *Mercia Sound* in Coventry and hosting the station's breakfast programme. While in Coventry Paul also worked at the local cable TV station, reading the news each evening. That led to work with *Music Box TV*, and the 'Pepsi Live' programme with Nino Firetto.

The following year Paul joined the *Chiltern Network* as Programme Director and while he was there they added stations in Northampton and Milton Keynes (*Horizon*) as well as *Severn Sound* and *FTP* in Bristol,

an ethnic station which Phe current success story, *Galaxy*.

In 1991 he joined the BBC as Editor of Daytime Programmes at *Radio One*, and was responsible for programmes hosted by Bruno Brooks, Steve Wright, Simon Mayo and Mark Goodier.

Two years later he was promoted to be Managing Editor of the Network and then was headhunted by the BBC's radio supremo, Liz Forgan. His new job is Head of Strategy for a ten year development plan for all radio, which involves developing new directions for all five national BBC networks, with a special emphasis on developing youth-interest strands, such as the Internet.

An excellent administrator with a good balanced taste in music, Paul was also a leading columnist in the Coventry Evening Telegraph for eight years.

Peter ROBINSON
Peter is the producer of sports and leisure programmes at *BBC Radio Suffolk*.

Richard ROBINSON
Richard is the Chief Executive at *Horizon Radio* in Milton Keynes.

Rony ROBINSON
The main mid-morning presenter at *Radio Sheffield* for many years, Rony is now heard on the station six mornings a week.

Alan ROBSON
Rock music presenter and popular late night phone-in host at *Metro FM*.

Kim ROBSON
After presenting at *Victory FM*, joined *Wey Valley Radio* in Alton in 1995 to present a lunchtime programme.

David ROBY
Born in Hong Kong in 1954, David was schooled in London and Singapore and went into advertising when he left school. He then trained as a journalist in Darlington and joined the Leicester Mercury in 1974.

After a period at *Radio Trent* in Nottingham he moved up the M1 to Sheffield and became Deputy News Editor at *Radio Hallam*, before moving back to the East Midlands to be News Editor at *Centre Radio* in Leicester.

He then moved to *LBC* for a while and in 1983 joined the BBC as a news producer at *Radio Nottingham*. In 1984 he was appointed News Editor at *BBC Radio Bedfordshire*, and in 1987 moved to *Radio WM* in Birmingham, becoming Assistant Editor.

In 1990 it was back to Leicester and a job at the BBC outlet there as Acting Programme Organiser, and in 1995 he was appointed Editor of *BBC Three Counties Radio*.

Paul ROBY
Weekend DJ at *Gem AM* in Derby in 1995.

Harry ROCHE
Harry is Chairman and Chief Executive of the Guardian Media Group, an investor in many ILR stations.

Vaughan RODERICK
Presenter at *CBC* in Cardiff in the 1980s.

David RODGERS
Chief Executive at *Orchard FM* and Managing Director of *Gemini Radio* in Exeter.

Phil ROE
Presents the 'Phil Roe Soul Show' each Tuesday evening at 7.30 on *Radio Maldwyn*.

David ROGERS
Chairman of *London News Radio*.

Keith ROGERS
Began his radio career on *Radio North Sea* in the 1970s (as Dave Rogers) and then moved to *Essex Radio*; now heard on *Breeze AM*.

Jean ROGERS
Born in Middlesex in 1942 she trained at the Guildhall School of Music and Drama and first broadcast on ITV in an episode of Emergency Ward 10.

Jean had a permanent role in Crossroads and for eleven years was Dolly in Emmerdale Farm, however her radio role is even more prolific, with over 1500 broadcasts as a presenter and writer on 'Listen With Mother' as well as being a regular presenter of Poetry Corner on *Radio Four*.

She has two children and four step-children and enjoys wine-making, yoga and gardening.

Mark ROGERS
Presenter on *Marcher Sound* in Wrexham.

Alex ROLAND
Until 1984 he was a presenter at *The Pulse* in Bradford and in 1995 he became Programme Controller of *CFM* in Carlisle.

Bill ROLLINS
Bill began his radio career on board one of the navy forts in the Thames Estuary in 1966 where he was one of the first voices on 'Radio Tower'.

For many years he was assistant to ace jingle and radio memorabilia king, Ray Anderson (qv), and was the technical genius behind many of East Anglian Productions recordings.

In the 1980s he joined *Mellow AM* in Frinton where he is still one of the station's main DJs.

Who's Who in British Radio

Neil ROMAIN

Head of Finance at the Radio Authority.

Mark ROMAN

A wartime baby with a chequered career, Mark once part-owned a jazz club in Ilford and worked for a while selling and then club DJing.

It was in deepest Wimbledon that he was discovered by Radio London DJs who appeared as guests from time to time,and in 1965 he found himself out on the North Sea presenting his programme 'The Roman Empire'.

In 1968 he joined Radio One and released a single 'Cuddly Toy' on the Deram label. In August 1968 he left the BBC and emigrated to Australia, where he worked in radio and television and then moved to New Zealand as a consultant programmer.

In October 1974 he returned to the UK but couldn't find any radio work at the new ILR stations so took a job as chief executive in charge of commercial production at an advertising agency.

He also voiced the 40 programmes of 'A Year to remember' of Pathe News as well as dozens of radio and TV commercials for UK and European stations. He now lives on a five acre farm in Norfolk.

John ROSBOROUGH

After attending the Royal Belfast Academical Institution, John graduated from the city's Queen's University with a degree in Electrical and electronic engineering. He joined Downtown Radio as a sound engineer before the station launched in 1975 and has become a permanent fixture there. Two years later he was promoted to be the station's production Manager and then in 1979 he took over his current role, Programme Director.

Ten years later the station split frequencies and John assumed control of both stations' output; the same year he became a Council Member of the Radio Academy, an organisation he is a founder member of. He is also an Equity member and an Associate Member of the Institute of Electrical Engineers.

John doesn't have much time for hobbies, but loves socialising in witty company and world-wide travel. He keeps abreast of all current affairs and is a satellite TV junkie, which he tries to excuse by claiming it helps polish up his German linguist skills.

A sixties and seventies pop and rock music buff (especially rare stuff) he also enjoys new age and cool jazz.

Sue ROSCOE

Sales controller at *Chiltern Radio Group*.

Howard ROSE

Born in Great Bookham, Surrey, on 17th March, 1953 and developed an interest in radio during the sixties. His first professional broadcast was on *Radio North Sea International* in early 1971 (Howartd's most terrifying moment was being on board the ship Mebo II when it was petrol bombed!).

His interest in news developed during this time when the station reported up-to-the-minute news bulletins on a US moon mission. Coming ashore, he joined *BBC Radio Brighton* but was soon back at sea and on the air at *Radio 199* (a Caroline offshoot), and *Radio Atlantis*.

Coming ashore he joined *Swansea Sound*, and hosted the mid-morning strip, as well as *Radio Top Shop*, and *The Voice of Peace*, where he was Programme Director.

In 1983 Howard was the mastermind behind the launch of *Radio Sovereign* in London, which was the UK's first 'all gold' station. He then spent some time back on *Radio Caroline* (as J. J. Jackson) before moving back into ILR at *Viking Radio, Radio Aire* and *Hereward* .

In the late eighties he launched a weekly radio industry magazine, called NOW RADIO, and also founded the group, KCBC, which successfully bid for the Kettering ILR licence.

When KCBC launched Howard was the station's programme controller, a position he held until his resignation in March 1992 to pursue other interests with *Goldcrest Broadcasting*.

This company launched the UK radio industry weekly 'The Radio Magazine' which he has edited since.

A member of the Radio Academy and a committee member of the Radio Festival, Howard and Patricia live with children Hannah, Thomas and Rachel in a miniature zoo in Rothwell, Northamptonshire.

Martyn ROSE
Director of *Fortune 1458* in Manchester.

Tara ROSIER
Tara is currently the Traffic Manager at *Breeze AM* and *Essex FM* in Southend.

Hilary ROSINGTON
Programme Producer at *BBC Radio Shropshire*.

Emperor ROSKO
Born Michael Pasternak on Boxing Day, 1942 in California into a well-known movie family he grew up in LA and spent most of his time listening to such radio luminaries as Moon Dog Johnny Hayes and Tom 'Big Daddy' Donohue. He was particularly influenced by Emperor Hudson on KYA and yearned to be in radio himself.

Rosko's chance came while in the US Navy where he got a shift on an internal station on an aircraft carrier - far better than polishing brass!

He also acquired a new name - Michael Prescott, and after coming to Europe joined Barclay Records to host sponsored programmes in France and Belgium.

After a chance meeting with Henry Henroi, later his manager, he joined *Radio Caroline* where his pacey American style soon made him one of the station's best known DJs. He then moved to *Radio Luxembourg* where Caroline boss Ronan O'Rahilly was acing as a consultant and built the station's first DJ-operated studio.

In 1967 he joined the BBC to host weekly programme on *Radio One* - his style was so breathtaking for the BBC that during his programme one of the newsreaders ad-libbed "now here is the news in English". After many years on Radio One he returned to the USA and continued his European presence with a series of taped programmes heard on the English service of *Radio Luxembourg*.

In the 1990s his programmes continue to be heard on many ILR stations.

Alan ROSS
Has worked at many stations in Yorkshire, including *Pennine Radio* and *Viking Radio* and is now a presenter at *Touch AM* in Cardiff.

Andy ROSS
Presenter of Scottish music programmes at *Moray Firth Radio* where he is also a director.

David ROSS
Born in Nottingham, David left school to became an apprentice carpenter, but after a while he got a job as a DJ in a night club and worked for Mecca and First Leisure, winning the regional final of 'DJ Personality DJ of the year' twice, using his own name, Glen Ross. At that time he also became involved in hospital radio with *Radio Witham* in Grantham and then at Nottingham Hospitals, where he became Programme controller.

In 1991 he won the *Radio Trent* competition to find the best presenter on hospital and campus radio, which led to relief work at *GEM AM* and *Trent FM*, where he now hosts weekend evening programmes as David Ross.

As well as his radio work, David also writes columns for local newspapers. He likes fast food and hates inconsiderate drivers.

James ROSS
James began his career with *Radio Caroline* in 1975 and stayed with the station for three years before moving to *Swansea Sound*.

He then joined the AA Roadwatch as a regular announcer (using his real name - Kelvin O'Shea) and is now a news reporter, often seen on-screen, with *Sky News*.

Who's Who in British Radio

Joel ROSS

Born on the 31st May, 1977, in Scarborough, Joel worked for Granada TV (not on screen, but selling TVs in their showroom!) until 1994, while also doing weekend shifts at *Yorkshire Coast Radio*. He'd joined the station the day after its launch and wasn't at all impressed with his first programme "My voice has come down a couple of octaves since!".

The highlight of Joel's career so far was seeing RAJAR figures for his show for the first time and the station winning a Bronze Sony Award. The most humourous event was mistaking a director of the station for a listener collecting a prize; he likes most pop music and well produced radio, but not club DJs.

He now hosts the weekdays evening slot (6 to 10pm) and a Saturday afternoon sports show as well as Sunday morning breakfasts.

Jonathan ROSS

A London-born Scorpio who was a researcher for TV game shows before becoming a TV presenter. In 1986 he was hired as a host by *Radio Radio*.

Les ROSS

Presenter at *BRMB* in Birmingham since 1980.

Paul ROSS

Presenter at *Virgin 1215*.

Robin ROSS

Was apart of the relaunch team at *Radio Caroline* in 183 and became one of the station's most popular DJs before moving north to *Red Rose Radio* in Preston, Lancashire, doubling audiences on both evenings and lunchtime, as Head of Music and Deputy Programme Controller.

He was then poached by neighbouring *Piccadilly Radio* in Manchester to be the Head of Music and Production at *Key 103*.

From there he moved to *Radio Radio* but left after the decision was taken to move the operation to Manchester and set up his own production company. He also took over the breakfast show at *Marcher Sound*, turning around a three year decline in listening and became Programming Consultant to the *Radio Wave* application for the Blackpool ILR licence.

Robin continued this line by consulting to *Fortune 1458* for their successful application for a major Manchester licence and hosted the station's breakfast show. Robin left Fortune because he felt the station was going into areas he didn't think were right and feels vindicated in his decision by the 4% (RAJAR) reach figure.

Robin Ross productions now supplies material to over 80 stations and his clients include Phil Collins, Take That, Mike and the Mechanics, Bonnie Rait, Bob Seger and Cliff Richard. In 1995 his company was awarded the management contract for *KIT KAT Radio* across Blackpool Pleasure Beach, one of the North's top summer attractions which Robin describes as "the most fun I've had in years." (Tel 01 253 304086).

Tom ROSS

After education at St Chad's in Birmingham, Tom had several jobs and worked at Birmingham's hospital network before his first broadcast, which was in August 1975 on *BBC Radio Birmingham*, reporting on a soccer match between Birmingham City and Ajax.

The following year he moved to ILR station *BRMB* and then nine years later was made Sports Editor of *BRMB* and its sister station *Xtra AM*.

As well as his sports work at BRMB, he is also a kick-boxing commentator and has appeared many times on the UK's second city's cable station, including a comedy sketch with Jasper Carrot.

There have been three major highlights in Tom's career - reporting from the players' bench at Wembley in a cup final, an unbelievable hour with boxing legend Don King and an interview with Mohammed Ali. He likes humour and honsety, as well as reggae, soul and Springsteen, but doesn't like liars, cheat and backstabbers.

John ROSS-BARNARD

John always wanted to be in radio: "I always had what can only be described as 'The Urge' and after a series of rejections from the BBC, I was finally offered a role by BFBS who found a vacancy out in Aden, at that time a violent hot-bed of trouble."

In the nick of time he found a new station in 1964 which offered him a job on its fort-based station off Whitstable. After training in fuelling diesel generators and other heavy-duty tasks, then de rigeur on such stations, John became a fully-fledged presenter. The term 'dj' did not fit the format on the stations which evolved from Invicta - *KING Radio* and *Radio 390*, the Women's Magazine of the Air (even then he was politically correct!)

He also supported the other staff - as senior announcer he dared to ask for their wages to be incresed by £2 for repeat fees on a proposed relay on a ship off the Isle of Man. For this brave attempt at 'equity' he was awarded the order of the boot by the sea-sick prone proprietor. [John wrote an amusing account of his experiences in 'Pop Went The Pirates' - see the bibliography].

He was out of work for two whole days before he was offered a job newsreading on *Radio Caroline* plus the £2! But *Britain Radio* and its fine owner, Don Pierson had deeper pockets. he offered John £15 a week - a 54% increase.

John wasted no time driving to Felixstowe where he ran into Patrick Hammerton (Mark Sloane), also from 390 who had just landed a job on Radio Caroline South.

Thirty years later John and his wife Connie still meet Pat/ Mark for breakfast, usually on a train to London.

At Christmas 1966 John was accepted as a 'narrator' (posh word for an announcer) on BBC 2 TV. He shares with noone the doubtful benefit of being the first annoiuncer to be heard 'in colour' when the facility was launched at Wimbledon the following June.

After that whe moved to BBC 1 and moved on to become network director, later directing the regional contributions to 'Nationwide' from Manchester, and then returning to London to become an Assistant Presentation Editor for BBC 1 and BBC 2 (TV) in 1970.

In 1974 he returned to radio as Manager of the BBC's Foreign Recordings douibling occasionally as a newsreader on *Radios One* and *Two*. (that old 'Urge' once again!)

In 1978 he returned to TV to start from scratch what is now BBC Video, the largest commercial contributor to the BBC after the Radio Times.

Always game for something new and dangerous, John left the BBC in 1984 to become the CEO of *ThornEMI Cable TV*. Since cable was then goiong nowhere (is it now?) after three years he took on the BT monopoly at its own game and launched *Satellite Media Services (SMS)*.

This company freed Independent Radio from the tyranny of the Red Star Parcels service and BT mono landlines by transmitting commercials by satellite direct to the stations. SMS was the first company, anywhere in the world, to transmit commercials in digital stereo. Today it sends news services, programmes and data throughout the world using a range of technologies including the Internet.

Promoted from CEO to deputy Chairman in 1994 he now provides broadcasting advice to the UK Parliamentary Committee PITCOM and its European equivalent EURIM. John is Chairman of the Radio Academy's trading arm, RATL and in 1996 will become the Chairman of the Royal Television Society in the Midlands.

Looking back overmore than 30 years in broadcasting John says has a lot to be thankful for - to broadcasting and to its people.

Jane ROSSINGTON

TV actress best-known for her role as Jill, the daughter of the owner of the Crossroads Motel. She was hired by *Beacon Radio* in the late 1980s to present morning programmes on their newly launched WABC easy listening service.

R. ROTHWELL

Station Director of *Brunel Classic Gold*.

Who's Who in British Radio

Brian ROWBOTHAM
Director of *Fortune 1458* and the Chairman of *Radio Mercury* in Crawley.

Steve ROWE
After three years at the GWR Group he moved to the Orchard Radio family in 1995 to become the group's Sales Director. Steve is based in Taunton and handles regional sales for *Orchard FM, Gemini Radio, Wessex FM* and *Lantern FM.*

Peter ROWELL
Presenter at GWR. West FM in Bristol.

Alex ROWLAND
Programme Controller at *CFM* in Cambridge.

Jerry ROWLANDS
Jerry is the station manager of *Asda FM*, the satellite delivered in-store radio station.

Samantha ROWLANDS
After education at a Roman Catholic school in Staffordshire, Samantha was a saleswoman before embarking on a nursing career. While working in one hospital she was cajoled into helping out with the hospital radio station because of her unique and warm voice and this led to a gig at *Marcher Round* in Wrexham - she found her first broadcast "absolutely nerve racking".

After a year of overnights at Marcher she landed a show at *Metro FM* (becoming the only girl on an otherwise all-male line-up) in Newcastle where she stayed for three years.

The highlight of her career came at Metro when she doubled the late night listening figures,and she was also headhunted by regional TV broadcaster *Tyne Tees TV* to host an arts programme called 'East Coast Mainline'. Since September 1994 Samantha has been at *Signal Radio* in Stoke and also working in a local nightclub while she studies drama with actress ambitions.

The funniest event of her career was trying to broadcast from a moving ride inside the Metro Shopping Centre - she ended up in hysterics on the air! She likes sincere people, especially on the radio but dislikes and pities anoraks.

Kevin ROWNTREE
Kevin is the host of a Sunday morning phone-in programme on *BBC Radio Newcastle.*

Walter ROY
Managing Director of *Broadland FM*

Richard RUDIN
Richard's radio career began with hospital radio in Birmingham when he was only 16, and after three years as a reporter in local newspapers he joined *Beacon Radio* in 1979 . He then moved to *BFBS* in Germany as one of their last broadcasting trainees and began the Berlin Breakfast Show in 1982, and two years later moved back to the UK when he joined Metro in Newcastle to host their mid-morning show and a weekly phone in programme.

After two years there, Richard moved to Preston to become senior presenter at *Red Rose Radio* and in 1989 joined *BBC Radio Leeds* as Programme Organiser and deputy Manager. He then moved south to *Radio Sheffield,* combining management with the station's Drivetime Programme.

In 1992 he was head-hunted by *Radio City* in Liverpool to run the station's new AM station, which also heralded a return to mid-morning programmes for Richard, and he stayed there as Programme Controller until early 1995. He now works, through his own company CAT, for *Fortune 1458* in Manchester, *Red Rose Gold* in Preston and *Signal Gold* in Stoke, and lives in Lancashire with his wife Alison and son David.

Mark RUDOLF
This Mark Rudolph is apProducer at *CNN Radio.*

Ian RUFUS
Director at *Leicester Sound FM* and Area Director at *Mercia.*

Robin RUMBOLL
Chairman of *Channel 103* in Jersey.

Mike RUMSBY
Presenter of a rock show each Wednesday evening at 7pm on *Radio Maldwyn.*

Who's Who in British Radio

Leigh RUNDLE
Leigh is one of the producers at BBC Radio Devon and Dorset.

June RUSHTON
Company Secretary at *Wey Valley 102*.

Willie RUSHTON
Born in Chelsea in August 1937, Willie was co-founder of 'Private Eye' magazine and a keen actor. He joined the team of 'That was the Week That Was' which led to regular radio work on *Radio Two* in programmes such as 'I'm Sorry I Haven't a Clue' and 'Trivia Test match'.

Willie was also a regular support actor on Kenny Everett's TV programmes and is a panelist on 'Through the Keyhole'. His hobbies include long weight, gaining weight and parking his car.

Martin RUSHWORTH
Financial Controller and company secretary at *Radio City* in Liverpool.

Paul RUSLING
Born in Bridlington on 17th November, 1953, and educated in East Yorkshire, Paul's interest in music began at Saturday morning disc sessions at the local Mecca ballroom.

Always an avid radio listener and radio amateur, he ran a DJ fan club and later organised a listener organisation which campaigned for the legalisation of commercial radio.

His DJ career began while still at school and he pursued qualifications in radio engineering while working in night clubs in Hull.

After a period with *Radio Caroline* (as Paul Alexander on its 'international pop-music service') he studied radio in the USA and worked as an engineer and DJ at a variety of stations in Europe and the USA.

Since 1980 he's worked as a consultant for over two dozen stations, including some on ships, UK ILR stations and national stations in Holland, Germany and France as well as Radio Moscow's World Service. He has been successful in obtaining licences in several countries, including a high power international one for the long awaited Baltic Radio International and a national FM network in Holland.

Paul is founder and a director of *Yorkshire Coast Radio* and is currently working on the launch of an international station to broadcast from the Isle of Man, as well as advising radio and TV broadcasters in Holland, Spain, Germany and the UK.

In addition to radio consultancy, he enjoys writing and his work is regularly seen in various technical magazines, including the 'Radio Magazine' and 'World Broadcast News'.

He lives in Yorkshire with his family and likes enthusiasm in radio, large cars (big enough for lots of radios) and good food. He hates bland food, bland radio and bland people as well as unadventurous, narrow-minded licensing authorities who stifle growth in radio.

Chris RUSSELL
News producer at *BBC Radio York*.

Dave RUSSELL
Head of News at *Isle of Wight Radio*

James RUSSELL
Presenter on *Clyde One* in Glasgow.

John RUSSELL
John is a presenter at *Classic FM*.

Stuart RUSSELL
Began his radio career on *Radio Caroline* in the 1970s and returned there in 1980s. He has also presented at several local radio stations.

Tom RUSSELL
Music presenter at *Radio Clyde*.

Liz RUTHERFORD
Liz is currently a reporter at *BBC Radio Solent*.

Mike RUTHERFORD
Presents Saturday lunchtime programme called 'On The Road' on *London News Radio*.

Stephen RYAN
Presenter at *Pirate FM 102* in Cornwall

Chris RYDER
Under the guise 'Caeser The Geezer' he was one of the high profile 'shock jock' presenters at talkradio UK when the station launched in February 1995. After many complaints to the Radio Authority about his programme the station fired him in September 1995.

Ken RYELLS
Ken is a producer at *BBC Radio Cleveland*.

Mark RYES
Presenter at *2CR* in Bournemouth.

John SACHS
One of the sons of comedy actor Andrew Sachs (Manuel in Fawlty Towers). Presenter for many years on *Capital Radio* in London and more recently hosting a morning music-based show for *BBC Radio 2*.

Neil SACKLEY
After occasionally attending school Neil trained as an electrical engineer, and the story of how he got into radio is a very long one.

His first broadcast was at *BBC Radio Northampton* one Sunday evening - from there he moved to *Northants Radio Supergold* as drive and Sunday AM presenter.

The highlight of his radio career hasn't yet happened, and he's moved to *Xtra AM* in Birmingham as breakfast and daytime presenter as well as doing some weekend shows.

The funniest event in Neil's career came as a young DJ; when asked to run a competition for Rolling Stone magazine he assembled a Rolling Stones montage thinking the mag was about them!

Bhagwat SAGOO
Presenter of Asian programmes at *BBC Three Counties Radio*.

Rachael SALAMAN
Rachel is the host of a late night show called 'The Eleventh Hour' on *London Newsradio FM*.

Mike SALISBURY
Presenter at the *New Leicester Sound*.

Peter SALT
Peter is a presenter at *JFM* in Manchester.

Mark SAMARU
Managing Director of *Fortune 1458*.

Jane SAMPSON
Jane is the News Producer at BBC Radio York's Scarborough studio.

Dave SANDERS
Station organiser at *Chiltern Radio*

Mark SANDERS
A news reporter at *BBC Radio Solent*.

Mark SANDLER
Presenter at *Swansea Sound*.

Rebecca SANDLES
Host of the early evening programme at 6pm each weekday on *BBC GLR*.

Tommy SANDS
Traditional Irish Music presenter at *Downtown Radio* in Belfast.

Geoff SARGIESON
Geoff was a producer at *Radio Aire* when the station launched in the early 1980s. he then joined the BBC and became Station Manager at *Radio Humberside* and in the early 1990s joined *BBC Radio York* in a similar role. Geoff also produces and presents folk music programmes for *Radio 2* and *Radio 4*.

Paul SAUNDERS

Born on 20th February, 1969 in Windsor, Paul attended Windsor Boys School and worked in sales for five years before starting his radio career.

He got into the industry after enduring a two hour interview for the now defunct cable station *WSM*, based in Slough and then moved to *Devonair* where he hosted weekday afternoon programmes.

Paul then presented daily business programmes on both *Devonair* and *Plymouth Sound* and produced political programmes for *BBC Radio Five*. The highlight of Paul's career to date was a very sad moment, when his was the last voice on Devonair before the station closed.

On a lighter note he once put another studio on air by accident, whilst the DJ was attacking the equipment - physically and verbally, oblivious to his massive audience. He has freelanced on *Mix 96, Fox FM* and *Ocean FM* and in 1995 joined *Viking FM* in East Yorkshire where he hosts the weekday drive time programme.

Paul also co-founded and set up West Coast Radio, an RSL station which has enjoyed tremendous success in Minehead.

Peter SAUNDERS
A director at *Radio Mercury*.

Steve SAUNDERS
Presenter at *10-17* in Harlow, Essex.

Remy SAUTER
Director of *CLT* and its subsidiaries, *Atlantic 252* and *Country 1035*.

Joanne SAVAGE
Presenter at *Cool FM*.

Sir Jimmy SAVILE
Born in Leeds on 3rd October, 1926 Jimmy is a former coal miner, whose DJ career began spinning records in a Mecca Ballroom. He became one of the circuit's most outlandish figures and joined *Radio Luxembourg* in 1963 to host a sponsored programme.

In 1963 as one of the first regular presenters of Top of the Pops he became a national institution, thanks to his shoulder length locks, often dyed in a tartan pattern.

He also took part in several charity-celebrity wrestling bouts in the 1960s and was probably the country's best known DJ outside the *Radio One* by the end of the decade.

Radio One finally persuaded him to present programmes for them in the 1970's and 'Savile's Travels' achieved high ratings, even given the prime Sunday lunchtime slot. While at Radio One he continued to host a weekly TV programme making children's dreams come true (Jim'll Fix It) as well as other appearances.

In the mid 1980's *Metro Radio* pulled off a coup, signing him to host a weekly Gold programme, networked on other stations, which he still hosts today.

An untiring charity worker, Jimmy where staff had once saved his life back in the 1950s, and he also works at the Stoke Mandeville Hospital in Buckinghamshire.

Brian SAVIN
Head of creative services at *BRMB*.

Pete SAYERS
Presenter at *BBC Radio Cambridgeshire*.

David SCHNEIDER
Born in London in May 1963, he is an accomplished actor with many TV programmes to his credit. He is the writer and presenter of two series of 'On The Hour' and also the 'Knowing Me , Knowing You . . with Alan Partridge' serie. on *Radio One*.

Phillip SCHOFIELD
Born in Oldham, Lancashire on April Fools Day, 1962, his family emigrated to New Zealand when he was two years old and Philips' first broadcast was with Auckland station, *Radio Hauraki*. One returning to the UK he appeared in many TV programmes and on a regular programme on *Capital Radio*. That show then moved to *Radio One*, following which he took a lead role in a London theatre presentation.

Mel SCHOLES
After four years in the Manchester Fire Brigade during which period he was a part time DJ, mel did some hospital radio work and then joined *BBC Radio Blackburn*, before moving south to the Corporation's *Radio Stoke* outlet.

Who's Who in British Radio

He then went west, to *KIQO* in California, and also worked at *KVEC Radio 92*, where his afternoon show was the highlight of his radio career. After spending two years stateside he returned to the UK and joined *Signal Radio* in Staffordshire and is now a regular weekday jock (doing lunchtimes - 10am until 2pm)at the station's Gold outlet on 1170AM.

As well as radio work, Mel is also the resident host at Jollees Cabaret Club in Stoke and was voted 'Compere of the Year' three times.

He has compered two Royal shows and says fronting the "Pub of the Week" programmes on Signal was the funniest thing which has happened to him. Doesn't like bad manners or bad driving and like working as a stand up comedian and after dinner speaker.

Tim SCHOONMAKER

New York born Tim joined EMAP in 1983 from the London Business School and worked with David Arculus on acquiring newspapers in the south. He ws apporached by Gordon McNamee to fuind an application *Kiss FM,* the unlicensed, was making for a London franchise.

Although they were initially unsuccessful, the EMAP Board had got bitten by the radio bug and Tim was given a huge pot of money to get EMAP into radio. He's since bought shares in Essex Radio, East Anglia and in 1994 bought Transworld from Owen Oyston and others.

In September 1995 their bid for the Metro Group became unconditional and Tim is currently based at Metro's HQ in Newcastle.

Tim is also Director and Chief Executive of the Association of Independent Radio Companies. He has his own recording studio at home and is a self-confessed country and western fan, although his real goal is to have a national rock station for the UK.

Chris SCOTT

Chris is the station director of *Brunel Classic Gold* and sister station *GWR FM-West*.

David SCOTT

David is now working as presenter at Invicta Supergold.

Digby SCOTT

David is the producer and presenter of farming programming at *Lincs FM*.

Don SCOTT

Engineer at *Essex Radio* in Southend.

Gregg SCOTT

Joined *Yorkshire Coast Radio* in 1994 and was the popular host of an early evening programme until early 1995 when he left to pursue a career in television - he's currently co-starring with Carol Vorderman in a schools quiz programme on Yorkshire Television.

Harriet SCOTT

Presenter at *Viking FM* until 1995 when she moved to *Hallam FM*.

Helen SCOTT

Secretarial assistant at *Yorkshire Coast Radio.*

Jerry SCOTT

First broadcast on *Radio Jackie* an unlicensed station in South West London. In 1992 he joined *Minster FM* where he presented the mid-morning programme until moving to the group's *Yorkshire Coast Radio* subsidiary in Scarborough in 1993 as Station Manager.

Mike SCOTT

Mike is the publicity and promotions manager at *Radio Forth* and *Max AM* in Edinburgh.

Sir Robert SCOTT

Director at *Piccadilly Radio* in Manchester.

Roger SCOTT   (see Greg Bance)

Wally SCOTT

Attended Dingle Secondary Modern School in Liverpool and then became a journalist, he was offered a job at *Radio City* in Liverpool, but can't remember his first broadcast as it was so long ago! Wally has been the Sports Editor of Radio City and producer of the Billy Butler programme on *BBC Radio Merseyside* as well as working in clubs and theatres.

The highlights of Wally's career were speaking to Doris Day and meeting Billy Butler - which is also the funniest thing to happen to him. A keen Liverpool FC fan, he hates the rest of the Premier League.

Jon SCRAGG
Breakfast jock at *Essex Radio* in the 1980s.

Steve SCRUTON
Steve is the producer of the phone-in programme each weekday afternoon on *BBC Essex*.

Graham SEAMAN
Graham is a programme producer and also hosts a programme each weekday afternoon on *BBC Wiltshire Sound*.

Mark SEAMAN
Mark's radio career began with the BBC where he produced and presented programmes in local and regional radio as well as reporting on regional TV news programmes.

He then moved across to *GWR* group where he was acting network controller, before joining *Premier Radio* in 1995. He is now Premier's Programme Director and also can be heard on its morning show.

Mark SEBBA
Mark is the Finance Director of Jazz FM in London.

Phillip SEDDON
Director and Company Secretary at EMAP station, *Red Dragon Radio*.

Ann SEDIVY
Ann is the producer responsible for all weekend output at *BBC Radio Leeds*.

Adrian SEEK
Schooled at Westcliffe High School, and King Alfred's at Winchester, Adrian did hospital radio from 1977 until 1981 at *Radio Basildon* and his first broadcasts were for Essex Radio's arts programme.

In 1981 he began a five year stint at the ILR station in Southend, before moving up to the BBC outlet in Chelmsford (*BBC Essex*) for two years in 1986. In 1990 he moved back to Southend and *Breeze AM* where he's done a lot of relief work and regularly anchors the Saturday afternoon show.

By day Adrian is a teacher, but he loves radio most and says "It makes a stimulating counterbalance to teaching." Not so much humourous as interesting, he enjoyed driving the soul shows which Steve Davis (the snooker player) presented from Essex.

Alison SERGEANT
Presenter at *BBC Radio Cambridgeshire*.

Chris SERLE
Born in Bristol in 1943, Chris became an actor before joining the BBC as a radio producer. he has been responsible for shows such as 'Brain of Britain', as well as appearing on TV programmes such as 'That's Life' and Sixty Minutes'.

Clive SETTLE
Colin was a journalist and then News Editor at *Radio Aire* until early 1995 when he moved to the BBC Radio general news room.

Ian SEWELL
Joined *Radio Forth* in 1975 as a Sales Executive and was appointed Local Sales Supervisor in 1980. In 1981 he became the first sales manager at *West Sound* in Ayr and in 1982 joined *Radio Tay* as Regional Sales Manager.

In 1986 he was promoted to be the station's Sales Manager and he continued to hold the position after *Radio Forth* took. In 1987 he returned to *Radio Forth* as Group Sales Manager and in 1989 was pointed to the Board. In October 1994 he was made a Director of Scottish Radio Network Sales.

Neil SEXTON
Presenter at *The Wave* in Blackpool.

Who's Who in British Radio

Arabella SEYMOUR
Producer of community programmes and organiser of charity events at *Spire FM*.

Mike SHAFT.
Mike is one of the country's most knowledgeable soul music DJs with an impressive track record. In the mid-eighties he was one of the team who launched *Sunset FM* an incremental station in Manchester. he has also hosted programmes on GMR in the city and is currently at Bay 96.9 in Lancaster.

Paul SHAH
Host of the 'Beach Party' programmes on new Midlands station, *Radio XL*.

Vijay SHARMA
Vijay is the main presenter of BBC Radio Leicester's Asian service which is on AM each day from 4pm onwards.

Pat SHARP
Pat was due to join *Radio Caroline* in the early 1980s but got tired of waiting around for the ship to turn up and so joined *BBC Radio One* instead.

Later he joined *Capital Radio* and hosted the station's evening weekday programme from 7until 10 each weekday until 1993 when he moved to the morning programme (10 until 1pm).

Rhod SHARP
His promising career as a student at Aberdeen and Princeton was cut cruelly short by graduation, Rhod organised a media conference in Scotland where he met the late great Jack Regan of BBC Scotland who inspired him to become a BBC news trainee.

His first broadcast was a talk for *Radio Scotland*, and then in 1977 he joined *Radio Leeds* on the early shift, then the BBC TV newsroom in 1978, before moving across town to IRN and LBC in 1979. By 1980 he was back in Scotland as the senior news broadcaster at the launch of *Radio Tay*. From there he moved out to San Fransisco as a stringer for the BBC until 1987, when he returned to *World Service*.

The BBC welcomed him back to the TV fold with a role as foreign duty editor in 1989, and a few years later his idea of an all night all news sequence using telephone lines was accepted by Jenny Abramsky and he launched 'Up All Night' as its weekday presenter in 1994.

The highlights of Rod's career are many and various, but his favourites are breaking news of the 1994 Republican landslide, being first reporter into Mexico City in the 1985 earthquake and getting Clayton Moore to read the Lone Ranger creed.

Rod once fell apart while sight reading live on air a story about a woman who told a court she'd shot her husband because she thought he was a large brown bear, causing fellow presenters to fall prostrate with mirth and listeners all over Tayside to spill their tea.

He likes the view from anywhere in San Fransisco and dislikes all the things an editor would tick you off for, such as not getting to the point!

Contact Rhod on e-mail - rhod@cityscape.co.uk.

Alistair SHAW
Alistair is a director of *Marcher Coast* and also the Managing Director of *Radio Developments Ltd*, an investor in many ILR stations.

Andrew SHAW
Andrew is a news reporter at BBC Radio Leicester.

Eddie SHAW
Presenter at *Lincs FM*.

Jack SHAW
Jack is the host of the Sunday morning breakfast programme on *BBC Radio Sheffield*.

Martin SHAW
Martin entered local radio in the 19909s and became deputy head of news and sport at *Mercia FM* in Coventry.

Mike SHAW
Mike was the executive producer for topical and entertainment programmes in the early 1990s at *BBC Radio Scotland*.

Michael SHEA

Born on the 10th May, 1938, Michael was educated at Gordonstoun and Edinburgh. He had a long career in the diplomatic service and was press secretary to HM the Queen for ten years. In 1987 he joined Hanson Plc in a similar role and is now vice-chairman of their *Melody Radio* station in London.

Dave SHEARER

Head of presentation at *Red Rose Radio*'s AM station in Preston.

Les SHEENAN

Les is a producer at *BBC Radio Lincolnshire*.

Lady SHEIL

Lady Sheil is a Member of the Radio Authority.

Andy SHELDON

Andy is a presenter at *Power FM*, Hampshire.

Paul SHELDON

Head of News at *Signal One* in Stoke.

Tony SHELL

Educated in Liverpool after which he became a milkman, window cleaner and builder he applied for a job which he thought was repairing radios, not actually broadcasting on them! His first broadcast was on *Radio Two* where he did a feature for 'Woman's Hour' in 1984. He then moved to BBC *Radio Merseyside* where he freelanced until 1985, when he joined *Radio City*.

It was at *Radio City* that the highlight of his career came - winning a Sony Award in 1987. He once fell in a moat while interviewing Jason Donovan at a Liverpool night club, the electric shock from the microphone gave him a good buzz.

Des SHEPHERD

Freelance broadcaster and trainer of staff.

Robbie SHEPHERD

Robbie was the presenter of the 'Take The Floor' programme each Sunday evening on BBC *Radio Scotland* in the 1990s.

Sue SHEPHERD

Sue is a news producer at *BBC Radio Newcastle*.

Wendy SHEPHERD

Wendy worked on *Radio Caroline* was a cook in the late 1980s and jointly presented several programmes with the stations Programme Controller, Steve Conway, who she later married.

Clare SHERMAN

Presenter at *Mix 96* in Aylesbury.

Alex SHIELDS

Engineer at *South West Sound*, Dumfries.

Andy SHIER

Andy is the Programme Controller and also Head of News at *Isle of Wight Radio*.

Alec SHUTTLEWORTH

Station Manager of *Central FM*.

Kevin SIDALL

Kevin is the Engineer in charge at *BBC GLR*.

Phil SIDEY

Phil was the launch manager of *BBC Radio Leeds* and the Head of BBC Network Radio based at Pebble Mill. He is currently chairman on *Swan 102*, an applicant for the Stratford on Avon ILR licence.

Chris SIGSWORTH (Chris MARKS)

Born in June 1970 in North Yorkshire, Chris got into broadcasting by working in hospital radio at York for four years, first as a presenter and then later as programme manager.

Under his direction they won 'North East Hospital Station of the Year' two years running. In November 1993, he joined *Yorkshire Coast Radio* at its launch as a freelance presenter, the highlight of his career to date.

Since then he's done a variety of different programmes at the station and in 1995 was promoted to Commercial Production Manager. Chris loves everything to do with radio (except the time he fell asleep on the mixer during a 48 hour marathon broadcast in York!).

Steve SILBY

As well as being Promotion Manager and Head of Sponsorship at *Mix 96* in Aylesbury, Steve also hosts programmes on the station.

Marc SILK

Marc is a programme presenter at *Mercia FM*.

Pete SIMESTER

Pete hosts weekend overnight programmes on *FOX FM* in Oxford.

Nick SIMMONS

In the 1980s Nick worked at County Sound as a daytime presenter on their 'Premier' service. He is now Head of the *AA Roadwatch* service.

Dave SIMONS

Dave was a programme presenter at *Hallam FM* in the early 1990s.

John SIMONS

John hosted the mid-morning show at *BBC Radio Nottingham* in the early 1990s and in 1994 became the Programme Controller at *Century Radio,* the regional station in the North East.

Susannah SIMONS

After many years as a presenter at BBC *Radio Four* and Business News presenter on *Channel Four TV*, Susannah is now a presenter of weekday lunchtime programme at *Classic FM*.

Lee SIMPSON

Formerly a comedian at the Comedy Store and various other venues in London, Lee is now one of the breakfast djs at *Heart 106.2 FM* .

Allen SINCLAIR

Allen was a broadcast journalist at BBC *BBC Radio Berkshire*, now merged with Radio Oxford to form *Radio Thames Valley*.

Dave SINCLAIR

Born in Kent in 1942, David joined *Radio Essex* (on a naval fort in the Thames estuary, 20 miles from Southend) in 1966. A keen Parliamentarian, he later moved to Yorkshire and *Radio 270*, which was run by former MP Wilf Proudfoot. David spent six months at the station, hosting the 'Lovely Ladies ' programme each morning at 9am.

in 1967 David moved back south and spent a period at *Radio 390* where the music was more to his liking - he likes big bands and is also a keen motor racing fan.

Malcolm SINGER

Malcolm is a producer of arts programmes at *BBC Three Counties Radio*.

Raj SINGH

Programme Controller of *Sunrise Radio* in the East Midlands.

Daphne SKINNARD

Presenter/Producer at *BBC Radio Cornwall*.

Richard SKINNER

Born in Portsmouth on Boxing Day, 1951, and while still at school he launched the city's first hospital radio station. His first paying radio job was with *BBC Radio Solent* in nearby Southampton, where he worked as a music presenter and reporter.

That route led him to fronting the *Radio One* lunchtime programme 'Newsbeat' where he became the station's main 'profile' presenter and music documentarist. He claims the honour of being the first DJ to play a CD on national radio.

In the 1980s he presented TV programmes such as Top of The Pops and Whistle Test, as well as Radio One's 'Round Table' and the prestigious Chart Countdown, before moving to local London station, *GLR*.

He hosted the Live Aid and Mandela concerts, and then joined *Virgin 1215* as Director of Music Programming. After Virgin's launch he resigned as Music Director to return to hosting radio programmes.

Keith SKIPPER

Went into local newspapers after school and, after seventeen years in the press, fancied a change. In 1980 he made his broadcasting debut with *Radio Norfolk* when it launched and has remained with the station since it began.

As well as radio, Keith has also written a dozen books about various Norfolk matters, and he is an accomplished after-dinner speaker and compere of concerts. The highlight of Keith's career was broadcasting from Wembley when Norwich City won the Cup Final, and finding out if Leslie Thomas sounded as good as he writes. He likes a good sense of humour, books, cricket and older women, but not traffic, noise, cynicism and older men.

Keith SKUES

Born on 4th March, 1939, Keith began his professional career in broadcasting as an announcer with the British Forces Network in Germany in 1958.

After two years in Germany he moved to Kuwait in 1961 and then spent three years in Nairobi, Kenya. while there he and an RAF team climbed the 19,000 feet high Kilimanjaro, as well as Mount Kenya, and he also wrote a series of articles for various newspapers.

His radio programmes won major awards in 1962 and 1963, and when Kenya gained independence the BFN station closed and he was transferred to Aden. After three months Keith resigned and returned to the UK joining *Radio Caroline* and spending eighteen months on the Mi Amigo.

Keith spent a short stint with *Radio Luxembourg* in 1965 and then swiftly moved back out to sea, this time on the good ship *Galaxy*, the home of Big L - more formally known as *Radio London*. During 1966 and 1967 he was one of Big L's stars and became a houshold name. He also interviewed many big name satrs of the day, too numerous to mention

Keith joined the BBC in 1967 and was one of the original team of DJs on Radio One and Radio Two. He remained with the Corporation until 1974 when he was appointed programme director of *Radio Hallam* in Sheffield.

In 1977 he won a national award for picking hits and compered the National Radio Awards for two years.

In the late 1980s as Hallam expanded to include eventually 13 transmitters, became Group Programme Controller and was responsible for the launch of the UK's first full time all gold station.

Keith has appeared on over a dozen different TV programmes, ranging from 'Top of the Pops' to The Kenneth WIlliams Show' and an award-winning series for the BBC "The Sory of Pop'.

His many varied hobbies include film making and aviation and he holds a private pilots licence. Keith is a squadron leader in the Royal Air Force Volunteer Reserve and saw service in the Gulf War. He is also a tireless worker for charity and is a vice president of the National Association of Youth Clubs.

Keith has a long track record as a writer and has penned the liner notes for albums and appeared in a film, Sunday, Bloody Sunday. Today he is a freelance writer, with several titles to his credit including 'Radio Onederland', and 'This is Hallamland' in 1975.

In 1994 his long awaited book "Pop went the Pirates" was published to wide acclaim and he continues to broadcast - currently full time with the BBC East Network with a daily programme.

Colin SLADE

While at college Colin booked bands for the Students Union, and got into radio in 1971 when the BBC opened a local station in his home town and needed someone for the rock show.

After three years at *Radio Medway*, Colin moved north to Sheffield and *Radio Hallam,* becoming the station's Head of Presentation in 1980. His most humourous moments were at Hallam, working with the late and much lamented Roger Moffatt.

After the merger which precipitated the *Yorkshire Radio Network* in 1987, Colin was assigned to Bradford's *Pennine Radio* and was also programme controller of *Grand Central Network* cable station from 1989 to 1992.

He freelanced for several BBC local stations for a few years, including periods at *Radio Humberside* and *Radio Leeds*, and in 1994 moved to Manchester to become Head of Programming and Music at Manchester's new easy-listening station, *Fortune 1458*.

Kate SLADE

Kate is the Breakfast Editor at *BBC Radio Humberside* responsible for the station's flagship 'Morningtide' programme.

David SLOAN

In the 1980s, David was the head of News and Sport at *Downtown Radio* in Belfast. In the 1990s he became the station's Managing Director.

Mark SLOANE

Born in March, 1942, as Patrick Hammerton, he became interested after visiting the Radio Luxembourg studios while on holiday in 1965. Chris Denning told him that Mike Raven was looking for broadcasters for *Radio 390* and after a voice test Mark found himself hired by KING RADIO, which broadcast from a fort, eight miles off Whitstable.

This later became Radio 390 and he became one of the station's most popular announcers. *Radio Caroline* offered him a job on the South ship, so long as he changed his name, and so he became Mark Sloan, after looking through a phone directory.

While on Caroline he took a short term contract at Radio Antilles in the Caribbean, before returning to the UK and a job at *Radio 355*. That station closed when the Marine Offences Act became law, so he moved to *Radio Caroline North*, however after the Daily Mirror published a story revealing his home address he decided to leave radio and went into advertising.

Mark then became a partner in City Marketing Group, a worldwide marketing group, and in the 1990s runs a company advising on advertising at airports from an office in Milton Keynes.

Rachel SLOANE

Rachel is a producer and also presents some programmes at *BBC Radio Suffolk*.

Tim SMALE

Head of sponsorship at *Capital Radio*.

Mary SMALL

Mary is the presenter of early evening programmes each weekday on *Radio Oxford*, now being merged with Radio Berkshire to form Radio Thames Valley.

Mike SMEETON

Engineer in charge at *Trent FM*.

Carol SMILLIE

A former columnist on the 'Sunday Scot' newspaper, Carol's radio career began at *Radio Clyde* where she hosted several programmes. She then moved to TV and has appeared on dozens of programmes, including her role as a hostess on 'Wheel of Fortune'.

She's recently presented a programme on *BBC Radio Five* called 'Carol Smillie's Blue Skies'.

Eric SMITH
Hosted the breakfast programme at *BBC Radio Humberside* in the 1980s and then moved to *Radio Shropshire* as programme Organiser and later he was made the station's Assistant Editor.

Gail SMITH
Head of Production at *Capital Radio*.

Ian SMITH
Director at *Invicta Radio Group* in Kent.

Linda SMITH
Linda is now the client marketing director at *Capital Radio*.

Mick SMITH
Country music presenter on *BBC Radio Lincolnshire*.

Mike SMITH
Born in Hornchurch Essex in April 1955, Mike always wanted to be in radio and began his career in 1974 on a hospital radio network. He then joined *BBC Radio One* as a researcher and stand-by presenter and in 1978 moved to *Capital Radio*.

Within a year he was hosting the Sunday afternoon Network Chart Show and appearing on various TV programmes.

In 1982 he was lured back to *Radio One* to host the station's prestigious Breakfast Show, and two years later left radio for a full-time role in TV as the host of 'That's Showbusiness' on BBC 1 TV.

Pete SMITH
Presenter of the Saturday teatime programme (from 1730 to 2100) on *Fortune 1458* in Manchester.

Phil SMITH
Engineer in charge at *BBC Radio Cleveland*.

Rosemary SMITH
General Manager and Financial Controller of the Metro Radio Group's Yorkshire stations.

Sean SMITH
Sean is the general office administrator of *KCBC* in Kettering.

Sandy SMITH
Sandy is the assistant editor responsible for news output at *BBC GLR*.

Terry SMITH
Terry was born on the 28th january, 1934 in Wakefield and attended the Wheelwrights Grammar School in Dewsbury. He was a journalist in the 1950s and in 1960 founded the Mercury Press Agency.

In 1973 he founded *Radio City* to apply for the Liverpool franchise and was the station's Managing Director from it's launch in 1974 until 1992.

Terry was also a leading member of the AIRC (which he chaired from 1983 to 1985) and was one of the people behind Broadcast Marketing Services (the BMS sales rep house).

In 1988 he joined the board of Independent Radio News and he joined Satellite Media Services in the same year.

Terry is also a director of EMAP Radio Ltd, of several charitable concerns, including the Liverpool Empire Theatre Trust. He is now the Chairman of the station and a keen football, golf and winter sports fan.

Tim SMITH
From *Metro Radio* in Newcastle he moved to *Radio Luxembourg* in the mid eighties, moved to *GLR* where he hosted the lunchtime weekday programmes in the early nineties. He now presents the breakfast programme each Saturday and Sunday at the station.

Jeffrey SMULYAN
Director of *Talkradio UK*.

Olive SNELLING
More than twenty years experience as a writer and presenter in radio and as a TV producer, specialising in human interest and religious programming. She recently worked at Channel Four TV with Gerald Priestland and in 1995 joined *Premier Radio*, the London Christian station, as a producer and presenter.

Hilary SNOWDEN
Hilary is a producer and programme presenter at *BBC Radio Devon and Dorset*.

Ken SNOWDON

Host of the mid-morning programme (from 9 until 1pm) on BBC Radio Cleveland.

Bob SNYDER

Born in Newark, Lincolnshire, Bob worked as a stage manager in several theatres in the East Midlands, South Yorkshire and Oxford while also working as a DJ in night clubs. He then attended a course in speech therapy at RADA and in April 1967 joined *Radio 270* off Scarborough. Just before 270 closed he jumped ship and set off for the Caribbean where he joined *Radio Antilles* where he became the station's programme director.

On returning to the UK he joined Thompson Newspapers and then Associated , working on applications for the first commercial radio licences in the 1970s. He joined *Piccadilly Radio* in Manchester when it launched at easter 1974 and became Presentation Controller. In 1975 he joined *Radio Trent*, the new station for Nottingham and a two year stretch as programme controller.

After a period at *Beacon Radio* in Wolverhampton, he moved to Canada and after work at several stations he settled in Dawson Creek where he works at CJDC.

Nick SOLARI

Client account manager at *Talkradio UK*.

Sal SOLO

A one time *Radio Caroline* DJ, Sal had chart hits with the eighties band 'Classics Nouveaux' who also had much success across Europe. In 1995 he joined *Premier Radio*, London's new Christian radio station, where he now presents a weekend chart shows.

Steve SOMERS

Afternoon presenter and producer at *BBC Radio Cambridgeshire* in 1995 Steve is also the senior producer at *BBC Radio Peterborough*.

Gordon SOMERVILLE

Works at *Orchard FM* as a presenter.

Jane SOOLE

Jane is the Head of News at *Wessex FM* in Dorchester.

Erika SORBY-FIRTH

Managing Director & Head of Sales at *Mix 96*.

Christopher SOUTH

Lunchtime programme host at *BBC Radio Cambridgeshire*.

Sammy SOUTHALL

Sammy is the head of presentation at *Radio Wyvern*.

Dave SOUTHWAY

Dave is a presenter at *Brunel Classic Gold*.

Stuart SPANDLER

A former Catholic priest, Stuart was a full time presenter with Ving Radio in the late eighties. He is now working on RSL's and in Christian radio.

Gordon SPARKS

Presenter on Plymouth Sounds's AM service.

Anthea SPEAKMAN

Anthea is a director of *Essex Radio*.

John SPEARMAN

A former high-flying advertising executive with a major agency in London, John joined *Classic FM* before the station launched..

Richard SPENCER

Richard is a presenter on *MFM* in Wrexham.

Helen SPENCER

helen hosts the mid morning g programme each weekday on *BBC Radio Newcastle*.

Richard SPENDLOVE

Late night phone-in host at *BBC Radio Cambridgeshire*.

Mark SPIVEY

Presenter of rock music and dance music programmes at *Trent FM*.

Pam SPRIGGS

Pam presents a programme each weekday morning from 9 until 11 on *BBC Three Counties Radio*.

Christopher SPURGEON

Christopher is the Finance Director of *Heart FM* in the Midlands.

Fiona SPURR

Presenter of the morning programme on BBC *Radio Jersey*.

Giles SQUIRE

Giles was the Programme Controller at *Metro FM* until the EMAP Group bought the station in September 1995.

Phil SQUIRE

Phil has been the sports reporter at *BBC Radio Humberside* since the late 1980's. he is married to a BBC local TV presenter and lives in East Yorkshire.

Norman ST JOHN

Born on 12th May in 1943, Norman was schooled in Melbourne, Australia, and wanted to be a farmer, but on finding it too much like hard work he got a job at a local station in his home town called 3UZ. He studied broadcasting at the Lee Murray School, who said he'd never make it!

Three years later he joined *3CS* and by the time he was 20 he'd worked at seven stations. After a period as a TV continuity announcer, he had a nervous breakdown and his doctor ordered him 'off the air' for twelve months. A trip round the world seemed ideal therapy, and after Japan and Hong Kong he arrived in the UK in 1965 where he joined a shipping company arranging entertainment.

He then applied for a job on *Radio Caroline* and joined the station, initially as a news reader at the height of its success. In May 1966 he left Caroline for a gig on nearby rival *Radio London*, and after another nine months on the North Sea, joined *Radio Luxembourg* as a staff announcer. After a stint in the Grand Duchy he returned to Australia.

Keith STAINER

Keith is a sequence producer at *Wiltshire Sound*.

Fiona STALKER

Recently became Programme Director at *Northsound Radio* in Aberdeen.

Dino STANDING

Sports commentator at *Capital Gold* in 1995.

James STANNAGE

Born in Stockton in 1950, James began his radio career at *Signal Radio* in Cheshire, where his late night phone in programmes caught the ear of Jasper Carrott who satirised him and brought him nation-wide fame.

James then moved to *Piccadilly Radio* and in October 1987 returned to his native Stockton to host a late night programme (a four hour phone-in) each weekday on *Radio Tees*. He later returned to *Piccadilly* to host programmes on their 'Gold' station and has stayed there ever since.

David STANSFIELD

Italian music and radio scene reporter for 'Music and Media' magazine, then Chief UK reporter. In Autumn 1993, David left M&M to host the weekly 'The Boots Bite Back', an Italian programme on *Spectrum Radio* in London.

Jonathan STAPLES

Host of the afternoon programme, from 1315 to 1600 each weekday, on *London Newsradio FM*.

David STARKEY

Hosted Saturday morning programmes on *Talkradio UK* at the station's launch.

Guy STARKEY

Born in 1959 in Bebington, Cheshire, Guy's radio career began with a three year stint at Chester Hospital Radio and doing mobile discos.

In 1978 Guy went to the *Voice of Peace* for a year, hosting most programmes and then returned to the UK and *University Radio Bath*. After two stints at *Radio Nova International* in Italy (where he hosted programmes in English and French) he moved to *BFBS Gibraltar*, where he stayed until 1986. While there he also produced a documentary for *BBC Radio Four*.

On returning to the UK Guy did six months with *Beacon Radio* in Wolverhampton, before moving to new station *Marcher Sound* for five years where he hosted the mid morning programme.

Who's Who in British Radio

In 1991 it was on to Liverpool's *Radio City* where he became Senior Producer and ran the AM programmes department.

In 1992 he took a job at the Farnborough College of Technology as a senior lecturer of OND students in radio production. He has also managed several RSL ventures over the last few years and writes for various publications including 'Radio Month'.

Patrick STARLING
Also known as 'Child Scientist' Patrick was one of the engineers on *Radio Caroline South* in 1964 and 1965 and often guested on Tony Blackburn's programme (being one of the few up so early in the morning!).

Katy STEAD
Producer and presenter at BBC Radio Devon and Dorset.

Paul STEAD
After working for several years in theatre and cabaret, Paul joined *Radio Aire* in Leeds as a freelance presenter. He remained with the station for eight years during which time he became senior producer and presenter. He has hosted all types of radio programme, from music-based shows to news, magazine, sport and religious programmes.

In 1990 Paul became head of promotions and sponsorship at *Radio Aire* and went on to become a senior manager operating a highly successful department which was a stand alone profit centre at the station.

In this role he oversaw all the radio station's major events and activities, working in close liaison with commercial clients, local authorities and voluntary organisations, winning widespread acclaim for his professional implementation of promotional events.

In February 1993 Paul set up his own independent production company which achieved an annual turnover of £500,000 in just eighteen months.

He has supplied many programmes to BBC and ILR stations and was responsible for bringing one of the country's best known and most popular TV and radio personalities, Dave Lee Travis, to the ILR network. It is now heard on 27 stations the length and breadth of the UK (a number which continues to grown steadily).

Richard STEAD
Richard is the weekend overnight (2 until 6am) DJ on *Minster FM* and *Yorkshire Coast Radio*.

Alan STEADMAN
Presenter of jazz programmes on *Radio Tay*.

Dave STEARN
Presenter of the weekend breakfast show on *Signal Radio* in Cheshire.

Nicky STEELE
Got into radio after being spotted in a night-club playing a Beatles medley by BRMB presenters. He has worked at *Xtra AM* since 1974 apart from a couple of years when he defected across town to *BBC Radio WM*. Says the highlight of his radio career was making the first live satellite broadcast from Disneyland and most humourous moment was gassing Katie Boyle's dog! Holds the World Record for a night club residency - almost 26 years at the Belfry Hotel in Birmingham.

Tom STEELE
Tom joined the company as it's first Head of News in October 1974 from Radio Clyde. Previously he was a reporter/producer with *BBC Radio Scotland* and BBC Local Radio after a spell in the House of Commons.

Tom was appointed Forth's Programme Controller in 1978, joined the *Radio Forth* board in 1980. He has also served a four year period as a director of *Radio Tay*.

Fiona STEGGLES
Programme Producer at *BBC Radio Cleveland*.

Alan STENNETT
Weekend breakfast programme presenter at *BBC Radio Lincolnshire*.

Who's Who in British Radio

Diana STENSON

Diane is the Producer of gardening programmes on *Classic FM*.

Brian STEPHENS

Brian was the producer of he *Radio Two* breakfast programme in the 1980s (when Derek Jameson presented it) and is now the station's Editor of Programmes and Music.

Mark STEPHENS

A director of *Premier Radio* in London.

Phillip STEPHENS

Phillip is the producer of all religious programmes at *Swansea Sound*.

Barry STEPHENSON

Barry was a news producer at *BBC Radio York* in the early 1990's. He then moved to *Radio Humberside* as an Assistant Editor and in 1995 was an Managing Editor for a time. He has recently been working in TV on attachment..

Kenny STEVENS

Kenny presents programmes on Central Scotland's regional station, *Scot FM*.

Mark STEVENS

Born in July 1956, Marks' radio career began in 1979 at *Radio CX36* in Montivideo, Uruguay. he then worked at *Radio Atlantica* in Santos, Brazil, and at *Radio Copacabana* in Rio de Janeiro.

In the mid eighties he joined a TV production company for a while and then ran an RSL station in Crawley.

In 1990 he joined *Aggelon Radio*, a production company, where he has produced and presented a variety of programmes - his current activity there is a jazz programme, and an alternative chart programme.

Mike STEVENS

Mike is currently a DJ on *Invicta Supergold* t.

Adrian STEWART

Attended Aldersbrook School in Solihull and then worked as an electrician for his local electricity board. His first radio work came in 1982 with the local BHBN and then in 1986 he was hired as a programme assistant with BRMB.

In 1988 Adrian got his first full time radio presentation role when BRMB launched a gold service, Xtra AM,and he's been there since.

Adrian recently recorded a special programme for *VH-1* TV channel, but the highlight of his career was his first ever live interview - it was with Paul McCartney on the phone. Likes Bacon and Eggs and Red wine, and dislikes any man over 30 who still has hair on his head!

Bob STEWART

One of the tallest UK DJs at 6 feet 5 inches, Bob was born in Liverpool in 1939 and joined the Army until 1962. He worked as a TV salesman and as a compere in Canada and got into DJing via his old friend, Pete Best, the former Beatles drummer. In 1965 Bob called Radio Caroline and asked if there were any vacancies.

There was and he joined Radio Caroline South for a week before moving to the North ship off the Isle of Man. Caroline management asked him to lose his scouse accent and he developed a mid-Atlantic twang.

In 1968 he joined *Radio Luxembourg* and quickly became one of the best known voices across Europe with the distinctive mid-atlantic drawl which belies his Liverpool upbringing.

He stayed with Luxembourg for twenty years, becoming an honorary citizen of Nashville for his promotional work for country music in Europe. Bob also worked at a station in Dallas, Texas, and is married to a Texan lady called Cynthia and has been widely heard hosting in-flight programmes for airlines.

He hosted the breakfast show on *Jazz FM* for a while and is now heard on *Capital Gold*. Among Bob's favourite things are his family, blue skies, sunsets and suntans - although he's not too keen grey weather, grey people and grey places. He's handled by Talking Heads - 0171 636 7755.

Ed STEWART

Born during an air raid on St George's Day in 1941, at a place called 'Caroline House' in Exmouth, Devon! His first broadcast was aged nine when he sang in a choir on the BBC North American Service and he attended public school in Oxford. While travelling the world he got into radio in Hong Kong and then joined *Radio London* in 1965 where he was given the nickname 'Stewpot' by ship-mate Dave Cash.

During 1966 Ed's popularity grew and grew, despite the cruel nicknames given him by his shipmates (Myrtle and Stewpot are the broadcastable ones). In February 1967 he became Programme Director of Big L , succeeding the much loved and revered Tony Windsor.

Ed joined *Radio One* when the station opened and had a regular programme each Sunday Morning called 'Happening Sunday' , but was replaced by Kenny Everett after just a few months. In 1968 he release a single called "I Like Toys" on MGM and hosted a TV programme and Junior Choice on *Radio One*. He then moved across to *Radio Two* where he stayed until 1983, following which he spent seven years at *Radio Mercury* in Sussex.

In the early 1990's Ed returned to *Radio Two* and now hosts a regular afternoon programme on the station.

Kevin STEWART

Kevin is the Managing Director of *Island FM,* Guernsey's ILR station, which has the best reach figures in the country. he is often heard on programmes on the station.

Kirsty STEWART

Senior producer at *Scot FM.*

Mike STEWART

Born on 30th January, 1946 in Dorking, Surrey, Mike worked in newspapers in the West Midlands before moving into radio. He helped start up a hospital radio station in Stafford where he became a presenter and News Editor.

Mike's first broadcasting was doing soccer reports on BBC Radio Stoke and in 1975 he joined *BRMB* as Senior Newsman. The following year became Head of News at *Beacon Radio*. After five years in Wolverhampton, he moved to Bristol and a similar position at *Radio West*; after two years he was promoted to become programme controller, a position he held from 1983 to 1984.

In 1984 Mike moved to Norwich and became Programme Controller at *Radio Broadland*; in 1991 he was made programme Director and now oversees the output of the Suffolk Radio Group stations *SGR, Broadland 102,* and their new *Amber Radio* station.

The highlight of Mike's career was getting into the business in 1975 in the early days of ILR at BRMB and also getting a 50% reach figure at *Radio Broadland* in 1990. He's saving his humourous moments for that inevitable book and confesses to liking tight punchy fun personality radio.

Paul STEWART

Head of News and Features at *KFM,* an ILR station in Tonbridge which launched in Spring, 1995.

Tim STEWART

Tim is a presenter and also responsible for playlists at *Invicta FM.*

Robert STIBY

One of the pioneers of the UK Radio industry, Robert started his long media career in 1959, joining the 'Croydon Advertiser' Group as reporter and sub-editor, eventually serving as Chairman and Managing Director between 1974 and 1983. He was President of the Newspaper Society in 1984.

Robert founded Radio Investments back in 1972. he is a founder-director of *Capital radio* and from this original investment, his company has expanded substantially and now holds a significant investment portfolio in over thirty UK radio stations.

Robert has over 20 years experience in independent radio and holds, or has held, a number of directorships in radio companies.

He is the Chairman of *KCBC* and Deputy Chairman of *Talkradio UK* and sit s on the board of many stations, including *Capital, Minster, Orchard, Wessex* and *Island*. He is also a director United Artists Communications, the South London Cable TV company.

He is very active in local affairs, being a magistrate on the Croydon bench, a director of the Fairfield Halls and a past president of the Croydon Boys Club as well as chairing local charities and trusts.

Al STIRLING

After an education at Heathfield High School in Congleton, Al became a chef for a while and then got into radio by answering the phones for an evening jock at *Signal FM*. His first broadcast was a one hour slot in the middle of the night, back in August 1993, but a month later he was given the weekend evening shows on *Signal One*, a job he's had for almost two years now.

Al also works as a broadcast sound engineer and the highlight of his career was broadcasting from a light plane flying above Stoke. He once did a three hour show with a fractured wrist (not at all funny at the time); he likes dance music and action movies, but hates brocolli.

Barry STOCKDALE

Barry began his radio career assisting at *BBC Radio Humberside* while still at school. He became a station assistant and worked his way up the ladder to become responsible for presentation at the station.

In the 1980s he moved to *BBC Radio York,* where he became Station Manager, and in the early 1990s he joined BBC *Radio Sheffield*, of which he is now Managing Editor.

Paul STODDARD

Paul is a weekday presenter on *Island FM*.

Tony STOLLER.

Born in London in 1948, Tony took degrees in law and history at Gonville and Caius College, Cambridge and joined the Thompson Regional News-papers Group as a graduate trainee before moving to the Liverpool Daily Post and Echo as Marketing Manager.

In 1974 he joined the Radio Division of the IBA, becoming Head of Radio Programming two years later. After a spell as Director of the AIRC, he becamne Managing Director of *Radio 210* in Reading for four years.

In 1984 he joined the John Lewis Partnership and was appointed Managing Director of a store in Southampton in 1986. In 1995 he was appointed the Chief Executive of the Radio Authority.

Tony is married with two teeneage children and his interests include cricket, sailing and music.

John STOLLERY

Professor Stollery is the Chairman of *Chiltern Radio* in Bedford.

Ivor STOLLIDAY

Ivor is the Chairman of *Gemini Radio* in Exeter.

Dick STONE

Programme Controller at *RAM FM*, Derby.

Mark STOREY
In the late 1980's Mark was a programme Producer at *BBC Radio One*, being primarily responsible for the Simon Mayo breakfast programme.

He then moved to *Piccadilly Radio* in Manchester where he was programme Controller until 1993 when he joined *Virgin 1215* as Programme Director.

Janice STRADLING
Janice is now a broadcast journalist at BBC Radio Berkshire.

Carol STRAKER
Carol is the P.C. of *Jazz FM* in London.

Maureen STREET
Maureen is the Promotions Manager at Island FM on Guernsey.

Craig STRONG
Presenter at *RAM FM* in Derby.

Colin STROUD
Colin is the Company Secretary and also a Director at *Swansea Sound*.

Ray STROUD
Ray got into radio after attending a presentation course on a local station, and his first broadcast was on the early breakfast show at *Pennine Radio* in 1978.

There followed many different programmes including a joint presentation with David Jensen (Network Chart Pop Quiz) run in association with local schools.

The highlight of Ray's career so far was beating *Radio One* for a Sony Award for "Best Outside Broadcast" for a programme he did from Disneyworld in Florida. Some of Ray's (and radio's generally) most humourous moments have come during his long-running feature "What have I got in my hand?" which has been running now for over a decade. He likes food and drink, but doesn't care much for poodles and babies.

Russell STUART
Managing Director of *Radio Broadland* in Norwich when the station launched in 1984, he is now MD of the entire Suffolk Radio group.

Barbara STURGEON
One of the longest serving voices on BBC Radio Kent, she also did some programmes for Radio Two for a while, and now has a daily talk show.

Claire STURGESS
Claire is a presenter on BBC *Radio 1* currently hosting the 12 midnight to 4am slot each weekday.

John SULLIVAN
John is the engineer in charge at *BBC Essex*.

Martin SUMMERS
Martin is a lawyer in Scarborough and a Board Member of *Yorkshire Coast Radio*.

Roger SUMMERSKILL
After school Roger did a variety of jobs before deciding to rain as a journalist. After a stint on a weekly newspaper he joined *Radio Merseyside* and made his first broadcast from a public phone-box, complete with the inevitable woman outside banging on the window and yelling that she had to make an urgent call!

He was originally a producer and reporter but had several spells in presentation. Was a newsreader on the original *Radio Five* and now presents the breakfast programme on BBC *Radio Merseyside* as well as a late night discussion programme on *BBC Five Live*.

Roger is also an accomplished pantomime actor and does compering work and has(touch wood) managed to avoid the "one-legged python" interview. Likes food, drink, holidays and money, but not people who are 'ratty' in the morning.

Alan SUTHERLAND
After leaving Tyneside High School he worked in the building trade and did discos by night. He got into radio by word of mouth, joining East Lothian Hospital Radio and then *Radio Lollipop* in Edinburgh, where he became programme controller and Chief Fund Raiser.

Three years later he joined *Central FM* and presented a weekly programme for some time before his big break on *Radio Forth FM* in 1993, and the programme 'The Big Noise'.

Who's Who in British Radio

In 1992 Al took part in the 'Challenge Anneka' TV programme and the following year on the Forth FM Summer Challenge had his (then very hairy) chest waxed, the most humourous event of his career so far. Big Al, as he's known in Edinburgh, likes a few beers and lots of laughs but not heavy metal and blues music and people who don't buy their round of drinks.

Mairi SUTHERLAND
Mairie was a producer at the BBC local station on the Solway Firth and then moved to TV in Glasgow. In 1995 she organised a bid for the Dumfries and Galloway ILR licence.

Rae SUTHERLAND
Chairman of *Nevis Radio*, Fort William.

Joseph SWAIN
Managing Director and Head of Sales at *Pirate FM* and Sales manager at *Star FM*.

Richard SWAINSON
Joined *Radio Caroline* in 1964 as a courier, ensuring all the necessary records and mail got out to the ship on time. Richard was also a prolific song-writer with a plethora of contacts in the music business and in early 1966 he joined *Radio London*.

He became head of administration with special responsibilities for the ship Galaxy until Big L closed. He then joined MGM records which signed up several ex Big L djs for single releases. In the 1970s he returned to broadcasting and a job with *Radio Luxembourg*.

Flavia SWANN
Flavia was Chief executive of *Wear FM*, the community radio station in Sunderland, until it was bought by Minster FM in 1995.

Mike SWEENEY
Presenter on *Piccadilly Gold*.

Ian SWEIGER
Communications Manager at *Spectrum 558*.

John SWINFIELD
A much-respected political programme producer with Anglia Television for almost thirty years, John is a director of *Radio Broadland*.

Malcolm SWIRE
Malcolm joined *BBC Radio Lincolnshire* in the 1980s as a programme producer and is now the assistant editor of the station.

Nicola SWORDS
Nicola is a news producer at *BBC Radio York*.

Colin SYKES
Colin is now assistant news editor at BBC *Radio GMR* in Manchester.

Colin SYKES
Assistant editor at BBC GMR.

Ian SYKES
Director of *Nevis Radio*.

Dave SYMONDS
Dave's first radio job was in New Zealand in the mid sixties and after he came to Europe in 1966 he joined the BBC and helped launch Radio One. His 'Happening Sunday' programme is still fondly remembered as one of the network's most distinctive.

After many years at the BBC Dave joined *Capital Radio* where he hosted the station's first breakfast programme in October 1973.

He left the station for a while and then rejoined in 1988 as part of the new *Capital Gold* team, hosting weekend shows until September, 1995.

'Catcher in the Rye' was his favourite book until a copy was found at John Lennon's murder - but he still likes indian food with a pint of bitter.

Graham SYMONDS
Managing Director and Head of Sales at *Sunshine Radio* in Ludlow, Warwickshire.

Derm TANNER
Derm is Sports Editor at *BBC Radio Leeds*.

Brian TANSLEY
Brian's radio career began by working for a local newspaper and for a freelance e agency - it was coverage of a Notts County FC game for *Radio Trent* in 1975. he served the station as sports reporter and then as Sports editor for twenty years and is now a weekday evening presenter on the station's gold outlet *Gem AM*.

Brian was runner up in the Rediffusion Sports Awards in 1981, and likes music, cricket and the theatre, but doesn't like the attitudes of the people currently running football.

Chris TARRANT

Born in Reading in 1946, Chris gained a BA(Hons) in English literature and taught English in a London school for a while. He came into broadcasting via programmes at ATV in Birmingham, and later Central, particularly 'Tiswas' and 'OTT' with Bob Carolgees.

In the 1980s Chris joined *Capital Radio* and has hosted their FM service's Breakfast Show, reportedly at the industry's highest salary, ever since.

In 1991 he received a Sony Award for 'Radio Personality of the Year' and the following year received a similar award from the Variety Club of Great Britain.

As well as broadcasting, Chris has also published two books, 'Ken's Furry Friends' and 'Fishfriar's Hall'. His hobbies are fishing and cricket.

Simon TATE

After school in Blackpool, Simon spent a period in catering management and being a club DJ. In 1978 he sent a tape to *Radio Luxembourg* and was invited to appear on the station as a guest celebrity DJ, and a year later he got a regular programme at *Radio Victory* .

He then spent four years at *Radio City* in Liverpool and then nine years at *Red Rose Radio* in Lancashire.

In 1992 he moved along the M6 to Morecambe and became the Programme Controller of *Radio Wave* - being there at the launch of the station in 1992 was the highlight of his career. His most humourous moment was having to turn the spools of tape for the Queen's Christmas Speech by hand in 1980 at *Radio City* - Simon loves Bovril crisps and chocolate, but hates filling in forms and questionnaires!

Simon is still at his home town station, *Radio Wave*, and is now programme director and music controller.

Andrew TAUUSSIG

Andrew was educated in Scarborough and has had a long career in the BBC. He is now the Head of Region responsible for Europe at the *BBC World Service*.

Dave TAVINER

Hosted weekend breakfast programmes at *Radio Humberside* in the 80s and 1990s and was also responsible for the station's religious output. He is now t Sequence Editor.

Barbara TAYLOR

In the late 1980s Barbara was the Programme Organiser (and for a while the acting General Manager) of Radio Merseyside. Barbara is now the Managing Editor of BBC Radio Shropshire.

Darren TAYLOR

Darren is a producer at *BBC Radio Cleveland*.

Dennis TAYLOR

Dennis is the Computer Services Manager at *Capital Radio*.

Digby TAYLOR

The Presenter of the mid-morning programme at *Signal Radio*'s station in Cheshire.

Jessie TAYLOR OBE

Jessie is a director at Piccadilly Radio.

John TAYLOR

John hosts a weekly nostalgia programme on *BBC Radio Norfolk* called 'Radio Times'.

Jonathan TAYLOR

Journalist at BBC Radio Lincolnshire.

Margherita TAYLOR

Margherita obtained a BA in media and Communications at the University of Central England and got into radio by winning BRMB's 'Search for a Star' in 1993.

She made her first broadcast during the August Bank Holiday weekend that year and spent the next 18 months doing overnight shifts for *BRMB*, as well as some weekend breakfast shifts. In March 1995 Margherita moved to *Capital FM* in London where she now does overnights and swing work.

As well as radio, she does voice over work and TV presenting, but the highlight of her radio career so far was co-hosting a road show in front of a crowd of 100,000 people. Her most humourous moment was forgetting lines on her first PA, she revels in music, sunshine, food and skydiving.

Patrick TAYLOR
Patrick is the Business Development Manager and also the Group Finance Director at *Capital Radio*. he also sits on the board of *Essex Radio*

Steve TAYLOR (1)
Sunday Breakfast presenter at KIX 96.

Steve TAYLOR (2)
Promotions accounts Manager at Virgin 1215.

Trevor TAYLOR
Producer of 'Gardeners' Question Time' at *BBC Radio Four*.

Wayne TAYLOR
Head of Sales at *Red Rose Radio*.

John TAYNTON
John does the 9pm until midnight programme each weekday on Midlands BBC stations, such as *Radio Leicester* and *Radio Stoke*.

Andrew TEAGUE
Breakfast presenter on *Radio Humberside*.

Kate TEBBY
Kate hosts the afternoon programme (2 until 5pm) on *BBC Radio Stoke*.

Gill TEE
Group Concert Manager at *Capital Radio*.

Richard TEIDEMAN
Richard's interest in sound recording led him to joining *RTM*, a community radio station in south London as commercial production assistant.

Richard then moved to *Allied Radio* for a while before moving on to the *GWR* Group where he wrote commercials for 26 radio stations.

He is also a music producer and produced the *Premier Radio* jingle package, where he is now the station's Commercial Media Manager as well as host of several programmes.

Mike TEMPLE
While in the Royal Navy, Mike began his radio career, broadcasting to shipmates on internal radio systems. After coming ashore he joined *Plymouth Sound* and then BBC *Radio Devon*. In 1995, he joined *Premier Radio* in London where he hosts 'Premier Lifeline'.

Eddy TEMPLE-MORRIS
Eddy is Presentation Producer at *Radio One*.

Ray TERET
Born in Wiltshire, Ray made his first public appearance aged 11 and had a variety of jobs before working in clubs in the north west. It was there that he befriended Jimmy Savile who arranged for him to audition for *Radio Caroline North*, anchored off the Isle of Man.

Ray joined Radio Caroline in August 1965 while just 19 years old and became one of the ship's best known DJs, hosting his 'Ugly Bug Ball' not only on the air but at clubs and other venues all over the North.

His sister Janet married Ray's colleague Mick Luvzit live on the air - the first wedding ever conducted on an radio ship! After Radio Caroline closed Ray worked on several ILR stations and in clubs in the north.

John TERRETT
John presents the 'First Edition' programme from 8 until 10pm each weekday evening on *London Newsradio FM*.

Ruth TERRETT
Ruth was a newsreader on *BBC Radio Wales* in the late 1980s, reporting on Gwent stories.

Christopher TERRY
Christopher presents the 'Ahead of the Game' programme each Friday, and a Saturday morning breakfast show, on *London Newsradio FM*.

Joan THIRKETTLE

One of the hardest working backroom girls without whom *Radio Caroline* would have closed down many years before it did.

Joan was secretary and PA to *Radio Caroline* director Philip Solomon who ran the station in the mid sixties and after it became illegal. She was responsible for keeping the station on the air after it closed its London office and organised the DJs travel arrangements to Holland and other essential maintenance.

Joan later trained as a journalist and now works for ITN, where she is frequently seen on major news bulletins as a reporter.

Darrell THOMAS

Darrell is the General Manager and Head of Sales at *CFM* in Carlisle.

Jeff THOMAS

Jeff is a DJ at *Touch AM* in Cardiff.

Jerry THOMAS

Jerry worked in television before joining *Talkradio UK* as Programme Director in 1995.

John THOMAS

John is the Sales Controller and a Director of *Swansea Sound*.

Kevin THOMAS

Presenter at *Red Dragon Radio* in Cardiff.

Mark THOMAS (1)

Initially a presenter at *BBC Radio Essex* in the mid 1980s when the station launched he became a General Producer and then moved to Radio Lancashire where he became acting Programme Manager.

Mark also presented the 'In the Mix' Programme on *BBC Radio Five* in the early 1990s, and then moved to *BBC Radio Devon and Dorset* where he is now a producer and presenter.

Mark THOMAS (2)

Director of Engineering at the Radio Authority.

Martin THOMAS

Martin is Chairman of *Marcher Coast*.

Alan THOMPSON

After school in Essex, Alan was fired from his first job after putting Fairy liquid in a director's tea. He got into radio via newspapers and made his first broadcast at *WBZ* Radio in Boston, Massachusetts in 1972, where he stayed for two years. returning to Europe he joined *LBC* as assistant news editor.

Later he freelanced as a reporter for *BBC Radio London* and, in the mid-seventies, at Capital Radio and Radio 210 Reading.

The years from 1979 to 1981 were spent researching and assembling a milestone in commercial radio : 'Searching The Ether' which traced the history of independent radio, with the legendary Bob Danvers-Walker, which was heard on twenty ILR stations.

After a period with *Wiltshire Radio*, the forerunner of GWR, he then joined the London Press exchange as Head of Media, but continuing to work in ILR. alan then joined BBC Wiltshire Sound for its launch as Programme Organiser, which achieved a 27% share in its first 12 months under his stewardship. Alan then moved to BBC national radio and produced several programmes for *Radio Two*, including shows presented by Angela Rippon, Acker Bilk and Kenny Ball. Other stations which have featured in Alan's radio career have included *Severn Sound* (as General Manager) *Sunshine 855* in the West Midlands, *Essex Radio* and BBC Television.

In 1991 Alan set up his own production company, ATC, which produced several programmes including the much admired 'Meek Reunion'.

The highlights of Alan's career have been 'The Kennedy Years' and getting into US radio, including the work he did on the Rick Nelson Tribute on *KRLA* in Los Angeles in 1986.

Alan doesn't like insincere people, and is currently producing a TV game show with Marcel Steeleman of 'Countdown' fame as well as hosting the weekday breakfast programme on *Eleven Seventy AM* in Slough, where he is also the Head of Programmes and a board member.

Alexis THOMPSON
Alexis was the Promotions Director at *Fox FM* in Oxford and in 1994 left the station to join *London Newstalk* as Head of Promotions and Sponsorship.

David THOMPSON
David was the General Manager of Radio Aire in Leeds for much of the 1980s and early 1990. He is now operating a book manufacturing 'talking books' for blin people and still lives near Leeds .

Erik THOMPSON
Chairman of *Stray FM*, in Harrogate.

Sir Gill THOMPSON
Sir Gill is a Director of Fortune 1458, the easy-listening station in Manchester.

Jeff THOMPSON
Director of *Piccadilly Radio* in Manchester.

Paul THOMPSON
Paul is the senior presenter at *KCBC* .

Don THOMSON.
In the 1980s Don was the Sales and Marketing Director at *Piccadilly Radio* in Manchester before joining a National Sales Agency. In 1995 he joined *Heart FM* as Sales Director.

Mark THORBURN
The host of a daily programme on *Metro FM*.

Gaston THORN
Gaston is a senior executive within CLT and is the Chairman of *Atlantic 252*.

Mike THORN
Business Development Manager at *NTL*.

Colin THORNE
Sales Director at *South West Sound* in Dumfries and at *West Sound* in Ayr.

Debbie THROWER
Born in Nairobi, Kenya on 17th November, 1957, Debbie got a BA(Hons) in French at Kings College in London. She became a local newspaper reporter in South London and Kings Lynn before joining *BBC Radio Leicester* as a reporter.

She moved to *BBC Radio Solent* to work in news and then became a reporter-presenter on regional news programmes, both with the BBC and the Southampton-based ITV regional TVS and Meridian.

Debbie also presented 'You and Yours' on *Radio Four* and stood in for Nick Ross on his weekly phone-in programme.

In recent years she has been a regular holiday relief at *BBC Radio Two*, standing in for Derek Jameson, Gloria Hunniford and John Dunn, as well as hosting programmes in her own name. She has been married to Peter since 1983 and has two children and a black Labrador which she enjoys walking near her home in Hampshire.

Jane THURLOW
Jane was a reporter and is now a news producer at *BBC Radio Suffolk*.

Emma THWAITES
Emma was a producer at *BBC Radio Berkshire,* the station now merged with Radio Oxford to form Radio Thames Valley.

Andrew TICKNER
Assistant to the Promotions and Marketing Manager at *Great Yorkshire Gold.*

Shaun TILLEY
In the late 1980s he worked at *Radio Luxembourg* and is now a presenter at *Mercia FM* in Coventry.

Brian TILNEY
Before getting into radio he worked as a manager at the London Palladium and then joined *Radio England* in 1966.

Ian TIMMS
Presenter of the Sunday Breakfast programme, plus weekday drive time programme on BBC Radio Leeds.

Sue TIMPSON
Sales Manager at *The Pulse*, Bradford.

John TINDALL
John is currently hosting overnights each weekday on *Great Yorkshire Gold* .

Paolo TISH

News reporter at *Capital Radio* in the nineties, mainstay of 'The Way It Is' programme.

John TOLANSKY

Presenter at *Classic FM*.

Russ TOLLERFIELD

Russ is one of the industry's most experienced radio engineers, having worked on Big L - Radio London's ship the MV Galaxy in the 1960s.

In the early seventies he joined *Radio Victory* in Portsmouth and he is now Chief Engineer at the Ocean Group of stations.

Mark TONDERAI

Hosted overnight programmes on *Radio One* in early 1980s.

Mike TOOLAN

Presenter at *TFM* in 1995.

Graham TORRINGTON

Graham began his career at *Buzz FM* in Birmingham and then moved on to *KIX 96* in Coventry where he now hosts the lunchtime programme and is Programme Director.

Mark TRAVERS

Engineer in charge at *BBC Radio Oxford*.

Dave Lee TRAVIS

Born in Derbyshire on 25th May, 1945, Dave was educated at the Central Grammar School in Manchester. Intent on a career in design, he began his career at the Oasis Club in Manchester as a part time DJ and later went full time at the Mecca Ballroom in Burnley. and toured the USA with Herman's Hermits, one of Manchester's local bands who made it big stateside.

In the Summer of 1965 he joined *Radio Caroline South* and six months later made national news when he was one of the DJs who had to be rescued when the ship went aground on Frinton Beach.

In 1966 he also compered some programmes for German television (Radio Caroline had a big audience on the continent) and these have recently been seen on satellite TV (e.g. West 3) once again.

At the end of 1967 Dave joined *Radio One* and fronted the station's output from Manchester. In 1971 he got his own daily programme and he also presented the station's breakfast show for a while. In 1976 he and Paul Burnett made a send-up record called 'Convoy GB (as Laurie Lingo and the Dip-sticks) which got to number four in the UK charts.

His weekend programmes on *Radio One* led to a variety of TV work with BBC, but in 1993 he criticised the BBC management on his programme and sold his story to The Sun newspaper, which resulted in him, being taken off the air two months before his contract expired.

Paul Stead (qv) then promoted his programme to several local stations and he is now heard weekly on the GWR network as well as several smaller independents. An avid photographer he is also heard on the BBC World Service with his 'Jolly Good Show'.

Keith TRAVIS

Keith is a presenter on *Amber Radio*, the new station in Anglia launched in September 1995.

Petroc TRELAWNEY

After a period on *Classic FM*, Petroc joined *London News Radio* in 1994 where he now presents the mid morning programme from 10am until 1pm on the FM service.

Nicholas TRESILIAN

Director of development at *GWR Group* and the chairman of GWR East in Swindon.

Jon TROWSDALE

John was the Programme Director of the two *Northsound* stations in Aberdeen until September 1995 when he joined NTL as their DAB Manager.

Tommy TRUESDALE

After school in Ayr, Tommy's first job was as a coal miner, and also as an electro plater, before starting his own pop band, Tommy Truesdale and the Sundowners which toured the UK in the 1960s. He became so well known as a vocalist on the local cabaret and club circuit that he was invited to join Ayr ILR station *West Sound* as a presenter.

His first programmes were a vintage rock'n'roll music and country music shows in October, 1981 - when West Sound launched and he's stayed with the station ever since.

Tommy has also appeared on several TV programmes as a vocalist and thinks the highlights of his career so far have been interviews with Johnny Cash, Brenda Lee, Glenn Campbell, Marty Wilde and Charley Pride. Tommy is currently seen nationwide on ITV Channel 3 in the IRN BRU commercial driving a yellow Capri called 'Sparkling'.

His programmes give a clue to his favourite music and he is also an avid boxing and 'Rock and Roll Years' TV watcher. Tommy doesn't like cruelty to animals and has his own record company called Scotdisc.

Gerard TUBB
Presenter at *BBC Radio York* and *BBC Radio Essex* in the 1980s.

Will TUDOR
Born and bred in Shropshire, Will worked for British Telecom as an engineer and then began his own mobile discotheque business. While doing a Young Farmers gig in the West Midlands, he was discovered by *Beacon Radio*'s Programme Director, Pete Wagstaff who gave him a regular programme in the mid 1980s. He is still there on the station's FM outlet in 1995.

Penny TUERK
Penny is the Commissioing Editor of English Programmes at the *BBC World Service*.

Nic TUFF
Presenter at *The Pulse* in Bradford.

Tom TURCAN
Tom is a Business Development Executive at *Capital Radio*.

Mark TURNBULL
Mark has been a journalist for 15 years working for nearly every national and regional daily newspaper in the country at one time or another in his capacity as a freelance writer in law, travel and sport as well as news and general features.

He came in to radio in `91 when he joined *Radio Cleveland* as a reporter. Since then he has presented phone-ins and general programmes and has also worked as a News and Programme Reporter and Researcher.

Alan TURNER
Born in South London on 29th March, 1939, he had a variety of jobs, policeman, salesman, engineer and joined *Radio Caroline North* in 1964.

Andrew TURNER
A former BBC journalist who was one of the main anchors on *Radio One's* 'Newsbeat' programme in the early 1980s, Andrew then joined *Laser Hot Hits* when that station launched in 1986. In 1989 he joined *Atlantic 252* and has been the station's Head of News ever since.

Christopher TURNER
Chris is currently the Finance Director of *Media Ventures International* who are big investors in INR3 station, *Talkradio UK*.

Helen TURNER
A director of *Fox FM* in Oxford.

Ian TURNER
Presenter at Marcher Coast.

Katy TURNER
In 1995 Kate became Managing Director of *Viva! 963*, the London station aimed at women, of *Jazz FM* and she is also a director of the parent company, Golden Rose Communications Plc.

John TURNER
Host of a lunchtime programme each weekday on *BBC Radio Bristol*.

Lowri TURNER
Lowri hosts the afternoon drive time programme on *Talkradio UK*

Juan TURNER
Host of evening programmes on *Manx Radio*.

Nigel TURNER
A producer/presenter at *BBC Wiltshire Sound*.

Robert R TURNER
A former senior bank official, Bob is now the Company Secretary with the Minster Group of stations.

Vikki TURNER
Presenter at *Q-103* in Cambridge.

John TUSA.
(Get full details from Who's Who or his book) In 1995 he was appointed the Managing Director of the Barbican Centre in London.

Jim TWYNEHAM
Presenter at *Mercia FM* in Coventry.

Martin TYAS
Director of *TRAX FM Ltd*, applicant for Doncaster FM licence in 1995.

John TYNDALL
Grew up and schooled in Stoke, and went to Nottingham University where he graduated in geography in 1994. While there he got tired of waiting for the campus station PC to 'pass' his demo tape, so he did a show one Sunday Breakfast time and took him the tape later!

He did virtually every show on URN, including a new concept - a drive time show without traffic news (most students are not mobile).

Likes Kim Wilde and bananas (?) and dislikes novelty doorbells,the doppler effect and Michael Bolton. Currently working on overnights at *Signal Radio* in Cheshire.

Tel 01 782 515543.

Umberto UMBERTO
Presents programmes on P*iccadilly Gold*.

Terry UNDERHILL
Head of Presentation on *Signal One* in Stoke and hosts the 10 til 1 show on the station.

Mike UNGERSMA
Presenter at *Touch AM* in Cardiff.

John UPHOFF
Head of Music at *Channel 103* in Jersey.

Gregg UPWARDS
After school Gregg became a video DJ and got into radio at *Severn Sound* in Gloucester because "no one else wanted to work for such naff money."

He did the station's breakfast show for three years before joining *Galaxy FM* in Bristol for a similar role in 1993. the following year he returned to *Severn Sound* to host drive-time programmes, but continued with a Sunday programme at Galaxy, both of which he still presents. Gregg would love to appear on TV or in films and to him the highlight of his radio career is every time he opens the mike, knowing that his next few words could well be his last on the air!

When asked about the funniest event in his radio career, Gregg suggests his pay cheques - and the things he likes most are his RAJAR figures, funny and creative DJs and his beloved Reading FC. Doesn't care at all for 'rip and read' style radio and people who winge about fame "they can pass it on to me anyday!" He's still looking for an agent who can make him number one - until then he can be reached on 01 452 731923.

Wally VALENTINE
Wally is a presenter of programmes on various RSL stations and also on KCBC in Kettering.

Rover VAN DER WEYER
Presenter on *Radio Cambridgeshire*.

Neil VAN NUIL
After school in Edinburgh (Forrester High) Neil had many jobs, ranging from being a driver to an office manager, during which time he operated a mobile disco. He got into radio by sending in many audition tapes, and a lot of perseverance.

His first broadcast was an early evening programme at *Central FM* in Stirling. where he also did the station's chart countdown. After a move to *Radio Tay* he did a programme featuring sixties music.

Neil then moved south to *Radio Borders* where he presented a mid afternoon programme as well as a country music show, and then moved to *Max AM*, another Radio Forth outlet, to host overnights leaving him time to do continuity announcing on Scottish TV.

Hosting a nationwide programme was the highlight of his career and he likes honesty and loyalty, but not violence lies and bad weather.

Rob VAN POOSS
Sales Controller at Essex FM and Breeze AM.

Chris VAN SCHAICK
Station Manager at *BBC Radio Solent*.

Tommy VANCE
A Londoner with show business in his blood, Tommy went to school in North London and his first job was at the Hyde Park Hotel. He ran away to sea as a cabin boy when he was 16 giving him a taste of real radio in the USA. Back in the UK he entered show-biz by way of a local rep' company and saved enough money to go back to the USA. There he got into radio by working for nothing at a local station and eventually got full time gigs at stations in Washington state as his girlfriend lived in nearby Vancouver (Canada).

Moving to Los Angeles he worked at top stations KOL and KHJ, who had a sung jingle package ready for a 'Tommy Vance' who never joined the station, so he was asked to use that and has been "TV on the radio" ever since.

Drafting in to the US Army in 1965 loomed large so TV headed back to the UK (his trip paid for by Ian Whitcomb - great singles on Stateside!) in time for Christmas, 1965.

Tommy got a job immediately on *Radio Caroline South* where he stayed until later in 1966 moving to *Radio Luxembourg*, but didn't like the set up so it was back to Caroline again.

In the 1966 Tommy recorded several singles which were released on EMI's Columbia label, the best of which is undoubtedly "Off The Hook", but sadly none ever got enough airplay. Just weeks before the dreaded MOA, he switched ships for *Radio London*, just a mile away (or six meters up the MW wave band) because he'd heard they planned to start a new service beaming in a station from the continent, a la Radio Luxembourg.

A move to Radio One was the next stage, co-hosting "Top Gear" with John Peel, but BBC producers feared Tommy's professionalism, cutting back his hours. He then launched *Radio Monte Carlo International* with Kenny Everett and Dave Cash.

They bought time on the high power MW station and broadcast to the UK late at night on 205 mtrs, but religious groups offered more money and took the time. The BBC also suppressed the station's success by transmitting continuous tone on a transmitter on an adjacent frequency for hours on end, marring reception over a wide area.

Tommy then broke into UK television, fronting one of the first series of Granada TV's popular 'New Faces' programmes and in 1973 joined *Capital Radio* in London. After six happy years there he returned to the BBC (*Radio One* and *World Service*) to host various rock-oriented programmes, including stints on 'Top of the Pops'. His was THE main voice on Sky Television's trailers and promotions for several years until becoming a main day time jock on *Virgin 1215* when it launched in 1993.

Tommy still lives in London with his wife Stella and the children.

Bryan VAUGHAN
Born on 23rd February, 1941 in Sydney, Australia, he worked as a recording engineer and later became programme controller at *2CH* in Sydney.

After a period touring Europe he arrived in the UK in 1964 and was offered a job as a studio manager by the BBC. He decided to take a slightly more glamourous role with *Radio Atlanta* where he became the station's chief DJ. When the station merged with *Radio Caroline* he stayed on, broadcasting a variety of programmes from the south ship and eventually becoming the station's Chief DJ.

After a break in Australia he returned to the UK and joined *Radio Luxembourg* hosting a programme sponsored by Polydor Records. He then moved to Glasgow and a job with *Radio Scotland* before joining EMI in Australia and then Phillips Records. Bryan still lives near Sydney and is a senior executive with the Readers Digest organisation.

Richard VAUGHAN
Host of a programme each Sunday evening (7 until 10pm) on *London Newstalk*.

Who's Who in British Radio

Mark VAUGHAN-LEE
A Director of *Orchard FM* in Taunton.

Keith VAZ
A prominent Member of Parliament (for Leicester East) Keith was asked to host a current affairs programme in May 1995 and now has a regular weekly programme called 'On Air Surgery' every Sunday lunchtime on *Spectrum International*.

Will VENTERS
Will has a long career in broadcasting, having begun as a news reporter, and risen to become Programme Controller at *Pennine Radio* for much of the 1980s before moving into regional television.

He is currently a news editor with Yorkshire Television, and lives in Huddersfield.

David VERCOE
David was the Editor of Music Programmes at *Radio Two* in the 1980s and is now the station's Managing Editor.

Chris VEZEY
Former BBC Producer at *Radio One*, he joined *Classic FM* as a Music Producer in 1993.

Mike VIBERT
Assistant editor at *BBC Radio Jersey*.

David VICK
Born on the 15th December, 1951, David attended Latymer Upper School and Peterhouse Cambridge where he obtained an MA. He joined the IBA in 1975 and two years later became Radio Services Officer.

After four years in that role he was promoted to be Senior Radio Officer, and then after 1987 Principal Radio Development Officer. When the Radio Authority took over radio activities of the IBA, he became the Authority's Head of Development.

David is a member of Amnesty International, the British Film Institute and the Radio Academy. A keen Everton supporter he also enjoys travel, sports and the cinema.

Alison VICTORY
Alison worked at *Mediacom* before joining *Atlantic 252* in Summer 1995, where she is now Research and Marketing Manager.

Mike VIMPANY
Sports editor at *Ocean FM* and *Power FM*.

Gary VINCENT
Presenter at *GWR FM East* in Swindon.

Noel VINCENT
Religious Producer at *BBC Radio Four*.

Stuart VINT
Stuart began his radio career as a technician on *Radio Caroline* and *Laser 558*; he has been involved in several other stations and is now the engineer at *Invicta Radio* in Whitstable.

Mike VITTI
Mike is the host of the afternoon drive time programme on *The Wave* in Blackpool.

Chris VOCE
Chris is the station engineer at *Scot FM*.

Steve VOCE
Steve hosts programmes on *GEM AM*.

Alistair WADDELL
Director of Allied Radio Group.

Lisa WADE
Promotions executive at *Atlantic 252*.

Tony WADSWORTH
Tony is a senior producer of programmes and also the weekday breakfast programme host at *BBC Radio WM/ CWR* in the Midlands.

Jim WAGSTAFF

Jim is the Chairman of *Radio Maldwyn*.

Pete WAGSTAFF

Born on 12th March, 1954, in Nottingham Pete started a hospital radio station in the city in 1971 and four years later was hired by the new ILR station, *Radio Trent*.

Four years later he moved to Australia and worked at *Transcontinental Broadcasting*. While there came the highlight of his radio career - watching the Programme Director of Sydney's 2WS eat three Big Macs and down two beers in one lunchtime!

On returning to the UK he joined *Chiltern Radio* and two years later moved to *Beacon Radio* in Wolverhampton, where he was soon promoted to be the group's Programme Director. He organised the successful launch of split operations with a new separate FM service for Shropshire, and in the late 1980's launched a third service - *WABC* on Beacon's AM channel.

Pete likes football and Nottingham Forest and Howard Stern.

Rob WAGSTAFF

Rob is the Programme Controller at *Trent FM*.

Jacquie WAIN

Producer at BBC *Radio Devon and Dorset*.

Michael WAKELiN

Michael is the Producer of 'Pause for a Thought' each day on *BBC Radio Two*.

Ian WALES

Ian's career began with Napier College in 1968 becoming Chief Technician for Educational Technology in 1971. He joined *Radio Forth* in 1974 as assistant to the station's Chief Engineer and took over his boss's job a year later.

Since then he's been responsible for the technical facilities at a number of new radio stations in Scotland and has participated in several industry committees and also serves on the organising committee for the Radio Academy's Techcon. He is a member of the IBS, the RTS and a Friend of the Lord's Taverners.

Andrew WALKER

A journalist all his working life, he began in newspapers and moved to the *BBC World Service* in the 1950s. He worked as a correspondent in a variety of places and was later a defence correspondent. On retiring in 1985 he wrote an excellent book on the history of the World Service 'A Skyful of Freedom'.

Angus WALKER

Angus is the Head of Creativity at *Scot FM*.

Carole WALKER

Sales Manager at *Xtra 1152* in Birmingham

Cliff WALKER

DJ on *Atlantic 252*, currently on -air mid-mornings.

David WALKER

David was the Finance Director of the *Chiltern Group* until August 1995, when he resigned following the take over by the GWR Group.

Johnnie WALKER

Birmingham-born Johnnie left school at 16 and moved to Gloucester to become a motor mechanic. When he was 20 he returned to Birmingham to work as a car salesman and at the local Locarno as a DJ.

He did an audition for Radio Luxembourg, who said 'You'll never make it as a DJ because you haven't got the voice or the personality."

Undeterred, he auditioned for the biggest and brashest new offshore station, *Swinging Radio England* and was hired in April 1966, just before the station launched. The American-owned station already had a jingle package with sung jingles for DJs, and he was told he must adapt the 'Johnnie Walker' name.

In October 1966 he moved to *Radio Caroline South*, taking Rick Dane's 9pm to midnight slot, where he excelled.

He quickly made the slot his own with features such as the "Kiss in the Car" licence, and having listeners in cars flash their headlights out over the sea from nearby cliffs. The programme soon became the UK's most listened to late night programme with Johnnie championing the still emerging soul music, rarely heard on the BBC.

His 'hero' status soared when stayed on board when the MoA came into force, while most of his colleagues jumped ship for a cosy job at the BBC (or oblivion!) declaring that Radio Caroline now belonged to its listeners.

When *Radio One* launched in late September, Johnnie was switched to the breakfast show to counteract Tony Blackburn (who was merrily playing all the old Caroline and Big L jingles) but couldn't stand the early mornings. He says he was personally devastated when the ships were towed away while he was on holiday in Spain the following March. "Caroline was a way of life for me at that time," he told Keith Skues recently. "I've never had so much satisfaction in my life."

In 1967 he was voted the World's Number One DJ in a poll in the Sunday newspaper, 'News of The World'. In a music paper poll in February 1968 he was still ranking number 4, quite a feat considering the massive exposure the Radio One team had in the run up to it.

After a year off the air while Caroline languished in harbour, Johnnie joined *Radio One*, hosting a Saturday afternoon programme where he was allowed to play some of the soul music he'd pioneered in previous years. This led to a daily strip and he stayed with *Radio One* for seven years until he could take no more of the station's orders: "play the Bay City Rollers, Neil Reid and other teeny-tunes."

Johnnie took his family off to the USA to work in Californian radio, where he had a good measure of success, particularly at *KSAN*. He also prerecorded programmes for *Radio Luxembourg* for a while, so his name continued to be heard in the UK.

In the early 1980s he was scheduled to rejoin *Radio Caroline,* which was due to return in a big way with a huge signal.

Johnnie moved his family back to Kent to prepare for the big event, but Caroline spent yet another year in harbour amidst money wrangles, so he joined *Radio West* and *Wiltshire Sound*. In 1995 he was snapped up by *Radio One* once again for Saturday afternoon programmes - at that time his programme was the only one *Radio One* had in stereo.

Since then he's also done regular work on the BBC World Service and at *GLR,* London's 'local' BBC station and also at the ill-fated *Radio Radio* syndicated programme service. In the 1990's he became one of the most popular programme hosts on *Radio Five* and until October 1995 he fronted the Saturday afternoon sequence on *One FM,* produced by his own production company - Wizard.

He then did a series of broadcasts for *Radio Caroline* and sailed up the Thames into London with the ship. In November 1995 he was heard on *Talkradio UK*.

Johnnie is also frequently seen on rock oriented programmes such as 'Top of the Pops 2' and Channel Four TV's 'Glastonbury' programmes. An avid motorcyclist, he also enjoys swimming, computers, surfing the Internet and sailing narrow boats.

Johnnie can be reached at 0181 960 5007 - or by e-mail: wizrad@cix.compulink.co.uk.

Mark WALKER

Mark looks after the music playlists at *Power FM* and *Ocean FM* and also hosts some programmes.

Rodney WALKER

Chairman of *Aire FM* in Leeds and a director of EMAP Radio.

Willy WALKER

Born in Bermuda in July 1939, Willy had a host of jobs (such as dentist, yacht navigator, male model, etc) before getting a job on *Radio Bermuda,* where colleagues Duncan Johnson and Mike Lennox (qv) convinced him that England was THE place to be. He moved to live with his sister in England and joined *Big L* (Radio London) in May 1966, staying with the station until it closed.

Willy then moved to Germany working in clubs and as a model and the moved to the USA to compete in the Newport Rhode Island Yacht Race. he now lives in Fort Lauderdale in Florida and manages and charters yachts.

Simon WALKINGTON

Presenter at Piccadilly's FM station, *Key 103.*

Jonthan WALL

Sports presenteron BBC *Radio Humberside.*

Robert WALLACE

Producer and presenter at *BBC Radio Dorset .*

Roy WALLER

Originally a coordinator for the AA, Roy applied to become a football commentator when *Radio Norfolk* began and his first broadcast was covering a game with Liverpool at Carrow Road. He did several programmes and AA broadcasts as well as commentaries for hospital radio and then was given a drive time slot from 3 to 5pm as well as a country music programme each Saturday morning. After a commentary at Wembley he did some work on *Radio Five.*

He has worked at the AA for 24 years and also promotes country music shows and comperes them too. The highlights of his radio career were being gunged on the Noel Edmonds TV programme and broadcasting live from an oil rig out on the North Sea.

The funniest thing which happened to Roy was having to kiss a sea-lion; he likes country music and good manners, but hates smoking.

John WALLIS

John is the Head of Commercial Scheduling at *Capital Radio.*

John WALSHE

John is the Finance Director of Sunrise Radio.

Clive WALTERS

Director of *Oasis Radio* in St Albans.

Colin WALTERS

Colin was a director of *Piccadilly Radio* in Manchester until the takeover by EMAP in the early 1990s. He became a director of *Minster FM* and also of *Fortune 1458* in Manchester as well as acting as an independent broadcast consultant.

Inga WALTERSON

Born in West Burrafirth on Shetland and educated in Walls, Aith and Lerwick in Shetland and in Aberdeen. Managing Director, Programme Controller and Head of Music of Shetland Islands Broadcasting Company in Lerwick.

Inga's is the most heard voice on commercials, news and promotions on the station, which broadcasts 24 hours a day. She is also 50% owner of the station. the other 50% being owned by her husband Ian Anderson (see separate entry). Her responsibilities include management, programming, music and traffic.

Robert WALTON

A native of Auckland, New Zealand, he worked on *Radio Caroline* in 1964 and 1965.

Becky WANT

Becky is the weekday breakfast host at *Fortune 1458* in Manchester.

Frank WAPPATT

Host of a nostalgia programme called "Golden Hour' each Sunday on *BBC Radio Newcastle.*

Bruce WARBURTON

Chief Engineer at *Beacon Radio,* Wolverhampton.

Dave WARD

Presenter at *Piccadilly Gold* in Manchester.

Judy WARD
Senior producer at BBC Radio Leeds

Martin WARD
Drive Time Editor at BBC Radio Kent.

Sandra WARD
Administrator at *Radio Maldwyn*

Sarah WARD
When Sarah, one of the best known voices in London first joined *Capital Radio* in 1975, she represented the first overnight programme broadcast by the station.
More recently with *Capital Gold,* she has been mixing late-night music programmes with phone-ins.

Simon WARD
Head of sales and marketing at GWR Group.

Don WARDELL
Resident DJ on *Radio Luxembourg* in the 1960s and seventies.

Keith WARMINGTON
Keith hosted folk music programmes on *Radio Solent* as well as a regular lunchtime programme on *BBC Radio Bristol* with Stephen Lamb in the 1980s; now the Assistant Editor at the station.

John WARNETT
Co-presents a Sunday afternoon sports programme on *BBC Radio Kent.*

Mike WARR
Mike is a director at *Channel 103* on Jersey.

Clive WARREN
Host of the 4 to 7pm weekdays programme on BBC Radio One and also hosts a Sunday morning g show on the station.

Duncan WARREN
Presenter at *Pirate FM* in Cornwall.

Dave WARTNABY
Evening shift host at *Ten 17,* in Harlow.

John WARWICK
Presenter at *Great Northern Radio.*

Martin WATERMAN
Martin a Commissioning Executive at *BBC Radio Three.*

Donald WATERS
Donald is a director at *Moray Firth Radio.*

Matt WATKINSON
Producer and presenter at *BBC Radio Humberside* in early 1990s.

James WATT
Has a long and varied radio career including periods at *Invicta* in Kent, *Yorkshire Radio Network, TFM* in Stockton, and *Island Sound Radio* in Malta where he was the station's Head of Presentation and breakfast show host.

Jame s is now heard across Europe on *BFBS* with a weekly phone-in game show and every weekday morning with his outrageous breakfast show. Contactable on 01 81 265 0179.

Sarah WATTS
Presenter of 'Topsoil', a gardening programme, each Saturday afternoon on BBC Radio Solent.

Steve WATTS
Steve hosts a four hour programme each weekday on *Southern Counties Radi*o.

Ruby WAX
Better known for her stage and TV appearances, Chicago-born Ruby also had a brief flirtation with the ill-fated *Radio Radio* syndication programme in 1987, presenting a late night programme interviewing guest artistes.

David WAY
David is the Station Manager of *Wey Valley 102* in Hampshire.

Alistair WAYNE
Station Director of *Q-103* in Cambridge.

Andrew WEALMSLEY
Director of *Downtown* and *Cool FM*, Belfast.

Gary WEAVER
Presenter at *Red Dragon Radio* in Cardiff.

David WEBB
Presenter / producer at *BBC Radio Suffolk.*

Elliot WEBB
Presenter at *The Pulse* in Bradford.

Who's Who in British Radio

Graham WEBB

Born on 19th April, 1936, the son of a Parramatta barber, Graham was a telegram runner in Sydney and was encouraged to apply for a job at a radio studio by Rod Taylor, who'd hired him to deliver a joke telegram and was impressed by his voice and delivery.

After a period in his native Australia he decided to try his hand in Europe and got a job at *Radio Monte Carlo* before moving north to the *Norwegian Home Service*. In 1966 he joined *Radio Caroline South* where his catchphrase was 'Spinning Tops with Spider Webb' and where he also became programme controller for a while. He brought the 'Caroline Newsbeat' style to the station and was one of the team shipwrecked on Frinton Beach in January 66.

In 1967 Graham returned to Australia and hosted 'Blind Date' on TV, a programme later copied by Cilla Black in the UK and then two years later was heard again in the UK on *BBC Radio Two* as the host of the Australian segment of Family Favourites.

He is still heard on leading Sydney station *2SM* and is frequently seen on TV.

Tim WEBB

Tim is the Head of News at *Fox FM*, Oxford.

Jennie WEBSTER

Jennie hosts a programme from 6pm until 8pm most weekdays on *BBC Radio GLR* in London.

Mark WEBSTER

Born in Kent on the 10th July, 1961, Mark is an avid blues fan who became assistant editor on the respected 'Blues and Soul' magazine.

This led to his becoming a weekly guest and then presenter on TV programme 'Boogie Box' and '01 for London' on Thames TV. He is the co-presenter of the breakfast show on London dance station *Kiss FM*. A very keen music lover he's also a West Ham supporter.

Martin WEBSTER

Reporter at *BBC Radio Solent*.

Rod WEBSTER

Rob is the Managing Director, the Programme Controller and also the Head of Sales at *Radio Borders*.

Tony WEBSTER

The Northallerton producer for *Radio York*.

John WELLINGTON

John is now a non-executive director of Allied radio, the owners of Radio Mercury.

David WELLS

David is the Managing Director of Eclipse FM in Sutton (Surrey) a cable station who intend to bid for a terrestrial licence for West London when one is advertised.

Mike WELLS

Engineer at *BBC Radio York* in the nineties, he's also been heard on some programmes.

Steve WELLS

For twelve years he presented Metro's breakfast and drive-time shows. Since then, Steve has free-lanced for *Ocean Sound, Chiltern, Radio Aire and GWR.*

Mark WESLEY

Born in January 1948 in Southend, Mark (real name Martin Goble) was educated in Hadleigh where he founded a cine club and joined a group called 'Their Rivals' as lead guitarist. he then transferred his talents to 'The Spectres' , whose manager Vince Allen (qv) helped set up *Radio Essex*. As a result, Mark became the station's first voice on the air, and stayed on the station's offshore fort base for several months getting experience as a DJ (and also making probably the only film of the station in 8mm cine).

Radio Essex closed just before Christmas 1966 and Mark was hired by *Radio 270* off Scarborough changing his name to Marcus West.

After a few months off Scarborough he continued his journey north to join *Radio Scotland* staying until the station closed. Mark then returned to London and worked for Acuff Rose Music Publishers for a while as a record plugger and then worked as a song-writer and had some material released by CBS.

In 1970 he was summoned to join *Radio North Sea International* before returning to the music business and a job at DJM records. In May 1971 he joined *Radio Luxembourg* and stayed with the station for ten happy years. In 1981 on returning to England he joined *Radio Orwell* .

In the 1980s he set up his own commercial music production company in Saffron Walden In Essex and has produced thousands of jingles and commercials for a variety of stations.

Mark also runs his own film production company called 'Media Futures' and in 1993 he joined *Capital Radio,*.

Alan WEST

Londoner Alan began his career as a DJ at the Top rank Ballroom in Sunderland and joined Radio Lodnon in 1966 as a teenager on the good ship Galaxy where he learned the basics of broadcasting on the knee of Tony Withers, thanks to whom he quickly became established as a reliable, competent announcer with distinctive voice and style.

Following Tony's advice, he picked up experience at many other stations - the next stop was Radio England, but after a month there Alan moved on to Radio 390, picking up some valuable experience and other things on the Red Sands Towers.

Alan then moved north to *Radio 270* where he became well known as 'Ross Randell' (also as the five foot bundle of joy!) and stayed until the station closed.

Alan then joined BBC Radio Leicester, the first BBC local station, and a later appearance on the Radio One Club didn't result in a deluge of work, so he became one of the first to join *Radio North Sea's* multi-painted ship. A year later he achieved global fame by transmitting the world's most powerful mayday call ever, after the ship was petrol-bombed and set ablaze.

With smoke billowing under the door he remained on the air asking amazed listeners to call for help; thousands did, resulting in overloading of telephone exchanges from Holland to Switzerland and unprecedented TV and press coverage for any programme!

Returning ashore he set up programming for *Leicester Sound*, and did the same for *Wiltshire Sound* a few years later.

In the 80s, West left the UK to work in radio stations in Europe, a career which has seen him resident in Holland, Belgium, Luxembourg, Italy, France, Monaco and Israel.

After six years with *Riviera Radio* in Monte Carlo as breakfast host and the Cote d'Azur's most popular anglo-phone radio personality, Alan moved across the border into Italy to create his own station, *STAR*108*, which achieved good ratings and was subsequently sold to a Monegasque family.

Moving back to London at the end of 1993 Alan fronted an excellent breakfast programme at *Buzz FM* in Birmingham and is now producing and presenting *RTM Radio's* breakfast sequence (doubling the audience - source RAJAR) as well as being involved in developing a number of broadcasting projects in Gibraltar.

Brian WEST
Brian has been director and Chief Executive of the Association of Independent radio Contractors for over fifteen years.

Colin WEST
Chief accountant at *Isle of Wight Radio*.

Who's Who in British Radio

Dave WEST (1)
Dave joined *Radio Caroline International* in June 1973 but fell prone to the offshore radio dj curse - seasickness. On returning ashore he joined *Swansea Sound* to p;resent rock music programmes and then moved back north to his native Manchester.

In 1989 he and his wife Barbara moved to the Isle of Man after a job offer from *Manx Radio* and in 1994 he helped found a new international station on the island.

Dave WEST (2)
Host of a programme on BBC Radio Stoke from 5pm until 6.30 each weekday .

Helen WEST
Country-music programme host at *BBC Radio Cambridgeshire* in 1995.

Paul WEST
Paul's career began on hospital radio in Reading in 1993. The following year he took a radio skills course at *Leicester Sound FM* and recently joined BECTU as a freelance radio presenter. Contact No. 0850 532703.

Simon WEST
Presenter at *Invicta FM*.

Stephen WEST
Kent born Stephen got into radio on the red Sands Towers, eight miles from Whitstable, when he joined the crew of *King Radio* in early 1965. A huge, softly-spoken man, he grew a beard while spending two years on the fort,. during which time he also worked on *Radio 390* - becoming one of the last voices on the air when the station closed in 1967.

Andy WESTGATE
Presenter at *Brunel Classic Gold* and on the GWR East FM station in Swindon.

James WHALE
Before his radio career James had some interesting jobs, including a period as a trainee buyer at Harrods. Fortunately he got the radio bug and his career has let others share his wit - including listeners at *Radio Aire* in Leeds and *BBC Radio Humberside* where he was heard (all too briefly) briefly as stand-in host of a phone in programme.

He now presents 'James Whale Radio Show' for ITV, and is heard on *Talkradio UK*.

Julian WHARAM
After school in West Hull, he went to Trinity and All Saints College at the University of Leeds where he gained an honours degree in geography and Public Media. One day a friend called and asked if he fancied helping out with sports input at *Viking Radio* and as a result he made his first broadcast in 1988.

He's since worked part-time in catering and in a camera shop as well as for a TV commercial production company in Australia.

Julian also did a six week attachment at *BBC Radio Humberside* doing general programme assistant duties, and was then Station Manager at *TASC Radio*, a campus station, where he was responsible for all aspects of station operation.

Under his control broadcasting was increased from 7 to 32 hours a week and was once locked in the studio all night with nothing but two pizzas and a bottle of scotch for company!

In 1994 he joined *Radio Aire* in Leeds hosting six programmes a week, including a high profile CD Album Chart countdown each Sunday. Julian likes sunshine and socialising but not being hungry and cold.

Richard WHATMORE
Director of *Channel 103* in Jersey.

Carl WHEATLEY
Carl presented the early morning programmes at BBC *Radio Humberside* until 1995, when he was awarded an arts programme each Sunday.

Richard WHEATLY
Richard is the Chief Operating Officer of Golden Rose Communications, the parent company of the two *Jazz FM* stations and *Viva 963*.

Karen WHEELER
Presenter at *TFM* in Stockton.

Nick WHEELER

Born in sight of the pyramids in Egypt, Nick's career began in newspapers and he got his radio break at BBC Radio Stoke. After leaving the BBC he joined *Independent Radio News* where he became The Editor, leaving only to join *Capital FM* in May 1985 as a founder member of "the Way It Is' newsteam.

Under his direction, the programme has pioneered popular news coverage in commercial radio and won awards in New York, London and Europe. Nick has interviewed royalty, prime ministers, supermodels and Kermit the Frog.

He almost gave up the newsroom for the catwalks after a modelling assignment in the 'For Him' magazine (but wasn't tall enough to take it up full time). He's broadcast while sky-diving from 6,000 feet and in racing cars and warships. Lives in south-east London and has two daughters.

Steve WHEELER

Steve is one of the librarians at CRMK.

Rodney WHELAN

Engineer at *The Bay* in Lancaster.

Mike WHITAKER

A Regional Operations Manager with the *BBC World Service*, Mike is a specialist in administrative and technical aspects of broadcasting and teaches radio skills with 'Instant Radio'.

Vanessa WHITBURN

Editor of 'The Archers' on *BBC Radio Four*.

Charles WHITE - aka Dr Rock

 One of the few true medical doctors of the radio world, Charles is a fully qualified chiropodist tending the feet of weary Yorkshire folk at his Scarborough practice by day, but by night (and every weekend, and holidays too!) he becomes the amazing Dr Rock, soulmate to the stars.

Born on the west coast Ireland just before the end of the war, Charles was stunned when he first heard rock'n'roll and has been totally devoted to it ever since. He came to England to study medicine in 1961 and while at college in London in 1961 he met his wife, fellow chiropody student Anne, who spirited him back to Scarborough where he's remained ever since. There have been many sojourns to Hollywood to see his friends Jerry Lee Lewis and Little Richard, both of whom commissioned him to write their biographies. So successful have these been that a film telling the true story of The Killer is now in the offing.

His first broadcast was on Any Questions with David Jacobs in 1975, since when he's been a regular programme host on *Radio Tees,Radio Humberside , Radio London, KPFA* in Los Angeles, top New York Station WINS, and on *Capital Radio* with Stuart Coleman.

In 1994 Yorkshire TV sent across a film crew to chronicle his trips to Hollywood and for several years he's been one of the most respected presenters at *BBC Radio York,* with a weekly programme at peak time each Saturday extolling all types of music, but mainly rock'n'roll.

Charles is also one of the founders of 'The Sons of Neptune', a local pressure group dedicated to saving the Yorkshire coast from ecological disaster. His most embarrassing moment was asking Vidal Sasson what he did for a living and he likes swimming (off Scarborough of course!) as well as a good pint (not of the North Sea!).

At Wembley Stadium in June 1995, Little Richard dedicated part of his show to his biographer, which Charles thinks is the best accolade to date, while that honorary title 'Dr Rock' was given by the 'Daily Mail' when they ran a story about a course he was running at Scarborough college . . about rock'n'roll of course!

David WHITE

Weekday presenter at *BBC Radio Cornwall*.

Fiona WHITE

Sales Manager at South West Sound, Dumfries.

Herdle WHITE

Host of the weekly reggae show each Saturday evening at 8pm on *BBC Radio Leicester*.

Jim WHITE
Jim is chief engineer at Plymouth Sound.

Jon WHITE
In 1995, a presenter at *Orchard FM* in Taunton.

Ken WHITE
Presenter at *CFM* in Carlisle.

Marcus WHITE
News Editor at *Gemini Radio* in Exeter.

Mary WHITE
Head of BBC Radio International.

Maureen WHITE
Maureen is the Station administrator at *Isle of Wight Radio*.

Peter WHITE
Peter presents a programme from 9.30 to 1.30 each weekday on *BBC Radio Solent*.

Phil WHITE
Born on 30th August, 1960, in London, Phil attended Ashford Grammar School in Kent and obtained a BA Hons degree at the Trent Polytechnic in Nottingham. His entrance into radio was quite nonchalant "I just kinda wandered in one day" and he made his first broadcast on *BBC Radio Nottingham*.

In June 1985 he moved up the A1 to Middlesborough and a Programme Assistant role at *BBC Radio Cleveland*.

After three years with the BBC, Phil moved to *TFM* in neighbouring Stockton as a presenter. After two years he became the Features Producer at TFM and in March 1993 he was promoted to become Programme Controller at the Metro Group's *Viking FM* in Hull. After two years he was made Programme Director at Viking and it's now hard to imagine the station without him.

Still working on the highlight of his career, Phil likes all the good things in life - food, drink, TV and radio plus of course life itself, but he hates inefficiency.

Simon WHITE
Simon is the producer of the Saturday Breakfast Programme at *BBC Somerset Sound*.

Steven WHITE
Group accountant at *Capital Radio*.

Stewart WHITE
Presenter and producer at *BBC Radio Suffolk*.

Tim WHITE
Born in 1968, Tim joined *Radio Aire* in Leeds in 1988 as Sports Editor. In 1994 he was made the deputy News Editor, and in 1995 Head of News.

Tony WHITE
Programme Director at CRMK.

Chris WHITEHEAD
Chris hosts a programme each weekday from 11 until 2 on *BBC Three Counties Radio*.

Richard WHITELEY
Bradford-born Richard joined ITN after Cambridge and then moved to *Yorkshire TV* when it launched in 1967. He has become the TV station's best known face after a quarter of a century hosting the regional news programme 'Calendar', and in 1982 his was the first face seen on Channel Four TV as the host of 'Countdown' - a role he still enjoys.

His interest in radio goes back many years - he was part of the consortium which applied for the Bradford ILR licence in 1975 when it was first offered (but won by rival group *Pennine Radio*) and in 1992 one of his dreams came true when his 'Voice of Yorkshire' group merged with Minster Radio.

In September 1995 Richard was appointed Chairman of the Group's York station.

Rod WHITING
News Editor at *Lincs FM*.

John WHITNEY
John Whitney was the co-founder and Chairman of the Local Radio Association, a campaigning group in the 1960s and 1970s. In 1973 he became Managing Director of *Capital Radio*, a position he held for ten years.

While at Capital he also chaired the AIRC for its first two years, and again in 1980.

In 1982 he left Capital to take the position of Director General at the Independent Broadcasting Authority which he presided over until 1989.

John is a companion of the TV and Radio Industries Club and was President in 1985/6 and is an associate of M A Media Partners, a leading consultancy in UK newspapers and broadcasting. He is also the Chairman of the Really Useful Group, as well as of RAJAR and the Sony Awards Committee.

Sue WHITTLE

Sales Promotion and marketing manager at *Marcher Coast* and sister station *MFM*.

Michel WHITWELL

Marketing Manager at *Jazz FM* and *Viva 963*.

Graham WHYTE

Educated at King George Grammar School in Southport he then became a local newspaper reporter and did some hospital radio work in Southport before moving into radio in the mid-eighties while working for a press agency in Liverpool. He did some shifts at *Radio Merseyside* and as a result was offered a twelve month contract in the newsroom.

After two years at the BBC, Graham moved across town to *Radio City* as Night Editor in December 1988. Four years later he was appointed Deputy News Editor and later News Editor, the highlight of his career. His fondest moments are of being part of the 'media pack' on HMS Beaver for the Fleet review off the coast of North Wales for the Battle of the Atlantic commemorations in 1993 - he was one of the few who were not seasick.

Since 1993 he's also been freelancing for Sky News and likes Startrek, Dublin and Guinness, but not wasting time - "life's too short!"

Ian WHYTE

Presenter at *Marcher Gold*.

Sandy WILKIE

Station Manager and director at *Radio Tay.*

Jennie WILKS

Jennie is the host of a three hour programme each Sunday lunchtime at 12 noon on BBC WM/ WCR in the Midlands.

David WILKINSON

Managing Editor at *BBC Radio Lincolnshire*

Jeff WILKINSON

Member of the news team at *Radio Cornwall.*

Dave WILLCOCKS

After leaving Guthlaxton Grammar School in Leicester, Dave did some hospital radio at *Radio Gwendolyn* and spent a period in printing.

Dave then joined *KCBC* in Kettering before moving to Northants Radio's *Supergold* operation, where the highlight of his career has been being trusted to present a prime time programme, and the team spirit he's found among his colleagues.

Dave likes lots of fun, the countryside and music but not selfish people and late trains.

Dave WILLIAMS (1)

Born in Oswestry, Dave did his National Service in the RAF and then worked as a photographer in the RAF's Public relations section. He hosted some programmes on the camp station and then left to join *Radio Caroline* as the station's first proper journalist. He ran the newsroom on Caroline's 'North' ship, anchored off the Isle of Man.

Dave WILLIAMS (2)

Educated at Guilsborough School in Northamptonshire, he got into radio through *Radio Cracker* charity broadcasts and the Midlands Radio Action Trust in Coventry. His first job in radio was at *Northants Radio* in an engineering role and station assistant and became a presenter with the *Chiltern Network* in September, 1994.

The highlight of his career so far has been giving away £1000 worth of electrical equipment to a pensioner who didn't know what most of it was for. His most humourous moment has been presenting an overnight programme with the fire alarm clearly ringing in the background.

[see also RAY CLARK]

Godfrey WILLIAMS
Managing Director of *Marcher Coast.*

Lee WILLIAMS

Lee has been involved in country music for over a quarter of a century, a vocation which began by singing in bands on the London club circuit and in military camps.

After several years on the road fronting bands, he became a manager and agent looking after many well-known big-name artistes.

Lee got into radio quite by accident, by helping a the presenter of a country music programme on *Radio 210* who didn't know anything about country music! Lee enjoyed the break from the pressure of promotion and was eventually offered his own programmes on *Wiltshire Radio* in Swindon as well as *BBC Wiltshire Sound* and BBC *Radio Oxford* where he's still heard every Sunday afternoon.

In 1991 he was asked to join pan-European satellite station *QMR*, and the following May Bank holiday he was a leading light behind the station's all day country music programme, which was so successful, it spawned *QCMR (Quality Country Music Radio)* the following May, launched in a blaze of glory by Crystal Gayle on Carlton Television.

After its first year the cost of transponder hire shot up, so a new arrangement with US based *Country Music Television* was arranged, and the station developed into *Country Music Radio* with a new base in Alton in Hampshire.

The station can be heard all over Europe on the same channel as CMT and is now owned by Lee, who plans to bid for terrestrial licences as these become available. Lee also presents a programme on London's new station, *Premier Radio* likes America and good food.

Mark WILLIAMS
Born in the mid-fifties at Maesteg, County Glamorgan, Mark worked for three years at a Top Rank Ballroom in Swansea. He finally got into radio by never taking no for an answer, a philosophy he's kept to this day.

The big break came in September 1974 on Metro's Saturday Night Party Show. His career encompasses *Metropolitan Radio, Radio City, Beacon Radio, Radio Trent, CBC Cardiff,* and *Centre Sound* in Leicester.

Mark then moved across the North Atlantic to *CFNY* in Toronto, which he describes as being the highlight of his career, and it involved broadcasting from the Toronto TV tower, then the highest in the world.

On his return to the UK he joined Birmingham's *Buzz FM* for a time and then in 1994, *Radio Maldwyn* as Station Manager where he also doubles a programme controller as well as running *Birmingham Cable Radio* which has 200,000 potential listeners.

The funniest moment of Mark's career was probably having to hold up Buzz FM's antenna after it fell down.

He likes movies, music radio and travelling but hates mindless formatted radio. After twenty one years in radio he's still totally in love with the industry.

Rob WILLIAMS
Overnights and weekend presenter at *Signal One* in Stoke on Trent.

Ruby WILLIAMS
After attending John Bright Grammar School in Llandudno she joined a local newspaper and finally, when she was 26, achieved her lifelong ambition - to work in radio.

Ruby had been a DJ in her spare time and made her first broadcast on *BBC Radio Merseyside* as a guest DJ on a summer roadshow. She then joined Liverpool ILR station *Radio City* and did a variety of programmes over a 13 year stretch with them, before joining *BBC Radio Merseyside* in the early nineties where she remains to this day.

The highlight of Ruby's career was trying to broadcast from HMS Bulldog during the Atlantic Celebrations in 1993 during a Force 9 gale. She likes driving, relaxing, sunshine and making people, happy but dislikes rudeness, aggression and male drivers. And she is still waiting to be discovered as a rock singer.

Russ WILLIAMS

Born in Lancashire, he spent a lot of time listening to *Radio Caroline* and was inspired to work in radio, beginning with a show on hospital radio in Eastbourne which ran for eleven years.

After training at the National Broadcasting School in programming and journalism, he won the school's "Most Outstanding Student" award and began working for Southern Sound as a journalistic presenter.

Russ then secured a job on *Radio One* - the one in Helsinki, where he met his wife Laura.

A move to *Metro Radio* in Newcastle was the next step in a career which led him to *Capital Radio* in London (with three years on the weekend breakfast show, achieving its highest ratings ever) and frequent holiday reliefs for Chris Tarrant (with Tarrant's contract that meant about 16 weeks a year!)

He moved to *Virgin 1215* in 1993 and now double heads the station's breakfast show 'Russ'n'Jono's Breakfast', as well as continuing his role of soccer presenter on Sky Sports and doing voice over work for British Airways, British Gas and many record adverts.

Sarah WILLIAMS

Sales Manager at *Plymouth Sound* and also a presenter on the station's FM service.

Tony WILLIAMS

In 1995 he was working as a journalist, and the main host of drive time programmes at *Ten-17*, Harlow's ILR station.

Simon WILLIS

Programme controller and presenter at Plymouth Sound's FM station.

Peter WILLISON

Head of Information Technology and broadcast systems at Capital Radio.

Colin WILSHER

Programme Controller. and Presenter at the New Leicester Sound.

Alan WILSON

After a few years in television with Scottish and Granada, Alan joined *Radio Forth* six months before the on-air date of 22nd January, 1975. He is closely involved in the financial control of a number of sister stations, including Radio Tay, Max AM and Radio Borders.

Andrew WILSON

Weekend breakfast host at *BBC Radio Cambridgeshire* in 1995.

Ian WILSON

Head of Public Relations at BCR, in Belfast.

Lynn WILSON

Senior Programme Producer at BBC Essex.

Nick WILSON

Sports Editor at *RAM FM*.

Paul WILSON

In 1995 he was hosting the lunchtime programme on Harlow's ILR station, *Ten-17*.

Pete WILSON

Born on the 15th April, 1972 in Norwich, Pete attended the Coleraine Academical Institution in Northern Ireland and then the Manchester Metropolitan University. He originally intended to go into press journalism, but got into radio instead as a sports reporter at *TFM* in Stockton. Further work at *BBC GMR, Piccadilly Radio* and Red Rose's *Rock FM* led eventually to his current station, *KISS 102* in Manchester.

Pete is football crazy and his favourite team are Manchester United.

Peter WILSON

Director of *Stray FM* in Harrogate.

Robert WILSON

Director of *Stray FM* in Harrogate.

Ron WILSON

Chairman of CFM, the ILR station in Carlisle

Scott WILSON

Scott was educated at Holyrood High School in Edinburgh where he excelled at sport and was signed by Dundee United as a goalkeeper and captained his country three times at volleyball. After further education at Edinburgh University and Napier College he qualified in Artificial Intelligence and Electronic Engineering.

His love of radio was spawned by experience of mobile discos at the age of 13 which evolved into several years of involvement with unlicensed stations before he joined Mayfield Hospital radio, which gave him aspirations of getting into 'real radio'.

In 1987 *Northsound Radio* in Aberdeen offered him a daily evening show, which he had to turn down due to work commitments, but his next tape brought two graveyard shifts at *Radio Clyde 2* in Glasgow. He was swiftly promoted to weekend daytime programmes.

Radio Forth approached Scott to host weekend breakfasts on their new AM service, *MAX,* which was ironic given that they'd rejected his previous eleven demo tapes, but he didn't need to be asked twice and was delighted to join his brother at his home city station.

As well as radio work, Scott has also appeared in two episodes of 'Taggart' the mini-series 'Your Cheating Heart' and has had to turn down a lot of other TV work due to other commitments.

He cites the highlight of his radio career as presenting five programmes live from Jamaica in 1993 with co-host Jay Crawford. An ardent Hearts of Midlothian FC fan, he's heavily into computing, golf, squash and his family but doesn't care much for the French, bad drivers or for bigotry.

Steve WILSON

Match commentator for *Capital Gold* in 1995.

Tracy WILSON

Reporter at BBC Essex

Eric WILTSHER

Eric arrived on Planet Earth in a pod along with Clark Kent and left school without even the mandatory DJ qualification (O-Level in woodwork) but with some success in English and Maths. After an apprenticeship with British Telecom, he worked for 12 years in sales for a tobacco company, but was already moonlighting for a variety of radio stations, some even naughtier than the tobacco.

Eric's tour of duty in radio has taken in such ports as began in hospital radio, *BBC local radio, QEFM, CMR, Euronet* and *World Radio Network*.

He lists being asked to open WRN and Country Music Radio as among his most memorable achievements, and winning the award for the 'Most popular show on satellite radio'(Satellite Surgery). The Surgery is heard across europe every Wednesday evening on CMR. Another highlight was conducting an interview inside a TV licensing van and discovering his own TV licence had expired!

Eventually set up the international media news and information service, TESUG, now the Europe leader in satellite expertise. In this context he's also appeared on *Superchannel*, anchored two experimental TV station on satellite and fronted news items on terrestrial TV.

Dave WINDSOR

Dave has worked for many stations over the last fifteen years, including the *Voice of Peace* and *Radio Caroline*. In 1995 he joined Kent's new ILR station in Tonbridge as breakfast presenter.

Monica WINFIELD

Host of the Saturday breakfast show, from 6 until 10am on *BBC Radio Leicester*.

Richard WINFREY

Director of the EMAP Group of stations.

Darren WINGHAM

Darren is now a Presenter at *Invicta FM*

Geoffrey WINN

Geoff is a leading chartered accountant with practices in several towns in East and North Yorkshire. He became the Company Secretary of *Yorkshire Coast Radio* in 1993 at the time the station was awarded the licence for Scarborough and resigned from that role in 1995, although he continues to sit on the board of the station.

Michael WINSON

Chief Engineer at *Swansea Sound.*

Andy WINT

In September 1995 Andy joined Capital Gold.

Ian WINTER

Sports producer at BBC WM and WCR.

Robert WINTER

Robert is the Business Development Manager at BBC Resources.

Dale WINTON

Dale comes from a theatrical family (his mother was Sheree Winton, who was known in the 60s as the English Jayne Mansfield) who encouraged Dale into show business.

He always loved radio and wanted to work in it; he joined the *United Biscuit Network,* a closed-circuit station which served thousands of workers in biscuit factories in the seventies. He acknowledges the UBN station as being among the best training ever for radio DJs - a sentiment echoed by many of his contemporaries.

He then worked at Nottingham ILR station, *Radio Trent* for eight years and then on to *Blue Danube Radio* in Vienna, Austria. In the mid 1980s Dale moved to *Beacon Radio* and in the nineties crossed into television. He was the host of 'Pets win Prizes' and now hosts a game show on daytime TV called 'Supermarket Sweep'.

Chris WISE

Presenter at *BBC Radio York* in the 1990s.

David WITHEROW

David is a senior engineer at the BBC and in 1995 he was appointed the DAB Project Director.

Terry WOGAN

Born on the 3rd August 1938 in Limerick, Ireland, Terry was educated at Crescent College in the town and at Belvedere in Dublin.. He worked in a bank for five years before joining the *RTE* in 1961. His first broadcast was reading the cattle market report. He progressed through such programme duties as reading the requests for people in hospital and became one of RTE's most popular programme hosts.

Eventually the lure of the big wide world brought him to London where he joined the BBC in time to be one of the launch DJs on *Radio One* in 1967. Initially he hosted 'Late Night Extra' on the station, in the days when much programming was shared with Radio Two, but was soon heard on daytime programmes.

He became one of the chief presenters on *Radio Two* in the seventies, eventually taking the station's 'Breakfast Show' where he injected much humour.

One example was his 'Fight The Flab' exercises and he even cut a record exhorting listeners to participate in the exertions, however his best know release was a vocal dub onto 'The Floral Dance', which despite a recent outing into the Top Ten, also sold in sufficient numbers to make number 21 in the chart.

Television lured Terry away from radio for a while; he hosted 'Come Dancing' for years and the 'Eurovision Song Contest' now seems synonymous with his name, however he's recently returned to *Radio Two* to host the breakfast programme once again and his ratings are now higher than ever.

He's won the TV Times 'Most Popular TV Personality' award for ten consecutive years and lives on the banks of the Thames with his wife Helen and their three children.

Charlie WOLFE

Charlie was born in the USA and worked in several stations there before coming to Europe in mid 1984 to join *Laser 558*.

He rapidly became one of the station's best known DJs, being the regular host of the 8pm until midnight slot, but perhaps better known for winding up the DTI, the Radio Authority and neighbouring ILR stations with taunts and other verbal attacks.

He left Laser in mid 1985, just a few months before the station closed down following chronic mis-management.

Charlie was then hired by *Atlantic 252*, and he now works as a presenter at GWR's East FM station in Swindon. He also writes a column in the magazine AM/FM.

Colin WOLLEY

Presenter at the New Leicester Sound.

Sue WOMERSLEY

Sales Manager at *Island FM* on Guernsey.

Doug WOOD

After school in Canterbury, Doug worked briefly in retail and pub management while making dozens of broadcasts on various land pirate operations in the seventies, then moved through hospital radio to the *Voice of Peace* where he spent two years. In 1983 he moved to *Radio Nova* on the Cote d'Azur, and later that year moved back to the UK and joined *Signal Radio* in Stoke on Trent, where he's been to the present day.

Doug also works as a stage show compere and does voice over and production work. The highlight of his career was beating Steve Wright's audience figures in the Signal Radio coverage area in 1986 and 1987, and being a part of the launch of *Signal Gold*.

He was once startled live on air; while interviewing Bananarama a dog shoved its nose up his trouser leg! He fervently hopes 'gold' stations will soon be heard on FM.

Lynne WOOD

Managing Director at *Radio City*, Liverpool

Phil WOOD

Born on the 9th April, 1951, in Manchester, his first job was in an advertising agency where he rose to become and account executive. In 1974 he was involved in the launch of *Piccadilly Radio* and made his first broadcast in April that year. Over the next few years he hosted most programmes on the station and by the early 1980's was the regular host of the station's afternoon programme.

In 1994 Phil joined *Fortune 1458*, the new MOR station in Manchester where he now hosts evening programmes on weekdays.

As well as radio he's appeared in Pantomime with Russ Abbott and Basil Brush and was the first to interview Julio Iglesias on UK radio. Phil likes the cinema but hates dentists.

Adam WOODGATE

After Tadcaster Grammar School, Adam did a BSc (Hons) in Economics at Brunel University and got into radio as a freelance at *BBC Radio York* in 1983.

After staying there for three years he took off to *KSFM* in Sacramento in California and in 1990 joined *KFM* in Stockport for a year.

In 1991 Adam, known as 'the man with the clipboard', moved south to London and joined *Kiss FM* in the capital before moving back north to join *Radio City*, where he remains to this day - now as Head of Music. Adam loves working in radio and hates bad radio stations.

Mike WOOLRIDGE

Born in 1947 in Surrey, Mike attended Bournemouth School for Boys and joined a local newspaper in Lowestoft when he left school. After three years he moved to Uganda as a volunteer with VSO and made his first broadcast there in 1969.

The following year he returned to the UK and joined the BBC, working in the newsroom for BBC External services until 1978. He then spent four years with the domestic radio newsroom and in 1982 was appointed the BBC's East Africa Correspondent and moved to Kenya.

Caroline WOODRUFF

Hosts a programme from 13:30 until 16:30 each weekday on *BBC GMR* in Manchester.

Karen WOODS

Karen is the Head of News at Ocean Sound FM, Power FM and South Coast Radio.

Ian WOOTON

Ian is the sales controller at Chiltern Radio's Bedford office.

Richard WOOTON

Host of a programme each Friday evening at 8pm on *BBC GLR* in London.

Kath WORRALL

Kath is a BBC trained radio producer who has worked in Canada and in the UK. She undertook a study of radio whilst on a Commonwealth Relations Trust Bursary and also worked with BFBS for a while.

She managed three of the BBC's most successful local radio stations and was Chief Assistant to the MD of the BBC's Regional Broadcasting Directorate, which she helped to establish.

After a period at BBC Scotland, Kath joined Border television and is now a director of the company's radio interests, which include *CFM* in Carlisle and *Century Radio*, the regional station in the North-east. She was also a key member of the team which launched *Scot FM* and Kath is also a leading member of the Radio Academy and BAFTA in Scotland.

Nigel WORSEY

Presenter at Beacon radio in Wolverhampton

Mark WRAY

Assistant Editor of *BBC Radio Essex*.

Chris WRIGHT

One of the music business true visionaries who loves the music too, Chris is chairman of the Chrysalis Group which now runs regional stations *Galaxy* and *Heart* in the Midlands and the 'local' station *Heart 106.2* in London.

Dan WRIGHT

Dan is the Head of Music and Programming at *Country Radio 1035* in London.

Elizabeth WRIGHT

Elizabeth is Head of the Asian and Pacific Region of the BBC World Service.

Graham WRIGHT

Born a Yorkshireman, he spent 3 years in Mexico and 13 years in Nottingham where he joined a hospital radio network. After a tip-off from a bloke called Dennis, he got into professional radio in January 1987 at *Leicester Sound*.

In October 1988 he was one of the team which launched *Gem AM* in the East Midlands and has stayed there ever since - he is currently doing weekday overnights on the GEM network in Nottingham and Derby.

As well as radio, Graham also finds time for TV and voice over work and is also an unpaid helmsman and canal spokesman. The highlight of his career was interviewing the former BBC Political Editor John Cole at the House of Commons, who he found to be a very nice man. Likes boats and Terry Wogan, but not modern pubs or Chris Evans.

Mick WRIGHT

Born in London in 1950, he began playing in a band when he was only 13 and worked as a musician on cruise liners and in clubs before an EMI Records rep suggested he send an audition tape to UBN, the factory cable network in the seventies.

After a year entertaining biscuit bakers, Mick joined *Beacon Radio* at it's launch in 1976 and two years later became the station's Head of Music.

He stayed at Beacon for 14 years, and the highlight of his career there was being flown to Philadelphia by Arista Records to interview Dionne Warwick for a networked documentary while the 'Heartbreaker' album was top of the charts.

Mick left Beacon to pursue his own clothing business but has obviously been bitten hard by the radio bug as he returned to the air in 1991 at Birmingham 'gold' station *Xtra AM* .

As well as doing voice overs for industrial and training videos, Mick is also trying to write novels at the moment. He likes music food and money, and hates a lack of any of them.

Nick WRIGHT

In 1995 is the host of the breakfast programme each weekday morning at *Heart FM,* the regional light-rock station in the Midlands.

Steve WRIGHT

Born in Greenwich in August, 1954, Steve's schoolboy ambition was to work in the entertainment business. He also ran his own radio station at Eastwood High School in Essex.

Steve also set up his own small jingle business, and worked in hospital radio in his spare time from his daytime jobs as an insurance broker, an electronics engineer and working backstage at a theatre.

During a period working in record promotion he supplied pre-recorded programmes to *Radio Atlantis,* a pirate radio ship anchored off the Belgian coast and then did some work for *LBC,* the London news and talk station.

Steve eventually joined the BBC, initially as a researcher and later in the record library. He left the BBC in1975,and joined *Thames Valley Radio* in early 1976 where he co-hosted shows with Mike Read (as 'Read and Wright on the Radio'). At the end of a three year stint in Reading he moved to *Radio Luxembourg* in early 1979 and presented his own nightly show.

In January 1980, Steve joined *Radio One* where his adaption of the American 'zoo' format to the UK was much admired in the 1980s. His 'Steve Wright in the Afternoon', complete with a cast of characters , was the mainstay Radio One's afternoon sequence for many years.

Steve released several singles in the 1980s, three of which - 'I'm Alright', 'Get Some Therapy' and 'The Gay Cabbeleros' - were chart hits. He also had several books published, including one highlighting items from his 'Another True Story' feature.

After much pressure he was persuaded to move to the *Radio One* breakfast programme in the early nineties. In 1994 he began a new TV series for BBC TV on Saturday teatime, and in early 1995 finally left Radio One. An avid radio fan we knew he would soon be back at one station or another and as the book went to press he was in negotiations for a series on *Talk Radio* and starting a new series networked on many ILR stations each Sunday morning.

Tony WRIGHT

Tony is now a DJ on *Touch AM* in Cardiff.

Joseph WU

Educated in Hong Kong and England, he is bilingual in Cantonese and English and got into radio after an interview with Lesley Cheung in 1985. He joined *BBC Radio Manchester,* to present their first Chinese magazine programme, 'Eastern Horizons'. Later he joined Manchester independent *Sunset Radio* to launch their 'Dragon Voice' programme and now works at *Spectrum International* in London on the Chinese programmes there.

As well as his work at Spectrum, Joseph also presents programmes on *TCC- The Chinese Channel* on Astra and is a musić columnist of the Siung Tao Chinese Newspapers. Joseph launched the Chinese Golden Award in 1990 and a Chinese New Year Celebration Concert in 1995.

Likes to surf the world wide web and isn't very happy during the hay-fever season.

Agent: Skyview 0171 434 2835

Mike WYER

Mike is a DJ on *WABC,* the easy listening station of Beacon Radio in the Midlands.

Sian WYN-DAVIES
Presenter at Swansea Sound

Gareth WYN-JONES
Welsh language DJ at *Swansea Sound*.

Simon WYNNE
DJ on *Marcher Coast*.

Chris YABSLEY
Weekend presenter at *BBC Radio Bristol*.

Tim YALE
Born in West London in 1945, Tim was a *Radio Caroline South* DJ in 1966.

Henry YELF
Henry was now the Managing Editor of BBC *Radio Berkshire*.

Sandra YEO
Chairman of *Lantern Radio* in Devon.

Alistair YOEMANS
Alistair is the producer and presenter of the sports programmes on BBC *Radio York*.

Gabrielle YORATH
Presenter at *TFM* in Stockton.

Peter YORK
Born on 2nd May 1948 in Stoke on Trent, he was educated at Lawton Hall in Cheshire. His first job was in a local nightclub (the Embassy in Stoke) for the princely sum of £1 a night in 1964. He was also a speedway commentator for a while and then in 1966 joined *Radio City* (the offshore one, in the Thames Estuary). The same year he won a Melody Maker poll to become 'South Coast DJ of the year'.

In 1968 he began broadcasting on *Radio One*, first doing 'Radio One Club' and then with a weekly programme on Saturday evenings. From 1970 he presented a weekly 'Album Show' on the *BBC World Service* and then five years later joined *BBC Radio Birmingham* (now Radio WM) to host the station's 'Breakfast Show'.

A few years later Peter moved back into commercial radio in Wolverhampton and joined *Beacon Radio*, and in the 1980's returned to host a morning programme at *BBC Radio Oxford*.

Bill YOUNG
Weekday presenter at *Great Northern Radio*.

Colin YOUNG
Programme producer and presenter of the weekday drive show (5 to 7pm) on *BBC Radio Shropshire*.

Chris YOUNG
News team member at *BBC Radio Cornwall*.

Jayne YOUNG
Presenter at *The Pulse* in Bradford.

Jimmy YOUNG
After education at East Dean Grammar School in Cheshire, Jimmy spent the war in the RAF and made his first broadcast on the *Light Programme* as a signer in 1949.

He then spent a year as a bandleader and pianist in London and in 1951 his first record "Too Young" became the UK's best seller of the year.

In 1953 he made his broadcasting debut as a presenter on a programme called 'Flat Spin' and two years later became a regular host of 'Housewives Choice'.

That same year he had two more number one hits: 'Unchained Melody' and 'The Man from Laramie', making him the first British singer to have two consecutive Number One hits.

In the late fifties and early sixties he hosted several programmes on the old *Light Programme* and had his last chart hit in 1963. In 1967 he joined *Radio One* to host a mid morning programme, also heard on *Radio Two* and in 1968 was named 'Radio personality of the Year' by the Variety Club.

In 1973 his programme was taken off *Radio One* and he became a *Radio Two* regular. His programme was later moved to a lunchtime slot and given extra weight with regular magazine features on health and legal advice, to replace the inane recipes and catch-phrases (BFN and 'this is what you do') which had given him such notoriety on Radio One.

In 1979 he was made an OBE and has since presented his programme from foreign countries, including Australia, Israel and Russia.

Paul YOUNG

Born and educated in Edinburgh, Paul has the distinction of being the first person to broadcast on commercial radio in Scotland - he opened *Radio Scotland* on 1st January, 1966.

Shortly after leaving school he went into television and was co-presenter of the childrens TV show 'Roundup' on which the Beatles appeared several times.

Paul has also appeared in several films, including 'SOS Titanic' and 'Chato's Lad' with Charles Bronson and Jack Palance, directed by Michael Winner. Paul now lives in Glasgow with his wife Sheila and two daughters.

Philliipa YOUNG

News reporter at *BBC Radio Newcastle*.

Robb YOUNG

Robb is the Sales Director of the Suffolk Radio Group, based in Ipswich.

Ross YOUNG

Ross looks after administration, financial matters and personnel affairs at BBC *Radio Suffolk*.

Steve YOUNG

Steve was born in Penarth, near Cardiff, in 1943 and brought up in Canada. His first job was as a TV announcer at CHAT TV and he then moved across to radio working at several local stations.

In 1965 he toured Belgium and France and arrived in England. In August 66 he joined *Radio Caroline South* and quickly became known as 'the curly haired kid in the third row' - after an off-the-cuff remark by Rosko during a programme changeover.

Steve held down the station's overnight shift (midnight to 6am) for quite some time. stayed until the Marine Offences Act in 1967, hosting an afternoon programme on the station.He returned to Canada after his stint on Caroline and now lives on Vancouver Island.

Robb YOUNG

Group sales director at East Anglian Radio and Suffolk Group Radio.

Sam YOUNGER

Born on the 5th October, 1951, Sam was educated at Westminster and at New College in oxford and worked in magazine publishing until 1978. he then joined the BBC as senior assistant in the Central Current Affairs Talks Department, and in 1985 became a senior producer in the World Serv ice's Current Affairs Department.

After a year as an Executive Producer he became Assistant Head of the Arabic service in 1986 and in 1989 was promoted to head that section. In 1992 Sam was made the controller of Overseas Services and in January 1995 he became Managing Director of the World Service.

He enjoys choral singing and he and his wife Anne have a son called Edward.

Wasseem ZAKIR

News reporter at *BBC Radio Newcastle*.

Mike ZELLER

Mike is currently working as a DJ at *Viking FM* in Hull.

Gary ZIEPE

Gary's first job involved zooming around on a milk float, followed by a period as a telephone operator, during which time he pestered radio stations with demo tapes galore. In 1976 he got his first break on the 'Young DJ' spot on *Capital Radio* where he also worked as a record librarian and programme assistant.

Gary later joined *Radio Victory* in Portsmouth and then followed a period with the A Roadwatch department and Metro Traffic Control. After a spell at the short lived *Airport Information Radio* and several RSL operations, he joined Essex Radio's *Breeze AM* outlet.

He's also worked as a film extra and has done a lot of voice over work. The highlight of his career was working with Kenny Everett and Roger Scott, but the most humourous aspect of his career has been a constant barrage of calls from a female listener who threatens to turn up naked in the station car park to meet him!

Likes positive people and working in wireless, not to mention his girlfriend Lorraine and hates negative attitudes.

Bernard ZISSMAN

Bernard is a Director on the Board of *BRMB*, .

Gerry ZIERLER

Born in Woodford Green in Essex, Gerry got hooked on radio technically while still at school, spending most of his time listening to offshore stations.

He got some experience by playing records at school dances and then passed an audition for *Radio Essex* (the one on an abandoned naval fort off the Essex coast) in June 1966.

Gerry joined the station as a bright eyed 18 year old while still sitting A-levels, but convinced that fame and fortune was beckoning - he was doing six hours a day on the air progressing from overnights to breakfasts.

He stayed there for several months, including the period when it became *Britain's Better Music Station* and then moved north to a bigger gig at *Radio 270*, anchored off Scarborough, where he broadcast as 'The Wise Guy' Guy Hamilton.

He quickly became one of the station's best known presenters - some listeners really believed he was the legendary film producer whose name he'd borrowed!

Gerry then moved into the world of advertising, working at several agencies by day yet still doing the odd gig (some of them very odd!) by night.

Gerry helped put together one of the country's biggest air time sales agencies, AIR Services, where he became Managing Director, although he often popped up as Guy Hamilton on various client stations, such as *Piccadilly Radio, Orwell, BRMB* and *Radio Hallam.*

In the early 1980's, Gerry started a little station in Swindon for the West Country called *Wiltshire Radio* (now better known as GWR) and also one called Northdown Radio, now known as *Invicta.*

After a period in television, he set up his own TV and radio sales agency, selling airtime on eight cable and satellite stations. He still enjoys doing freelance disc-jockeying and voice-over work for both the BBC and for many commercial stations.

Gerry is sure that the highlight of his career was working off Scarborough on the radio ship, *Radio 270,* in the sixties.

A page for you to note the very latest changes
(Dont forget to send us details too, for the next edition)

In Memory

We salute those who are no longer able to take part in British Radio,

Don Allen
Reg Calvert
Leonard Dale
Alan Dell
Samantha Dubois
Dave Eastwood
Kenny Everett
Paul Kaye
Paul Kramer
Ed Moreno
Roger Scott
Stephen Williams
Tony Windsor

~ your presence still echoes through the ether

BIBLIOGRAPHY

The following books were consulted during assembly of the *Who's Who in British Radio* and, where these are available, they are recommended reading.

Pop Went The Pirates by Keith Skues
A first rate account of how radio ships forced the start of Radio One by one of the UK's leading broadcasters, Keith Skues. He worked on Radio Caroline and Radio London before joining Radio One, and then was in senior ILR management for almost twenty years. This is a highly recommended and lavishly illustrated account of the stations, the DJs and the fun of the UK radio scene over the last thirty odd years.
Copies available from Eurobroadcast Publications at £15, plus £1.75 post and packing.

Last of The Pirates by Bob Noakes
An amusing and controversial tale of life on *Radio Caroline*, including some very personal details of some of the DJs! A fun and rivetting read, but only for the broad-minded.

The Lid off Laser 558 by Paul Alexander Rusling
This is a first-hand account of the launch of one of the most effective offshore radio stations ever. Photographs, technical drawings and descriptions of how the equipment works. The ship is still broadcasting, as *Veronica Hitradio*, in Holland.
A few copies left from Eurobroadcast Publications at £7.99.

Emperor Rosko's DJ Book by Rosko and Johnny Beerling.
An excellent guide to Top 40 presentation in the seventies.

Who's Who in Pop Radio by Peter Alex
A look at several dozen leading pop music DJs and the stations operating in Summer 1966.

Who's Who On Radio by Sheila Tracy
An early 1980's directory listing some broadcasters on BBC and ILR stations at that time.

Butterfly upon the Wheel by Peter Moore
Radio Caroline's manager these last ten years describes the 'operation' of the 'organisation'.

Wheel turned Full Circle by John Burch
A 'Dear Diary' account of how an RSL station was set up as an offshore station in 1992.

Independent Radio by Mike Baron
Story of the development of commercial radio in the UK up to 1977.

Station of the Stars by Richard Nichols
A 50 year history of Europe's best-known pop station, Radio Luxembourg,

Who's Who in British Radio

will be published every year in December

Preparation is already under way for next year's edition of the ***Who's Who in British Radio***.   This is a continuous process, as the information is also made available electronically (further details below). As the radio business is continually evolving, changes and new entries are being added all the time, so each year's edition will be different to the last.

To ensure you receive the new 'Who's Who in British Radio" each year, register your order now. You can have a standing order for the book, by telling us your credit card details, or sending an official order if you are an incorporated body, such as a radio station. We will then invoice you when copies are available and you will be among the first to receive a copy.

You can send your order by mail to :

Who's Who in British Radio
Eurobroadcast Publications
P O Box 12
Willerby.
HULL   HU10 7YT

(Please make cheques payable to *Eurobroadcast Publications*)

or fax your Credit Card details to   01 482 658227

Please send your Credit Card Number (16 digits) and the card expiry date (eg 12/96) and do not forget to include your Name and Address, which must be the same address as the card-holder account. Include a phone number and state clearly if it's the next edition of the book you require and how many copies.

[Credit cards will not be charged until books are dispatched]

Electronic Version

Who's Who in British Radio is also to be made available on diskette. The 'text only' version can be supplied as ASCII files or in *Word, Filemaker Pro, QuarkXpress* or many other DTP formats.   The cost of this service is £10, plus £1.15 pence post and packing, and updates will be available each month. Remittance details as above.

LATEST INFORMATION

In 1996, the fastest way to find out what's happening in the radio business is to call one of the various Information Lines and subscribe to the trade press. The following Information Lines are updated twice weekly (except the Radio Caroline line, which is often a little less frequent)

0836 404088   *The RADIO Magazine*   This premium rate line has the latest job vacancies in the UK industry as well as late breaking stories from the weekly magazine. They also operate a fax on demand service of news - dial 0336 423088 on a fax machine and press 'start' (premium rates apply).

01 426 910390   Jaybee Newsline   This is cheap to call as it is on a BT Mail Box, costing about 20 pence per three minute call on average. The news is mostly about offshore stations and other unusual operations. The operator relies on callers to make a voluntary donation to his £1000 a year BT rental ; his address is 23 Grove Road, Grayes, Essex, RM17 6JY

0336 404575   *LINE ONE* is run by Steve Conway and covers latest developments in UK radio. It is a Premium Number operated commercially but Steve billboards items on the line at the start of each message so callers don't waste money on news they don't want to hear.

0839 669990   Radio Caroline Newsline is run by Station Manager Peter Moore and is another Premium Rate line. Its news is usually a report of the latest equipment renovations and gossip about members of the Caroline family.

NOTE 'Premium Rate' lines cost 48 pence per minute peak rate, slightly less at other times.

REGULAR PUBLICATIONS
The following publications give news of developments in radio.

The RADIO Magazine
Weekly magazine aimed purely at the UK radio industry. It costs £1 per issue and is available by subscription.
[If you call 01 536 418558 and mention the *Who's Who in British Radio,* they will send a sample copy, free of charge.]

BROADCAST
A weekly large format newspaper for the TV industry, with some radio stories and an occasional radio feature.

MUSIC AND MEDIA
Published in Holland this is a weekly glossy magazine with music radio oriented developments from around Europe and airplay charts.

MUSIC MONITOR
Weekly publication with music industry news, and airplay charts.

AM/FM
Glossy magazine with radio station features and columns. Also publishes a fortnightly newsletter updating stories.

WORLD BROADCAST NEWS
Monthly glossy magazine aimed at station operators, discussing new equipment and licensing developments worldwide - radio and TV. Mailed FOC to radio staff by WBN, PO Box 12901, Overland Park, Kansas 66282-2901, USA.

PLAYBACK MAGAZINE
A monthly review of radio developments, UK, Europe and USA, with a section on satellite radio stations.

OFFSHORE ECHOES.
Quarterly magazine looking at offshore radio, mostly nostalgic.

UPDATES

Production of the *Who's Who in British Radio* is a continuous process, as an electronic version is being made available each month (text only).

Please ensure we receive details of your career advancements, be it a new role or a new station.

Please mail updates (and photos) to:

**P. O. Box 12,
Willerby. Hull,
HU10 7YT,**

or fax them to **01 482 658227,**

but note :

*ALL EDITORIAL CHANGES
MUST BE IN WRITING.
No telephone advice accepted.*

HOUNS◉MES
Rock◉ase
PLUS

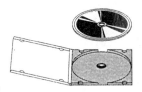

The Ultimate Rock Database

Searchable details on nearly **400,000 tracks**
from **120,000 albums** and **100,000 singles**
by **40,000 artists**.

All on CD ROM on YOUR computer.

The data was collected over nearly 20 years by Terry Hounsome, who compiled the defini-
tive reference books for rock music collectors *Rock Record 6* and *The Single File* (similar in
concept to the *Guinness Book of Hits* and *Music Master* books). This information has now
been converted to a computer-readable database and is now available on CD-ROM.

What can you do with RockBase Plus ?

- **List all the known releases for any artist.**
- **Discover which musicians played on which albums**
  or what album contained a particular track, (>280,000 musicians listed)
- **Search by artist, album, single title, track, country of origin,**
  musician, instrument, record company, catalogue no. and year of release.
- **Print lists of album and/or single titles for any featured artist.**

FOR EXAMPLE List all the LPs produced by Eric Clapton and discover that Ry
Cooder played guitar on 'Money & Cigarettes'. Then search all the recordings Cooder
made with other artists and thus discover a little known album made by Marc Benno.

The data relates mainly to Rock and Pop with some Soul, Reggae, Blues, Jazz, Country,
and Folk. Most of the data for singles relates to the period from the 1950's to the late
1980's. Album information covers the period from 1950 to 1995. Information about each
known release of a title is available, so if an album was released on CD and vinyl in
Europe and the USA there will be four entries giving full details.
Entries for singles contain 'A' and 'B' side titles. Many album listings have a list of all
the tracks as well as the musicians featured and the instrument(s) they played.

This user-friendly Windows based program runs on any IBM Compatible PC (486 or above recommended)
running Microsoft Windows version 3.1 (or later) or IBM O/S 2 Warp for Windows. The programme comes
on a CD-ROM (Double speed or above strongly recommended), and you'll need 4Mb RAM (8Mb+ strongly
recommended), 4Mb hard disk space for the programs, (or 100Kb from CD-ROM) plus space for temp files.

For your copy of **Hounsome's Rockbase Plus**, send a cheque for £49.95 (incl' post and
packing) or full credit card details to:

Business Data Ltd, 107 Woodland Drive, Anlaby, HULL HU10 7HP

(Credit card orders may be faxed to 01 482 658227 for immediate dispatch)

NEW PUBLICATIONS
in 1996
from *Eurobroadcast Publications*

Writing A Broadcast Licence Application

Written by a panel of broadcast experts, this easy to reference guide makes it clear how to obtain the necessary forms from licensing authorities, how to complete them. What sort of help you will need to consolidate the myriad of research and other information required. How to physically produce the documentation with a minimum of effort and administrative 'snarl-ups' and a thousand and one other helpful hints.

Due to contractual limitations, the final price for this book has not yet been set, but if you wish to be placed on the Mailing List for a flyer when one is available, please send a Business Card or a fax to Eurobroadcast Publications at the address below.

European Radio Licensing

This is a country by country guide to the licensing systems of all EEC countries and some other EFTA countries. This guide is being written by Paul Rusling and his team of consultants, who have been involved in ten successful licence applications in various European countries in recent years, including three national licences and two international licences.

European Radio Licensing describes the different regulatory systems prevailing, the legislation governing new frequency grants and licence issues and lists useful contacts and other information.

For full details of these publications, publication dates and cover price, please request a fly-sheet by writing to

Eurobroadcast Publications
P O Box 12
Willerby. HULL
HU10 7YT.

or   Fax your enquiry to   **01 482 658227**

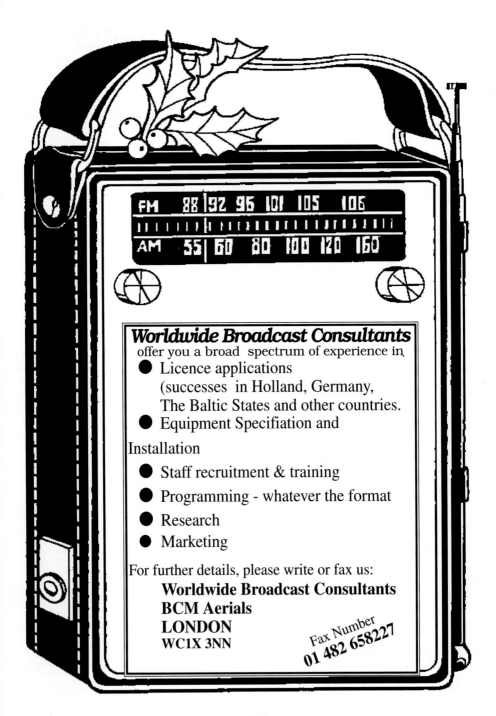